The Church in Response to Human Need

edited by

Vinay Samuel *and* **Christopher Sugden**

Wipf and Stock Publishers
EUGENE, OREGON

Wipf and Stock Publishers
199 West 8th Avenue, Suite 3
Eugene, Oregon 97401

The Church in Response to Human Need
By Samuel, Vinay and Sugden, Chris
Copyright© January, 1987 Oxford Centre for Mission Studies
ISBN: 1-59244-148-3
Publication Date: February, 2003
Previously published by William B. Eerdmans Publishing Company, January, 1987 .

Contents

Acknowledgments

We would like to acknowledge the work of John Waters of Oxford and John Allan of Swindon for their work in copyediting the manuscript.

We would also like to thank the World Evangelical Fellowship, the Paternoster Press of Exeter, England, and the Westminster Press of Philadelphia, Pennsylvania, for permission to print Tom Sine's article "Development: Its Secular Past and Its Uncertain Future," which has been revised for this volume from an earlier version that appeared in *Evangelicals and Development: Toward a Theology of Social Change,* edited by Ronald J. Sider (Exeter: Paternoster; Philadelphia: Westminster, 1982).

Introduction

Several years have passed since the Wheaton '83 Consultation on the Church in Response to Human Need. The publication of conference papers, with the process of revision and editing, inevitably takes time. But the time has enabled further reflection on the place of Wheaton '83 in the development of evangelical missiological reflection and on the state of the debate now, several years later.

Looking Back—The Lausanne Movement

Evangelical involvement in relief in this century began to grow in earnest after the Second World War, and especially in the aftermath of the Korean War, when Bob Pierce began a ministry of compassion among Korean orphans which led to the founding and growth of World Vision. In the United States the civil rights movement of the 1960s gave great impetus to evangelical reflection on social involvement. We do not mean to imply by this, however, that this was the beginning of evangelical involvement in social work. Indeed, evangelicals involved in missions had long concerned themselves with social work as an expression of their compassion and care. They ran schools, worked for famine relief, developed education and literacy programs, pioneered medical work, and developed progressive and modern agricultural activities in the countries where they were working. While it may be true that some evangelicals in the United States were uneasy about their response to their own social issues, it would not be true to say that they have not responded to social needs on the mission field. Yet although evangelicals demonstrated laudable advances in social action, mission workers themselves usually saw these efforts as secondary. For them, the success of their efforts lay mainly in the impact of the gospel on individual lives rather than in the positive change in society brought about by their efforts.

In the sixties and seventies, the world seemed to shrink with the growing ease and speed of long-distance travel and the revolution in communications and news reporting. Television viewers in the United States saw the war in Vietnam on their screens every evening, and far-off famines, disasters, and crises came to everyone's doorstep. The world had truly become a global village, a fact that had a major impact on the evangelical world. In November

1973 a group of evangelicals in the United States felt called to respond to the situation in the world and they produced the Chicago Declaration of Evangelical Social Concern.

The process of evangelicals proclaiming their social concern continued in July 1974 when evangelicals from around the world met in Switzerland at the Lausanne Congress on World Evangelization. Participants included those with practical experience in the field of social involvement, such as George Hoffman, director of the newly established Tear Fund, and those involved in evangelization in the context of poverty and oppression, such as C. René Padilla and Samuel Escobar. The participants presented papers and shared their reflections on the role of the gospel in their particular contexts. Some of them represented mission societies that had already been active in both evangelism and social care. Others encountered a new dimension at Lausanne: a concern to apply, as part of Christian mission, biblical principles to the social issues that lay behind human needs. The combination of practical experience and biblical reflection at the congress gave birth to the Lausanne Covenant, which affirmed social involvement as part of the mission of the church, and also to a statement on radical discipleship, which called for a holistic approach to missions.

The atmosphere generated at Lausanne was euphoric—the "Lausanne spirit." Evangelicals had united around their basic concern, the evangelization of the world, and had affirmed the place of sociopolitical involvement in the mission of the church. Evangelical relief and development agencies around the world received fresh energy because they could now appeal to the evangelical constituency as "family" without the fear of either being rebuked for preaching the "social gospel" or being charged with compromising on evangelism. Mission theologians who came in contact with the relief and development movement at Lausanne found a vast area of mission involvement that raised crucial issues for the statement of evangelical theology and the practice of evangelical mission. By and large, relief and development agencies welcomed their interest. The agencies found themselves facing escalating demands on their services along with the continuing opportunity to refine their answers to the questions about the relation of relief and development to missions. Both relief workers and mission theologians found that they had much to learn from each other. In this way the dialogue of mission theologians and workers in relief and development at the Lausanne Congress catalyzed a whole movement for the development of holistic ministry.

A Five-Year Process

The Wheaton '83 Consultation on the Church in Response to Human Need takes its place in the line of dialogue begun at Lausanne almost a decade before. This dialogue began in earnest in September 1978, when five concerned evangelical leaders from around the world (Wayne Bragg, Bruce Nicholls, John Robinson, Vinay Samuel, and Ronald J. Sider) proposed a long-term process of study and reflection on the nature of development from a biblical perspective. This process continued the Lausanne spirit of concerted evangelical action in holistic ministry and eventually culminated in the Wheaton '83 Consultation.

But Wheaton '83 was by no means the only outgrowth of this process. In June 1980 the Lausanne Committee for World Evangelization held the Consultation on World Evangelism in Pattaya, Thailand. During the consultation, a group of the participants circulated a Statement of Concerns to which others were invited to contribute. (The Statement of Concerns is published in *Texts on Evangelical Social Ethics, 1974–1983,* vol. 1, ed. C. René Padilla and Chris Sugden [Bramcote, Nottingham: Grove Booklets, 1985].) Soon nearly a third of those present had signed the Statement, which was later submitted to the Lausanne Committee. The Statement of Concerns was a reminder to the Lausanne Committee that the overwhelming majority of the unreached were the poor and the powerless and the oppressed of the earth. It emphasized that "evangelism and socio-political involvement are both part of our Christian duty," that the former cannot be separated from the latter.

Another landmark along the way was the Consultation on the Theology of Development, held at Hoddesdon, England, also in 1980, by the Unit on Ethics and Society of the Theological Commission of the World Evangelical Fellowship. The papers of that conference have been published in *Evangelicals and Development: Toward a Theology of Social Change,* edited by Ronald J. Sider (Exeter: Paternoster; Philadelphia: Westminster, 1981). Also included in that volume is a statement of intent issued as a result of the discussion at the Hoddesdon consultation. The participants decided that a three-year program—Christian Involvement in Human Development: A Program of Evangelical Study and Action—was needed to implement the statement; and they appointed a steering committee that defined the goals of the program as follows:

> Goal I: "We seek to promote theological reflection on attempts to meet human need in concrete local development situations." Persons involved in concrete development work (in both local, Third World development projects and international and national agency offices) will be invited to write up, analyze, and reflect theologically on case studies of development work. Of special concern in the process will be the attempt to ask how biblical norms and perspectives do and/or ought to shape the concrete character of development work. What are the relevant biblical criteria for evaluating development work? How should a concern for evangelism, justice, Christian community, servanthood, redistribution of power, partnership, etc., be integrated into goal-setting and evaluation? A large number of case studies will be collected and brought to a Stage I consultation in June, 1982. Additional groups will be invited to collect additional case studies in preparation for Consultation '83, a major international consultation on evangelical development work.
>
> Goal II: "We seek further clarification of theological issues related to development." Vigorous disagreement exists over the relationship of development to the total mission of the church. To what extent is it legitimate bibli-

cally to engage in development without attention to questions of both evangelism and social justice? Six theological papers will be prepared, analyzed by the local groups preparing case studies, and presented at the Stage I Consultation of 1982. After revision, further analysis by additional local groups and regional consultations, they will be presented at Consultation '83, revised once more and then published as a monograph.

In addition to the activities designed to implement the above goals, the three-year programme will seek to develop new models for theological reflection on development and promote the dissemination of development curricula for theological schools. We hope and pray that the Lord of the church will direct and guide these various programmes in order to improve and strengthen evangelical involvement in development. [See Ronald J. Sider, ed., *Evangelicals and Development: Toward a Theology of Social Change* (Exeter: Paternoster; Philadelphia: Westminster, 1981), introduction.]

The Wheaton Consultation

The Consultation on the Church in Response to Human Need met in Wheaton, Illinois, in June 1983 as the third track of a larger conference sponsored by the World Evangelical Fellowship under the title "I Will Build My Church." The papers presented at Wheaton '83 have been revised in the light of the discussion there and are now published in this book. Also included here is the statement "Transformation: The Church in Response to Human Need," which was produced as an outgrowth of the consultation. This statement does not attempt to be a comprehensive statement of the whole counsel of God on the issues of development, but it reflects the thoughts of the participants at the consultation as they were expressed and modified in the papers and the discussion that followed.

We wish to share the papers in this way to give practitioners of ministry with the poor and those in training for ministry a window on the theological issues underlying such work—issues that have been exercising evangelicals for a number of years. As soon as one asks whether the Bible indicates any *method* for ministry among the poor one raises numerous other questions about the place of the poor in God's plan, about God's purpose and the movement of human history, about the nature of the gospel of the kingdom, and about the interrelation of the gospel and culture. While we could never hope to give any hard-and-fast answers to these questions, we hope that the reflections in these papers are helpful to others in beginning their own process of discussion and questioning.

The process envisioned in 1978 is still active. The Wheaton "Transformation" statement is itself not a goal but a landmark. It represents a commitment to the ministry of the gospel of the kingdom to bring change at all levels among every people. As the statement itself says: "According to the biblical view of human life, then, transformation is the change from a condition of human existence contrary to God's purposes to one in which people are able to enjoy fullness of life in harmony with God. (John 10:10; Col. 3:8-15; Eph. 4:13)" (Paragraph 11).

VINAY SAMUEL AND CHRIS SUGDEN
OXFORD, EPIPHANY 1987

Development: Its Secular Past and Its Uncertain Future

Tom Sine

We are appalled to know that about 800 million people, or one fifth of the human race, are destitute, lacking the basic necessities for survival, and thousands die every day. Many more millions are without clean water and health care, without opportunities for education and employment, and are condemned to eke out a miserable existence without the possibility of self-improvement for themselves or their families. They can only be described as "oppressed" by the gross economic inequality from which they suffer and the diverse economic systems which cause and perpetuate it. . . . All these are rooted in the profound sinfulness of humankind, and they demand from the people of God a radical response of compassion. In addition to worldwide evangelism, the people of God should become deeply involved in relief, aid, development, and the quest for social justice and peace. [1]

Consultation '83, under the general title, The Church in Response to Human Need, stands not in isolation but in a line of consultations stretching back to Lausanne in 1974. In our discussion here we take as our context the progress made in the past, most recently at the Consultation on the Relationship between Evangelism and Social Responsibility (CRESR) held in Grand Rapids in 1982. Though Consultation '83 has its own agenda, the CRESR report quoted in the epigraph above provides a clear backdrop for our discussion here, so we affirm the commitment of Consultation '82 to the larger mission of the church in both evangelism and social responsibility.

I seek in this paper to understand more fully the context within which we work with the poor, not only today but tomorrow. We who work in development must learn to anticipate new needs, constraints, and opportunities before they arrive, so that we will have time to create new forms of response without interrupting our work.

While Vinay Samuel and Chris Sugden, in their paper in this volume "God's Intention for the World," focus on the future largely in terms of the advent of God's present and coming kingdom, I discuss the future almost exclusively in terms of anticipating tomorrow's challenges and opportunities. I wholeheartedly agree with Samuel and Sugden that God's transcendent king-

dom is breaking into history by the power of the Spirit today. My task of out-
lining the new challenges the church must face in the 1980s and 1990s does not
undermine the importance of their kingdom vision. In addition, any insight
about the rapidly changing context in which we will be doing development in
the future must first be grounded in a critical evaluation of the philosophical
and theological premises of our development activities in the present and the
past—hence the other part of my task. I cannot help but write from my own
context—North America—yet I have attempted to raise questions with which
the church in all nations must struggle as all Christians together seek to advance God's kingdom.

Development: Its Secular Past

Before we attempt to articulate a biblical premise for working with the
poor, not only do we need to anticipate more effectively tomorrow's challenges
but we need to analyze more critically the secular origins of the concept of development and the ways it has been interpreted and put into practice, especially
in Western social history. First, the concept is essentially secular in origin.
Implicit in the term *development* are numerous Western values that may unwittingly have become our values in Christian development programs in non-
Western contexts. Thus we must discover to what extent Christian development programs may be turned away from biblical goals and the ideals of Christian mission by the influence of secular values of Western development. Then
we will be able to articulate a biblical premise for our work with the needy in
the future.

I hope to illuminate Western development's implicit values through a
series of questions and answers on development and a better future, development in relation to God and his universe, development and the nature of persons, and development and the pathway to that better future. At the end of each
section below I have given questions for further thought and discussion. These
seek to ask how Christians are to respond in real-life situations in the attempt
to formulate Christian theories and programs of development in distinction
from, but also in relation to, secular Western theories and programs.

What Is the Implicit View of the Better Future
in Western Development?

Western development is a child of the European and American Enlightenment. It is based on the implicit belief that human society is inevitably progressing toward the attainment of a temporal, materialistic kingdom. In fact,
the certain belief that unending economic and social progress is a natural condition of free persons has become the secular religion of the West.

Somehow the millennial expectation of the inbreaking of a new transcendent kingdom was temporalized and secularized into the expectation of a future
of unlimited economic and technological growth. Francis Bacon's book *The*

New Atlantis gives the first vision in Western history of a technological paradise achieved solely through human instrumentality.

Implicit in this progressive view of the future was the firm conviction that economic progress would automatically result in social and moral progress. This view of the better future is primarily economic, focusing largely on human activities of production and consumption. The "good life" became synonymous with self-seeking and the ability to produce and consume ever-increasing quantities of goods and services.

As the Industrial Revolution began, the expansive nature of the Western dream of progress motivated Westerners to go beyond their own national boundaries in search of both resources and markets. The realization of the American dream was made possible by the appropriation of enormous areas of land and the resources they held from Native Americans. The great leap forward of industrial and economic growth in the West would not have been possible without the abundant, relatively inexpensive resources acquired through the colonization of countries in the southern hemisphere.

We Christians must realize that "missionary activity has gone hand in hand with colonization for almost two millennia. No matter how we interpret the underlying relations between the two orders, it is self-evident that political expansion and the church's expansion in the world have covered the same ground, geographically and chronologically."[2] So we must ask: To what extent have the values of secular Western development permeated a Christian view of development?

As we enter the eighties, virtually no one believes any longer in the inevitability of economic, technological, and social progress other than Marxists. (As a point of information, Marxist ideology was born out of the same ferment of Western industrial and political expansion and sees society moving toward a temporal future that is singularly economic and political. The Marxists believe that this future is inevitable, and they attempt to ensure that all peoples will participate in it.) The seventies sounded the death knell for the Enlightenment belief that humanity could achieve a utopia here on earth. Yet the essential image of the better future as synonymous with economic growth, which is implicit in contemporary development theory, has not significantly changed since the beginnings of Western expansion. Nations that have experienced major economic and technological growth are described as "developed"; those that have not are characterized as "underdeveloped," in spite of the growing awareness of the negative human and environmental consequences of unrestrained growth.

The apparent superiority of the "developed" image of the ideal future has directly influenced the definition and goals of contemporary development programs. Thirty years ago the primary goal of Western development in the Third World was "maximization of GNP per capita." Today the goal increasingly focuses on "basic needs" to raise the economic level of the world's poorest people.[3] John Sommers argues that "the measuring of development on the materialistic basis of per capita gross national product is inadequate and often misleading."[4] He advocates that development should be defined in spiritual and cultural terms as well as economic.

Some non-Western models of development based on a broader understanding of the scope of development are consequently more useful than the models we now use. For example, Gandhi's vision for the future of his people was very different from the vision that is implicit in the typical Western model of development. "The Mahatma was wholly opposed to those who argued that India's future lay in imitating the industrial technological society of the west. India's salvation, he argued, lay in 'unlearning what she had learned in the past 50 years.' He challenged almost all of the Western ideals that had taken root in India. Science should not order human values, he argued; technology should not order society, and civilization was not the indefinite multiplication of human wants, but their limitation so that essentials could be shared by all."[5]

Gandhi's image of the better future for India was a nation of some six hundred thousand decentralized, highly self-sufficient villages in which traditional culture, religion, and family life would be strengthened. While longing to see grinding poverty ended, he opposed the sort of development that would create material affluence because he was convinced that affluence would lead to cultural erosion and moral bankruptcy. His vision for the future gave primacy to the development of the inner spirit and the reinforcement of positive values and reconciled relationships within traditional culture.

Have we been as successful as Gandhi in determining what is essential in a truly Christian view of development? Do we have a biblical view of the future that transcends economic progress and expanding consumerism?

What Is the Implicit Image of the Better Future among Christians Working with Those in Need?

1. Are we unconsciously trying to help the poor climb aboard the escalator of Western progress?

2. Is the better future we are trying to help people attain essentially economic?

3. Is the good life the "individualistic pursuit of happiness," or is it something else?

4. What are the images of the better future that are implicit in development projects Christians are working with?

5. While we obviously need to address the urgent economic needs of the poorest of the poor, do our development projects imply that our image of the better future includes concern for the spiritual, cultural, and relational dimensions of life?

6. What image of the better future are we "showcasing" in our own lives and values and in the organizations we work for?

7. What is a biblical image of the better future? What are God's intentions for the human future, and how should we be consciously working to promote God's intentions through our development processes? How can we work

for righteousness, justice, peace, reconciliation, and love through our present organizations?

What Is the Implicit View of God and His Universe in Western Development?

Western views of development are tied to secular views of God and his universe that have their origins in the Enlightenment. In sixteenth-century England, Francis Bacon drew a historic line between the "words of God" and the "works of God." He thus promoted a new dualistic view of the universe. He lumped all in the natural order that can be experienced through the senses into the "works of God," and he pigeon-holed the revelational and spiritual aspects of existence under the "words of God."

Thus not only God but all sense of divine intention and sacred mystery were forcibly evicted from the natural world. Much of Western culture was left with an empty, meaningless universe freed from any divine presence or purpose. The Enlightenment encouraged this scientific secularization of the universe, insisting as Bacon had that it is a realm that can best be understood through empirical science, not divine revelation. For many, if God existed at all he existed outside the natural universe, impotent, passive, and unable to intervene in his world.

The Enlightenment thinkers saw the creation as a passive realm. Westerners learned to think of the world around them as nothing but a collection of passive, malleable resources to be exploited in the drive to fulfill their materialistic dreams for the future. In this "enlightened" age, Adam Smith offered a new, secular, doctrine of providence to justify and make possible their achievement. For Smith, providence was merely the guiding force in the economy and the personal accumulation of wealth. He insisted that the "divine Hand" of the marketplace determines winners and losers and brings us to a new age of plenty. He too relegated God to some place outside our world, which is left the arena for human exploitation.

This dualism has borne its fruit in our age. In contemporary development theory and practice, as in much of Western culture, there is no belief that the God of the Bible lives and acts in history. The world and its future are perceived to be solely in the hands of humankind. Contemporary development literature gives not the slightest consideration to the possibility that God is present in our world, or that he has any influence on human affairs. It tends to deny even the existence of any realm beyond sensory experience. Partly as a result of this, development theory assumes that "developed" people have the responsibility, through rational development planning, to enable as many of the "underdeveloped" people as possible to join the inner circle of economic growth and prosperity.

The massive exploitation of global resources has made us realize that the earth is not infinite. The "First Report to the Club of Rome" in 1973 brought this to everyone's attention. Far from being simply a passive malleable resource, God's world seems to be able to respond in some way to every act we commit against it. We can no longer thoughtlessly exploit the natural order but must consider the consequence of our every act. We are being forced to perceive ourselves as stewards not of passive resources but of a vast, active, fragile planetary system. This contemporary insight more than any other has put to rest the Western belief in the possibility of all people fully participating in the Western dream.

What Is the Implicit View of God and His Universe in Our Christian Development Activities?

1. Have we unconsciously bought into the secular illusion that God is "out to lunch" and that work among the poor is completely up to us?

2. Do we see "nature" as nothing but passive, malleable resources to be used in our development activities, or do we see the natural order in more sacred terms, as filled with the presence and purposes of God? What is our theology of earth-keeping?

3. Do we tend to see the world dualistically in defining church planting, evangelism, and disciplemaking as a part of the larger spiritual order of things and development programs as essentially secular activities—though perhaps done in Jesus' name?

4. Do development proposals Christians are working with mention the active participation of God? Would our proposals have more explicitly mentioned God's involvement if they were focused on evangelism instead of development?

5. Do we make any effort to discern how God is active in a culture before we begin our projects so that we may build on God's activity rather than disrupting it?

6. Someone has said, "In our areas of strength, we are all practicing atheists." Do those of us who are trained and experienced in development tend to be more dependent on our own initiative than are those who are involved in more "spiritual" ministries?

7. What is a biblical view of the involvement of God in mission to the poor, the sick, and the forgotten? Can God's initiative evidenced in the life and ministry of Jesus and the early church in supernatural acts of deliverance, healing, and miracles be available to the church today in our work with the poor? Should we seek insights from charismatics and Pentecostal believers in reexamining our doctrine of the Holy Spirit in mission to those in need?

What Is the Implicit View of Persons in Western Development?

Closely related to the view of God and his universe is Western development's implicit view of humanity. When Francis Bacon divided the natural and the sacred realm he unwittingly divided body from soul. Even as the universe was reduced to nothing but the sum of its physical properties, many in the West learned to view persons as nothing but the sum of their biological core and their behavioral surface. In a universe freed from divine presence and purpose, human beings were increasingly seen as alone. Their lives were seen as having no sense of divine intention or innate worth.

In an essentially economic worldview, human worth is largely derivative: the individual has worth only to the extent that he or she contributes to the collective economic growth. John Locke was the archapostle of what became a new Enlightenment doctrine: that if individuals pursued their own private self-interest it would eventually work for the common good. This doctrine has survived into the present. People in Western culture tend to identify themselves by and, indeed, to derive significance and meaning for life from their ability to produce and consume. Self-interest and self-seeking thus became the basis of this new society of economic progress and growth. "With Locke, the fate of modern man and woman is sealed. From the time of the Enlightenment on, the individual is reduced to the hedonistic activity of production and consumption to find meaning and purpose. People's needs and aspirations, their dreams and desires—all become confined to the pursuit of material self-interest."[6] Indeed, Locke even condemned the North American Indians for living on land filled with abundant resources and not exploiting them in order to live lives of personal affluence.

A person's sense of meaning, identity, and worth have come to be derived from his or her ability to successfully participate and compete in an essentially economic world. Increasingly, North Americans have learned to derive their very identity from what they produce and what they consume. The more we own, the more we are. In this regard Pope John Paul II has declared that while communism reduces people to economic things, capitalism reduces them to consuming things. Westerners tend to see those in their culture who are not able to fully participate in the economic rat race as a threat to the entire system. They further reduce them in human value based on their economic value to the larger technocratic order.

The self-seeking attitudes encouraged by Locke and also by Thomas Jefferson have become an absolute mania in contemporary Western culture. The good life for the individual is strongly oriented toward acquisitive, consumptive, and status-seeking behavior—even among Western Christians, who also participate in using up an unjust share of limited planetary resources.

Modern development theories tend to talk about human personality, human activity, and human goals in largely economic terms—such as human resources, beneficiaries, and so on. Therefore, modern development activity tends to foster a reductionistic view of human personality and activity, often ignoring the areas of spiritual, cultural, and relational development.

What Is Our Implicit View of Persons in Our Christian Development Programs?

1. Do we unconsciously tend to think of persons as nothing but the sum of their biological core and their behavioral surface—the product of random genetic activity?

2. Do Christian development agencies tend to focus only on people's economic and physical needs and leave the spiritual and relational needs to the church?

3. Do we tend to define persons in largely economic terms? Do we describe groups as "developed" or "undeveloped," or persons as "beneficiaries" or "resources"?

4. Do we tend to assign worth to individuals or groups based on their productivity and the level at which they are able to participate in the larger consumer society?

5. Do our development activities tend to encourage the values of individualism, materialism, and acquisitive behavior, undermining community and traditional values?

6. How do those working in ministries of evangelism and disciplemaking tend to see persons differently from those working in development?

7. How should the biblical view of persons as image bearers of God, as spiritual, relational beings created for corporate life, change the way in which we do development?

What Is the Implicit View of the Pathway to this Better Future in Western Development?

The proponents of Western progress believed that the attainment of a materialistic paradise on earth was inevitable. But they saw human instrumentality, not the initiative of God, as essential to create this new age.

Bacon proclaimed that he had discovered a new Promethean power that would enable humanity to subdue a passive nature and fashion a new technological, materialistic utopia. Rationality and the exercise of the reason enabled humanity to empirically examine the natural world. The knowledge that would result was, for Bacon, the power that would lead to a brighter future.

John Locke, believing that all human activity is based on materialistic self-interest, encouraged self-seeking as yet another pathway to achieve this enlightened paradise. Thomas Jefferson incorporated in the "Religion of America" the Lockean goal of the individualistic pursuit of happiness as a cardinal doctrine.

Building on the philosophy of Locke, Adam Smith created a new economics of growth that became an essential pathway to the temporal kingdom of progress. His economics had no sense of morality. He postulated that individuals and organizations should have complete freedom to pursue self-interest in their quest for economic gain. The invisible hand of natural law would then ensure the achievement of the common good through private selfishness. This foremost premise of capitalism eventually leads to a Darwinian economic theory. "Smith championed the cause of a growing class of manufacturers who saw their interests stifled by government monopolies and the closed ranks of the mercantilists. Just as Locke had promoted the social interests of bourgeois merchants and traders, Smith appealed to 'natural laws' based on

Newtonian-Baconian science to legitimatize the economic interests of the new industrial entrepreneurs."[7]

Since contemporary advocates of development no longer view progress as inevitable, and since they recognize no God, even more depends on human initiative to set the world right. Until recently, many people believed that global development could best be achieved through the intervention of high technology and advanced science. With the publication of E. F. Schumacher's classic *Small Is Beautiful: Economics as if People Mattered* in the mid 1970s, people began to shift their attention to smaller and more appropriate technological responses to development needs in the Third World. But many people still see science and technology as a primary pathway to the better future, though they now realize the importance of appropriate application for community health, sanitation, and agriculture.

The laissez-faire economics introduced by Adam Smith, which is based on the belief that private selfishness will secure the common good, is not the only scheme that sees development solely in terms of economics. During the past seventy years a host of socialist regimes have sought to demonstrate a pathway of planned economics that elevates the common good above private gain. Marxist ideology opposes Western economics and development planning as obscuring the need to overthrow and replace unjust structures. However, Marxism often constrains civil freedoms.

As long as the better collective and personal future is defined almost exclusively in economic and physical terms, contemporary development has no pathways to that future other than the appropriate application of science and technology, growth economics, and utilitarian education.

What Is the Implicit View of the Pathway to the Better Future in Christian Development?

1. Do we rely primarily on our human initiative or on the initiative of God in our work with those in need?

2. In our efforts to help the poor, do we place our confidence in the "can do" capability of Western science and technology? Do we begin with our own desires, with felt needs, or with God-given dreams?

3. When we leave a successful development project, have the people been made more dependent on Western science and technology or on God?

4. Do we place our confidence in Western economic models to bring people to a better future, assuming that the pursuit of private self-interest will work to the common good, or are we working from another philosophy?

5. What seem to be the primary pathways to the better future implicit in the development projects Christians are involved with? How are they integrated with ministries of church planting, evangelism, and disciplemaking?

6. What is a biblical image of the pathway to the achievement of the future intentions of God, and how drastically would its implementation alter our existing Christian development activities?

7. In the New Testament, the mission of the church is not carried out through individual human initiative working through institutional structures but through organic fellowships of believers empowered by the Holy Spirit. How could we create methods of Christian development that flow organically out of Christian communities of shared life empowered by the Spirit of God, so that we could advance his kingdom in response to the challenges of tomorrow's world?

Development: Its Uncertain Future

"Suddenly—virtually overnight when measured on a historical scale—mankind finds itself confronted by a multitude of unprecedented crises: the population crisis, the environmental crisis, the raw materials crisis, just to name a few. New crises appear while the old ones linger on with effects spreading to every corner of the earth until they appear in point of fact as global, worldwide crises. . . ."[8] These global crises indicate that we have entered a period of dramatic planetary change. We can no longer predict the future by studying the past; nor can we assume any longer that the future will simply be an extension of the present, as current long-range planning tends to do. Those of us working with the poor for the kingdom must learn to anticipate tomorrow's challenges before they arrive so that we will have time to create new ministry responses. Attempting to forecast the future is very difficult and uncertain, but the only other option is to be surprised by change.

The best example of anticipatory planning I know of was done by the Philippine Council of Evangelical Churches, which analyzed the economic, social, and technological trends in the Philippines between now and the year 2000. They concluded that the continuing high rate of inflation would have a particularly harmful effect on most Christian families, who often survive on subsistence incomes. As a result, mothers of families would be forced to join the labor market simply for the families to survive, "leaving children unsupervised, thus weakening the home."[9]

To ward off this future challenge the Council of Evangelical Churches began creating some economic development projects to enable women to earn the necessary supplemental income at home, while they care for their children. This project cannot reverse the course of inflation, but it can attempt to counter its immediate effects. The Philippine Council would never have thought to create the supplemental income projects for women in their own homes if the need were unanticipated.

Those of us who work with the poor must critically examine both the theological assumptions on which our Christian development programs are premised and our assumptions about the future. Only as we learn to anticipate the needs, threats, and opportunities of tomorrow's world do we have any hope of mobilizing resources and directing ministry to those areas of greatest need. Many challenges are likely to confront those working in global mission during the last years of the twentieth century, and their anticipation demands much work and thought. I hope that by sketching out some of the questions that global trends raise for us theologically and relationally I can suggest some new ways we might foresee and respond to future challenges.

The Future of Our Global Ecology

A report from The U.S. Office of Technology Assessment projects that future levels of combined economic and population growth will seriously threaten the carrying capability of our finite planet through massive pollution of air and water, deforestation, desertification, elimination of wildlife habitat, depletion of fisheries, and in general the progressive simplification and homogenization of nature. The report concluded that these pressures on global systems will create escalating rates of inflation, which will take their greatest toll on the poorest of the poor.[10]

In many parts of the Two Thirds World, the major energy crisis is a shortage of firewood. So much wood has been cut in some areas that the people have deforested vast tracts of land and have caused extensive erosion of croplands. This means that those of us who work in the Two Thirds World need to focus not only on immediate human needs—cooking fuel—but also on the ecological context—the ultimate depletion of fuel supplies, erosion, and all the further consequences. We need to monitor those geographical areas that are threatened with destruction by human growth, and together with others we need to try to find ways to protect the environment—and ultimately those who live there as well. If we fail our biblical responsibility to be "earth keepers" and stewards of the ecological context within which we live and work, our efforts at economic development may be pointless.

The Future of the Global Poor

Approximately seventy million people are in imminent danger of starvation, four hundred million are chronically malnourished, and fully one billion do not get enough to eat. Two billion people, or almost half the world's population, make less than two hundred dollars per person per year.[11] And if the present situation is not bad enough, the plight of the poor will likely only worsen as we approach the year 2000. The "Global 2000" report, published recently by the government of the United States, states that the world's poor are in a growing state of jeopardy. This is the world in the year 2000: "more crowded, more polluted, and even less stable ecologically, and more vulnerable to disruption than the world we live in now, unless the nations of the world act quickly and decisively to change current policies."[12] Former West German chancellor Willy Brandt warns in his "North South Report" that the growing global inequity between North and South threatens world peace and stability. Consequently he has called for a major international program by industrialized nations to help the poorer parts of the world become self-reliant.

The problem is that neither independent nations nor private voluntary agencies are acting decisively. Some experts predict that we will have twice as many hungry people by the year 2000 as we have today. But those of us in

Christian organizations have not paid adequate attention to these signals—we have not mobilized an adequate response to address the growing issues of hunger and poverty that will be even more pressing in our world tomorrow. How can we make the church and all Christians aware of the growing challenges and then motivate them to mobilize their resources to provide a more adequate response to future needs?

The Future of Global Urbanization

The unprecedented urban explosion—already an enormous problem—will only worsen from now to the end of the century and beyond. In Africa, Asia, and Latin America the number of landless poor—those rural people who own little more than their own bodies and who can stay on the land only as long as they are strong enough to work it—now stands at some six hundred million. By the end of the century their number will likely be around one billion. Their situation is far from settled today, and, as Erik Eckholm forecasts, the "conflict rooted in the inequality of land ownership is apt to become more acute in country after country."[13]

Millions of these landless people have given up hope for the land and are flooding into the cities of the Two Thirds World. "By the end of the century, three-quarters of all Latin Americans and one-third of all Asians and Africans will be living in cities."[14] By the year 2000, Latin America will be more urbanized than Europe. The largest city in the world by the century's end will be Mexico City with thirty-two million inhabitants, and São Paulo, Brazil, will be second with twenty-five million.[15]

Again, very few government or voluntary agencies are paying attention to this critically important trend. To avert a potential human holocaust in these critically over-populated corridors, those directly involved must take immediate action and others must provide support to provide some plan for land use and for rural and urban development. Evangelical agencies have historically worked intensively in the areas of rural development but have had very modest involvement in programs of land reform. Only in the last several years have a few agencies, World Vision and World Concern, for example, begun to consider the area of urban development. We in the church, in concert with others, must also initiate programs to return land to the landless and begin new creative urban ventures to enable people in the exploding cities to become self-reliant in meeting their basic survival needs.

The Future of Global Refugee Migrations

We must respond not only to the unprecedented urban migrations of today and the future, but also to the emerging refugee movements of tomorrow's world. Refugee movements are a by-product of political destabilization, which is likely only to increase in the future. Therefore, we need to analyze the politically unstable regions of the world and identify where the next refugee flows are likely to come from. In cooperation with the United Nations and government agencies, refugee programs need to be developed *in advance* of new refugee movements.

The Future of Global Economics

Of course the issues of world hunger, global ecology, and large-scale human migrations are inextricably connected to global economic and political structures. Thus some of the most difficult challenges confronting the church in the future are economic and political—but also ethical, for any country's economics and politics will affect those of many other countries. Richard Barnet predicts that "there are enough resources in the world to support a decent life for the predicted global population of the year 2000, but not to support lopsided opulence or continual ecological plunder," which is a characteristic of our world today.[16]

In the seventies we abruptly awakened to a new image of our planet as a finite pie. Unquestionably, a major contributing cause to the rapid depletion of nonrenewable resources and their escalating costs has been the dramatic economic growth of countries in the northern hemisphere. Robert Heilbronner points out that until recently the industrialized North has been growing at a rate of about 7 percent a year, or doubling about every ten years. If that rate continued for another fifty years, and all else remained constant, the North would have to extract resources from the earth at a rate thirty-two times that of today.[17]

We in the North have assured ourselves, and those with whom we share the planet, that our trajectory of high economic growth is not only good for us but will bring benefits that will trickle down to all the earth's inhabitants. However, recent evidence seems to raise serious questions as to whether our high economic growth benefits or penalizes those with whom we share the finite resources of the world. Alvin Toffler charges that this "trickle down economics" has failed: those of us in the North have treated the rest of the world as though it were not a cobeneficiary but merely our "gas pump, garden, mine, quarry, and cheap labor supply."[18] Yet despite this failure and the growing concern among many both North and South about economic justice, there is little evidence of serious change in international economic structures. Indeed, the call for a new economic order in 1974 by Two Thirds World countries and the proposals they raised have been virtually ignored.

In fact, the industrialized countries tend to ignore even those problems that much more directly affect them. Even though the issue of Third World debt is a growing concern to the economic capitals in the North, lending nations are doing little to resolve the issue. Therefore we can expect the gap between rich and poor nations to continue to widen as we approach the year 2000. "Under the influence of the U.S. Government, World Bank has fundamentally changed directions. These changes will probably influence its activities through the Eighties. The World Bank is becoming more of an umbrella agency through which private investment is channeled to the Third World. Essentially, under the new focus, instead of the Bank being a cushion against the market, the Bank will now be the market, tying interest rates to the market. It seems likely that these changes will have a negative impact on the poorest countries."[19]

The changes at the World Bank reflect the dramatic change in the foreign policy of the United States brought by the Reagan administration. Mr. Reagan has taken a more ideological approach to both domestic and foreign policy than has any U.S. president in fifty years. Partly as a result of this there is a growing disparity between the interests of the United States and those of Two Thirds World countries. Of primary policy concern to the U.S. at this time is "national security," and American policy makers see the whole world in terms of American-Soviet relations.

The areas of policy that do manage to lie outside the sphere of American-Soviet relations are seen in terms of the American ideal of success. At the Cancun Summit, Mr. Reagan lectured the poorer nations to follow the American example and pull themselves up by their own bootstraps. Yet even though the U.S. is offering some private sector assistance, its foreign aid to poorer nations is declining, and one wonders how resource-poor nations are supposed to pull themselves up in a global economy rigged in favor of the rich and influential nations and against the poor.[20]

Even though most industrialized nations have experienced a slowing of economic growth in the wake of the global recession, the engines of growth are beginning to start up again. As Christians we must ask—and we must find out—who will benefit and who will lose if the North begins to experience a higher rate of economic growth. Is it really an unmixed blessing for all people in the world? Should we really leave the future of the poor to Darwinian economic theories? Do the church and Christian relief and development agencies have any responsibility to influence government policies in our respective countries, or is our only responsibility to patch up those victimized by unjust economic structures—to work only on relief and leave prevention to others?

In view of prophetic warnings from Isaiah to Amos about God's judgment against those who live affluently at the expense of the poor, Christians who hope to live in accordance with the Bible must come to grips with the issue of social justice and its implications for global economics and the use of planetary resources. We need a policy of more equitable growth in the North that will ensure justice for all those that share this finite planet.

The church as a whole must address these issues. We need a more biblical and more responsible theology of stewardship. Nowhere in the New Testament is the tithe normative for stewardship. We cannot divide our lives up into two portions, the one for God and the other for ourselves. Rather, we need to affirm again that all "the earth is the Lord's" and that following Christ is always a whole life proposition.

Therefore, if the earth is truly the Lord's, the question is never "How much do I have to give up?" but "How much of God's do I get to keep as I seek to live in a just relationship with others?" So before we build a multimillion dollar church in America, we must check to see if a church in Bolivia can afford a metal roof. Before we buy a luxury item for ourselves, we must find out whether a family in another part of the world can afford to feed their children. We need to begin stewarding all our personal and institutional resources of time, education, money, and facilities with the realization that they belong to God and his church international, not to us. The International Fellowship of Evangelical Students promotes one model. Their executive committee is comprised of twelve members, eight of whom are from the South. Even though financial resources come largely from the North, they belong to the Fellowship as a whole, and this committee has the authority to determine their use in ministry.

If the earth is the Lord's, then relief and development agencies in the North need to consider bringing brothers and sisters in the South into full partnership in the use of resources that belong to the international body of Jesus Christ, and Northern agencies need to internationalize their leadership. All of us in both North and South must reduce overhead so that a greater share of the resources gets to those who need it. Two new agencies in the United States—Harvest, in Phoenix, Arizona, and Good Deeds, in Seattle, Washington—have found ways to reduce overhead by simplifying operations, and they have found nontraditional ways to raise money to cover all their remaining overhead costs. As a consequence, they are able to send 100 percent of designated gifts to the field.[21]

The proclamation also calls all of us who work with the poor to reduce the costs of our own lifestyles significantly and to live much more simply so that more of God's resources are available for the work of his kingdom among those in need. If we do not authentically incarnate the values of the kingdom in lifestyles of simplicity, how can we work with the poor in integrity?[22]

The Future of Global Political Confrontation

Closely related to the larger issue of economic justice is the issue of political freedom and world peace. Recently the nuclear arms race and the Cold War between the superpowers has dramatically escalated. Christians and others concerned for peace in western Europe and the United States have challenged this buildup.

Unless the Soviet Union and the United States agree to freeze production and deployment of nuclear missiles and begin actually reducing their nuclear stockpiles, they will not have the moral clout necessary to persuade nations without nuclear weapons to sign a nuclear nonproliferation treaty. Without such a treaty some forty nations will develop and possess nuclear weapons by the year 2000. And some of those nations are likely to use their weapons.[23]

Does it make sense for Christians, churches, and Christian agencies to labor to save the lives of the poor from the ravages of hunger and economic injustice and yet not speak out against nuclear war, which would be the ultimate violence against persons? In working for the kingdom, is our sole task to run the ambulance service at the bottom of the cliff, treating the victims of injustice and violence, or do we also have a responsibility to challenge the forces that push the innocent off the cliff? Should we, for example, speak out against human rights violations in Russia, Iran, and El Salvador? Should we seek to stop the flow of arms into the Middle East or Central America, or should we leave the policy issues to others? What does the Bible's call to work for peace and reconciliation mean in our world today and tomorrow?

The Future of the Globalization of Culture

A less visible but perhaps more pervasive use of human control and intimidation is the introduction, and often imposition, of Western values into traditional cultures. Some accurately observe that North America has become the image of the better future for many in the Two Thirds World. Through transnational marketing by multinational corporations, we appear to be creating a global consumer society in which everyone listens to the same kind of music, drinks the same soda, and buys into the same individualistic, materialistic values.

Powerful Western interests are using advanced communication systems to gain control of communications networks in the Two Thirds World. Using technology ranging from satellite television to laser radio, they are promoting a new global culture, in the process changing local customs, tastes, and values.[24] Increasingly, Two Thirds World countries are responding by pushing for "a new information order." Christopher Nasciemento, a cabinet member in Guyana, argues that the West dominates and controls the direction, flow, management, and content of information internationally. The creation of a new information order which would provide for indigenous direction and management of communications systems could fundamentally alter consciousness all over the world. Not only might this slow the Westernization of the world, it might very well raise some consciousness among those in the First World as well.[25]

Those of us involved in global mission need to ask to what extent we are unconsciously promoting the Westernization of indigenous traditions and cultures and to what extent we are working for kingdom agendas that are transcultural. Should Christian development projects seek, as a conscious planning goal, to help people preserve and augment their traditional values in the face of growing Westernization? Should Christian organizations help indigenous organizations gain greater control of media and information systems within their own countries in response to the growing challenge of external, Western control?

The Future of Global Christian Faith

The global rate of Christianity's growth is slowly declining. There is also a significant shift in the demographics of the church. "Presently, some 1.433 billion people consider themselves Christian and are affiliated among over 20,800 distinct denominations. The percentage of Christians to the total world population has been slowly declining: from 34.4 percent of the world's population in 1900 to 32.8 percent in 1980. Massive gains in the Two-Thirds World countries are offset by growing apostasy in the One-Third World."[26]

The changes in the church will reveal new prominence by groups and areas that previously formed only a small part of the church. Throughout the world, the groups experiencing the most rapid gains are the Pentecostals and the charismatics. And by the year 2000 over half of all the Christians will be citizens of the Two Thirds World. According to Walbert Buhlmann in his book *The Coming of the Third Church: An Analysis of the Present and Future,* we are witnessing a fundamental shift, not only in demographics, but potentially in the leadership of tomorrow's church. Those of us in the First World will have to listen more and talk less. For example, we will have to read theology from our brothers and sisters in Africa, Asia, and Latin America.

We need to be clear on the implications of working in true partnership North and South, freely sharing leadership with those who are the growing edge of the church. The dying church in the North will be forced to turn to the growing church in the South for renewal and revitalization. Churches in the Two Thirds World will play an increasingly aggressive role as mission agencies, not only in sending missionaries to the unreached but also in organizing relief and development work. In view of the mounting challenges discussed in this paper, Christian agencies must work more cooperatively—North and South together, increasingly under Two Thirds World leadership—witnessing our unity in Jesus Christ.

In view of the unprecedented global challenges that confront the church already and that will only continue to confront it in the last two decades of the twentieth century and beyond, it is essential that those of us working with the poor learn

1. to more effectively anticipate the needs, challenges, and opportunities that are likely to be a part of tomorrow's world;

2. to identify the implications that those challenges will have for the church and its biblical mission to the world;

3. to create imaginative new ministries that will more effectively respond to the anticipated challenges in each part of the world in which we are working;

4. to act more justly and conscientiously—in both our personal lifestyles and our institutional programs—as stewards of the resources of time, education, and money that God has entrusted to us, thus freeing up much more for the work of the kingdom to be used in partnership with those in the Two Thirds World;

5. to set aside all competition and conflict, and to join together cooperatively in our common mission to the poor, increasingly relying on the leadership and vitality of the church in the Two Thirds World—and receiving their ministry to us;

6. to articulate a theology of biblical mission to human needs that is responsive to the context of a very rapidly changing future; and

7. to pray as we have never done before that God's kingdom will come and that his will may be done on earth through his church as it seeks to act in response to the escalating challenges of tomorrow's world.

A business-as-usual approach to these anticipated challenges—responding to the ever-increasing needs simply by increasing our budgets and activities by some fixed percentage over the previous year—will not make any significant difference to the plight of many in the world. We must mobilize our constituencies and organizations to a much greater commitment to global mission in the 80s and 90s in both proclaiming the love of God and demonstrating his love in a lifestyle of justice and service. We need to articulate and implement a coherent theology of social transformation in the context of a rapidly changing future.[27]

Notes

1. "Evangelism and Social Responsibility: An Evangelical Commitment," the Grand Rapids Report (from the Consultation on the Relationship between Evangelism and Social Responsibility held in Grand Rapids in 1982), Lausanne Occasional Papers no. 21 (Lausanne Committee for World Evangelization, 1982). The papers presented at Grand Rapids are published in *In Word and Deed,* ed. Bruce Nicholls (Exeter: Paternoster, 1985; Grand Rapids: Eerdmans, 1986).

2. Walbert Buhlmann, *The Coming of the Third Church: An Analysis of the Present and Future,* ed. Ralph Woodhall and A. N. Woodhall, orig. *Kommt die dritte Kirche* (Maryknoll, N.Y.: Orbis, 1977), p. 42.

3. David Morawetz, *Twenty-Five Years of Economic Development* (Washington, D.C.: World Bank, 1977), p. 7.

4. John G. Sommer, *Beyond Charity: U.S. Voluntary Aid for a Changing Third World* (Washington, D.C.: Overseas Development Council, 1977), p. 3.

5. See Larry Collins and Dominique LaPierre, *Freedom at Midnight* (New York: Simon and Schuster, 1975).

6. Jeremy Rifkin and Ted Howard, *The Emerging Order: God in the Age of Scarcity* (New York: Putnam, 1979), p. 33.

7. Ibid., p. 34.

8. Mihaljo Mesarovic and Eduard Pestel, *Mankind at the Turning Point* (New York: Dutton, 1974), p. 1.

9. Augustin B. Vencer, *1980 Annual Report* (Manila: Philippine Council of Evangelical Churches, 1980), p. 15.

10. U.S. Office of Technology Assessment, *Technology and Population* (Washington, D.C., 21 August 1978), p. 2.

11. These figures are from Michael Harrington, *The Vast Majority: A Journey to the World's Poor* (New York: Simon and Schuster, 1977), pp. 14-15.

12. See the article "Global 2000: A Warning," *Agenda,* September 1980 (Agenda is an official publication of the U.S. Agency for International Development).

13. Erik Eckholm makes this point in the article "Study Urges Crop Reform," *Christian Science Monitor,* 2 July 1979, p. 2.

14. Jan Tinbergen, *Reshaping the International Order* (New York: Dutton, 1976), p. 31.

15. See these figures in "Hemisphere Trends," *Americas,* January 1979, p. 71.

16. The quote is from Richard Barnet, *The Lean Years: Politics in an Age of Scarcity* (New York: Simon and Schuster, 1980), p. 309.

17. Robert Heilbronner, *An Inquiry into the Human Prospect* (New York: Norton, 1975), pp. 47-48.

18. Alvin Toffler, *The Third Wave* (New York: Morrow, 1980), p. 345.

19. Robert Manning, "The World Bank Feels the Pinch," *South,* March, 1982.

20. See Roger D. Hanson, *U.S. Foreign Policy and the Third World: Agenda 1982* (New York: Praeger, 1982), pp. vii-xii.

21. See further Robert Moffitt's article "The Local Church and Development" in this volume.

22. Increasingly, the policies of evangelical relief and development agencies in this area are becoming more visible. See "A Giver's Guide," *The Other Side,* March 1983.

23. See Ruth Legger Sivard, "World Military and Social Expenditures," Bread for the World Background Paper no. 21 (Washington, D.C.: Bread for the World, February 1978).

24. See Cees Hamelink, *The Corporate Village* (Rome: IDOC International, 1977), pp. 135-37.

25. Christopher Nasciemento, "A Third World View of the New Information Order," *Christian Science Monitor,* 18 December 1981.

26. These figures are from "Status of the World," an unpublished research paper (Monrovia, Calif.: MARC, 1982).

27. An earlier version of this article was published in *Evangelicals and Development,* ed. Ronald J. Sider (Exeter: Paternoster; Philadelphia: Westminster, 1981), the proceedings of an earlier conference leading up to Wheaton '83.

From Development to Transformation

Wayne G. Bragg

Rain clouds began to mask the equatorial sun above Soy, a village in the high plateau of western Kenya. Inside the thatched house the Reverend Shadrack Opoti and his wife were meeting all day with their church leaders to discuss evangelism and social programs for their people. Outside, millet was spread on a hardened cow-dung drying area.

When the afternoon rain broke, we suspended the meeting to help sweep up the millet. We stashed the millet sacks, holding a season's basic food, in the crowded room. I sat on one sack and listened all afternoon to the musical Luo language, understanding nothing except Shadrack's occasional interpretation. Later, a girl brought a bowl of steaming cornmeal ugali, another of water, and a towel for our hands. After washing, we passed the bowl around and scooped out handfuls to eat.

Following dinner Shadrack leaned back and said to me: "We have been talking today about how to respond to needs as the church. You have seen the conditions of life here—how we live on the edge of existence day after day. As Christian leaders we want to be able to offer some hope of improvement for our families and communities, as well as the message of eternal salvation. But what kind of improvement can we offer? Our government talks of development but things get worse. Our young people who get education leave for the big cities, and our crops bring low prices if we can sell them at all. We have few tools and no credit, even though we were returned our land after independence. Food is still short, and sickness takes it toll. What can we do?"

I was suddenly aware of the silence as they all looked at me across the kerosene lamps on the table. What could I say? What is the church's role in addressing human need? Is it to bring the benefits of modern technology to the Third World? Is this really development or is it just a false panacea? Indeed, what is development?

"You have heard of the United States," I said, and paused for translation.

They nodded in agreement.

"You must think of the United States as very advanced and rich, with tall buildings and motor cars like in Nairobi."

They nodded again.

"But what would you think of a place where families can live next to other families without ever knowing their names? Where people can live and work and never need anyone else in the community? Where money is more important than anything?"

Murmurs and glances among themselves.

"What would you think of a country where many old people are sent away to spend their last years apart from their homes and their families? And where many children are abused or even killed by their parents? Where millions of young people run away from home?"

Looks of amazement and horror crossed their faces.

"And what would you think of a society that allows its people to pollute its air and water with poisons and wastes? What would you say about that kind of life?"

A rapid crossfire of dialogue in Luo ensued. After ten minutes, Shadrack turned back to me and said, "They don't think they would like to live like that."

It became apparent as we talked about development that economic or material wealth does not necessarily constitute the "good life." As E. F. Schumacher noted, this approach to the good life has created "a system of production that ravishes nature and a society that mutilates man."[1] What the Luo desire is a little more security in terms of better health care, crop prices, tools, and nutrition. They do not desire to give up a way of life that stresses family cohesion, group cooperation, and the value of each member of the community. In this sense, the Luo possess qualities that the industrialized West seriously needs to learn from.

The sort of development pursued by government and private agencies is based on a model of a better life that is inappropriate to the needs and goals of people like the Luo. Christian church and parachurch agencies seem to have accepted uncritically the basic premises of the Western ideal of development. Tom Sine suggests that these premises are derived more from the secular humanism of the Enlightenment than from Christian thought, and that they are "based on the implicit belief that human society is inevitably progressing toward the attainment of a temporal, materialistic kingdom. . . . Implicit in this progressive view of the future was the firm conviction that economic progress would automatically result in social and moral progress."[2]

There are numerous current approaches to development, each of which usually contains both elements of value, through God's common grace, and also distortions and failings. I have examined four major approaches in particular along with their basic assumptions in order to understand the strengths and weaknesses of each. On the basis of this examination, I seek to move beyond the current conceptualizations and practices of development and so to formulate some general criteria on the nature of development. I hope that these criteria will both help the church examine any theory of social change for its inherent advantages and disadvantages and also help guide it toward a new approach more adequate in particular contexts than any current approach alone.

Four Approaches to Development (and Underdevelopment)

The dominant contemporary approach to development is the Modern-ization theory, which has contributed much to a popular understanding of development and which today commands the majority of programs, human resources, and money. The three other approaches—Dependency, Global Re-formism, and Another Development—are either variations of Modernization or reactions to it.

Modernization

Since the modern industrial and technological era ushered in unparal-leled economic growth and prosperity for the West (more correctly, the North), the idea of making its fruits available to the rest of the world has motivated governments, intergovernment institutions, and private voluntary organiza-tions. Modernization theorists sought to spread those fruits by attempting to replicate the Western process of industrialization and technological growth in other parts of the world as well. In the words of Francois Perroux, Modern-ization is the "combination of mutual and social changes of a people which enable them to increase, cumulatively and permanently, their total real produc-tion."[3]

Modernization theorists gained impetus and acceptance after World War II especially as they sought a response to the Cold War and the needs of new nations. They hold that the way to development is to diffuse the industrial system of the West to these "less-developed" countries (which is why Modern-ization is also called diffusionism). Their ultimate goal is to increase produc-tion and economic growth which, they say, will raise the standard of living and provide a "good life" for as many as possible.

A corollary motivation is to combat the rising tide of international com-munism. By spreading the economic benefits of the capitalist market system, Modernization theorists hope to destroy the need and desire for socialist move-ments. Walt W. Rostow, a political adviser to various U.S. presidents, wrote his *Stages of Economic Growth: A Non-Communist Manifesto* with this ideo-logical bias in mind.[4] He saw the process of development as a succession of natural stages from "traditional" to modern, a sort of Spencerian social Dar-winism[5] in which societies develop from a backward stage through the evolu-tionary process until they "take off" into sustained economic growth.

This process accelerates, according to the theory, through the transfer of knowledge, technology, and capital from the "advanced" to less-advanced na-tions. The transfer closes the technological gap between the two and creates an economy in the latter that supposedly matures until it reaches the final stage of high production and mass consumption. At this point, the benefits would trickle down within that economy from the modern industrialized sector to the poorer sectors, creating a society and economy that would look very much like those of Western Europe, the United States, or Japan. The ultimate stages of

Modernization will be the eventual post-industrial society, described by Daniel Bell.[6]

Some Assumptions and a Critique of Modernization

Modernization theory is based on at least five flawed assumptions.

1. Modernization theorists assume that traditional (that is, rural and agrarian) societies are in some absolute sense underdeveloped and that their values and institutions cause underdevelopment as well as express it. "Resistance to development" came to be a perjorative criticism of any non-Western society, as though the Western model of development were the summum bonum of human existence and those who declined to accept it were backward and too ignorant to accept it.

Such attempts to define what is good merely against the standard of one's own experience are the height of ethnocentrism. Is "progress" preferable to the adaptive patterns developed over centuries? The Maasai elder who refuses to send his son to a government school rightly sees Western education as teaching him to despise the ways of his ancestors. Is his position ignorant?[7] Some writers suggest that traditions are not necessarily a hindrance to true development but can be positive forces to build on.

2. Modernization theorists assume that their idea of development is an inevitable, unilinear process that operates naturally in every culture. They tend to assume that all traditional societies are alike, and they fail to explain the variations brought about by random change and by interactions between societies.[8] The theory that modernization naturally occurs in a series of stages likewise assumes that "developing" countries today are similar to the "developed" countries at an earlier stage of their growth and that they can therefore modernize in the same way. In actual fact, the internal and external socioeconomic conditions acting on countries are greatly different now from what they were during the development of the present industrial countries. Trade and the market do not operate in the same way today that they did in early capitalism. It takes many more bags of coffee to buy a tractor today. Rich countries today can determine, through their purchasing power, their use of tariffs, and other rules of trade, not only what is grown in the poorer countries, but also what the prices of the product should be. Raul Prebisch sees the function of trade as "only benefiting the economically stronger countries," not stimulating the growth of the weaker ones.

3. Modernization theory assumes that productivity equals development, and that large-scale capital-, energy-, and import-intensive systems are the most productive and thus the most developed.[9] Benjamin Higgins counters by saying that "productivity is not development, but merely the possibility of development."[10] There is a qualitative aspect to development that productivity ignores.

What may be exported along with the Western ideal of modernization is universal alienation and industrial bondage. Indeed humanity can be reduced to a unit of production, *homo faber*, with all the anomie and alienation that goes with it. In Hong Kong, where the Modernization theory is having its greatest influence, multinational corporations are exploiting some thirty-four thousand children under the age of fourteen, half of whom work ten hours a day.[11] Human beings are multidimensional with the psychological need for dignity, self-esteem, freedom, and participation. To reduce them to mere producers and consumers is to assume that some basic materialism is the goal of life. Of course, meeting human material needs makes life possible, but as Maslow's hierarchy of needs shows, it is not sufficient for human self-realization.[12]

Modernization theory contemplates economies of scale as the most efficient means of production, hence the emphasis on sophisticated technology and capital-intensive production. However, this creates more problems than it solves. Large industrial plants situated in urban centers tend to exacerbate rural to urban migration and create squalid squatter settlements, as well as cause pollution and ecological destruction. Capital-intensive production not only creates large external debts (Brazil's foreign debt is now approaching $100 billion) but also in most cases destroys smaller local companies. Furthermore, it worsens structural unemployment and underemployment by destroying traditional sector jobs, especially in agriculture, thus creating a pool of cheap surplus labor.[13] Another cost of articulation into the international capital market system is that local markets become vulnerable to the fluxes of the international market. Partly in response to such flux, Ford Motor Company in Buenos Aires recently fired six hundred workers, all from San Fernando, an urban squatter town.

4. Theorists and politicians commonly assume that the benefits of the system will trickle down to the poorest of the poor. The infusion of capital at the top supposedly creates jobs so that the "economic pie" grows and benefits everyone with a bigger slice. This neoclassical economic theory is alive and well in the United States in supply-side economics. This simplistic and reactive formulation assumes conditions of a previous era of capital formation.

The phenomenal rise of transnational or multinational corporations (MNCs) has altered the rules of the international game. With maximization of profits as the primary goal, MNCs use their mobility to create a neomercantilism that serves only the ends of the corporation, not those of the countries in which they operate or those of their own employees.[14] The favorable conditions for MNCs in less-developed countries have created a new comparative advantage that works for the corporation: cheap labor, looser controls on pollution, fewer safety regulations, longer work days, better labor discipline, and little or no trade union protection of workers—all resulting in higher profits.[15] Some MNCs have become so powerful that they can even exert their will over that of independent nations.[16]

Peter Evans documents a case history of MNCs in Brazil and concludes that "the industrializing elite alliance (of local, multinational, and state capital) that currently holds sway in Brazil is inherently incapable of serving the needs of the mass of the population."[17] Inflation in Brazil has outstripped the increase in salaries by some 235 percent during the period of the "economic miracle." The poor, invariably, are the worst hit—all over the world. In Seoul, Korea, the work week is often 84 hours, seven days a week, and in São Paulo poor workers may have to ride buses four to six hours a day to reach their work.[18] Furthermore, the jobs that MNCs create are often volatile—when wages rise, companies move. In Hawaii, Castle and Cooke company (founded by missionaries!) closed down its pineapple production and moved to the Philippines where land and labor are cheaper. In doing so, not only did they disrupt labor markets in Hawaii but they also began to force Philippine peasants off their traditional farmlands. Obviously, the trickle-down approach has little demonstrable success in creating stable jobs or distributing the benefits of wealth to the poor.

5. Modernization theory is based on the assumption that nation-to-nation aid fosters development. In the United States, the U.S. Agency for International Development (USAID) was conceived as a mechanism to transfer technology and foster institutional growth in Third World countries. In actual fact the aim of foreign aid was much more self-seeking. Richard Nixon put it very baldly in 1968 when he said, "Let us remember that the main purpose of American aid is not to help other nations but to help ourselves." Eugene Black, former president of the World Bank expands on this theme: "(1) Foreign aid provides a substantial and immediate market for United States goods and services. (2) Foreign aid stimulates the development of new overseas markets for United States companies. (3) Foreign aid orients national economies toward a free enterprise system in which United States firms can prosper."[19] The expansion of markets for U.S. goods in the Third World has by now become essential to the prosperity of the U.S. economy. *Agenda,* an official USAID publication, indicated that some 1.2 million U.S. jobs depend on exports to the Third World.

The self-seeking nature of U.S. "foreign" aid is revealed by estimates that 75 percent of USAID funds for the Third World are in fact spent in the U.S. But what does AID money do when it does get overseas?[20] The authors of *Aid As Obstacle* conclude that by dwelling on food aid, we divert attention from the process of how hunger is created and only maintain the conditions that necessitate food grants.[21] Consistent with this call for an aid moratorium, a recent USAID director saw some programs as in fact exacerbating the plight of the poor in situations where land tenure practices are inequitable. He went on to assert that such assistance has only served to create or strengthen an agrobusiness elite as well as to support relatively few U.S. corporations abroad.[22]

Unintended Results: The Social and Ecological Costs of Modernization

Social Costs. There are several unintended results that actually threaten any future "development" of certain peoples. "The estimated 200 million tribals, hunters and gatherers now on the receiving end of 'progress' are among the world's largest and most endangered species. Hunger, disease, development and war are their enemies."[23] Tribal peoples are bearing the brunt of the accelerated pace of Third World modernization because their way of life is not tied into the money market, and therefore is considered unimportant.

These so-called primitive peoples are jeopardized simply by where they live, for they often occupy land that is rich in resources and very desirable for developers. The aborigines of northern Australia began losing sovereignty over their tribal lands when uranium was found; North American Indian groups are under pressure because of the resources, especially oil, of the lands given to them by treaty; and the Indians of the Amazon basin are threatened by the rush to exploit the gold, strategic minerals, and timber of the area, all aided and abetted by Brazilian expansionist policies. Brazil's Indian population has declined from somewhere between three and six million at the time of the first European invasion four centuries ago to approximately two hundred thousand today. Brazilian settlers intent on getting the Indians' lands sometimes gave them clothing infected by smallpox, a technique pioneered in U.S. Indian warfare by British General Jeffrey Amherst. The anthropologist Jean-Patrick Razon in an interview with *Newsweek* stated that by the year 2000, all but a few of the Amazon tribes will have been eliminated.[24]

Beyond the ethical and moral questions of the destruction and assimilation of such tribal peoples, the rest of the world also faces the permanent loss of their insights and knowledge about local wildlife, medicinal plants, and ecology. Barbara Bentley of Survival International contends that a plan of modernization that depends on overwhelming tribalism and native ways is "like destroying a library of information. If we get rid of these people we're effectively destroying a part of ourselves."[25]

The loss of traditional values and whole cultures through the cultural imperialism of Westernization is increasing. The *Hastings Center Report* recounts that the Mayuruna, a small remote Amazon Indian tribe, have found Western civilization so devastating to their tribal and cultural identity that they have apparently decided to kill their babies rather than let them grow up in an alien culture.[26] The Mayuruna had never encountered Western culture until the 1960s, when rubber tappers entered their lands. Since then the Western impact on their tribe has been enormous. In 1972, there were an estimated two thousand Mayuruna; now there are only about four hundred. While at first they killed only their female babies, they are now killing their male children as well, according to Paulo Lucena, a Brazilian anthropologist.

Ecological Costs. The Western scientific movement is based on the materialistic theme "man over nature," the idea that nature is to be subdued rather than respected. This attitude was exported with the Modernization approach to development, and the results have been disastrous in many parts of the world. Already the societies that we call modern consume a disproportionate amount of the earth's renewable and nonrenewable resources. The consumption of the few has become a strain on the many. For example, a North American consumes during his or her lifetime five hundred times the resources that a person in India does.[27] The physical resources of the earth certainly cannot support a whole world that consumes on the level of the West.[28]

One critical area of concern is the degradation of the earth's fertile land. Already 43 percent of the earth's landmass is desert or semidesert, due partly to overcutting, overgrazing, improper cultivation, and changing settlement patterns. "Fully one-third of today's arable land will be lost in the next 25 years, while the world's need for food will double," according to Boyce Rensberger.[29] Osvaldo Sunkel reports especially high soil erosion in three countries in Latin America: Colombia, Chile, and Mexico.[30] The loss of arable land in this way only makes the loss to urbanization an even greater problem.[31]

Haiti was once covered with a tropical rain forest and as a colony produced more income for France than any other. Now it is so denuded that the government tags every large tree in an effort to preserve it. In any rain forest the trees to some extent control the weather: they retain the moisture that falls then return it to the air for the next rain. But with the destruction of the forest, rainfall, except for hurricanes, has dropped 90 percent in some areas of Haiti. Furthermore, the rains that still do fall are no longer caught by the trees but now rush off the slopes, washing boulders down dry gulches and further eroding the topsoil. In many other parts of the world, tropical or true rain forests are being destroyed at the rate of around 650,000 square kilometers (250,000 square miles) each year. In Latin America alone, the deforestation is around 60,000 square kilometers (23,150 square miles) per year, according to the Food and Agricultural Organization. The land that looks so fertile when it is covered with forest is in fact rather unproductive. Even the grasslands that replace the forests become rapidly depleted. At first, 2.5 acres may be sufficient to support one cow, but in five years it may require from 12 to 17 acres.[32] When the topsoil is eroded away by rain and wind and the land no longer produces without fertilizer, the colonizers, including the peasants of Haiti, push onward into virgin timber higher up the mountainsides and so begin the process all over again.

The modern export crop economy introduced to the Third World demands an ever-increasing application of pesticides, which are harmful to workers who have not been taught how to use them and which threaten the environment, where residues build up to an intolerable level. The danger is perhaps greater in the Third World than in the United States, for people often drink from, wash clothes in, and bathe in the same streams that carry the effluents of agricultural runoff. Contamination is a fact of life for many people in the Third World; blood samples in Central American children have shown fifty times the safe level of some toxins.

Pollution, both from manufacturing and from the hydrocarbons produced by automobile engines, is a sure sign of Western "progress." The restraints on pollution in the First World, with the corresponding cleanup costs, have often merely forced polluting multinationals overseas.

Conclusion

The elders of Soy village in Kenya quickly perceived that the social costs of the American model of modernization might be too high, but still they, like millions of the deprived of the earth, look at the West longingly for the kind of progress that would allow them to lead longer, better, and easier lives. Modernization has provided a radical improvement for one-fourth of the world's population. But the flaw in Modernization theory is the assumption that the only way to achieve more satisfying lives for the rest is through the exportation of Western values, goals, and lifestyles. It does not recognize its ethnocentric assumptions and deleterious social costs. But perhaps the greatest cost of Modernization to the rest of the world is that it fosters—perhaps requires—the continued dependency of the have-nots on the haves, of the modernizing on the modernized.

Dependency and Underdevelopment

> Dependence is a conditioning situation in which the economies of one group of countries are conditioned by the development and expansion of others. Interdependence between two or more economies or between such economies and the world trading system becomes a dependent relationship when some countries can expand only as a reflection of the expansion of the dominant countries, which may have positive or negative effects on their immediate development.[33]

The Dependency theory has arisen in reaction to the increasing disparities between rich and poor nations. The figures used to measure per capita income and standards of living hide the inequitable distribution of the growth brought through Modernization. Gustavo Lagos notes that in one recent year the Gross National Product of the United States was almost 7.2 times that of all of Latin America, while the population of Latin America was greater by almost a third than that of the United States.[34] He indicates that the top 5 percent income group in the U.S. has more wealth than all groups in Latin America combined—ten million privileged North Americans have more than the entire Latin American population!

Dependency theory is an attempt to understand this phenomenon. The root cause of underdevelopment in one part of the world, according to these theorists, is the advance of development in another part.

André Gunder Frank's thesis in "The Development of Underdevelopment" encapsulates the new trend in development thinking that arose in Latin America in the 1960s.[35] He distinguishes "centers" or "metropoli" (the developed countries) from "peripheries" or "satellites" (the underdeveloped countries). He sets forth the thesis that underdevelopment is not the product of a country's own characteristics or structures but, rather, is generated by the development of capitalism itself; the development of the periphery or satellite is greatest when its tie to the center is the weakest. Thus, he argues, the regions most underdeveloped today are those that had the closest ties with the centers in the past. Indeed, he says, Latin America has experienced its most productive growth in times of world crisis, such as during the world wars, when it has been isolated from the United States.

According to some theorists, dependency can be a factor in relationships within a national economy as well. It is because rural sectors of Third World economies are dependent on urban sectors that there is such an income disparity between the two.[36]

Dependency theory stresses the vulnerability of economies that are not autonomous. Dependent countries are those whose involvement with the world market has led them to specialize in the export of a few primary products—and to become dependent on them. For these countries, the world market price of just a few export products can have a great impact on the nation's ability to accumulate capital. For the center countries, however, each product they import—even if it is a primary export of a dependent country—is only a small fraction of total imports, and price fluctuations can have little effect on the economy. Bananas, for example, are not central to the North American economy even though North Americans eat a lot of them. For the economies of Ecuador and Costa Rica, however, bananas are pivotal, and small changes in prices or exports can make a lot of difference to the livelihoods of people there. As Evans points out, the dependent country requires a good market for its product in the center; therefore, economic fluctuations in the center can have severe negative consequences for the periphery.[37] On the other hand, an economic crisis in the periphery offers no real threat to the centers. Thus the state of dependency is "a structural condition in which a weakly-integrated system cannot complete its economic cycle except by an exclusive or limited reliance on an external complement."[38]

This reliance on an external complement is often maintained by foreign control of industry in a given periphery country. José Míguez Bonino notes that in 1975 the ownership of 41.6 percent of Brazilian industry was in the hands of foreigners.[39] Certain industries, such as the automobile industry, were 100 percent foreign controlled while others came close to that mark, including the chemical industry with 94 percent external control and the rubber industry with 82 percent. Bonino concludes that Brazil has become a warehouse of multinational corporations for which the Brazilian population is a reserve of cheap labor.

Dependent economies often suffer uneven growth patterns. Capitalist development, according to Alain de Janvry, is neither linear nor homogeneous, and the accumulation of capital occurs through a succession of periods of advance and stagnation.[40] Furthermore, advance and stagnation can occur simultaneously in different areas of the same developing country. De Janvry suggests that development in particular regions is dialectically paired with stagnation or deformed development in dependent regions, which only perpetuates the dependency syndrome.

Some Assumptions and a Critique of Dependency Theory

1. Dependency theory takes as a given that neocolonialism prevents indigenous capitalistic development. Fernando Cardoso and Enzio Faletto argue, however, that industrialization *is* being carried out in the peripheral countries, though it is controlled largely by multinational corporations.[41] Thus it is possible to have a "dependent development," although that seems a contradiction in terms. Peter Evans's study of Brazil's development shows that capital accumulation does take place in the periphery even under conditions of classic

dependence and that Brazil has been incorporated into the capitalist world economy in a new—still dependent—way.[42]

2. Mainstream dependency theory assumes that the centers grow at the expense of the peripheries, which languish in dependent doldrums. Alain de Janvry argues, however, that the power of the centers has been altered by multinational corporations, OPEC, and revolutions in Africa, Central America, and Southeast Asia.[43] He shows that growth is actually increasing in the periphery and declining in the center. From 1969 to 1979 the rate of capital formation was much higher in Latin America than in the United States.

3. Dependency theory assumes that exploitation of the Third World arose with colonialism and is perpetuated by international dominance of the periphery by the centers. Furthermore, the theory assumes that capitalism is the sole cause of dependency and its ills. However, history is replete with examples of exploitative relationships and dominance of one class by another or of one nation by another when capitalism is not a factor. In Mexico the Aztecs cruelly subjugated and exploited other tribes, and in Peru the Incas oppressed the Huancas and Aymaras long before Pizarro landed.

4. Dependency theory upholds the primacy of economics, as does Modernization theory. Yet a truly developed human society has moral and cultural needs as well, and desires and goals that cannot be reduced to material well-being.

5. Dependency theory discusses "underdevelopment" in the abstract, without seriously considering practical strategies for "development." It optimistically assumes that the demise of a periphery nation's dependent relationship with a center nation, however that is to happen, will automatically usher in development.

6. Dependency theorists have assumed only a one-way dependency: some countries are dependent and others are independent. In fact all countries are interdependent. Industrialized states are dependent on some Third World countries for the supply of strategic minerals and raw materials necessary for defense and high-technology products.[44] As vital resources, nonrenewable or renewable, diminish or are controlled by developing countries, as oil has been, developed countries will have to scramble and pay higher stakes in order to maintain their lifestyles and their militaries. Dependency is a two-edged sword today as the formerly dependent countries begin to realize their power. The Third World is already using its leverage to call for a reordering of the world economic system, the New International Economic Order.

Conclusion

Having lived through colonial rule, Pastor Opoti and his people in Soy would concur with the analysis of the Dependency theorists. They saw the best lands in the western Highlands taken by whites, and they bore the burden of an export economy directed to satisfying the needs of the West. Kenya's political independence meant only the redistribution of land and a concomitant sense of national pride. Jomo Kenyatta bought out the white landowners, but the

Kikuyu and Luo farmers had no management knowledge, tools, or capital to run their farms. Any cash crop production, such as the tea produced in the Kericho region, still flows largely to the external market. Even under political independence economic dependency continues to maintain its grip.

Global Reformism: The New International Economic Order

Another reaction to global inequity, sparked partly by the critical analysis of neo-Marxist dependency theorists, is a worldwide political call for a more just economic order. In 1974, the United Nations Sixth Special Session of the General Assembly presented a "Declaration of the Establishment of a New International Economic Order" (NIEO) under the leadership of Third World representatives. The subsequent Seventh Special session in 1975 adopted the resolution "Development and International Economic Cooperation" based on the "Charter of Economic Rights and Duties of States." All these documents demonstrate the dissatisfaction of the poorer dependent nations with their share of the world economic pie, and their disposition to challenge seriously the international economic status quo.

In a sense this challenge grew out of the post–World War II decolonization process and was a reaction to growing periphery-center dependency. The NIEO was, and continues to be, a cry for economic interdependence based on a more equitable international distribution of wealth. The NIEO proponents, the famous Group of 77 Nations, stated that this interdependence demanded equitable and fair trade agreements among equal and autonomous nations rather than the continuation of the status quo interdependence in which the poorer countries merely exchanged raw goods for manufactured wares.

The NIEO proposal for global reform was based on some sound principles: autonomous control by developing countries over their own economies and resources, international cooperation, active aid assistance by developed countries, a greater participation in decision making, better terms for the transfer of technology, greater facilities for industrialization in the Third World, food security, and changes in the international monetary system.[45] Yet the NIEO has been politically ineffective, in part because these goals are resisted by many of the developed nations, which are in fact carrying out policies contrary to the NIEO. At the 1982 meeting with Third World leaders at Cancun, President Reagan reaffirmed his belief in market strategies for development rather than in a reformed international economic system.[46]

Some Assumptions and a Critique of Global Reformism

The proposed new economic order retains many of the old assumptions of Modernization, with all their flaws.

1. The NIEO does not propose radical change in the economic structures. It is still a form of trickle-down economics. It differs, however, in that it provides a theoretically faster way for the poorer economies to catch up with the rich—it would open the growth spigot for a faster trickle to run down from developed to developing economies. This does not depend on radical change. By

calling for more development aid, for example, the NIEO falsely assumes that aid necessarily results in development. While aid may spark economic development, it may often accomplish just the opposite. "The functions of aid have been many: to make 'weak' economies capable of joining the international capitalist market, to make them more able to suppress internal rebellions, to link them to one or the other of the main political blocks and to facilitate the spread of the Western model of development, but rarely to give an impetus to development."[47]

The NIEO program assumes that the route to development is more trade with industrialized countries and more Western technology, rather than alternative local solutions. In fact, increased access to high technology through more favorable trade arrangements will only exacerbate the social cost of rapid industrialization in developing countries. A "new" economic order would allow the developed nations to maintain control over the direction and pace of "development" in the Third World. An increased emphasis on technology and industrialization would only increase the strength of the multinational corporations.[48]

2. The NIEO assumes that world resources are infinite and highly resiliant. It disregards the deleterious impact of technological development on environments in the Third World. Not only would increased industrialization add to the population migration to large metropolitan centers, it would also encourage polluting industries of developed nations to move to the Third World.

Rising expectations and demands for consumer goods in developing countries would deplete even more rapidly the world's nonrenewable resources—as well as some of the normally renewables like topsoil, forests, and potable water—and it would threaten even more seriously the earth's fragile biosphere. Global Reform would only expand Western consumption patterns to the rest of the world.

3. Reformism idealistically presupposes that the "have-not" countries (including formerly have-not OPEC countries) can maintain cohesiveness in their demands for equity and resist the divide-and-conquer tactics of the "have" countries. Not only have the regional trade associations and common markets formed by developing countries mostly failed, but cracks have even appeared within OPEC. Is it reasonable to assume that in the future countries will band together for the common good and not revert to self-seeking or nationalistic tendencies? How then can a global strategy of reform hope to break the syndrome of dependence and initiate a worldwide change in the economic rules?

4. Reformism assumes that the trickle-down approach works. Yet there is little evidence that trickle down works from nation to nation or from group to group within a developing nation. The program of Global Reformism is unable to meet mass needs because it tends to cater to the small minority in a developing society who want to catch up with and adopt Western ways of life.[49] But the benefits they accumulate do not often reach those below. Rather, the NIEO would further the growth of a rich internationalized bourgeoisie among and within developing countries. The beneficiaries would not be the

neediest, and indeed the poor in a so-called developing country might actually see their lot becoming more difficult and oppressive as others reap the benefits. According to the Cocoyoc Declaration framed by a United Nations expert seminar, "We are still in a stage where the most important concern of development is the level of satisfaction of basic needs for the poorest sections of the population in society. . . . A growth process that benefits only the wealthiest minority and maintains or even increases the disparities between and within countries is not development. It is exploitation. . . . We therefore reject the idea of 'growth first, justice in the distribution of benefits later.'"[50]

5. Global Reformism presupposes that its program will enable the now-dependent countries to control their own destinies with honor. Yet what honor is there when the palliative provided by "easy" imported solutions further erodes a society's own capabilities to deal with its problems from within? S. L. Parmar, an Indian economist, notes, "A society must begin with its reality. If poverty and injustice are the main facts of economic life, the potentiality of the poor must be the main instrument for overcoming them. This would be possible if the people in developing countries discover a sense of dignity and identity within their socio-economic limitations. To assume that only when we have more, when we are nearer to the rich nations, we will have dignity and identity, is a new kind of enslavement to imitative values and structures."[51]

Reliance on quick technological and economic "fixes" also delays any real social transformations within the Third World. Dom Helder Camara, bishop of Olinda, Brazil, asked, "How can there be a new international *economic* order without a new international *social* order?"[52] Radical social reform is a priority in poor countries if "development" is to encompass more than just economics and if all of society is to benefit from a new economic order.

Conclusion

If the proposed changes in the world economic system were to reach the village level in western Kenya, which is doubtful, my friends in Soy might well lament them. Just as many of the poor in Brazil have fared worse under interdependent development on the Western model, the Luo would find the changes under Global Reformism ultimately deleterious and threatening to their lifestyle. They would see Kenya turned more rapidly into a polluted and impoverished backyard for rich nations and corporations, and they would see an even greater gap between themselves and the Kenyan elite. If the politically improbable and personally undesirable should occur, the rural peoples of Kenya would be compelled to exchange their birthright for a technological "fix."

Another Development

In 1975 a UN study group in Stockholm produced the Dag Hammarskjöld Report, which presented an alternative to the NIEO. The report outlined a new framework in development strategy: "Development is a whole. Its ecological, cultural, social, economic, institutional and political dimensions can only be understood in their systematic interrelationships, and action in its service must be integrated. Similarly, needs cannot be dissociated from each other: the satisfaction of each need is at one and the same time the condition and the result of the satisfaction of all others."[53]

This new approach is based on three pillars: the eradication of poverty, endogenous and self-reliant development, and ecological soundness.

Eradication of Poverty

Another Development emphasizes that basic survival needs are not met in the greater part of the world, neither in the Third World nor in the pockets of poverty that still exist in affluent societies.[54] It then proposes a unique strategy to meet them.

Another Development recommends direct attention to meeting basic human needs and the redirection of development priorities from producing more goods to sharing what already exists.[55]

In addressing the basic need for food, for example, Another Development theorists emphasize redistribution: "Hunger and malnutrition are indeed due to the fact that the poor are deprived of the means either to produce or to purchase their food, the socio-economic mechanisms being so organized as to ensure that the lion's share goes to the rich and the powerful."[56] Another Development theory stresses that the provision of habitat, health care, and education should be directed at the neediest, not at the middle class or an upper-class elite. Consequently, development of habitat demands a balanced emphasis on rural and urban areas; and it must place a priority on public transport, clean and stable water supplies, and self-help construction for the poor.

Another Development perceives as the most pressing health need a public, preventive health care system founded on the use of local resources. This approach implies a radical decentralization favoring the participation of local communities, with the more sophisticated hospitals only dealing with problems that cannot be solved at the local level.

The implications of Another Development for education, similarly, are that benefits and resources must be shifted from the minority elite to the masses.[57]

Endogenous and Self-Reliant Development

Perhaps the most striking feature of Another Development is its emphasis on endogenous and self-reliant development. The concept is rooted in Third World experiences and arose as an antithesis to the dependency syndrome. Experiences in Gandhi's India, in pre-1900 Japan, and, more recently, in Tanzania, China, and Sri Lanka (as well as in other places) point the way to self-reliance. Johan Galtung considers self-reliance an important political strategy of contemporary history that seeks to undo five centuries of dependency on the West.[58] "The search for a new international economic order requires a reformulation of the basis for the overall system of relationships between Third World countries and the international system. Instead of total integration into the international system, what is needed is selective participation. This proposition responds to the basic reality that development comes from within, not from without."[59]

In 1967 the TANU party met in Arusha, Tanzania, to develop strategies for that recently independent country. The Arusha Declaration spelled out the Ujamaa (socialist) ideal: "In order to maintain our independence and our people's freedom we ought to be self-reliant in every possible way and avoid depending on other countries for assistance. If every individual is self-reliant, the ten-house cell will be self-reliant; if the cells . . . wards . . . Districts . . . [and] Regions are self-reliant, then the whole nation is self-reliant and this is our aim."[60] Under President Julius Nyerere's leadership, Tanzania has pursued the goals of national identity and self-reliance without depending on either the communist or capitalist blocs. Tanzania wanted development on its own terms and by its own initiative. Nyerere perceived that only by withdrawing from the world capitalist system was it possible to act autonomously and develop on its own terms.[61]

Self-reliance is not autarchy or isolationism, however, as the Dag Hammarskjöld Report points out: "Self-reliance applies at different levels: local, national, international. At the national level, it gives the economic content to political independence. It is not synonymous to autarchy, but with the autonomous capacity to develop and to take decisions, including that of entering into relations, on an equal footing, with other countries, which nations are bound to do."[62] "Above all," in the words of the Cocoyoc Declaration, this autonomous capacity "means trust in people and nations, reliance on the capacity of people themselves to invent and generate new resources and techniques, to increase their capacity to absorb them, to put them to socially beneficial use, to take a measure of command over the economy, and to generate their own way of life."[63]

Thus the self-reliant approach to development is a strategy for more appropriate development, based not on external constraints and potential dependency but rather on internal needs and criteria. Structurally, self-reliant development would equalize and redistribute power among nations and among people within nations. Glyn Roberts argues that power is an important factor in development at both the macro and micro levels.[64] It is the ability to control the environment or people physically, economically, or culturally. Without structures that allow for a democratization of power there is no authentic development, he says. The concept of self-reliance within a nation thus involves a decentralization of power, which would "allow all those concerned, at every level of society to exercise all the power of which they are capable."[65] This redistribution of power is necessary for the exercise of fundamental human rights: the right to express oneself without repression, the right of equal opportunity, and the right to control one's own destiny. Thus self-reliance is sought in order to promote the participation of all members of society, from the lowest levels up.

Self-reliant development could also be called "appropriate" development because it uses technologies derived from local conditions to meet local needs. Since E. F. Schumacher popularized in his book *Small Is Beautiful* the concept of small-scale, decentralized technology that he discovered in India, the idea of appropriate or intermediate technology has taken hold in development circles. Appropriateness in terms of cost, generation of employment, simplicity of construction and maintenance, compatibility with the environment (not "harsh technology"), renewability, and effectiveness lends technology the ability to contribute to individual and national self-reliance.

Appropriate technology need not be high technology; appropriate development need not be development on the Western model. It may often use local resources rather than transferred high technology. President Nyerere of Tanzania strongly holds to this belief:

> I've been telling my own people, "We've got to change, we must mechanize, we must have better tools." But what are better tools? Not the combine harvester. If I were given enough combine harvesters for every family in Tanzania, what would I do with them? No mechanics, no spare parts. . . . It would be a very serious problem—unless, of course, I sell them for hard cash. But we still have to give the people better tools, tools they can handle, and pay for. Americans, when they speak of better tools, are talking about something quite different. We are using hoes. If two million farmers in Tanzania could jump from the hoe to the oxen plough, it would be a revolution. It would double our living standard, triple our product![66]

Ecological Soundness

It follows that a development that is self-reliant, appropriate, and directed at meeting basic needs should also be ecologically sound. Another Development theory seriously questions the dominant thinking among development theorists today that emphasizes unlimited growth and maximum exploitation of the earth's resources. Another Development stresses that on the one hand reckless growth distributes its benefits unequally and on the other it depletes the earth's resources at the expense of future generations.

The earth's resource base is finite, according to Another Development theory. Yet some nations consume more than their share—which in a closed system implies that other, less powerful, nations are left with less than their share. Indeed, the industrial market economies, with 18 percent of the world's population, consume 68 percent of the world's production of nine major minerals while the 50 percent of the world's population that lives in the Third World consumes only 6 percent. What is done with these minerals is yet another issue. Many of them are used for the production of arms. The $244 billion spent on armaments in 1973 by just four industrialized countries represents nearly half the combined 1972 Gross National Products of all the nations of the Third World. "The situation is clear: at the global level, it is neither the poor nor the satisfaction of their needs that is endangering the outer limits, but the monopolization and misuse of resources by a few."[67]

The effects of traditional development strategies have been devastating on Third World environments. Wastes from factories contaminate rivers and kill fish; indiscriminate logging threatens the continued existence of tropical rain forests and creates soil erosion; and automobiles pump their noxious fumes into congested urban areas. Yet the concern for the environment is not predicated only on a love for nature as such. The preservation of our environment is essential for meeting the needs of the poor today and in the years ahead. If we care for the environment now it may suffice to meet our needs; if we destroy it we know that it cannot. "In Another Development, . . . the preservation and enhancement of the environment are inseparable from the satisfaction of needs."[68]

Some Assumptions and a Critique of Another Development

1. Another Development theorists assume that in seeking self-reliance it is possible for a country to be politically neutral. The realities of North-South, East-West, and other global tensions, however, make absolute neutrality for a poor nation extremely difficult. Even when some country tries to be neutral and attempts to adopt a nonaligned position in international politics, it is viewed with great suspicion—especially by the Western power bloc. President Nyerere notes: "When I say 'From China we can learn,' they say we are going Red."

2. These theorists also assume that the necessary conditions for declaring self-reliance are present in the Third World. Yet self-reliance in the real world can be founded only on a political state that is strong enough to resist the political and economic manipulations of the international power structure—the very thing that most Third World countries do not have. Weak nations cannot simply reverse the built-in bias of the world market mechanisms, the cancellation or severe limitation of credit, embargoes, economic sanctions, subversive use of intelligence agencies, repression, counterinsurgency, and even full-scale intervention. In the face of such manipulation by the powerful, the political cost of a self-reliant strategy on the part of any weak nation will be high. Nicaragua has felt the full impact of these strategies of destabilization since 1979 because the Sandinista revolution dared to adopt the policy of nonalignment and sought to meet its basic needs before it attended to the pressures of the international market.

3. Another Development theory also presupposes a state of collective consciousness at the grass-roots level. It assumes that workers, laborers, and farmers are informed and that they share with politicians and leaders common goals and common ideas on how their nation should approach those goals. Ujamaa, the socialist ideal in Tanzania, has suffered because it attempts to solve problems only from the top down. Those people who were moved into rural settings were often not prepared materially or conceptually for the tasks at hand. If grass-roots participation based on education and a sharing of common goals is lacking, the results will contradict the principles of the self-reliance that was sought in the beginning.

4. Another Development theory views people as easily conformable, rational, and nonegoistic—which makes the theory susceptible to the charge of being too utopian and overly optimistic about humanity in the face of human nature. For example, though we can state that some intermediate technology is appropriate for a certain place and time, will those who live in that context be satisfied with that technology when they see the fruits of high technology everywhere? What theorists propose as best for a country may be wholly different from what the people really want and desire. Can any nation in today's world insulate itself from the market economy that promotes Western consumer lifestyles? Papua New Guinea has deliberately prohibited television in the attempt to do so, but how long can that be successful? Some Third World leaders even reject the whole idea of appropriate technology as a new form of imperialism to keep them from achieving the standard of living enjoyed by the industrial states. They demand the right to a modern (that is, Western) lifestyle and end up paying the high social cost, as has happened in Brazil.

Conclusion

The people of Soy would like the process of change to meet their needs, and they would also like it to begin from within their own context. This sort of development will not threaten their heritage, lifestyle, land, or environment. Their traditional patterns of life would become the basis for creative improvements in food production, nutrition, health care, habitat protection and development, and education. Power would be retained at the village level. They would be able to manage the appropriate technological innovations introduced to help them gently harness the resources without making them dependent on others. However, this image is overshadowed by the question of whether international political conditions and Kenya's internal resource base will ever let the country and my friends realize the dream.

Beyond Development to Transformation

Development, it is clear, has come to mean a wide variety of things, depending on a given set of culturally defined assumptions. Theologians and Christian development workers, like their secular counterparts, have struggled to understand what true development is. In the light of the ongoing discussion, I propose an alternative framework for understanding human and social change from a Christian perspective, which I will call *transformation*.

What Is Transformation?

Transformation is a concept that permeates the biblical record, from the Old Testament images of *shalom* and the reign of God in Israel to the New Testament church and the kingdom of God. Throughout the Bible, we see how the existing reality is transformed into a higher dimension and purpose: a rag-tag slave group in Egypt is changed into the Hebrew nation; a small band of powerless Jews are transformed into the church that altered the course of history. Christ's ministry was transformational too—he changed water into wine, a few loaves and fishes into a feast, a Passover supper into powerful symbols of his death and communion, and even the Roman executioner's cross into a sign of victory. Transformation is to take what is and turn it into what it could and should be.

Transformation is a part of God's continuing action in history to restore all creation to himself and to its rightful purposes and relationships. Sin, "the social and cosmic anti-creation,"[69] has distorted God's original design and purpose for creation. This is visible in the way every dimension of life has been distorted from the original design of the Creator. Oppression and injustice, racism, alienation, and exploitation in the structures of communities and nations are the results of idolatry and disobedience to God.[70]

The power of sin cannot last, however, for through Christ "God chose to reconcile the whole universe to himself, making peace through the shedding of his blood on the cross—to reconcile all things, whether on earth or in heaven, through him alone" (Col. 1:20).[71] Transformation, then, is a corrective to both individual and institutional sin. It does not extract people from their earthly contexts for otherworldly piety, but rather changes the contexts as well as the people.

> It is this transforming power of the Gospel that distinguishes it from mere religion. In many religions "salvation" is conceived as a way out of the realities of social, political, and material life. It might be compared to a drug that helps people to have an imaginary flight out of reality. But Christ creates a new man within reality, and through the new man transforms reality. God had a purpose in creation and when men turn to Christ, a process begins in them by which they grow in the fulfillment of the original purpose of God.[72]

God's purpose for humanity is that men and women be the imago Dei— that they live as his image in the world, his cocreators and stewards, rather than as predators of creation. God intends that social structures reflect and promote justice, peace, sharing, and free participation for the well-being of all. The goal of transformation is that God's purposes be realized, as is revealed in the Old Testament concept of shalom—harmony, peace, health, well-being, prosperity, justice—and in the New Testament image of the kingdom, which is both present and coming. Transformation seeks to repel the evil social structures that exist in the present cosmos[73] and to institute through the mission of the church the values of the kingdom of God over against the values of the "principalities and powers" of this world. The church is at the center of God's purpose for society, "in order that now, through the church, the wisdom of God in all its varied forms might be made known . . ." (Eph. 3:10). Ron Sider suggests that "perhaps the genuinely unique contribution of Christians to development is precisely the people of God—the Church—as a new community where all relationships are being transformed and redeemed."[74]

Transformation is a joint enterprise between God and humanity in history, not just a mechanistic or naturalistic process. It involves a transformation of the human condition, human relationships, and whole societies. The so-called "developed" modernized world needs transformation to free itself from a secular, materialistic condition marked by broken relationships, violence, economic subjugation, and devastation of nature; and the "underdeveloped" world needs transformation from the subhuman condition of poverty, premature death, hunger, exposure, oppression, disease, and fear. Whereas "development" tends to be a term that the West applies to the Third World, transformation is equally applicable to both the "overdeveloped" and the "underdeveloped" worlds.

Characteristics of Transformation

The idea of transformation is not posed as an alternate development strategy but as a Christian framework for looking at human and social change. As such, it contains a set of principles against which any theory of development may be measured. As we look at these principles, discussed in no particular order, let us also examine how the four theories discussed earlier fulfill or fail to fulfill them.

Life Sustenance

Any plan for transforming human existence must provide adequate life-sustaining goods and services to the members of society.[75] When a society has only minimal food, water, shelter, and clothing, existence becomes subhuman, distorting God's provisions for humanity's well-being. The Old Testament establishes God's desire to meet those basic needs: "Is not this what I require of you as a fast: to . . . set free those who have been crushed? Is it not sharing your food with the hungry, taking the homeless poor into your house, clothing the naked . . . ?" (Isa. 58:6-7). Jesus said that the struggle to meet the needs of the poor—for food, water, shelter, clothing, health care, and spiritual nurturance—would be seen as an indication of true salvation on judgment day (Matt. 25:31-46). Similarly, the apostle James indicates that out of a true and vital faith will spring the desire to supply the bodily needs of others (Jas. 2:15-16).

Modernization has met these basic needs for the majority of the people in the industrialized West (though there are still pockets of poverty). It is no wonder that the Third World looks longingly toward industrialization, even though the social costs are high and its benefits are unevenly distributed. Dependency and Global Reformism fail to meet the basic needs of the poorest of the poor. Another Development seeks to meet these needs as well by lowering consumption standards and stressing the basics, rather than emphasizing growth for the minority and a trickle-down of "benefits" to the majority. Yet even so, meeting these basic needs, while necessary, is not a sufficient condition for social transformation. The provision of life-sustaining necessities and an overall increase in society's wealth provides a quantitative change. But this can form only the basis of what is really needed—a qualitative change.[76]

Equity

A second characteristic of transformation is an equitable distribution of material goods and opportunities among the peoples of the world. Whatever the causes, the fact remains that two-thirds of humanity is suffering deprivation while a minority lives extremely well. The United States wastes more energy than Japan uses, and it spreads more fertilizer on lawns, golf courses, and cemeteries than China consumes in all applications. Furthermore, even within many Third World countries there is skewed income distribution. If the wealth of the upper 5 percent of the population were more evenly distributed, equity would be served. Land tenure, for example, is probably the biggest problem in Latin America, the dominant upper class often holding (and profiting from) as much as 80 percent of the arable land and available water, as in El Salvador.

"The Christian favors a kind of development that is within the reach of the majority," according to John Taylor.[77] Equity is essential to transformation because all people are God's children, with the same needs and potentials. As shown by the jubilee laws and prophetic teaching, God has a special concern for the have-nots—the poor, the defenseless, the weak, the marginalized, the sick, and the hungry. The early church shared this concern and gave of what they had to the needy (Acts 2:42-47). When Paul commented on the sharing by the Macedonian church he stressed equality: "It is a question of equality. At the moment your surplus meets their need, but one day your need may be met from their surplus. The aim is equality; as Scripture has it 'The man who got much had no more than enough, and the man who got little did not go short'" (2 Cor. 8:14-15).

If social progress is to be equitable, the advantages must reach the most needy. Frances Lappé and Joseph Collins argue that the world can produce food enough for ten billion inhabitants if, among other changes, the people in need were given access to the land.[78] In the United States, which every year stores large farm surpluses, over thirty million people hunger under the poverty line. In the world economy, meanwhile, the poor nations are getting poorer and further in debt, because Modernization has failed to distribute its fruits to the poor.

Dependency theory points out the inequitable distribution of Modernization. Global Reformism aims at a redistribution of resources among nations without stressing a more equitable distribution among all levels of the population within nations. Another Development in theory at least stresses the needs of the poorest of the poor and a "fairer redistribution of resources satisfying the basic needs" in a "harmonized cooperative world" in which everyone seeks to live "at the expense of no one else."[79] This is exactly what a Christian ethic of sharing also proposes.

Justice

Justice goes beyond mere redistribution. One can have a fair share of material goods and services without enjoying justice: slaves were often treated very well—better than some free people—but they were still bound within unjust relationships. Unjust relationships and power structures need to be transformed into just ones, eliminating privileges for the few that are bought at the cost of the many. The class and caste systems, institutionalized racism, the subordinate status of women, the domination of the elite, and international trade rules all need transformation. "A just vision of the transformed world is: where every man, no matter what his race, religion, or nationality can live a fully human life, freed from servitude imposed on him by other men or national forces over which he has no control."[80]

Isaiah 58 describes in detail the justice that God desires. Indeed, the justice of God himself and his desire that it be instituted in human society is one of the major themes of the Bible. God's desire for justice reveals who he is; his nature and sovereignty are inextricably tied to it: "for the Lord your God is God of gods and Lord of lords, the great, mighty, and terrible God. He is no respecter of persons and is not to be bribed; he secures justice for widows and orphans, and loves the alien who lives among you, giving him food and clothing" (Deut. 10:17-18). Lest anyone think that God alone seeks justice and that humanity can leave it up to him, Deuteronomy adds, "You too must love the alien."

Modernization is blind to justice; the profit motive and the capitalist free market system tend in fact to create injustices. The anchovies of Peru go into cattle feed to make marbled beef for rich palates, while the diet of the Quechua Indians in Peru is protein deficient. Dependency theory and Global Reformism allow exploitative structures to remain intact: independent states may escape the domination of other states but they can still oppress their own people. Nor would a new world economic order prevent elite groups from exploiting those under them.

Another Development, in contrast, does seek to redress unjust relationships. It would allow every level of society to exercise local democratic power, promote equal rights, and throw off any oppressive relationships. Oppressed or endangered tribes, for instance, would be granted the right to live as they always have on their lands; they would not unjustly be forced to live the lifestyle native to others.

Dignity and Self-Worth

True transformation also depends on the establishment and the affirmation of all people's dignity and self-worth—especially as society is changing. People need self-esteem to be fully human. As Edgar Stoesz puts it, "Development is people with an increasing control over their environment and destiny, people with dignity and self-worth."[81] It is a very difficult thing either to give or to receive with dignity. Many development projects have been vitiated by relationships that rob those who are already oppressed and in need of their dignity. The very language used that characterizes people as "target groups" or "recipients" creates, even in programs founded on the best of intentions, power structures and paternalism. It is no wonder that the "recipients" sometimes internalize a feeling of inferiority.

Self-identity requires a good dose of self-esteem. Demeaning and condescending attitudes by the rich nations and agencies need to be transformed into attitudes of partnership and equality. We must learn from Christ, who knew how to serve without condescension and how to give with dignity. His birth into a poor home in an oppressed colony of the Roman Empire put him on the side of the weak and thus gave dignity to the powerless. He even gave dignity to his persecutors, those who we might think deserved no respect at all, when he said of them, "Father, forgive them; they do not know what they are doing" (Luke 23:34).

Relationships under the Modernization approach have been extremely paternalistic and demeaning, and the Dependency and Global Reformism theories have sought to rearrange these on behalf of the periphery nations. Global Reformism calls for better terms of trade and a relationship between nations that is equal. Another Development theory carries this even further, calling for a reevaluation of the true needs of people and countries that would free weaker economies from the control of the stronger. By seeking self-reliance, it "excludes dependence . . . that can be converted into political pressure,"[82] and it desires to instill trust in people and nations based on their autonomy, thus affirming the worth and dignity of all.

Freedom

Freedom is a vital component of transformation. Throughout history, as people have struggled to change their societies they have seen their goal in terms of freedom from subservience and slavery. Goulet sees one of the objectives of development as freeing people from servitude—servitude to nature, to ignorance, to other people, to institutions, and to beliefs considered oppressive.[83] Christian transformation must work to liberate people from these bondages, and also from bondage to themselves. In John 8:36 Christ tells his followers that "if then the Son sets you free, you will indeed be free"—that is, free to achieve all dimensions of the human potential God has endowed us with.

Concretely, social transformation for most Africans is freedom from the vestiges of colonialism, racism, and neocolonial modernization. President Nyerere of Tanzania underscores this: "Freedom from colonialism and the preservation of some of our local traditions are at least as important as the accumulation of Western-style wealth. It is more important to us to be human than to be merely rich."[84] For Latin American peasants and tribal peoples, transformation is freedom from oppressive national and international structures that marginalize them in society, force them from their land, crowd them into cities, or exploit them as cheap labor.

Dependency theory and Global Reformism strike a blow against the neocolonial system but still fail to assure freedom from local varieties of elitist, often repressive, regimes. Another Development theory, however, does aim at liberating people from unjust international and national powers by stressing local control and participation in the structures and decisions that affect the people.

Participation

Related to freedom is the need for the affected people to play a meaningful part in their own transformation. If people participate in the process of their own transformation it becomes meaningful, effective, and lasting. The best-laid plans of "developers" have been wrecked by a top-down approach that disregards the participation of those involved. Local initiative and control from the beginning of any project are essential for people to commit themselves to it as their own and to carry it forward. Any other approach only perpetuates the relationships of dominance and dependency and the patronizing attitudes of outside developers. President Nyerere said that "all men who are suffering from poverty need to be given confidence in their ability to take control of their own lives."[85]

God has always given high value to human participation in his plans for the world. Even in salvation, the individual response of the human will is indispensable. God has always allowed, even required, human beings to participate in the shaping of history, both personal and collective. Christians are called fellow workers with God and stewards of the earth's resources. True human transformation comes about only when people are able to act upon their own needs *as they perceive them* and progress toward a state of wholeness in harmony with their own context.

In other models of development, power is alienated from the masses. Another Development in contrast fosters the full participation of the affected people at every level and encourages them "to invent and generate new resources and techniques, to increase their capability to absorb them . . . to generate their own way of life."[86]

Reciprocity

Progress and social change result both from independent discovery within a culture and from intercultural contact and the transfer of innovation. All societies receive benefits from others and all depend (in the positive sense of the word) on others. No one, and certainly no society, is self-sufficient. The modernized countries have tended to assume that they alone have the key to success in social change and will generously use it to help the world "develop." But they have forgotten that they too can learn from the poorer countries, especially in the area of cultural identity.

The positive values of traditional societies can instruct modern societies in many ways and may help free them from their insularity. The Dag Hammarskjöld Report reminds us that "there is a vast area for cultural cooperation which would help the industrial societies to recognize finally that the human experience is rich, and to redefine their styles of life."[87] The Cocoyoc Declaration affirmed that the poorer countries should "help the affluent nations, for their own well-being, to find a way of life less exploitative of nature, of others, and of themselves." This implies reciprocity and, as Goulet says, vulnerability. Are the rich societies willing to open themselves up to learning reciprocally?[88] Likewise, can the dominant elites in the Third World learn from the peasants and the marginalized? Under the approach of Another Development theory, reciprocity would uniquely be possible.

Cultural Fit

Transformation must always be appropriate to the culture that is to be transformed. All cultures are a part of God's good creation. By his blood, Christ "purchase[d] for God men of every tribe and language, people and nation; [he has] made of them a royal house, to serve our God as priests; and they shall reign upon earth" (Rev. 5:9-10). Christ honored all cultures by entering fully into Jewish social and religious life with all its traditions. No culture is pure and holy, but we know from Christ's attitude toward it that all have intrinsic values that can be redeemed and used as a basis for social transformation.

Too often modernizers have ignored customs and social patterns in an attempt to bring material benefits to the "backward." In fact they often regard local traditions as deterrents to change and technology without understanding the rationality of a society's accumulated wisdom. They simply do not stop to listen to the peasant! The result has been cultural imperialism and the destruction of indigenous values—even of whole cultures.

The Westernized elite in Third World countries who clamor for a new international economic order also tend to view the benefits wholly in terms of increased wealth and consumer goods for the people. They sacrifice the cultural heritage of their own people to the "progress" of industrialization and extractive economies. Dependency theorists have no better record when they come to power—witness the problems that Indian subgroups have faced in Mexico and Peru under "revolutionary" regimes. If any culture is destroyed, a part of creation and of all humanity dies.

In Another Development theory, however, the vital importance of the cultural heritage and creativity of all people is respected as a biblical idea. In Another Development, any change must be appropriate because it would arise out of the culture endogenously.

Ecological Soundness

Transformation should also be environmentally sensitive. Our world is a closed biosphere (with only solar energy coming in) that is delicately balanced for the existence of all life, including human life.[89] We should care for the world around us, be its stewards, and preserve it. This is clear in the Bible.[90] In Leviticus, for example, God gives the injunction that the land should not be worn out but should be rested one year in seven, and this year should be "a sabbath of sacred rest" (Lev. 25:4).

The pressures on the ecosystem are increasing with population and industrialization, particularly the high and harsh technology required by Modernization theory and allowed by Dependency theory and Global Reformism. Unless we seek development through "gentle" technology that works with nature instead of abusing it, our grandchildren will live (if they can) in a much less hospitable world depleted of nonrenewable resources and choked by our own wastes. The Cocoyoc Declaration emphasizes that everything we do must be done in the context of "preserving a base of production compatible with the necessities of future generations." Another Development stresses that any technology must be appropriate in its cultural and environmental context, both now and on into the future.

Hope

Ultimately, transformation is hope. Without an attitude of expectation, even optimism, change rarely occurs. When peasants or landless slum squatters have already experienced so much disappointment and hardship in their lives, there is little reason to take any additional risks unless there is a good chance that some change to their advantage will result. Pessimism has become encrusted in entire cultures and traditions and stands as the nemesis of positive social change.

A vital Christianity attempts to replace this pessimism with hope. In Christ, God intervened in human society and gave it a sense of movement: no longer are the problems of society only human problems because God is working on them with us. In the Incarnation God demonstrated that he was active in relieving people's ills. The continuing lordship of Christ now gives us the rationale and the responsibility to continue his work, to make the changes that will prefigure the day when every knee shall bow and every tongue confess that Jesus Christ is Lord.[91] Because of what Christ has done, we know that God hears the cries of a burdened humanity and that there is a way out of the human predicament. God is on the throne, and evil will not always prevail. Through Christ, we are enabled to realize here and now something of the kingdom's presence. "The kingdom has come near" (Matt. 10:7), and even in its present inchoate form it engenders hope for the future.

Modernization theory holds out the hope that the "good life" will trickle down to all people, and Global Reformism is optimistic about the prospective benefits for all of a restructured world economy. But experience gives little reason to trust the hopes these approaches raise for the masses. Another Development holds the most realistic hope for the "little" people of the world. It proposes small solutions at a local, community level and seeks guidance from and gives control to the local participants. By beginning with small, realistic programs, it can also offer hope at the national and world level.

Spiritual Transformation

The core of human and social transformation is spiritual. Without the change in attitudes and behavior implicit in *metanoia* (conversion), human beings remain self-centered creatures. They are unlikely to transform the external structures and relationships of their society. The power in society of sin, both individual and institutional, is a basic deterrent to positive change. Many "development" programs have failed because of human greed, power politics, graft, or plain lethargy. Even programs that increase production and income may concede to sinfulness if they divide communities, create a new elite, or merely serve to furnish a better quality whiskey.

Human nature is rapacious, and the existing order (the *cosmos*) is distorted by inequalities and injustices. Jim Wallis sees redemption as a "world event in which the individual has part."[92] Spiritual transformation must begin in the individual but must spread to encompass the transformation of all of society, indeed, of all creation. Samuel Escobar shows that this is a biblical model. "When men turn to God and are transformed by the Spirit, their individual lives as well as the structures in which they live are affected. This is evident in the book of Acts where the end of idolatry is a danger for the business structure of a city (Acts 19), where the spiritual liberation of a girl also affects the social and financial life of a group of people and brings political accusations against the apostles (Acts 16:16-23)."[93]

As social, economic, and psychological relationships are redeemed, structures and institutions are transformed. Redeemed structures, in turn, allow people to be more fully human. We see this in the historical interactions between Christianity and society where slavery, child labor, and the degraded status of women have been fought. While we do not expect this transformed "new order" to fully arrive on earth until Christ returns, we rejoice in the good news that it has already begun: "When anyone is united to Christ, there is a new world; the old order has gone, and a new order has already begun" (2 Cor. 5:17).

None of the development theories we have examined (even Another Development) adequately accounts for the distortions introduced by sin. All have a somewhat rosy view of human nature and social institutions. They do not see spiritual regeneration as a goal to be sought in development, or even as a means to encourage progress. Yet spiritual regeneration must accompany and encourage transformation and thus distinguish it from mere development.

From Development to Transformation

No development program in the real world and no development theory adequately meets all the characteristics of transformation, though each reflects to one degree or another some of the essential elements. Even Another Development falls short of a holistic biblical perspective. "Development" becomes "transformation" when all the elements discussed above are present. The transformation that the Bible calls us to is a transformation of both individuals and social structures that allows us to move toward increasing harmony with God, with our fellow human beings, with our environment, and with ourselves. As Escobar puts it, "It is not just a better life but a better way of living among men as whole persons."[94]

Notes

1. E. F. Schumacher, *Small Is Beautiful: Economics as if People Mattered* (New York: Harper and Row, 1973).

2. Tom Sine, "Development: Its Secular Past and Its Uncertain Future," in *Evangelicals and Development: Toward a Theology of Social Change,* ed. Ronald J. Sider (Philadelphia: Westminster, 1981), pp. 71, 72. See the revision of Sine's article in this book; the quote is from the section "What Is the Implicit View of the Better Future in Western Development?"

3. Francois Perroux, "Le Notion de Developpement," in *L'Economie de XXe Siecle* (Paris: Presses Universitaires, 1964), p. 155.

4. Walt W. Rostow, *Stages of Economic Growth: A Non-Communist Manifesto* (Cambridge: Cambridge University Press, 1960).

5. An excellent brief description of modernization theory as it applies to Latin America is found in J. Samuel Valenzuela and Arturo Valenzuela, "Modernization and Dependency: Alternative Perspectives in the Study of Latin American Underdevelopment," in *From Dependency to Development: Strategies to Overcome Underdevelopment and Inequality,* ed. Heraldo Muñoz (Boulder: Westview, 1981). See also the first three chapters of Ian Roxborough's book *Theories of Underdevelopment* (Atlantic Highlands, N.J.: Humanities, 1979), in which he deals with the transition from traditional to modern society, and its replicability, from a social theory perspective.

6. Daniel Bell, *The Coming of Post-Industrial Society: A Venture in Social Forecasting* (New York: Basic Books, 1973).

7. Colin Turnbull and Chinua Achebe have described at length the anguish of the young African caught between tradition and modernity. See Turnbull, *The Lonely African* (New York: Simon and Schuster, 1962); and Achebe, *Things Fall Apart* (Greenwich, Conn.: Fawcett, 1974).

8. See Roxborough, *Theories of Underdevelopment,* pp. 14-15.

9. See Osvaldo Sunkel, "Development Styles and the Environment: An Interpretation of the Latin American Case," in *From Dependency to Development,* ed. Muñoz.

10. Benjamin Higgins, cited by Helene Castel, ed., in *World Development: An Introductory Reader* (New York: Macmillan, 1971), p. 11.

11. See Teresa Hayter, *The Creation of World Poverty: An Alternative View to the Brandt Report* (London: Pluto, 1981), p. 106.

12. Abraham Maslow, *Motivation and Personality* (New York: Harper and Row, 1954).

13. See Sunkel, "Development Styles and the Environment," p. 98.

14. Richard J. Barnet and Ronald Muller describe the contradictions between the interests of host countries and the interests of the MNCs in *Global Reach: The Power of the Multinational Corporations* (New York: Simon and Schuster, 1974).

15. Hayter, *The Creation of World Poverty,* pp. 45ff.

16. Abdul Said and Luiz Simmons, *The New Sovereigns* (Englewood Cliffs, N.J.: Prentice-Hall, 1975).

17. Peter Evans, *Dependent Development: The Alliance of Multinational, State, and Local Capital in Brazil* (Princeton: Princeton University Press, 1979).

18. Hayter, *The Creation of World Poverty,* p. 107.

19. Hayter cites Eugene Black in ibid., p. 85.

20. William Paddock, a USAID consultant, and Elizabeth Paddock toured the supposedly successful AID projects worldwide and wrote a devastating critique, a documented exposé of the failure of foreign aid and the reasons behind it. See *We Don't Know How: An*

Independent Audit of What They Call Success in Foreign Assistance (Ames: Iowa State University Press, 1973).

21. David H. Kinley, et al., *Aid as Obstacle: Twenty Questions About Our Foreign Aid and the Hungry* (San Francisco: Institute for Food and Development Policy, 1980).

22. See John Gilligan, *Aid Policy on Agricultural Asset Distribution: Land Reform,* PD.72, 16 January (Washington, D.C.: U.S. Agency in Development, 1979).

23. "The Vanishing Tribes," *Newsweek,* 12 October 1981, p. 92.

24. For more on the destruction of native cultures in Brazil see Shelton H. Davis, *Victims of the Miracle: Development and the Indians of Brazil* (London: Cambridge University Press, 1977).

25. "The Vanishing Tribes," p. 93.

26. *Hastings Center Report,* February 1977.

27. Barbara Ward and René Dubos, *Only One Earth* (New York: Norton, 1972), p. 119.

28. See John V. Taylor, *Enough Is Enough: A Biblical Call for Moderation in a Consumer-Oriented Society* (Minneapolis: Augsburg, 1975).

29. Boyce Rensberger, "14 Million Acres a Year Vanishing as Deserts Spread Around the Globe," *New York Times,* 28 August 1977.

30. Sunkel, "Development Styles and the Environment," p. 102.

31. Ibid., pp. 104-5.

32. See Norman Myers, "Cheap Beef and Priceless Rainforests," *Chicago Tribune,* 3 January 1982.

33. Teotonio dos Santos, "The Structure of Dependence," *American Economic Review* 60, no. 5 (1970): 231.

34. See Gustavo Lagos, "The Revolution of Being: A Preferred World Model," in *From Dependency to Development,* ed. Muñoz, p. 130.

35. André Gunder Frank, "The Development of Underdevelopment," in *Dependence and Underdevelopment: Latin America's Political Economy,* ed. James Cockcroft, André Gunder Frank, and Dale Johnson (New York: Anchor, 1972).

36. Rodolfo Stavenhagen calls this process of urban bias "internal colonialism." *Social Class in Agrarian Societies* (Garden City, N.Y.: Doubleday, 1969).

37. Evans, *Dependent Development,* pp. 26-27.

38. James A. Caporaso and Behrouz Zare, "An Interpretation and Evaluation of Dependency Theory," in *From Dependency to Development,* ed. Muñoz, p. 48.

39. José Míguez Bonino, *Doing Theology in a Revolutionary Situation* (Philadelphia: Fortress, 1975), p. 28.

40. Alain de Janvry, *The Agrarian Question and Reformism in Latin America* (Baltimore: Johns Hopkins University Press, 1981), pp. 1-2.

41. Fernando Henrique Cardoso and Enzio Faletto, *Dependency and Development in Latin America* (Berkeley: University of California Press, 1978).

42. See Evans, *Dependent Development.*

43. De Janvry, *The Agrarian Question.*

44. Heraldo Muñoz calls this "strategic dependence." "The Strategic Dependence of the Centers and the Economic Importance of the Latin American Periphery," in *From Dependency to Development,* ed. Muñoz.

45. For the full text of the NIEO Program see Guy F. Erb and Valeriana Kallab, *Beyond Dependency: The Developing World Speaks Out* (Washington, D.C.: Overseas Development Council, 1975).

46. I am indebted to Bjorn Hettne for his excellent discussion of the problems of Global Reformism upon which I have based some of my critique. See his *Current Issues in Development Theory* (Stockholm: Swedish Agency for Research Cooperation, 1978).

47. Ibid., p. 25.

48. Gala A. Amin examines the relationship between multinational power and the NIEO in "Dependent Development," *Alternatives* 4 (1976).

49. See ibid., p. 393.

50. The Cocoyoc Declaration, a declaration by UNCTAD/UNEP, an expert seminar of the UN General Assembly, at Cocoyoc, Mexico, in 1974. Published in *Development Dialogue* (Uppsala), no. 2 (1974): 88-96.

51. Samuel L. Parmar, cited by Hettne, *Current Issues in Development Theory*, p. 29.

52. Dom Helder Camara, cited by John G. Sommer, *U.S. Voluntary Aid to the Third World: What Is Its Future?* (Washington, D.C.: Overseas Development Council, 1975), p. 142.

53. "What Now? Another Development," the Dag Hammarskjöld Report on Development and International Cooperation, published as a special issue of *Development Dialogue* (Uppsala), no. 1/2 (1975).

54. Ibid., p. 28.

55. Ibid., p. 29.

56. Ibid.

57. Ibid., p. 33.

58. Johan Galtung, "The Politics of Self-Reliance," in *From Dependency to Development*, ed. Muñoz, p. 173.

59. "What Now?" p. 18.

60. The Arusha Declaration, in Julius Nyerere, *Freedom and Socialism* (trans. of *Uhuru na Ujamaa*) (New York: Oxford University Press, 1967).

61. See Nyerere's speeches in his book *Freedom and Development* (trans. of *Uhuru na Maendeleo*) (Dar es Salaam: Government Printers of Tanzania, 1973).

62. "What Now?" p. 35.

63. Cocoyoc Declaration, p. 174.

64. Glyn Roberts, *Questioning Development* (Alverstoke, Hampshire: Alver Press, 1979), pp. 14ff.

65. "What Now?" p. 39.

66. Nyerere, quoted by William Edgett Smith, *Nyerere of Tanzania* (London: Gollancz, 1973).

67. "What Now?" p. 36.

68. Ibid., p. 37.

69. Rosemary Reuther, cited by Gutiérrez in *A Theology of Liberation*, p. 9.

70. Samuel Escobar, "Evangelism and Man's Search for Freedom, Justice and Fulfillment," in *Let the Earth Hear His Voice*, ed. J. D. Douglas (Minneapolis: World Wide Publications, 1975), p. 309.

71. All Scripture references are from the New English Bible.

72. Escobar, "Evangelism and Man's Search," pp. 309-10.

73. Stephen C. Mott, *Biblical Ethics and Social Change* (New York: Oxford University Press, 1982), pp. 6ff.

74. Ronald Sider, in a talk given at High Leigh, England, in 1980.

75. Dennis Goulet, *The Cruel Choice: A New Concept in the Theory of Development* (New York: Atheneum, 1975), p. 94.

76. Ibid., p. 333.

77. Taylor, *Enough Is Enough*, pp. 13-17.

78. Frances Moore Lappé and Joseph Collins, *Food First: Beyond the Myth of Scarcity* (New York: Ballantine, 1977), pp. 13ff.

79. Cocoyoc Declaration.

80. Pope Paul VI, "Populorum Progressio" ("Development of Peoples"), 26 March 1967.

81. Stoesz, *Thoughts on Development*, p. 3.

82. Cocoyoc Declaration.

83. Goulet, *The Cruel Choice*, p. 26.

84. Arusha Declaration, in Nyerere, *Freedom and Socialism*.

85. Julius Nyerere, in a talk at Maryknoll, New York, in 1970.

86. Cocoyoc Declaration.

87. "What Now?" p. 34.

88. See in this connection Bob Goudzwaard, *Aid for the Overdeveloped West* (Toronto: Wedge, 1975).

89. Only in recent history has the Western world begun to realize the precariousness of nature. Two pioneer books on this theme are Rachel Carson's *Silent Spring* (Boston: Houghton Mifflin, 1962) and Barbara Ward and René Dubos's *Only One Earth* (New York: Norton, 1972). A more recent work is W. Jackson Davis's *The Seventh Year: Industrial Civilization in Transition* (New York: Norton, 1979).

90. A good treatise on the stewardship of the earth is *The Earth Is the Lord's*, ed. Mary Evelyn Jegen and Bruno V. Manno (New York: Paulist Press, 1978).

91. John Howard Yoder, "The Biblical Mandate," *Seeds of the Kingdom/Sojourners* (1977): 18.

92. Jim Wallis, "The Vehicle for Vision," *Seeds of the Kingdom/Sojourners* (1977): 8.

93. Escobar, "Evangelism and Man's Search," p. 309.

94. Ibid., p. 274.

Social Transformation:
The Mission of God

Edward R. Dayton

The Road We Have Traveled

It is helpful to realize that twenty years ago there would have been no felt need among evangelical Christians, and especially among *Western* evangelical Christians, for the conference for which this essay was originally prepared. Whereas in the late 1800s evangelicals were still actively involved in trying to set the world right, by the 1930s many of them, particularly in the West, separated themselves from "liberals," who were viewed as being concerned only for the "social gospel." Although a great deal of development was being carried out by Western evangelical missionaries, it was submerged under the heading of "reaching the lost for Christ." It has only been in recent years that some evangelical agencies have specifically identified their purpose as doing something called "development."

Much of the debate that has been carried on within the church about the reasons for and the methods of development stems from the assumption on the part of some that we must of necessity see things alike and come to a joint agreement. There is a strong feeling that "if you knew everything I know, we would agree." But the Bible, history, and our own experience demonstrate that this is not the case. Just as the different churches of the New Testament were permitted to work out their Christianity from within the context of their own worldview, so must we permit one another to do the same. However, this should not keep us from speaking prophetically to one another. Accepting the local church in another culture does not mean accepting everything that church does. Nor can we be naive about our own history. As George Marsden has so well illustrated in his book *Fundamentalism and American Culture,*[1] what was "an American evangelical view" in 1870 was by 1925 being described as "liberal."

Furthermore, we are continually rewriting history. One has only to review the North American school books of the last 150 years to see how quickly we reinterpret the same situation as time goes by. The "vicious savage" became the "noble savage" who is now understood as a "Native American."[2]

Our understanding of our world is greatly shaped by our own culture. I am a North American. I have been brought up and educated in a culture whose values are sharply different from those of the rest of the world. It is not that North American culture is the one different culture while all other cultures are the same; it is only that, as Edward Steward points out, "On any culture scale, Americans seem to be at one end."[3]

Having said that, it may be helpful to realize how far we have traveled in the seventeen years since the Berlin Congress on World Evangelization in 1966. That event was the first time in history that a *world* conference had been called of those who identified themselves as evangelicals. Those at Berlin spent most of their time examining evangelical theology and particularly the need for evangelicals to look out again upon a world which was lost. The primary focus of Berlin was on the personal salvation of those who had yet to hear.

In the eight years between Berlin and Lausanne, there was tremendous movement in the evangelical part of Christ's church. We had come to know one another. We revived an interest in research in what God was doing in the world.[4] Lausanne was intended to be a congress of those actually involved in trying to reach the world; but the Holy Spirit was also enlivening the minds of men and women to expand our understanding of what it meant to evangelize. The Lausanne Covenant greatly broadened our worldviews. We were called to see that the task of evangelization was not confined to the sharing of information about Jesus. There was a *life* to be lived. We saw the need for the broad redemption of the world in all of its aspects.

The year of Lausanne—1974—might also be described as a watershed year in Western evangelicals' interest in social concerns. Much of this was triggered by the disastrous drought in the Sahel area of Africa. The result was the inauguration of a number of new Christian "relief and development" agencies and the rapid expansion of those already involved, such as World Vision International. These agencies appeared to be taking on a new task, but they already had the ability to raise large sums of money.[5] By 1981 the amount of income being received by evangelical agencies concerned for alleviating human need amounted to approximately $375 million. During the same time the total income of all other North American Protestant agencies working overseas equaled $1,465 million.

Evangelicals were "catching up." They were moving into an area where Church World Service and Catholic Relief Services, as well as other non-American agencies, had been for years. Most of them took the same approach as CWS and CRS—namely, drawing a firm line between "evangelism" and "social responsibility." In at least one denomination of evangelical tradition, a separate agency was set up to work alongside the "mission" efforts of the agency.[6] Many agencies were looking for a theological justification for what they were doing. Indeed, there was a nervousness as to whether one could have an *evangelical* relief and development agency.

But there were others who questioned whether the *way* that these agencies were going about attempting to relieve human misery was biblically sound. There were calls for a deeper understanding of the *root causes* of much of the suffering that these agencies were attempting to alleviate.

By the time of the Consultation on World Evangelization (COWE) in Pattaya, Thailand, in 1980, evangelical theologians were beginning to enunciate clearly the need for "a theology of development." During March of that same year the Consultation on the Theology of Development had been convened by the Unit on Ethics in Society of the Theological Commission of the World Evangelical Fellowship.[7] The discussion at this consultation led to the proposal for a subsequent consultation to be entitled "A Christian Response to Human Need." A program was inaugurated to gather case histories on how development was actually being carried out all over the world. Meanwhile, out of COWE there developed the Consultation on the Relationship between Evangelism and Social Responsibility (CRESR).[8] This consultation was convened, to quote John Stott's foreword to its final document, the Grand Rapids Report, "with a considerable degree of apprehension. The papers and responses, circulated in advance, had not only been critical of each other's positions but even in some cases sharply so. How then could we possibly expect to reach accord? Yet underneath our natural fears there was a confidence that God could unite us, if we humbled ourselves under the authority of His Word. And so it proved. . . . This is not to say that we agree about everything (as our report makes plain), but that our agreements are far greater than our residual differences."

But the Holy Spirit and the movement of history seemed to be pushing us along at a quickening pace. When the members of the interim steering committee of "A Christian Response to Human Need" met in 1982 and discussed with one another the work that we had done so far, we concluded that rather than attempt to develop a "theology of development," we should abandon the entire notion of development! We concluded that "development" had become so loaded with secular and humanistic freight that it was no longer useful to us. We struggled to find a term or phrase that we might use. The best we could do was to call it "social transformation."

And what is social transformation for the Christian? Is it not the entire business that God is about, namely, the redemption of the world? And is not the *mission* of the church social transformation in every dimension?

The Grand Rapids Report argued that "social responsibility" and "evangelism" were intimately intertwined. Those who came together at the CRESR meetings recognized that the Lausanne Covenant's affirmation, "In the Church's mission of sacrificial service, evangelism is primary," did not refer to an invariable *temporal* priority, because in some situations the social ministry will take precedence. Rather, the covenant refers to the *logical* priority of evangelism.

Defining Social Transformation

Tito Paredes defines cultural change as "any modification of the ideas, society, technology, economy, and ecology of a people due to factors working from within or without." He sees all cultures as constantly changing. Social transformation is going on all the time.[9]

But the question before the church is one of *intention*. What is it that God would have us *do* and *be?* It is perhaps helpful to avoid biblical language and thus hopefully avoid circular definition. Thus in this paper I will define "intentional social transformation" as *a process of external intervention intended to enable a people to become better than they were before.*

Let us examine this definition piece by piece: It is a *process,* something that goes on in time and assumes a series of consequences. It includes *external intervention.* In other words, it is assumed that if the people with whom it is concerned are left to themselves, it is unlikely that the particular change will take place. Someone outside must intervene. We should be quick to add here that the "external intervention" may well be the intervention of the Holy Spirit!

The purpose of this intervention is *to enable.* Thus it assumes that the potential to be different, to be better, already lies within the people.

The subject of social transformation is *a people.* The transformation we are talking about here is not only of the individual—it is *social.* It assumes individuals in relationship, in community. Finally, the assumption is that the people will in the end be *better* in some way than they were before this intervention. Yet the definition does not define "better." That has to be uniquely defined for each people in their own context.

We have, then, a serviceable general description. But it raises many questions that demand biblical answers. Is "external intervention" justified? And if so, under what conditions? And how do we go about defining "better"?

What Is God's Intention for the World?

The Bible opens by announcing God's evaluation of what he had created as good (Gen. 1:31). This goodness was then violated by Adam and Eve as they broke God's covenant with them (Gen. 3). The results of this rupture in God's relationship with humanity are disastrous.

> To Adam he said, "Because you listened to your wife and ate from the tree about which I commanded you, 'You must not eat of it,' cursed is the ground because of you; through painful toil you will eat of it all the days of your life." (Gen. 3:17-19)[10]

The balance of the Bible reveals God's intention for the world, namely, its *redemption.* This redemption is at once spiritual, physical, and social.

> Then I saw a new heaven and a new earth, for the first heaven and the first earth had passed away, and there was no longer any sea. I saw the Holy City, the

New Jerusalem, coming down out of heaven from God, prepared as a bride beautifully dressed for her husband. And I heard a loud voice from the throne saying, "Now the dwelling of God is with men, and he will live with them. They will be his people and God himself will be with them and be their God. He will wipe every tear from their eyes. There will be no more death or mourning or crying or pain, for the old order of things has passed away." . . .

I did not see a temple in the city, because the Lord God Almighty and the Lamb are its temple. The city does not need the sun or the moon to shine on it, for the glory of God gives it light, and the Lamb is its lamp. The nations will walk by its light, and the kings of the earth will bring their splendor into it.

"The kingdom of the world has become the kingdom of our Lord and of his Christ, and he will reign for ever and ever." (Rev. 21:1-4, 22-24; 11:15b)

The ultimate purpose of God for this world, as he has revealed it to us, is the gospel. This was the "good news" that Jesus and his forerunner, John the Baptist, announced: "Repent for the kingdom of heaven is near." This is also the "good news" that God has declared his victory over the powers of sin and evil. Jesus' ministry is introduced with the words: "Jesus went throughout Galilee, teaching in their synagogues, preaching the good news of the kingdom, and healing every disease and sickness among the people" (Matt. 4:23). Matthew emphasizes this by repeating the same words in Matthew 9:35. This kingdom is thus to be our primary focus: "But seek first his kingdom, and his righteousness, and all these things will be given to you as well" (Matt. 6:33).

The kingdom has been prepared for those who do God's will (Matt. 25:34). God's righteousness is worked out through those who in obedience to him are responsive to the world around them. "For I was hungry and you gave me something to eat, I was thirsty and you gave me something to drink, I was a stranger and you invited me in, I needed clothes and you clothed me, I was sick and you looked after me, I was in prison and you came to visit me" (Matt. 25:35-36).

This is the kingdom within which Abraham, Isaac, and Jacob will be found (Matt. 8:11). This kingdom is of the future, but it is also a present reality: "But if I drive out demons by the Spirit of God, then the kingdom of God has come upon you." (Matt. 12:28).[11] Paul agrees. He tells us we have been already brought into the kingdom (Col. 1:13).

Finally, "this gospel of the kingdom will be preached in the whole world as a testimony to all nations, and then the end will come" (Matt. 24:14).

But the gospel takes on a fuller meaning in the writings of Paul, who assumes that his readers will understand what he means by "this gospel." Paul tells us that it is the good news concerning God's Son: "The gospel he promised beforehand through his prophets in the Holy Scriptures regarding his Son, who as to his human nature was a descendant of David, and who through the Spirit of holiness was declared with power to be the Son of God by his resurrection from the dead: Jesus Christ our Lord" (Rom. 1:2-4).

God intends that the world be redeemed and that his kingdom be established. His instrument in the world is the church, which is the *sign* of the kingdom: "His intent was that now, through the church, the manifold wisdom of God should be made known to the rulers and authorities in the heavenly realms, according to his eternal purpose which he accomplished in Christ Jesus our Lord" (Eph. 3:10-11).

The task of the church is to make disciples of all nations, to baptize them, and to teach them to obey everything that Christ has commanded. Unfortunately the "Great Commission" has often been interpreted in a very limited sense. Even if one assumes that disciples are commissioned—"made"—as soon as they announce their acceptance of Christ (a view I myself hold), we cannot escape the fact that they still must be *taught to obey* everything that Christ has commanded.

What then were these commands? The people of God were to "preach this message: 'The Kingdom of heaven is near.'" They were also to "heal the sick, raise the dead, cleanse those who have leprosy, [and] drive out demons" (Matt. 10:7-8). This passage is contained in Matthew's second discourse (the mission of the twelve, 9:35–10:42). It is closely coupled with Jesus' response to John's disciples: "Go back and report to John what you hear and see: The blind receive sight, the lame walk, those who have leprosy are cured, the deaf hear, the dead are raised, and the good news is preached to the poor. Blessed is the man who does not fall away on account of me" (Matt. 11:4-6).

In Matthew's fourth discourse (18:1-35) Jesus spells out the ethics that are to exist within this kingdom, as he did in the first discourse, which we call the Sermon on the Mount (Matt. 5:1–7:27).

What we see then is that the gospel has *consequences* in the lives of those who claim it for their own. As Karl Barth has so aptly pointed out in his commentary on Romans, we should not be surprised that after eleven chapters of well thought out doctrine, Paul turns to the consequence of that doctrine: ethics—how we live![12] We are no longer to conform to the pattern of this world, with the consequence that we will "be able to test and approve what God's will is—his good, pleasing and perfect will" (Rom. 12:2). We are to fit together as the body of Christ by using our gifts for that body. Our relationships are to be above reproach.

The quality of the ethics of the gospel, the quality of this love, is so different that Jesus calls it a new commandment: "A new command I give you: Love one another. As I have loved you, so you must love one another. All men will know that you are my disciples if you love one another" (John 13:34-35).

God's intention for the church then is that it act out its citizenship within the kingdom in a spirit of love. Within the church we are to conform to the ethics of the kingdom. In our mission without the church we are to announce the news of the availability of the kingdom for all who will listen. No priority is given nor intended. Thus the question as to which has priority, evangelism or social responsibility, is of philosophical interest only. When the question is asked within a real-world context, the answer will usually be obvious. The road to Jericho sets its own agenda.

How Do We Respond to God's Intentions?

We live in an ever widening circle of relationships: our immediate family, the local fellowship of which we are a part, our neighborhood, the village, city, or town within which we live, our country, our continent, our world. The demands of these relationships will necessarily vary as a function of proximity. Obviously those close to us will always demand our attention and concern. "If anyone does not provide for his relatives, and especially for his immediate family, he has denied the faith and is worse than an unbeliever" (1 Tim. 5:8).

But there is also the broader injunction: "Let us do good to all people, especially to those who belong to the family of believers" (Gal. 6:10). The church is itself a community of gathered communities. And this church has been given a *mission* to move out from within its own environs to regions beyond—"to all people." Whereas everyday life within the community should be lived out with the purpose of doing good in whatever immediate circumstances one finds oneself, there is another dimension, an *intentional* dimension of *going forth* to announce the kingdom, to make disciples, and to teach them all that Jesus has commanded. Clearly some members of the community are to be set apart (Acts 13:2) for a special service, as Paul and Barnabas were.

It is noteworthy how many times Paul departed from his task of verbal proclamation to the task of carrying out missions of relief (see, e.g., Rom. 15:25). Indeed, it is striking that Luke states that Paul's first mission on behalf of the church was one of relief—carrying famine relief from Antioch to Jerusalem. Luke then follows this with the Holy Spirit's commissioning of Paul and Barnabas (Acts 11:27-30; 13:2). Paul does not seem to have any internal dilemma. Even though he sees himself as set apart as the "apostle to the Gentiles," concerned with proclaiming the good news of the gospel, he is still concerned with the physical needs of the Jewish church community.

Interestingly, the subject of giving financially for others is found throughout Paul's letters. For example, he writes to the Corinthians about the gift he is collecting from the churches. He also exhorts the people of God to work so that they can give.

Paul developed a strategy for bringing a particular message to a particular group of people (Acts 17:2-3). His intention was to intervene because he believed that the people he went to would become better people if they knew the saving power of Jesus Christ. He intervened in sending money to the poor in Jerusalem because he believed that they would be "better" if they had famine relief. He intervened in the life of the church at Rome by giving them instructions on sound doctrine and ethics because he believed that they would be "better" people if they gave heed to the gospel he proclaimed.

The Role of the Holy Spirit

Part of the mystery of the Christian life, the mystery of the gospel, is the intertwining of the personalities of the actors with that of the Creator. Perhaps the writer in Proverbs sums it up best when he says: "In his heart a man plans his course, but the Lord determines his steps" (Prov. 16:9).

Jesus told us that it was the Holy Spirit who would be the primary actor in the world (John 16:8-11). It is the Holy Spirit who will guide us as we seek to bring glory to God (John 16:13-14). Now this active involvement of the Holy Spirit is at once both an encouragement and a challenge. The Holy Spirit is involved (or should be!) in all that we do. Indeed, his involvement is so intimate that in Romans Paul tells us: "In the same way, the Spirit helps us in our weakness. We do not know what we ought to pray, but the Spirit himself intercedes for us with groans that words cannot express. And he who searches our hearts knows the mind of the Spirit, because the Spirit intercedes for the saints in accordance with God's will" (Rom. 8:26-27).

Mission: A Biblical View of Social Transformation

Whereas the world may have a desire to intervene on behalf of others for their own betterment, Christians are *commanded* to do so. "All the world" is the object of redemption, and the church and the Holy Spirit are the vehicles of that redemption.

The responsibility of each local body of Christians is to their fellowship and their community, as well as to the larger church and to the world. The very act of being a Christian assumes "doing good" for all humanity. Some believers will be gifted and called to act out their Christianity in the spontaneous ways of everyday living. Others will be gifted and called to be, at times, and in addition to their other social tasks, more active in intentional social transformation in the larger secular community of which they are a part: caring for widows and orphans, visiting those in prison, or seeking to change those aspects of society that oppress people. Then there will be those who, like Paul and Barnabas, have been gifted and set apart solely for such intentional social transformation both at home and abroad.

In all this we declare that the greatest good that one can do is to proclaim the kingdom effectively and convincingly so that others are attracted to Jesus and become his disciples. Evangelization is central to the work of the church, not only because eternal life is of supreme importance to the individual, but because the greater number of Christians in the world, the greater amount of good may be done for all humanity.

The Christian goal for social transformation is thus to *model* the good news so as to provide everyone with the opportunity both to respond to the commands of the gospel and to live in obedience to it.

There is no longer any question of *whether* social transformation includes evangelization. The question now is a question of strategy: how and when do we integrate the two.

Implications

How then do we go about the business of *Christian* social transformation? The answer is at once simple and extremely complex: We are called to *be* the church, the people of God in community, as the New Testament described that community to us. The question is not what we are to *do* but what we are to *be*—and to become and attempt to become.

In order for the church to be "salt and light" in the world it must first accept the task of transforming itself. In order for the church to proclaim justice in the world honestly, it must first create justice within itself. Thus we see that the church too is in the process of social transformation. We are in the process of becoming alive in the dialectic of a kingdom that has come but that is yet still to arrive. We live in the light of our own sinfulness, but somehow we must not let our own failures immobilize us.

We need to concern ourselves with the business of presenting our bodies as a living sacrifice by having our minds renewed (Rom. 12:1-2), even as we are about the business of "doing good to all men."

Our recent (and rapidly developing) evangelical history has brought us a complex legacy. First, it has reawakened our acknowledgment of our social responsibility. Second, it has led us to strive to meet that social responsibility through separate attention to physical and spiritual needs. But third, it has also brought a deepening understanding that if the church is to be conformed to the image of Christ it must act Christianly in all situations—without separating verbal and physical proclamation of the kingdom. And fourth, it has instilled in us a growing understanding of the necessary *wholeness* of announcing and demonstrating God's redemptive purpose in the world.

Notes

1. George M. Marsden, *Fundamentalism and American Culture* (New York: Oxford University Press, 1980).

2. Frances Fitzgerald, *America Revised* (Boston: Little, Brown, 1979).

3. Edward C. Stewart, *American Cultural Patterns: A Cross-Cultural Perspective* (Chicago: Intercultural Press, 1972).

4. The last attempt at research on the movement of the church in the world was the *World Missionary Atlas,* ed. Harlan P. Beach and Charles H. Fahs (New York: Institute of Social and Religious Research, 1925).

5. Of course, it was not only the relief and development agencies that had discovered ways of attracting funds through the mass media. The "electronic church" in America discovered the same response to its appeals.

6. A major exception to this trend toward separation was provided by World Vision International, which continued to attempt to find an integration between social responsi-

bility and evangelism and continued to announce to itself and to others that "evangelism was the bottom line."

7. See *Evangelicals and Development: Toward a Theology of Social Change,* ed. Ronald J. Sider (Philadelphia: Westminster, 1981).

8. See the Grand Rapids Report, "Evangelism and Social Responsibility," a joint publication of the Lausanne Committee for World Evangelization and the World Evangelical Fellowship.

9. See Tito Paredes's paper in this volume; the quote is in the section "Toward a Holistic View of Sociocultural Change."

10. This and all subsequent biblical references are to the New International Version.

11. See, in this context, George E. Ladd, *Jesus and the Kingdom* (New York: Harper and Row, 1964).

12. Karl Barth, *The Epistle to the Romans* (London: Oxford University Press, 1933).

Culture and Social Change

Tito Paredes

Introduction

The discussion of social transformation is rapidly becoming embedded in non-Western cultures—so much so that any discussion of Christian missions to those cultures must take account of it. Even though different evangelists or missionaries will obviously have different opinions on the methods and goals of social transformation, we can no longer deny that integral to the proclamation of the gospel of the kingdom is the proclamation of hope for social justice through social change. On the other hand, no truly adequate theory of social change can be stated without the hope of the coming of the kingdom of God, in which social transformation will reach its perfect fulfillment. I hope here to look at the relationship between culture, social change, and actual mission practice. I will consider first of all the concept of culture and outline its basic components. Then I will show some approaches to sociocultural change and explain their influence on current mission customs. And finally I will attempt to make the theme concrete in the context of Latin American Christianity.

What Is Culture?

We know from anthropological studies that the concept of culture should not be confined to a group of people with privileged access to selected aspects of their culture. Culture should not be identified with knowing and listening to classical music, reading the classic literature of one's country, or having formal (usually advanced) education. This limited view excludes from the group of "the cultured" the great majority of people who have not had access to formal educational systems connected with the Western tradition, or who are unlearned in Western music and literature. Yet this does not make them "uncultured" or devoid of a cultural tradition. Culture cannot be so readily identified with the customs and practices of certain groups in certain societies. All the people of the world, regardless of whether they know how to read or write, are repositories of rich cultural traditions developed through hundreds or even thousands of years. So they should not be belittled just because they do not fit our own or someone else's conceptions of what culture is.

Anthropology has rescued the term *culture* for use in a more inclusive sense, to refer in general to ways of life and thought of peoples everywhere. Yet a more exact definition of culture—and finding agreement on it—is not easy. There may be as many definitions as there are anthropologists—in 1952, A. L. Kroeber and C. Kluckhohn collected one hundred sixty-one.[1] "The Willowbank Report—Gospel and Culture," one of the papers from the Lausanne Committee for World Evangelization, says, "Culture is an integrated system of beliefs (about God or reality or ultimate meaning), of values (about what is true, good, beautiful and normative), of customs (how to behave, relate to others, talk, pray, dress, work, play, trade, farm, etc., etc.) and of institutions which express these beliefs, values and customs (government, law courts, temples or churches, family schools, hospitals, factories, shops, unions, clubs, etc.), which bind a society together and give it a sense of identity, dignity, security and continuity."[2]

This definition is a good start, but it is not inclusive enough. Culture has several dimensions that cannot be ignored. To use the formulation of Melville J. Herskovitz, we can say that "1. Culture is learned; 2. Culture derives from the biological, environmental, psychological, and historical components of human existence; 3. Culture is structured; 4. Culture is divided into aspects; 5. Culture is dynamic; 6. Culture is variable; 7. Culture exhibits regularities that permit its analysis by the methods of science; 8. Culture is the instrument whereby the individual adjusts to his social setting, and gains the means for creative expression."[3]

This diagram illustrates the most important components of culture:[4]

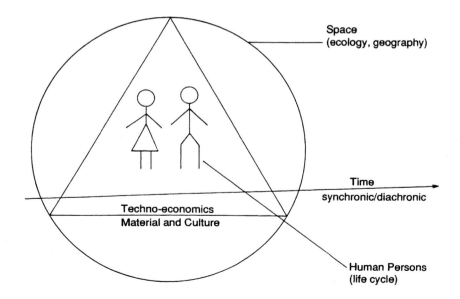

Space
(ecology, geography)

Time
synchronic/diachronic

Techno-economics
Material and Culture

Human Persons
(life cycle)

A serious study of a society that pretends to cover all the social dimensions depicted in the diagram will take a great deal of time. Furthermore, not everyone is interested in studying all of them in depth. Some students of society are only interested in the economic dimension, or the ideological one. Excessive specialization makes certain social scientists concentrate on some aspects of the phenomenon of culture, or on certain subcultures or social classes, to the detriment of their understanding of other aspects or subcultures or classes. If any approach to the study of the sociocultural reality of a people or society is to be accurate and profitable, however, it must take into account all dimensions.

Leslie A. White sees three subsystems in any culture. "The ideological system is composed of ideas, beliefs, knowledge, expressed in articulate speech or other symbolic form." It includes "mythologies and theologies, legend, literature, philosophy, science, folk wisdom, and common sense knowledge."[5]

"The sociological system is made up of interpersonal relations expressed in patterns of behavior, collective as well as individual." It includes "social, kinship, economic, ethical, political, military, ecclesiastical, occupational and professional, recreational, etc., systems."[6]

"The technological system is composed of the material, mechanical, physical, and chemical instruments" and techniques by which people interact with their surroundings. "Here we find the tools of production, the means of subsistence, the materials of shelter, and the instruments of offense and defense."[7]

Though White reduces the number of essential dimensions of a culture to three, others must be taken into account as well. Coincident at points with the technological dimension is the ecological dimension, which has to do with the natural environment's relationship with a society. The environment is the fountain of resources that allows the group to survive and shapes its development in certain ways. At the same time, human beings can shape the environment and exercise an effect on its development. They can misuse the environment and exploit it irrationally—even destroy vast parts of it—but they can also use it with care.

All social development takes place not only in a given natural space but also in a certain time dimension. To analyze the state of a society in any given time we can make a synchronic analysis: we refer to its existence and state at that particular time without regard to what led up to that point. Yet this obviously cannot tell everything about a society because all people and societies have a past, individual or corporate, that has conditioned and continues to condition the present. We can make a diachronic analysis, then, that specifically takes into account that society's change and development over time; this is the sort of analysis that takes seriously a people's historical development.[8]

Culture and the Human Being

With all this talk of societies and peoples, we would still only be talking in abstractions if we did not take into account the individual human person, a concrete reality whose behavior and life cycle are observable. Culture conditions people and enables them to function within it: they learn the sorts of behavior acceptable in that culture. But a human being is not a robot or a computer that has been programmed to behave in a certain way. Rather, humans are self-conscious—aware of many of their acts—and can choose to behave within the learned constraints or not and so pay the consequences. People are born, grow, become adolescents, adults, old people, and finally die, all within some social structure. During this life cycle many changes affect their society and culture—both from without and also from within as they create and modify their own culture.

Some anthropologists believe that one aspect of culture may determine a society. Leslie White states that "the primary role is played by the technological system. This is, of course, as we would expect it to be; it could not be otherwise. . . . Man must have food. He must be protected from the elements. And he must defend himself from his enemies. These three things he must do if he is to continue to live, and these objectives are attained only by technological means. The technological system is therefore primary and basic in importance. All human life and culture rests and depends on it."[9]

Max Weber places the emphasis on ideological factors, as exemplified in his classic work, *The Protestant Ethic and the Spirit of Capitalism,* while Émile Durkheim exemplifies a sort of sociological determinism.[10] The Marxist approach may be a determinist view not only of history but also of the economic and technological aspects of society.

Determinism is like the debate of what comes first, the chicken or the egg? For example, does a given society really rest on its technological system, as Leslie White says, or is that technological system actually the natural product and consequence of already extant social and cultural structures? The important conditioning factors of a social phenomenon or culture can be established only after very serious study and analysis, and even then, we cannot be sure that we have discovered them all. Consequently, we should talk, not of determining factors and structures, but of regularities and tendencies. We need to give due weight to all the variables at work within cultures.[11]

Biblical Perspectives on Culture

In addition to analyzing culture on its own, what perspectives can we glean from the Bible? We see that in the last analysis God is responsible for the creation of culture. He created not only the universe, the heavens, and the earth, but also men and women. Furthermore, he created all people with an orientation toward the supernatural beyond human individuals: human beings were created with the inherent need for God. As Pascal put it, there is within all people a vacuum that can only be filled with the lordship of Christ. We are created in God's image and likeness, and only when this vacuum is filled can we fulfill his purpose for us: to live in communion and fellowship with him. Apart from God, we cannot become what we were intended to be. "Man comes from God and because of this he encounters his destiny and he is able to realize all his possibilities only in Jesus Christ who is also man and God."[12]

God also gave humans physical, moral, social, and spiritual capabilities. These together grant them the potential to create their own culture. In Genesis God tells how he has placed man and woman in a special position over creation. They are to be administrators, caretakers, and cultivators of the whole earth and universe (1:26-28; 2:15); they are to use the capabilities given to them to interact creatively not only with God and each other but also with their environment; they are expected to elaborate, adorn, mold, and produce culture. As soon as God gave the command to take care of creation Adam began to give names to the animals: he was beginning to put to work that capacity to create culture and to shape the created order.

When God created the world he laid the foundations for culture. When he created man and woman he intended to have a special communion with them, and he intended that they would enjoy sinless relationships among each other and between themselves and the cosmos. But something went terribly wrong in our history: sin and evil entered into the created order (Gen. 3–4). The activity of Satan, the power of sin, and the Fall have damaged not only our relationship to God and to our fellow human beings but also our relationship to the earth. As a result of human rebellion, the whole earth was cursed. Since then all our labors have been accompanied by sweat, conflict, and weariness (Gen. 3:16-19; Rom. 8:19-22). Selfishness, pride, and ethnocentrism entered into human history and became basic causes of the struggles of individuals, families, and nations.

Yet despite their sin and need of redemption, all people in the created order still reflect in some way the grace, likeness, and image of the Creator; they are still able to do and to express much that is good. This remnant of good is a gift of God's grace, which he sends to both the good and the evil. Consequently, the Bible says, the rain and sun benefit not only the just but also the unjust; the land produces its bounty for all.

But this grace of God, which is able to bring good from even the evil, is not all that we must have and must strive for in the world. For although through grace many people have been given a sense of justice and beauty, and can express kindness and creativity, no matter how good they may appear, no matter how capable or beautiful their works, they still need salvation and liberation in Christ. Only the good news of the kingdom will make the good of the cultures even better. It is only the power of the gospel that will make the good citizen, student, or professor a better one. Only the power of the gospel can change what is evil or indifferent and make it good. Through the Fall came the need for a new humanity and a new creation. And through the saving work and liberation of Christ, which provides the possibility of renewal for human beings, nations, and all of creation, God has already laid the foundations of the new creation.

Sociocultural Change in the Anthropological Tradition

In the nineteenth century several prominent thinkers developed the groundwork for new theories of origin and development—Charles Darwin in biology,[13] Edward B. Tylor in religion,[14] Lewis H. Morgan in property, government, and the family,[15] and (following Morgan) Karl Marx and others in society. This interest in development theory was greatly motivated by the search for laws of progress applicable to all peoples, places, and times. Societies and cultures were seen as organisms that function according to certain laws. Many thought that if one could determine the stages of human and social development in one context, then that knowledge could be applied to peoples throughout the world.

Behind the search for the origins and development of humanity lay the assumption that human beings were on the road to perfection, not only economic, social, and ideological, but even moral. The idea of human degeneration and fall was seen as contrary to the new discoveries of evolutionary science—and was consequently denied. If all societies are in process of becoming more perfect, the reasoning goes, it stands to reason that some are further along the road than others. But it also stands to reason that sinful humans choose their standards close to home. With a built-in ethnocentrism that made them look upon their own societies as the highest in cultural development, nineteenth-century scientists established a hierarchy of societies most and least developed in the evolutionary scale. Usually non-Western societies were placed on the lower scales of cultural development, while Europe and North America became the model of development that all others were "supposed" to follow.

This Western ethnocentrism nourished much of the philosophy behind development theory and practice today. As Tom Sine puts it, "Western development is a child of the European and American Enlightenment. It is based on the implicit belief that human society is inevitably progressing toward the attainment of a temporal, materialistic kingdom. In fact, the certain belief that unending economic and social progress is a natural condition of free persons has become the secular religion of the West. . . . Implicit in this progressive view of the future was the firm conviction that economic progress would automatically result in social and moral progress."[16]

Cultural Relativism and Functionalism

The social evolutionist viewpoint is, of course, not without opponents and critics. Around the turn of the century, many anthropologists began to realize that much of the information on which it was based was shaky and unreliable. The assumptions on which it was built were mere conjectures and speculations about society and human beings that could not be supported by solid field data. Many people, including the Diffusionists and Historicists,[17] criticized the evolutionists for their unilinear schemes, poor handling of cultural data, ethnocentrism, and unwarranted speculation about the origin and development of society and institutions. They proposed a more careful use of data with more rigorous study of specific cultural areas instead of devising grand-scale theories that were supposed to be applied to the whole world.

Those theories that reacted against the evolutionist view contributed to the rise of the cultural-relative approach to the study of cultures. The basis of such an approach is the judgment that no cultural system can be adequately studied from the framework of another. Rather, each must be studied in its own context, on its own merits, taking into account its own peculiarities. No hierarchy of value exists that corresponds to a society's degree of development according to Western standards. Societies cannot be said to be superior or inferior, higher or lower, better or worse; rather, they are just different from each other. With the rise of cultural relativism and its rejection of judgment and comparison between societies, the concept of development as progress through fixed stages was devalued.

Another school is the functional school, which sees a society as a biological organism made up of many interrelated parts, each functioning for the maintenance of the whole. There is a tendency to see equilibrium and harmony in this approach. As a consequence, although an overall direction of change may be recognized, it is often not accounted for adequately, especially when it is swift.

The functionalist tradition within anthropology has contributed to a careful description and analysis of social groups and cultures within a limited frame of reference. It has helped us to understand how cultural systems function internally. However, since researchers have often preferred to analyze small-scale societies or social subgroups, their studies often have not taken full account of the larger social context. For example, a native culture in the jungle of Peru may, under this approach, be studied in isolation, without a very careful look at the larger context of Peru as a whole! The interactions between this culture and others around it, perhaps very influential in its determination, may not be adequately analyzed.

The cultural-relativist position and the functionalist tradition have both contributed to viewing societies as cultural systems that have a genius of their own. Both views grant the possibility for each culture to devise its own development programs which may be adequate and appropriate in their own context, even if they may not make much sense from a Western perspective. This possibility must be reckoned with in discussions about transformation, particularly by those whose bias is for preserving the status quo.

How is this approach worked out in the missionary task? We get a clear, but inadequate, answer in the work of William A. Smalley: "There is nothing intrinsically moral or right and wrong about social structure as such. The many different social structures as found today in the world are simply many different ways of organizing group behaviour into useful channels and of making life more valuable to the participants in the society. The missionary's role in relation to this as in relation to other cultural matters is to let history take its course and to concern himself with more important issues."[18]

Smalley would have us believe that there is no need to change social structures because they are amoral and do not impinge on the mission task. But the biblical perspective is that all social structures are under the judgment of God, and any that hinder his purposes are evil. In many places in the world today the rich are getting richer and the poor poorer. The structures that allow this—and that allow other unjust and sinful relationships at both the personal and international level—are sinful. The indiscriminate exploitation of natural resources and the pollution of the environment are often motivated by love of money and the desire to satisfy or create artificial needs. The structures that allow this are evil, too, and they must be changed.

So we cannot conclude that social structures are amoral. In this world there is much injustice, discrimination, indiscriminate exploitation of the environment, and exploitation of human lives. Sin and evil are concretely expressed not only in individuals but also in structures. When the Bible denounces the exploitation and domination of the poor, the injustice, corruption, and idolatry of Israel, it is judging not only the people who do this, but also the human relationships and institutions that manifest and make possible this sin.

In *Look Out—The Pentecostals Are Coming* C. Peter Wagner argues that "this is a book on the growth of the Pentecostal churches in Latin America. What the social stance of these churches should or should not be is a very fascinating subject, but it must be debated elsewhere. We here are basically interested in whether the socio-political position of Latin American Pentecostals in general helps or hinders the growth of their churches."[19] Wagner's point here seems to be that in the growth of the church it does not matter much whether the surrounding social structure is good or bad, or whether the gospel has something important to say to it. The only important thing for Wagner appears to be whether these structures hinder or contribute to the numerical growth of the Pentecostal churches.

A similar line of thinking is taken by Donald A. McGavran in his book *Understanding Church Growth*. Here there is a chapter entitled "Social Structure and Church Growth," but McGavran's major concern is not whether structures are good or bad but rather whether or not they impede the growth of the church: "The great obstacles to conversion are social, not theological."[20] In a later chapter, "Without Crossing Barriers," he states that "men like to become Christians without crossing racial, linguistic, or class barriers." He adds, "When marked differences of color, stature, income, cleanliness, and education are present, men understand the Gospel better when expounded by their own kind of people. They prefer to join churches whose members look, talk, and act like themselves."[21]

There does not appear to be much importance laid on the judgment of the social structures under which one lives. The "marked differences" are discussed not in terms of right and wrong but only in terms of their being an obstacle to the proclamation of the gospel. Whether the social structures that cause such differences are good or bad "is a very fascinating theme," worthy of being discussed, but one on which the gospel and the growth of the church have very little to say. What matters, as for Wagner, is the effect of a structure on numerical growth in the church.

McGavran does recognize that social action is a very legitimate activity for Christians. It must, however, be subordinated to evangelism, for the ultimate goal is reconciliation of humanity with God and the numerical growth of the church: "A multitude of excellent enterprises lie around us. So great is the number and so urgent the calls, that Christians can easily lose their way among them, seeing them all equally as mission. But in doing the good, they can fail of the best. In winning the preliminaries, they can lose the main game. . . . Among other desires of God-in-Christ, He beyond question wills that persons be found . . . that is, brought into a redemptive relationship to Jesus Christ where, baptized in His Name, they become part of His Household. . . . The more found, the better pleased is God." McGavran sums up the superior position of evangelization over and against social action by stating: "A chief and irreplaceable purpose of mission is church growth. Service is good, but it must never be substituted for finding."[22]

This neutral attitude toward social structure gives little attention to the evils that structures can cause in social relationships. It is functional, relative, and uncritical of the premises upon which the social sciences have been elaborated. Furthermore, this attitude also reflects a tendency in the Western world to segregate the material and spiritual dimensions of reality, as well as to put the spiritual over the material, rather than integrating them and looking at them holistically.

Wagner himself now recognizes that the church growth movement, of which McGavran has been called the dean, has often taken an uncritical approach to social structures: "Evangelicals during most of the twentieth century chose to concentrate largely on soul saving. Wes Michaelson is correct in his observation that the evangelical heritage has been 'dominant individualism,' with its great emphasis on 'converting,' while assigning a peripheral status to 'questions of discipleship, justice and the shape of the church.' The Church Growth Movement, firmly located in the evangelical camp, uncritically, and somewhat innocently, participated in this ethos."[23]

Wagner argues, however, that while this may have been characteristic of the church growth movement in the past, the movement is now mending some of its deficiencies regarding the cultural mandate. He insists that neither the cultural nor the evangelistic mandate is optional. This may reflect the "change of mind" that he says he himself has undergone as he has come to accept the idea of "holistic mission."[24] "True Christians, for whom Jesus is really Lord, do not have the luxury of sitting back and coolly deciding whether they will participate in carrying out one or the other. There is no such option. Serving God, the king, necessarily includes both the cultural mandate and the evangelistic mandate."[25]

He states that "the evangelistic and cultural mandates can be differentiated from one another, but must not be polarized"; yet even so he tends in practice to insist on the priority of the evangelistic mandate and the numerical growth of the church. He distinguishes between social service and social action, and prefers service over action because service is able to contribute more directly to the numerical growth of the church.[26] "Social service is the kind of social ministry geared to meet the needs of individuals and groups of persons in a direct immediate way. If a famine comes, social service will provide food for starving people. . . . Social action is the kind of social ministry geared toward changing social structures . . . by definition, [it] involves socio-political change. . . . The end goal of social action is to substitute just (or more just) for unjust (or less just) political structures."[27]

To approach social structures "statically"[28] reflects not only a particular theological reading of Scripture, but also a tendency to see societies as orderly mechanisms in a state of equilibrium. Although Wagner argues that church growth teaching both recognizes and promotes culture change, this is true at best only when that change is slow and when religious ideologies change as well: "The Church Growth Movement, which leans toward the functionalist camp advocates minimal cultural change and concentrates mostly on religious change."[29]

It would be simplistic to say that proponents of the church growth movement reveal only a functionalist orientation because "besides functionalism, they are drawing on ethnohistory, cognitive anthropology, symbolic anthropology, and other methodologies."[30] However, there is a functionalist priority in the methodology of the social sciences of the movement. Wagner recognizes the great influence of cultural anthropology, which in turn has been greatly influenced by functionalism: "Cultural anthropology has been the social science most influential on the Church Growth Movement. Particularly as it has touched the field of missiology, it has brought an orientation toward the anthropological school of thought called 'functionalism.'"[31]

As is not uncommon in a functionalist study, church growth specialists tend to treat cultures and dimensions of those cultures in isolation. They do not take enough account of the socioeconomic dimensions of a people, but instead put the emphasis on ideological variables. They also treat small or primitive cultures as homogeneous groups isolated from each other, and in the process they lose sight of the dynamic interrelations of the group under study with other groups.[32] The practical outworking of this orientation is support of existing social structures. In his preference for social service (feeding the hungry) over social action (changing social structures), Wagner unconsciously reveals a bias for the preservation of the status quo.

The Conflictive Approach

While functionalists tend to see equilibrium in cultural systems, those theorists who have ascribed to conflict theories see structural change everywhere.[33] These theories constitute the legacy of Karl Marx, among others. Ralf Dahrendorf points out that

> for Marx, society is not primarily a smoothly functioning order of the form of a social organism, a social system, or a static social fabric. Its dominant characteristic is, rather, the continuous change of not only its elements, but its very structural form. This change in turn bears witness to the presence of conflicts as an essential feature of every society. Conflicts are not random; they are a systematic product of the structure of society itself. According to this image, there is no order except in the regularity of change.[34]

For Marx, change and conflict are the engines of history and civilization—"the history of all societies up to the present is the history of class struggles."[35] The key to understanding structure and conflict at any period lies in the relationships created by the means and mode of production. These relationships are marked by conflict between the haves and the have-nots, between those who control the means of production and those who perform the labor in production. One social class is trying to maintain their primacy while the other is trying to wrest it from them.

According to conflict theories, three great historical periods stand in a dialectical relationship: primitive communism, mercantile capitalism, and developed communism. Primitive communism is characterized by collective cooperation in labor through the participation of family members. Community rather than individual interests take priority. There is no economic exchange. The diverse activities of hunting, fishing, and weaving are *social* functions whose fruits are given freely to the community—the family. Individual work activities act as part of collective family or community labor and form a distributive system.[36] During this stage of history people are free to an extent, but this freedom remains incomplete as long as all are chained and enslaved to nature. Although the division of labor, division into classes, and class conflict are absent, the freedom is dull and purposeless. The goal that gives meaning to labor will be realized only during the developed communism stage.[37]

The mercantile capitalism stage of social and historical development negates primitive communism. Capitalism is characterized by the division of labor, an exchange economy, and the dissolution of community property. Feudalism and present-day capitalism, marked by individualism and self-interest, are antitheses of primitive communism.[38] Technology grants some measure of control over nature, but because the mechanism for this control is the division of labor, people become alienated from each other, from their work, and from their true selves. The division of labor and the holding of private property create relations of domination and subjection, class formation, and struggles in ever-changing patterns.[39]

Modern capitalism, which is the developed form of this second stage, introduces into this exchange economy great contradictions and conflicts that eventually become unbearable. The separation between the proletariat and the bourgeoisie becomes so great that the struggle between these two forces issues in the classless society by virtue of the total victory of the proletariat. This is characterized by a return to communism, not limited as was the primitive stage, but a developed communism that benefits from the advances of technology and control of nature developed by the interim capitalism. Only in this stage can people realize themselves as free beings: "In Communist society, where nobody has one exclusive sphere of activity but each can become accomplished in any branch . . . society regulates the general production and thus makes it possible for me to do one thing today, and another tomorrow, to hunt in the morning, fish in the afternoon, rear cattle in the evening, criticize after dinner, just as I have a mind, without ever becoming hunter, fisherman, shepherd or critic."[40]

Marx saw that contradictions, conflicts, and struggles are constantly present in society, and he considered them especially acute in modern capitalism. He believed that it is the process of conflict and resolution that moves human history—from primitive communism to capitalism and eventually to developed communism. A Marxist analysis of any society tends to focus especially on the conflicts between the proletariat and the bourgeoisie. Instead of seeing stability and equilibrium in society as the functionalist does, Marxists see constant change. Furthermore, they do not just accept the status quo of social structures but see the opportunity to use and exploit struggle and tension to bring about revolutionary change. Marxists will not be satisfied with simple reforms or community development since these serve only to distract the proletariat from the real task of bringing revolution—a complete change in the underlying structure of society.

The Latin American Theory of Dependence

In Latin America,[41] the failure of the Alliance for Progress and the inability of reformist approaches to do anything significant about deteriorating social conditions have contributed since the late sixties to the emergence of the theory of dependency. This theory is a derivative of Marxist theories of imperialism and colonialism and as a result may itself be viewed as a Latin American expression of Marxism.

This theory attributes the underdevelopment of the Third World to its dependency on the developed capitalist world, which carries out its socioeconomic activities in its own interest. The underdeveloped world, tied to the international capitalist system through a long historical process of interactions with it, follows along, passive and powerless. The "metropolis," the center of power in the developed world, dominates the periphery, the underdeveloped world. Underdeveloped economies can do none other than revolve around the needs and interests of the developed world. This is sometimes called neo-colonialism or external colonialism, terms that reveal that this dependency is not merely economic, but encompasses all of society as the underdeveloped world finds itself dependent also in terms of culture, politics, and ideology.

This analysis is also applicable to the subnational context of indigenous cultures. The anthropologist Stefano Varese tells us that "in different kinds of degrees, through long historical processes, all the ethnic minorities find themselves in a situation of domination. They are victims of that national economic, social and cultural structure which has been defined as internal colonialism."[42] Through the same dynamic processes that can enforce the dependency of one nation on another, tribal communities that were autonomous and self-contained have been incorporated into a net of dependent and nonsymmetrical (that is, nonreciprocal and unharmonious) relationships. They are part of a pattern of conquest and colonial expansion that has taken place throughout Latin America.[43]

From this perspective, social studies or mission approaches that do not take seriously the dynamic complexity of the relationships between the developed and underdeveloped world are at best faulty or completely irrelevant and at worst may serve to perpetuate or even exacerbate the problem. To repeat a point made in regard to the functionalist approach, no study of a community can be truly valid that does not take seriously the political and historical context of a nation or region. People groups must always be studied in relation to their past and their future, in relation to other groups and classes, and in relation to larger national and international interests and goals.

The Conflictive Dependentist Approach in the Mission of the Church

In the "Final Document of the International Ecumenical Congress of Theology," a conference that took place in São Paulo, Brazil, in February and March 1980, we find what may be called a conflict-dependency approach to the mission of the church to social reality:

> The situation of suffering, misery and exploitation of the great masses of people which are concentrated especially, but not exclusively, in the so-called Third World, is so obvious as well as unjust. . . .
>
> However, the most important historical process of our time begins to be carried out by these people. . . . Their oppression has its roots in the colonial exploitation of which they were a victim for centuries. Their fight for life, for their cultural and racial identity which was denied by the foreign dominator, is as ample as the domination itself. . . .
>
> As the popular movement develops, the fundamental question put forward is the formulation of an historical project which basically is a critique of capitalism and imperialist domination. . . .[44]

The Final Document limits the concept of oppression almost exclusively to its social, economic, and political manifestation. Important here is the *effect* of injustice and domination in people's lives, not necessarily the underlying nature of the oppression. In the Bible there is also an effective attack on injustice and exploitation (Exod. 3:8-10; Isa. 58:3-12; Jer. 6:13-15), and the Lord raises his voice against it in protest and denouncement (Isa. 58:6-8). But God's strongest attack is not against the effects or manifestation of injustice; he reserves that instead for the *nature* of oppression—it is the result of the reign of sin in human beings and social structures.

This point can never be used to deny the importance of the liberation from the effects of evil, however. In the Exodus of the Hebrew people, we see the liberating action of God from this type of social and political oppression; and in the New Testament the gospel of Jesus Christ speaks against these manifestations of sin (Luke 4:16-20). But the Bible not only speaks about the oppression of sinful structures. It also speaks about the oppression of personal sin that all people experience: "What then? Are we Jews any better off? No, not at all; for I have already charged that all men, both Jews and Greeks, are under the power of sin, as it is written: 'None is righteous, no, not one; no one understands, no one seeks for God. All have turned aside, together they have gone wrong; no one does good, not even one'" (Rom. 3:9-12). This means that all people, rich and poor, oppressors and oppressed, have sinned and need the salvation of God.

The Final Document does not take full account of this, however. It says of oppressed peoples that "their oppression has its roots in the colonial exploitation of which they were a victim for centuries." The implication is that the oppression of Latin America all began in 1492 with the arrival of the Spaniards. Although there is a lot of truth to this, it is not the whole historical truth. The oppressors in the Americas were not always, or only, foreigners.

We have to recognize that in certain ways, and at certain times, the oppressors in Central and South America were the natives of the region, not outsiders. Before the arrival of the Spaniards both the Inca and the Aztec empires conquered and dominated other peoples who would have preferred to maintain their autonomy. The Chanca people were forced to accept Inca domination after an initial period of resistance. The Aymarás, rivals of the Incas, were also conquered but maintained a persistent resistance that has kept them linguistically and culturally strong even until today. The Araucanians of Chile were able to resist Inca conquest successfully, while the Huancas, though initially subjected, took the first opportunity to rid themselves of Inca domination by entering into an alliance with the Spaniards. This alliance became a factor in the eventual defeat of the Incas.

Sin, in the form of exploitation and colonization, obviously did not enter the Americas with the arrival of the Spaniards; it is not restricted to the colonial and postcolonial world. It has been in all times and places since the Fall; it is apparent in all peoples. The root problem of humanity is our disobedience and rebellion against God, and this has its manifestations in the personal and structural dimensions of life. We all need personal liberation from sin; and all social structures need to be redeemed from their sinful roots.

No social critique is adequate and true that refuses to see the universality of sin. Sin is present not only in capitalist but also in socialist systems. We cannot close our eyes to the experience of Czechoslovakia, Poland, or Afghanistan; nor to the tyranny of some of our dictators in Latin America. The structural manifestation of sin is not limited to any one sort of human system: *all* social structures need liberation from sin through Jesus Christ. Yet it is here that I notice a gap or silence in the Final Document: it condemns capitalism but not other systems and social structures.

It is time to evaluate more critically the different theoretical and methodological approaches that we use in the study of social reality. The Dependency Theory is just one of several approaches that help us see the macroprocesses of our social context at the national and international levels, but it, along with the others, has its inherent limitations. It can never be more than just one of the windows that give us light.

The categories of oppressed and oppressor, for example, do not do full justice to the complexity of social reality. To categorize one as oppressor or oppressed always demands a certain frame of reference; yet this frame is not always stated. For some peasants of the Peruvian jungles, the category of oppressor includes not only the great transnational companies that exploit their lands and resources but also certain other peasants from the highlands. The peasants from the highlands themselves consider the transnational companies the oppressor, but when, because of land scarcity, they migrate to the jungle to find new ways of livelihood, they become the oppressor from the point of view of those who have inhabited the jungle for thousands of years.

The conflict-dependency approach would probably put both groups together under the category of the oppressed. While this is true at a certain level of analysis, it does not shed light on the microprocesses of the interpersonal and intergroup relationships that take place between the peasants, nor does it take into account how they themselves perceive each other as oppressed or oppressor. This is only one instance of the whole complex of social relationships and differentiations that are present even *within* different groups, particularly within the so-called "oppressed" and "oppressors." Social processes are not as simple as dependency theorists seem to indicate. There is much more behind the scenes.

One important point that we can draw from this example is that all human beings have the potential to be oppressors. The oppressed can very easily, if only they once gain power, become the oppressors, not only of their former oppressors but also of those whom they are supposed to represent. This is always a present possibility because sin transcends social structures. It is people who build social structures and people who sin, and mere structural change will never alter that. Therefore it is crucial that there should be transformation not only of structures but also of persons. It is here that I see the challenge and the radicality of the gospel of our Lord Jesus Christ.

Although Christians do not share the historical vision of Marxism that expects the establishment of a classless and just society by human means alone, we should still be open to the contributions and critique that Marxism makes of our contemporary world. The conflict-dependency tradition has alerted us to the dynamic contradictory forces at work in the world bringing about a kind of development that is leading humankind to its final doom. Christians see the power of sin and the activity of Satan behind these conflicts, as he tries to draw us into a "development" that leads to hell. But the development that God wants for men and women, society, and creation will ultimately free all those who have come to know, understand, and accept the gospel of our Lord Jesus Christ.

Toward a Holistic View of Sociocultural Change

It is important that we not see this Christian freedom strictly in spiritual terms. The liberation that we are referring to is to be understood holistically— as integrating the spiritual, economic, social, and political dimensions of life in this world. The liberation that is proclaimed in the gospel never divorces one dimension from the other.

No culture is static: all of them change, though some change faster than others. This change can be any modification of the ideas, society, technology, economy, and ecology of a people due to factors working from within or without. For example, conversion to Christianity of a person, a family, or an entire people would be a change that begins at the level of ideas. The introduction of new crops or new machines such as rice hullers is change that begins at the level of techniques. Changes that begin at a certain level do not end there, however. A change introduced in one dimension is bound to affect the others. Technological changes affect the economy and the way people think. A change in the ideas of a people may well affect its social structure; it may even reflect back on its economy or on the technology it employs. Nor can changes be restricted within any culture because societies are now so intimately involved with each other. We now live in a "global village," in which the dealings and interests of one society affect and influence others. The actions of the superpowers, for example, affect the lives and the future of all peoples, often adversely.

Culture and sociocultural phenomena need to be studied together, in action in history, not separately as uniform units that seem to function smoothly in equilibrium. Cultures, although they tend to seek order, regularity, and equilibrium, are also ridden with contradictions and conflicts. Any development project must aim at the just resolution of these conflicts and contradictions: not just their symptoms but also their deep causes. It must seek the integral liberation of individuals, families, and peoples within the unique sociocultural context in which they live.

A problem common to many development programs is Western ethnocentrism. This is usually shown by the tendency of many such programs to define for the target group the problems and needs to be addressed and then to impose solutions. This is often partly due to Western ignorance of the culture of the people and blindness to the potential solutions that either spring from the soil of the culture itself (autochthonous solutions) or are at least grafted onto local ways (that is, solutions that combine outside and local techniques). Western development programs often ignore the long traditions of technology and know-how and other assets in non-Western societies that could be explored and used to address modern problems more effectively. For example, ancient agricultural, medicinal, and building methods are often ignored in community development projects because it is believed that Western techniques are more effective—but often this is not the case.

Although there is less talk now about developmental change along nineteenth-century evolutionist lines, we still divide the world in terms of developed or underdeveloped countries, mainly using technoeconomic criteria. When we talk about the developed world, we do so mainly on the basis of its industrial and technological advancement in contrast to the supposed lack of it in the underdeveloped world. But again, this cannot be isolated as the only aspect of a society that should be considered as a measure of its development. Ideology, worldviews, religion, social institutions, personal relationships, organizational forms, ecological factors, and even the historical testimony of a people—all these need to be brought into any evaluation of or action for development and sociocultural change.

Thus we need to see social change in its entirety and not just in its technoeconomic dimension—that is, our view of development and social change must be holistic. But just as important as this overall view is a contextual view of each culture. We must view the development of each culture in terms only of its own needs and goals—not all societies should or can follow the Western pattern. In this sense, the rise of cultural relativism is welcome in that it helps us free Western societies from thinking of themselves as superior to others just because they possess industrial technology, and it also makes us more able to tolerate differences between cultures. But at the same time we have to be careful not to condone unjust, sinful, and inhuman social conditions on the basis of functionalism and cultural relativism. Evil is not to be accepted in the name of cultural diversity.

We should learn from the mistakes of the nineteenth century not to impose upon other peoples our own idea of development. We should realize that sociocultural change in non-Western countries should come from the country itself and may not take the same route as Western development. In any case, it is preferable that the kind and direction of change be determined by the active participation of the people affected by it, under the direction of the Holy Spirit and the judgment of Scripture.

The Bible, Persons, and Society

The Bible has an opinion not only about human nature but also about human social structures and relationships. All, without exception, show the stain of sin and rebellion against God. Everyone is guilty and under God's judgment, and everyone needs the salvation of God in Christ Jesus. God's call, which is clearly directed to everyone, is to repentance and to a new life in the experience of his kingdom. As sin entered all through Adam, so in Christ is salvation offered to all. The sinful solidarity of the human race in Adam has its counterpart in the salvation that we find in Jesus Christ.

The consequences of sin are shown and made real at both the personal and the sociocultural levels. Sinful humans build and create imperfect and sinful social structures. "Sin is not only personal but it is structural. It is structural in the sense that it responds to the logic behind collective behaviour (Alves). Society is not the sum total of its members; it constitutes a very complex network of interpersonal, cultural and institutional relationships."[45] Even though not all human creation is bad (there is a lot of beauty in it), it is all imperfect, and much is even demonic. The imperfect and the demonic require the liberation and transformation that only the gospel of the kingdom of God can provide.[46]

Even as the Bible integrates the personal and the collective, it does the same for the material and the supernatural. It presents both to us as integral dimensions of the life of the world and of humanity. In the Old Testament, the liberation of the Hebrews from Egypt was not only sociopolitical but also spiritual. Physical oppression had affected their spiritual relationship with God. It is a fact that many of them were complaining and groaning for their complete liberation, but many of them perhaps did not see an end to their situation and may have lost their confidence and trust in God. God stood by them, however, and accomplished their material liberation even as he strived to renew his relationship with them.

The Lord Jesus in his ministry did not split apart the spiritual and material either. Whenever Jesus brought someone to himself, he did it in both dimensions. For some, he cured physical infirmity, for others he forgave sins, and for others he did both (Luke 5:17-26). The Bible, then, presents to us a complete vision of sociocultural reality, which integrates the physical and spiritual dimensions of humanity.

In the mission of the church, we cannot do less: "The fundamental missiological question before the Christian Church is not whether mission should be conceived of as vertical, horizontal, or both; not whether it should be thought of either as spiritual and personal, or material and social; nor whether we should emphasize in our practice one aspect or another. It is rather whether we can recover its wholeness and efficacy, whether we can see it as a whole and live up to its global objectives."[47]

Objectivity in the Study of Sociocultural Phenomena

One of the basic principles of the social sciences in the Western world is objectivity. This is understood as an effort to understand, describe, and analyze a social phenomenon or society without making value judgments, without judging whatever is studied as good or evil, superior or inferior.[48] A social phenomenon, a sociocultural reality, must be understood within its own frame of reference and must not be judged in relation to other realities. The academic effort of the universities in the West and the functionalist approaches to society nourish themselves from this research tradition.

This orientation often results in the divorce of researchers from their own sociopolitical praxis. In their effort to be objective, they do not want to commit themselves to the good of the people that they study or with whom they live. They want to be neutral, not to take a position, especially toward sociopolitical changes. The Colombian sociologist Orlando Fals Borda describes this attitude like this:

> The objectivity of the social scientists in the developed countries consists essentially in "not having any commitments with the social order that is being transformed. Thus it runs the risk of becoming a mere intellectual sub-product of the factors that are stopping the social historical change." This implies the belief in a dynamic and relative reality of social change, but in any event, it also recognizes independent qualities from the will of the observer. Objectivity of the problems of change and development, under these conditions, is that which directs, describes and explains painful truths that may go against created interests or that reveal the ideological biases of given groups.[49]

Objectivity can also be understood from within the framework of commitment and the struggle to transform society, that is, from a conflictivist point of view. The Peruvian ideologist José Carlos Mariátegui refers to this commitment in a very eloquent manner: "Once again I repeat that I am not an impartial or objective critic. My judgments are nourished by my ideals, by my feelings, by my passions. I have a very clear and energetic ambition: that is to witness and contribute to the creation of Peruvian socialism. I am as far away as possible from the professorial technique and the university spirit."[50]

For Mariátegui, to make value judgments and to commit oneself to the transformation of the social order that is studied is very legitimate and even imperative in any approach to social reality. Value judgments about Peru are nourished by the socialist vision that Mariátegui assumes. Fals Borda would argue that it is possible to be committed to social change without necessarily losing objectivity. Even as it is possible for social scientists in the Third World to be objective, so it is crucial that they be committed to the social context in which they live. "The non-neutral authors can be very disciplined and very objective. Not to be neutral does not imply to lose objectivity in the analysis."[51]

Christians cannot be objective either—in the sense of the word that implies neutrality. They have a commitment that is very acute and clear, not with the relativities of the sociological approaches, but with our Lord Jesus Christ, the Lord of history. Christians cannot only describe and analyze the phenomena before them but must commit themselves, with their Lord, to the transformation of persons and social structures that are unjust and anti-Christian.

I would like to recast the above passage quoted from Mariátegui from a Christian perspective, saying that as Christians "our judgments are nourished by our commitment and loyalty to our Lord Jesus Christ and to his holy word within the context in which he has placed us. This commitment is the engine that nourishes our ideals, our sentiments, our passions. We have a clear and energetic ambition: that of witnessing the expansion and establishment of the kingdom of God on this earth—not by the works of human beings alone, but through the decisive intervention of God." May it be so!

The Christian church and Christian institutions must work and minister with an integral biblical perspective of humanity in their actions and visions. Human beings, the family, the community, must be redeemed through Jesus Christ with and within the matrix of the society, economy, history, and ecology of which they are part. The Christian vision is not content just with higher crop yields, economic growth, or changes in the unjust structures of society; rather it demands that one minister with just as much energy for the salvation of people's lives, so that they too can become part of the people of God and his kingdom.

We like to talk about Christian growth, maturing, and discipleship. We like to talk about "developing" to the image of Christ. This is usually restricted to the individual and seldom is applied to the family or society. Here again, the Western individualistic bias must be questioned. What is the meaning of development within a cultural, family, or group context? What does God want people, society, and creation to become? Does God have a place for the individual in isolation from the community?

God is interested in development that includes the whole creation with the hope that, although we may not yet see its fulfillment, we can experience already today signs of the full development that awaits us. Using the criteria from God's word, which helps us to be holistic and integral in our approach, we can see that development applies not only to the transformation of individual minds and behavior, but also to the transformation of families, society, and the world. We need to apply the whole counsel of God to the whole of his creation, to address development at the level of ideology, worldviews, value systems, structures, and institutions of all sorts. We need to remember that development applies also to the physical environment and its exploitation, to the arms race and the rejection of wars, and to unjust relations between nations as well as within them.

We need to proclaim God's victory over satanic forces at work against his vision for the full development of mankind. Jesus Christ must be the paradigm of biblical development. The kingdom of God is already—but not yet—and this "already" sense must be a very intimate part of development in Christian missions. We must see, taste, and experience the kingdom of God right now. We must also be aware of all God wants for his people, that he will intervene to bring about the consummation of his kingdom, the full consummation of development that is "not yet."

A holistic and dynamic view of God's work in creation and his present activity in human culture must be the framework in which a holistic development project takes place. God's creation, human culture, and development are integrally related and we must give due attention to the material, spiritual, social, and personal needs of all people. Development is a "movement towards that freedom and wholeness in a just community which persons will enjoy when our Lord returns to bring the Kingdom in its fullness."[52]

Notes

1. A. L. Kroeber and C. Kluckhohn, eds., *Culture: A Critical Review of Concepts and Definitions* (New York: Vintage, 1952).

2. "The Willowbank Report—Gospel and Culture," Lausanne Occasional Papers no. 2 (Wheaton, Ill.: Lausanne Committee for World Evangelization, 1978), p. 7.

3. Melville J. Herskovitz, *Man and His Works* (New York: Knopf, 1951), p. 625.

4. See also Ruben (Tito) Paredes: *Hacia Una Misiologiá Latin-americana— Modelos Socio-Antropológicos en el Estudio de la Realidad Socio-cultural y Misional de los Pueblos y de la Iglesia* (Lima, Peru: PUSEL, 1981).

5. Leslie A. White, *The Science of Culture: A Study of Man and Civilization*, 2d ed. (New York: Farrar, Straus, Giroux, 1969), pp. 364-65.

6. Ibid., p. 364.

7. Ibid.

8. In the past there has been a tendency, particularly within the functionalist approach to anthropology, to ignore or at least not to pay enough attention to the historical past of cultures and societies. In this regard E. E. Evans-Pritchard has an enlightening essay, "Anthropology and History," that concludes: "I believe an interpretation on functionalist lines (of present in terms of present) and on historical lines (of present in terms of the past) must somehow be combined." *Social Anthropology and Other Essays* (New York: Free Press, 1962), pp. 187-88.

9. White, *The Science of Culture*, p. 365.

10. Max Weber, *The Protestant Ethic and the Spirit of Capitalism* (New York: Scribner, 1948); Émile Durkheim, in his *Elementary Forms of the Religious Life* (1915; reprint, New York: Humanities, 1976), gives us a sociological explanation of the religious beliefs and behavior of the Australian aborigines.

11. I agree with Walter Goldschmidt's assertion that "it is necessary to appreciate the variety and character of the existing explanations for the divergent social systems. . . . It is not only that each orientation should be tolerant of the other, that those who seek psychological explanation should give the sociologists their due. It is, rather, that each kind of explanation *requires* the others; that, say, in order to understand a phenomenon sociologically requires a proper psychological orientation, and so on." *Man's Way: A Preface to the Understanding of Human Behavior* (New York: Holt, 1959), pp. 54, 60.

12. Samuel Escobar, writing in the Certeza series (Buenos Aires: International Fellowship of Evangelical Students), no. 42, p. 33.

13. The publication of Darwin's *Origin of Species* in 1859 was a boost for evolutionary studies—not only in biology, but in social and cultural anthropology as well. Darwin's contribution lay not so much in pioneering evolutionary ideas as in popularizing them at a time when the social climate was against evolutionism. Though social scientists such as Thomas Malthus and Herbert Spencer had anticipated Darwin, *The Origin of Species* gave evidence for what Spencer had previously only speculated. Darwin's influence in the social sciences shows in the many analogies of biological and social evolution in Spencer's later

work, *Principles of Sociology* (1876, 1882, 1896). See in this context Robert L. Bee, *Patterns and Processes: An Introduction to Anthropological Strategies for the Study of Sociocultural Change* (New York: Free Press, 1974), p. 43.

14. Edward B. Tylor tried to show that religion evolved first out of the belief in the soul then into animism, polytheism, and finally monotheism. See his "Animism" (excerpted and abridged from his two-volume work, *Primitive Culture* [London: John Murray, 1873]) in *A Reader in Comparative Religion: An Anthropological Approach,* ed. William A. Lessa and Evon Z. Vogt (Evanston, Ill.: Row, Peterson, 1958), pp. 11-23.

15. Lewis H. Morgan, along with E. B. Tylor, is considered a classic representative of unilinear evolutionism, according to which society was assumed to develop through fixed stages, from lower to higher. Under this ethnocentric conception, European and North American societies were considered to be at the pinnacle of progress, which societies everywhere were expected to reach in due time. See Morgan's *Ancient Society; or, Researches in the Lines of Human Progress from Savagery through Barbarism to Civilization,* ed. E. B. Leacock (Cleveland: Meridian, 1963).

16. See Sine's article, "Development: Its Secular Past and Its Uncertain Future," in this volume; quote is from the section "What is the Implicit View of the Better Future in Western Development?"

17. For a discussion of these approaches that reacted against classical evolutionism and proposed alternatives, see Bee, *Patterns and Processes,* pp. 67-93; and Robert H. Lowie, *The History of Ethnological Theory* (New York: Rinehart, 1938), pp. 128-95.

18. William A. Smalley, "Planting the Church in a Disintegrating Society," *Practical Anthropology* 5 (September-December 1958): 232.

19. C. Peter Wagner, *Look Out—The Pentecostals Are Coming* (Carol Stream, Ill.: Creation House, 1973), p. 139.

20. Donald A. McGavran, *Understanding Church Growth,* rev. ed. (Grand Rapids: Eerdmans, 1980), p. 215.

21. Ibid., pp. 223, 227.

22. Ibid., p. 24.

23. Wagner, *Church Growth and the Whole Gospel: A Biblical Mandate* (San Francisco: Harper and Row, 1981), p. 3.

24. Ibid., pp. xii, 91.

25. Ibid., p. 51.

26. Ibid., p. 37.

27. Ibid., p. 36.

28. Orlando Costas traces this approach to an "anthropological-functionalist syndrome" in *The Church and Its Mission: A Shattering Critique from the Third World* (Wheaton, Ill.: Tyndale, 1971), p. 15.

29. Wagner, *Church Growth and the Whole Gospel,* p. 155.

30. Ibid., p. 164n.18.

31. Ibid., p. 153.

32. The homogeneous unit principle and the idea of "consecrated pragmatism" (see ibid., pp. 69-86) both reflect functionalist ideology.

33. This discussion of theories of conflict and dependency is an edited extract from my article "Different Views of Sociocultural Change," *Missiology* 9 (April 1981): 181-92.

34. See Ralf Dahrendorf's essay in *Theories of Social Change,* ed. Richard P. Appelbaum (Chicago: Markham, 1970), p. 82.

35. Ibid.

36. See Paul Dognin, *Introducción general a la doctrina de Carlos Marx* (Buenos Aires: Pontificia Universidad Católica Argentina, 1973), p. 2.

37. Dahrendorf, in Appelbaum, *Theories of Social Change,* p. 87.

38. Dognin, *Introducción general,* p. 3.

39. Dahrendorf, in Appelbaum, *Theories of Social Change,* p. 87.

40. Ibid., p. 89.

41. See my "Different Views of Sociocultural Change."

42. Stefano Varese, "Milenarismo, Revolución y Conscientia de Clase," *Educación,* 1st Trimestre (Lima, Peru: INIDE, 1975), p. 45.

43. Ibid., pp. 45-48.

44. "Final Document of the International Ecumenical Congress of Theology," p. 3. The Final Document has been published in *The Irruption of the Third World,* ed. Sergio Torres and Virginia Flavela (Maryknoll, N.Y.: Orbis, 1984).

45. See Orlando Costas, "Pecado y Salvacion en America Latina," in *America Latina y la evangelizacion en los años 80,* documents of the Congreso Latinoamericano de Evangelización II (CLADE II), Lima, Peru, November 1979, a congress under the auspices of the theological fellowship of Latin America (Lima: CLADE II, 1980), p. 275.

46. See "The Willowbank Report—Gospel and Culture."

47. Orlando Costas, *The Integrity of Mission: The Inner Life and Outreach of the Church* (San Francisco: Harper and Row, 1979), pp. xii-xiii.

48. This conceptualization is closely related to the relativity of the socioanthropological phenomena. In conceptualism, universals exist as mental concepts only. In relativity, knowledge is only of relations of reciprocal dependence between individuals and society.

49. Orlando Fals Borda, *Subversion and Social Change in Colombia,* trans. Jacqueline Quayle (New York: Columbia University Press, 1969), p. 121.

50. José Carlos Mariátegui, *7 Ensayos de Interpretación de la Realidad Peruana,* 10th ed. (Lima, Peru: Biblioteca Amauta, 1965).

51. Fals Borda, *Subversion and Social Change in Colombia,* pp. 124, 125.

52. Regarding this, I reassert what I wrote in my article "Different Views of Sociocultural Change," pp. 190-91: "Dependency theory alerts us to the macrosocial processes affecting the international and national context. How the dominant world economic and political powers from West and East relate to each other and to the Third World is bound to have an impact upon our nations and their future. The current situation . . . has been shaped by the relationships of world powers in the past. We are part of an international community whose destiny is tied with ours. Missions cannot ignore this. How we develop mission and ministry models in such a world is a challenge to our creativity and our openness to the Spirit of God and His Word."

Culture and Planned Change

Miriam Adeney

Do Westerners Support Only Successes?
Cultural Values of Development Agencies

Two Asians stood admiring a lake at an international Christian conference. One had supervised a highly touted indigenous socioeconomic program. Western Christian leaders had lionized him. But as he looked over the lake he mused to his friend—who reported it to me—"Have you noticed that Westerners support only successes? I wonder, would they be interested in me if I were to fail?"

Westerners give "development" high priority. If a project fails, all is lost. Other peoples certainly value change, too, but they balance this with other priorities. Some value roots. Some value the old and their heritage as much as youth and newness. Not all people are as eager as Westerners seem to be to bring change at any price.

As we discuss culture and planned social change, then, we would do well to consider the cultural values of change agencies, including missions agencies. Certainly their workers and project directors do not arrive on the scene value-free. This is equally true whether the workers move internationally or within their own nation. National social workers ministering to a different ethnic group—or even to a different social class—in their own country can be as imperialistic, as contemptuous of local values, and as rigid about the rightness of modernization as any Westerner working in a non-Western country. Nevertheless, because the United States is the place I know best and also the base for many relief and change agencies, let us consider relevant North American values as they affect change efforts.

In the United States, change is viewed as desirable. We expect new consumer goods, new amusements, new ways to get work done better. Aiming to be self-reliant, we North Americans leave our birth families behind. Without extended families, we become a nation of joiners. Voluntary associations flourish. Amid this flux, our social security numbers are more important than our names.[1] Since we ourselves lack roots, we often cannot take others' roots seriously.

We admire active, assertive, ambitious achievers—self-starters.[2] We admire pragmatic problem solving. We do not admire contemplation of the eternal mysteries. We view life in measurable terms. Money is valuable not only for its intrinsic usefulness, but also because it serves to measure intangibles. Can your organization afford a word processor? A video cassette system? Glossy paper in your promo magazine? If so, you must be doing something right.

From our rich and driven perspective, however, time is even scarcer than money.

> So "efficiency" requires the maximum use of advanced technical devices—all aimed at saving time. And this begins to affect our attitude towards all reality. Is the task evangelism? We immediately think of money for travel, honoraria, media, printing bills, rental of facilities. Is it healing bodies? This requires money for hospitals, X-ray machines and surgical theatres, doctors and nurses. Is the task education? We visualize expensive buildings, equipment, and professional staff. We quite literally lack the capacity to imagine doing things other than this capital-intensive, technology-intensive way.
>
> And we bring these ideas along wherever we do the Lord's work. Even where technology is inordinately expensive. Even where believers are all but destitute. And even where the most abundant resource is willing minds, willing hands. Soon, however, it becomes apparent that local Christians can't pick up the tab. And because they also lack the know-how to operate the system, we end up taking over.[3]

With these values, we suffer from a "success syndrome."[4] Should we support failures? Of course not! What is that Asian Christian leader by the lake thinking of?

This is not to say that other people outside the United States don't want change. Most people want to live beyond the age of forty-five. They want more than half of their babies to survive. They even want refrigerators. C. P. Snow has observed,

> It is all very well for us, sitting pretty, to think that material standards of living don't matter all that much. It is all very well for one, as a personal choice, to reject industrialization—do a modern Walden, if you like. . . . But I don't respect you in the slightest if, even passively, you try to impose the same choice on others who are not free to choose. In fact, we know what their choice would be. For, with singular unanimity, in any country where they have had the chance, the poor have walked off the land into the factories as fast as the factories could take them. . . .

The industrial revolution looked very different according to whether one saw it from above or below. It looks very different today according to whether one sees it from Chelsea or from a village in Asia. To people like my grandfather, there was no question that the industrial revolution was less bad than what had gone before. The only question was how to make it better.[5]

Most people have dreams. Nevertheless, change may fit into their scale of priorities—their dreams—somewhat differently from the way it does in the scheme of a worker from an industrialized country.

Anthropological Views of Culture

Description of Anthropological Theories

In this paper I explore both anthropological and theological views of culture. Anthropologists, the acolytes of culture, turn out to be like the fabled blind men describing an elephant whose mental image of the beast varied so greatly depending on what part of it they took hold of. Crudely differentiated, some anthropologists emphasize the material aspects of the human experience while others focus on intangible mental and social patterns. "Culture," then, includes a number of variables. Depending on the theoretical framework one advocates, certain variables will be seen to be more crucial than others. And it is important to remember that the variables one believes to be foundational will affect the approach to social change one comes to support.

What are the theoretical alternatives?

Evolutionists have asked: What forces of natural selection—what variables in the struggle for survival won by those who most effectively adapt to their environment—have operated in the development of this culture? Ecological anthropologists have considered culture "an adaptive mechanism for maintaining material relations with the other parts of man's ecosystem."[6] Marxist anthropologists understand social phenomena in terms of the dialectical relations that are believed to determine everything else. Beginning with private ownership of the means of production, moving to class struggle, culminating in the classless society, the dialectic is seen as materially based, directional and inevitable. Events either serve or hinder the coming revolution: that is the basis for analysis and evaluation. Any attempt to study them "objectively" is considered misguided.

Anthropology, then, must cease being a tool of the status quo, the Marxists say, and must start cooperating with the dialectic movement of history. But how? By selecting problems that are significant from a Marxist perspective. By researching data that Marxist groups need. By abdicating the attempt to study humanity per se and embracing the study of human beings as they are molded by their several socioeconomic contexts. By exposing our field ties with administrators who serve the imperialistic expansion of the West. Finally, by combining theory with praxis, by serving the revolution actively ourselves.

Against these materially focused theories stand many others. For structural functionalism, which comprises the mainstream of American and British anthropology, ideas, customs, and material artifacts are mutually interdependent parts of a whole integrated system, which operates like an organism or a complex machine. Social structure is central. The question is not how a variable adapts to the external environment so much as how it fits and functions in the overall cultural pattern.

The structuralism of Claude Levi-Strauss proposes that cultures are systems imposed on the random natural world by the structure of the human mind. That structure is a pattern of opposed binary contrasts. Cognitive anthropologists believe that systematic syntactic and semantic analysis will give clues to what a people holds to be the constituent entities and taxonomies of the universe. Many other anthropologists assert that idea systems exert a powerful influence. Among them, Clifford Geertz has defined culture as a historically transmitted pattern of meanings embodied in a system of symbols which grids action.[7] He has also referred to culture as "webs of significance," which we spin and in which we hang suspended.

Between the naturists and the nurturists, between those who emphasize the independent variable of the external environment and those who emphasize our response, are the psychological anthropologists. They focus on patterns of child raising, on the cultural conditioning of the personality, and on various areas in which the unconscious breaks through in culturally-patterned channels, such as art or mental illness.

Ethnic anthropologists hold that interpretations or explanations of a people must come from the people themselves, in their own terms. They follow in the tradition of nineteenth-century German scholars who distinguished *Geisteswissenschaften,* sciences of the human spirit, from *Naturwissenschaften,* sciences of nature. The method appropriate to the *Geisteswissenschaften* is *Verstehen,* empathetic understanding, which is an aspect of anthropology's preferred method of participant observation. Critics of the ethnicists argue that we are moved by many aspects of culture of which we are not conscious. In his research on the Tewa tribe, for example, Alfonso Ortiz found that none of his Tewa informants was aware of the whole system of beliefs that he pieced together. Yet they were certainly influenced by it all.[8] However much we empathize with an informant, then, that person may not be able to articulate his culture as comprehensively as we can after a systematic and somewhat more objective study.

A Critique of Anthropological Theories

Anthropologists who are concerned about social change argue over their theories. In particular, they argue about which is more determinative: material environment or intangible worldview and interaction patterns. Is a local approach to community development—one that is sensitive to values and concerned about value change—effective? Or does this assume an unwarranted power of ideas, rigidity of culture, and isolation of communities? Is a restructuring of national or international political and economic structures the more effective route to community development and cultural change? We must be clear on one thing. There is no one "right" theory. Different theories are appropriate for different research questions. Different degrees of reliability are acceptable, also, depending on the number and complexity of the variables and the amount of philosophy as opposed to empirical data. A study on nutrition *should* be more verifiable than one on religion. Ironically, the verifiability of a study often correlates inversely with its significance. As Thoreau noted long ago, "It is not worthwhile to go round the world to count the cats in Zanzibar." On the other hand, some of the most worthwhile questions perennially resist easy answers.

Because nature is one independent variable, the material environment *must* be included in an explanation of culture. Idea systems may indeed be powerful, but what shapes idea systems? For example, the "meek, docile, and peaceful 'hunting and gathering' Shoshone" changed "into the horse-riding, 'fierce, warlike' Comanche" almost overnight, not because of any new idea, but because of a new resource in their material environment: horses.[9]

To date, when we missionary anthropologists have given attention to material factors, we have done so in terms of a hypothetically integrated, semi-isolated, semi-static group of people. We have not developed our theory to encompass adequately the true range of variables in space, variables in time, and unequal power relations impinging so strongly on a people's way of life. We have not fully accepted that, for example, the hiring policies of Exxon may affect a people's culture more than their beliefs about their ancestors. For anthropologists sensitive to these variables, the theoretical alternative employed has often been Marxist. Certainly Marx is our forerunner in conflict theory. After Marx, no thinking person can look at the world in the same way. In particular, Marx formulated keen insights into the *origins* of conflict in a capitalist society. In the *development* of conflict, however, several of Marx's propositions appear to be false descriptions of what happens in the real world.[10]

While material factors are necessary in an explanation of culture, they do not appear to be sufficient. Studies in ethnicity, for example, suggest that when people share a distinctive history, even when there is no material advantage to be gained, they will often continue to affirm a distinct ethnic label for themselves because it provides a certain coherence, satisfies social structures, and gives a sense of primordial identity. Certainly, as some cultural materialists have pointed out, peoples are not imprisoned by their worldviews; they are well able to juggle alternatives. On the other hand, as the cultural materialists neglect to mention, there is a dearness to traditions. The ability to choose does not mean that the materially advantageous option will always be chosen. Price does not always equal value.

Given all these contrasting approaches to culture, is there any underlying common ground? Among themselves, anthropologists may fight tooth and nail for their favorite theories. But they will unite around a number of common values that agents of positive change, too, will do well to cultivate. Anthropologists want to be holistic. They want to study real behavior not just ideals, corporate groups not just individuals, culture in all its rich and confusing complexity not just a few selected variables. And they want to study cultures throughout space and time. Empathy, curiosity, objectivity, and tolerance for ambiguity are some of the attitudes anthropologists cultivate. Within this context, they evaluate theories for their simplicity, their elegance, their comprehensiveness, and for how well they generate significant questions and hypotheses.

Theological Views of Culture

Over the years, theology has taken various views of culture. At times people have thought that God was directing us to separate ourselves from culture; at other times people have thought that he meant us to work with and within culture. Some of these theological views have passed away, but many of them are still apparent in various forms yet today.

Christ Condemns Culture: Culture as the Binding Clutches of Satan

Like anthropologists, theologians have viewed culture variously. "India is the tragic story of a vast nation left for centuries to the binding clutches of Satan. . . ." So begins an article in a current magazine. God may well have ordained culture, but the customs and the reality that we observe around us no longer glorify God. Instead of loveliness, harmonious creativity, and admirable authority, we see fragmentation, generation gaps, alienation, lust, hate, corruption, selfishness, injustice, laziness, disorder, and violence. This is why some Christians throughout history have taken the position that Christ is at odds with culture. No part of culture remains pure. Science tends to serve militarism or hedonism. Modern art often becomes worship without God. The mass media are full of verbal prostitutes. Advertisers exploit sex. Those in business often pull shady deals. Politicians fill their own pockets with the people's money. Teachers don't bother about scholarship after a few years in the profession. Workers do shoddy work. Husbands deceive their wives. Wives tell their husbands only what they think will promote their own interests. Parents dominate their children. Children ignore their parents as persons.

At the cultural level, then, sin permeates all activities to some extent. Therefore the Lord tells us not to love the world. It is too easy for the cares of this world and the deceitfulness of riches and the lusts for various things to choke the word of God in our lives and make us unfruitful. We need, consequently, to take heed lest at any time we be overcharged with the concerns of this life. We dare not think that if we are rich and have lots of goods we are without need—when in fact we are spiritually wretched and miserable and poor and naked. What profit is it if we gain the world and lose our souls? The Lord advises us to set our affections on things above, not on the things of this world. Denying worldly lusts, we are to live soberly, righteously, and godly in this present world.

The elements of our culture don't come from our Father, but from human beings. They are going to disintegrate and pass away. So we are not to pin our hopes and joys on them. We are to keep ourselves from idols of any kind. For example,

> Christian women are not to be caught up in the latest fashions but are to cultivate a meek and quiet spirit. In politics we are not to agitate for some utopia

but rather to nurture one another to prepare for life together in the kingdom of Christ. In intellectual pursuits we are not to become absorbed in philosophy, because even a fool in Christ is wise. We are not to love money, not to worry about meeting expenses. We are not even to be slaves to schedules or productive work, as Martha was. We are not to worship aesthetic experiences; rather, we are to be like Abraham, willing to leave the centers of culture. Like Paul, who could stand on the Areopagus, looking out over one of the greatest artistic achievements of human culture, and shout that what is really worth knowing is Jesus Christ.[11]

Sin permeates culture. This is a basic Christian belief. Already in the first century some withdrew on these grounds from established cultural institutions. For them, the affirmation of Sojourners' Jim Wallis would have rung true: "When the church dares to be the church, it becomes self-consciously marginal to the mainstream culture."[12] By the second century, Tertullian was thundering, "What has Jerusalem to do with Athens?" and encouraging Christians to withdraw from public life where possible, because it "required a mode of life contrary to the spirit and the law of Christ. . . ."[13]

Since the second century, many have been convinced that Christians constitute a "third race" beside Jews and Gentiles. Some have dropped out to form model communities: monasteries are but one example.

In history these Christian withdrawals from and rejections of the institutions of society have been of very great importance to both church and culture. They have maintained the distinction between Christ and Caesar, between revelation and reason, between God's will and man's. They have led to reformations in both church and world, though this was never their intention. Hence men and movements of this sort are often celebrated for their heroic roles in the history of a culture which they rejected.[14]

Christ Generates Culture: Culture as a Treasure Chest of Symbols

Other Christians would argue that, far from being demonic, culture is God's gift. God has endowed people everywhere with his image, the image of a Creator, with the creativity that develops cultures. He has commissioned us with the cultural mandate (Gen. 1:28). Cultures are not, then, amoral rules holding Hobbesian man in check, but rather they are treasure chests of symbols for exuberant expressions of the image of God.

In the beginning God affirmed that it was not good for man to be alone. People were made to live in communities of meaning, so God established the family, the state, work, worship, arts, education, and even festivals. He spelled out laws that preserved a balanced ecology, ordered social relations, provided for sanitation, and protected the rights of the weak, blind, deaf, widows, orphans, strangers, poor, and debtors. And he gave a motivation for duty by relating it to himself.

God taught the Hebrews, and later the Christians, that life is abundant. "We are not to live in quiet resignation but to press toward the goal ahead. We are to do everything heartily, as to the Lord. Whatever our hand finds to do, we should do it with our might."[15] God blesses wholehearted activity.

And we are made "in God's image." What does this mean? Christian theology asserts, in Kierkegaard's words, that "every man is an exception." Surely, then, being in God's image also means creativity. As God is a creator, we are made creative. When we create, we exercise a characteristic that represents God. "When God made the earth, He could have finished it, but He didn't. He left it as a raw material—to tease us, to tantalize us, to set us thinking, and experimenting, and risking, and adventuring. And therein we find our supreme interest in living."[16]

Human culture, then, is not wholly alien from God, but rather is "the result of man's creative activity within God-given structures."[17] Many institutions, corresponding to the human needs for work, worship, play, and love, have been blessed explicitly by God. Indeed, God's early words to Adam

> call man to progressive growth in culture. Far from being something in conflict with God, cultural achievements are an essential attribute of the nobility of man as he possessed it in Paradise. Inventions and discoveries, the sciences, and the arts, refinement and ennobling, in short, the advance of the human mind, are throughout the will of God. They are the taking possession of the earth by the royal human race, the performance of a commission.[18]

Because human culture stems from God's gifts of creativity and common grace, people with little personal knowledge of Christ may show lovely traits.

> When I looked around at my neighbors in a Philippine community where I lived for several years, for example, I saw strong families. Warm hospitality. Lots of time lavished on children. Enduring loyalties. The ability to live graciously on little money. A heritage of economic freedom for women. Creativity in music. Sauces that deliciously extended a little meat to many people. A delight in sharing. Skill in the art of relaxation. Lithe, limber bodies. The ability to enjoy being with a large number of people continuously.
>
> Since every good gift is from above and since all wisdom and knowledge come from Jesus Christ, these beautiful qualities of Philippine culture must be gifts of God. It seems that, just as our Creator delights in a vast variety of colors and smells, just as he has brought millions of unique personalities into being, so he has ordained an amazingly wide spectrum of cultures. He has programmed into man a capacity for cultural variation that enables us to explore our potential in all its complexity, to increase the richness of His world.
>
> The early Christians accepted different cultures. When they preached to Jews, their framework was the law of Moses and the prophets. But when their audience was pagan, they dropped that emphasis and talked instead about how God provides for our physical and spiritual needs, and how God is stronger than idols. Peter learned to accept all peoples, including their food that was repulsive to him. Paul learned to be "all things to all men." Timothy was circumcised; Titus wasn't. Both were Paul's key men. The Epistles show that churches from different cultural backgrounds had different kinds of problems. So when the mother church in Jerusalem set standards, she decided not to ask new

Christians in other cultures to conform to her ways, since there was no difference "between us and them" (Acts 15:9).[19]

Because of God's gifts of his image, the cultural mandate, and common grace, there is much in the "secular" order of every culture, in traditional institutions, structures, ideologies, and world powers for which we can thank God and on which we can build. When we probe cultural patterns, then, we do so humbly, because, as some of the early physical scientists expressed it, we are "thinking God's thoughts after him." In this vein, A. N. Triton comments,

> We believe that Christian morals are for all men because God is the Creator and His law is given to everyone. It is not just the rule for the church. To break God's law is always injurious and God cares about the state of society even in non-Christian cultures. You do not have to be a Christian before you are told that you ought to keep the Ten Commandments. We want to say to the whole of mankind that God is the Creator; that He has graciously told us the basic moral principles; that they are always for man's good in the long run and that they should be obeyed both for that reason and also because God says so and we are His creatures.[20]

Christ Transforms Culture: Culture as a Fellowship of Creative Deviants

On one hand, we see that God blesses humanity's involvement with this world. On the other hand, he commands humanity to keep separate from it. How can these positions be reconciled? Because of humanity's paradoxical nature, we must hold disparate perspectives in tension, recognizing that

> this world is broken. Not absurd, not suspended between two vacuums, but something extremely precious and yet totally broken. The whole creation, which God proclaimed to be good, reflecting His glory, this world is broken. The more it is perfect, the more we can understand the tragedy, the tremendous sadness, of that brokenness. It is only when something precious is broken that we are sad. If something has no goodness in it, why cry about it?[21]

Yet, amid this brokenness,

> although sin infects the entire world, God is still in charge. He still owns the cattle on a thousand hills. He still sends rain on the just and the unjust. He ordains governments, according to Romans 13. The structures of nature and society are held together in Christ, according to Colossians 1. God is moving in history toward his own goal. This is still his world.[22]

God loves the world. He doesn't want us to go out of the world but instead wants us to keep separate from the evil—and to go into all the world to reconcile it to him. Marriage, food, politics, and all other aspects of culture are acceptable to God if they are experienced in the context of his authority, love, and holiness—if they are related to him as he really is. Unlike Buddhism, Christianity does not approve passivity. Christianity teaches wholehearted involvement in the life around us, not for selfish goals but for the glory of God.

Whether we eat or drink or agitate for political change, we should do it to the glory of God.

In all our affirmation, however, we must continually remind ourselves that Christ rivals all systems—even our religious ones. This is not to say that systems, or powers, are evil in themselves. Remember, the powers were created by Christ and are held together in Christ. But powerful systems become evil when they usurp the central place in ordering our values and beliefs. Given our tendency to idolatry, this happens frequently. Whether Marxism, sex, Islam, or money, some power constantly appears on the horizon to nudge Christ out.[23] We worship the creature rather than the Creator. We pray, "*My* will be done."

Human systems tend to take over. Because of this, according to 1 Corinthians 15, it was necessary that Christ's death dethrone all powers. His sacrifice did not necessarily destroy them, as some translations suggest, but it dethroned them. Following Christ who dethroned the powers, we too must see them in proportion, as merely one segment of creation, existing because of the Creator, and limited by other creatures. Beyond that, while we stand questioning the powers, we ourselves need to ask God for liberation every day from those powers that inhibit us personally.

We who stress "power encounter" in regeneration need also to apply it at more general levels. Anthony Campolo does this when, "view[ing] capitalistic institutions as principalities and powers," he argues, "I believe Romans eight tells us these institutions are 'groaning and in travail waiting for the sons of God' to help them serve the purposes for which they were created."[24]

The danger in affirming culture is that we may find ourselves lead on an insidious path of false reasoning toward triumphalism about our own culture. We tend to start thinking that ours is the best and is the standard by which others should be evaluated. Even evangelical Anglicans associated with the Clapham Sect, that small group of influential Christians in early nineteenth-century England who accomplished so much in eliminating the slave trade, nepotism in civil service, child labor, unsafe factory conditions, prison squalor, and harsh punishments—even some of these dedicated evangelicals, blinded by triumphalism, viewed Indians and Africans ambivalently, almost, in Kipling's famous phrase, as "half-devil and half-child." Charles Grant, "taking as his starting point the utter depravity and corruption of the Hindu race," argued that Britain must assume "the task of instructing the Indian population in Christian civilization which providence had so clearly ordained for it, by putting the country under British control," and further that "there was no foreseeable future 'in which we may not govern our Asiatic subjects more happily for them than they can for themselves.'" After all, as John Lawrence explained, "In doing the best we can for the people, we are bound by our conscience and not theirs."[25]

If triumphalism threatens those who affirm culture, other dangers lie in wait for those who hurl judgment down on it. Culture is, in fact, inescapable. Though the world may lie in wickedness, distinctions still must be made between relative rights and wrongs. Though we may withdraw from culture, we will do so only to create new subcultures. Some have advocated this, and Christian communities from the Benedictines to the Sojourners community have salted the earth. Yet they have at the same time drawn criticism.

"I don't think the young evangelicals are ever going to be substantive because they're utopian," said Bill Bentley, president of the National Black Evangelical Association, a few years ago. "They don't see the need to go back and be prophets in their own community come hell or high water. Until they do that, they're always going to be chasing rainbows. I regard the retreat into communes as just that. They've got to close their eyes, hold their nose, and jump back into their communities, taking whatever comes."[26]

God has planted us at one spot in time and space and history. Shall we cut off our roots? Deny our opportunities? Skip out of stewardship of the cultural resources over which God has made us managers? Build more enclaves in segmented society instead of building bridges with people of all social labels? Link up with likeminded peers in the prime of life, rather than with our natural parents who need human warmth?

In the final analysis, culture is necessary for the Christian

> because he is a Christian and a man. If he is to confess Jesus before men, he must do so by means of words and ideas derived from culture, though a change of meaning is also necessary. He must use such words as "Christ" or "Messiah" or "kyrios" or "Son of God" or "Logos." . . . These things he must do, not only that he may communicate, but also that he may himself know whom and what he believes. . . . In his effort to be obedient to Christ, the radical Christian therefore reintroduces ideas and rules from non-Christian culture in two areas: in the government of the withdrawn Christian community, and in the regulation of Christian conduct toward the world outside. . . .[27]

The Greek word for world *(kosmos)* in 1 John—"Love not the world"— is the same as that used in John 3:16—"For God so loved the world." This seems a contradiction, but we must let one passage balance the other. In the end, are we called to a counter culture? Or are we not rather called to God in the middle of every culture and institution in which we find ourselves? Niebuhr observes that after recognizing

> the importance of the role played by anticultural Christians in the reform of culture, we must immediately point out that they never achieved these results alone or directly but only through the mediation of believers who gave a different answer to the fundamental question. . . . The movement of withdrawal and renunciation is a necessary element in every Christian life, even though it be followed by an equally necessary movement of responsible engagement in cultural tasks.[28]

Culture—humanity's creativity within divinely ordained structures—is blessed by God. Relating it to him, we rejoice in it. But since culture is also involved in humanity's rebellion against God, we do not idolize it. Rather we balance affirmation with judgment. Expecting a struggle with sin in every area—education, art, recreation, politics, or personal relations—we want to be a fellowship of creative deviants.

How to Help a Culture Change: Culturally-Sensitive Transformation

Our review of anthropological theories has reminded us to admit a range of variables, stretching from macroeconomics to local values, as partially determinative of culture. To keep this range in mind when embarking on a project aimed at transformation, it may be useful to make a checklist: Does the project fit with local concepts? With traditional knowledge? With local religion or contemporary secular ideology? With local social structure (including law and politics as well as informal groupings)? With local economic resources, infrastructure, and technologies? With local family and child-training patterns? With local communication styles and media? With local aesthetics? With local recreations and celebrations? With the specific pressures for cultural change that this society is experiencing? Naturally, a culture will include multiple, sometimes contradictory formulations. Nevertheless, our humble attempt to adapt to its major themes remains important both pragmatically and theologically.

Some may object that this is an unduly positive approach to cultures. Confrontation, not appreciation, is what is needed, they may contend. Nevertheless, successful confrontation cannot occur until there is understanding of the context. Cultural integration is pervasive. It cannot be ignored or shrugged off while we get on with our confrontations. Superficial confrontations in fact often do more harm than good. Furthermore, understanding the context means appreciating the good gifts of God's common grace that are present there. A review of theological approaches to culture has cautioned us to be neither naively optimistic nor overly judgmental, whether about the culture of the poor or of the social workers trying to help them. This is equally vital whether the workers move internationally or within their own nation, from an educated background to a slum, or from an urban to a rural context. People are just as likely to develop through an admiration of their strengths as through a thundering condemnation of their deficiencies.

With this as background, let us consider several areas of culture where we must adapt if we are to facilitate successful change.

Does the Project Fit with Local Worldviews, Concepts, and Values?

Consider our approach to a polluted water supply, for example. In village after village around the world, this is a major source of sickness and death. Some experts estimate that 60 percent of the diseases in some areas could be eradicated if the water could be cleaned up. In many cases the solution is simple: cover the pool and install a pump. Yet, surprisingly, local people often resist this public health measure. Why?

In one Middle Eastern community described by Afif Tannous of the Department of State, the villagers explained their feelings.[29]

> "Our fathers, grandfathers, and great grandfathers drank from this water as it is, and I don't see why we should make a change now."
>
> "You say that you want to install a pump at the spring; but I for one have never seen a pump, nor do I know what might happen if it should be put there."
>
> "I tell you what will happen. The water will flow out so fast that the spring will dry up in no time."
>
> "Not only that, but the iron pipe will spoil the taste of the water for us and for our animals."
>
> "You So and So," put in one of Jibrail's elders, who are much more advanced than the people of [the village], "do you like the taste of dung in your water better?"
>
> "Well, I admit it is bad; but we and our animals are at least used to it."
>
> "You have told us that the water is the cause of our illness and of our children's death. I do not believe that, and I can't see how it could be. To tell you the truth, I believe that the matter of life and death is in Allah's hands, and we cannot do much about it."
>
> "One more thing. We don't understand why you should go to all this trouble. Why are you so concerned about us?"
>
> "You say that the pump will save our women much effort and time. If that happens, what are they going to do with themselves all day long?"

This story points up values and concepts that contrast with those of a social worker. Although many human needs and hopes are similar, values do differ from culture to culture. Some people value clean water supremely. Others value stability. Still others may value outlets for expression. Some value individual success. Others value family pride. Others may not care about advancement as long as they have an enjoyable life with their kin now. Some, immersed in ideas about imperialism, the bourgeoisie, and the people's struggle, will sacrifice everything else as they pour themselves into efforts for a social revolution.

In socioeconomic projects, value conflicts may occur between the social workers' emphasis on progress, modernity, and youth and the emphasis of others on age and tradition. Conflicts may also arise through different emphases on efficiency, different work rhythms, different socialization patterns expected, and different communication styles.

Culturally-sensitive development begins with what people value and know, and then expands on it. It proceeds from the known to the unknown.

Does the Project Fit with Local Social Structure?

Bruce Olson, who has lived with the Motilones of Venezuela and Colombia for nearly twenty years, confesses that he could do nothing to improve the people's health care system until he worked through and with local leaders.[30]

When he began offering a few simple medicines—after he had already slept in a hammock in the local longhouse for several years, had learned the

Motilones' language, and had run barefoot with them down thorny jungle trails—they rejected them. "Those medicines are fine for you," they said, "but we have our own herbs and treatments." So, helpless, Bruce saw the people fall prey to one illness after another.

One day an epidemic of conjunctivitis surged through the camp. Soon nearly everybody's eyes oozed and burned. Bruce stood by, frustrated because he had a medication that would clear up the inflammation immediately. Finally, desperate, he stepped over to a friend and poked his finger into the corner of the man's eye. Then he wiped the goo in his own eyes—and developed pinkeye himself. He then went to the local healer.

"Could you please give me something for my eyes?" he asked. "They're burning."

"Bruce, I wish I could help you," she answered, "but I've tried every herb and chant I know. Nothing works. I'm worn out."

Then Bruce pulled out his ointment. "Maybe this would help. Would you put it in my eyes?"

She did.

When Bruce's conjunctivitis cleared up, and when he gave the healer all the credit, she became willing to try the medication on others. In three days the whole longhouse was cured. As a result, she began to listen to Bruce's health suggestions. She was willing to look through his primitive microscope, and she marvelled at the wiggling demons that she had always known were responsible for disease. When they beat the longhouse for spirits periodically, she was willing now to add disinfectants to the beating. Within a few years, the Stone Age Motilones were running eight clinics. Motilones were doing the diagnoses and the treatments. Motilones were giving the injections. Even Spanish-speaking settlers were streaming to their clinics by the thousands. This shows the importance of working through a local leader.

Questions that will help us adjust our program to local social structures include: Who are the community opinion leaders? What is the community decision-making process? How do they settle quarrels? What are the natural lines of affiliations? These may tie individuals to several networks. Within the subgroups in the culture, what are the rights and obligations of members, the distinctive roles, the special rituals or celebrations, the myths or special reputation of the group, the models, the villains, the techniques of boundary maintenance, the distinctions between formal and informal behavior?

Frequently we may anticipate tension between an emphasis on the group and any plan that rewards individual incentive. Farmers around the world argue, "Why should I grow a bigger crop? It will just mean more relatives descending on me at harvest time." Cooperatives may mitigate the tension between individualism and group-mindedness. One way or another, proceeding from the known to the unknown, we must use the group wherever it is significant. Individuals are not as rootless as we may assume.

As an alternative to cooperatives, when capitalizing small shopowners in New Guinea, missionary Don Richardson counseled each one, "Go to the oldest man in your group and make a deal. Explain why you cannot give away your goods—the village soon would not have a store. Then ask him if you can refer to him all the relatives and friends who come asking for free goods. He can explain the situation to them. The refusal will be firm but indirect. Then you tell the old man that at the end of the year, as a token of gratitude, you will give him a shiny new ax." This plan has worked.

In other countries, similarly, businesses have reduced absenteeism by visiting the employees' home provinces and explaining to family elders why regular work attendance is essential.

Does the Project Fit with Local Economic Resources?

Juan Flavier, director of the International Institute of Rural Reconstruction, recalls how he learned to adjust to local economic realities.[31] When he began his medical career in the rural Philippines, one of his first patients was an infant with pneumonia. Standing in the simple bamboo hut above the convulsing infant, Dr. Flavier reached automatically for his prescription pad.

"Penicillin," he began to write.

The baby's relatives looked at each other.

"Doctor," the father interrupted, "the nearest drugstore is thirteen kilometers away. And it will never open at night, for fear of thieves."

Suddenly the child convulsed.

"At least let's get some ice. We have to get this fever down," Flavier said.

Again eyebrows rose.

"Doctor, we have ice here only once a year. During fiesta time."

Flavier's training had not prepared him for this. He was mentally wringing his hands when a wizened old woman tottered up. "Excuse me, Doctor. This is what we use here," she said. She placed a bundle on the child's forehead. Shortly, the fever declined and the convulsions subsided. Later, when Flavier had the bundle's contents analyzed, he discovered that it was the trunk of a banana tree chopped fine and soaked in water. It had a cooling effect when placed on the body.

That night when Flavier walked home he cried—and he determined that he would learn to work within the limits of the economic resources of the people.

Economic questions include: How convenient is transportation? How regular is the power supply? How dependable is the communications infrastructure? How available is water? Does the equipment have parts that are replaceable in the country at low cost? Is simplified accounting needed? How many trained personnel are available—or should an elementary skills training course be developed?

Less job-specific questions that will help make the development worker more sensitive to the economic milieu include: What is the average daily diet? Do the people consider themselves impoverished or not? What kinds of expenditure do they delight in (clothes, fiestas, insurance policies, investments, labor-saving gadgets, etc.)? What kinds of expenditures do they consider extravagant? What do economists think are the country's chief economic problems? Its assets? Its economic opportunities? If you are a worker there, what do your neighbors—the people themselves—think the country's chief economic problems are? How do they experience these? Is there a Marxist movement among university students? What are their specific complaints? Is there economic tension between ethnic groups?

In our priorities at World Vision International, we favor producing cheap food, low-cost housing, or intermediate technology, rather than luxury goods for wealthier people. We favor marketing to the poor. We favor locally made equipment, labor intensive methods, entrepreneurs with a simple lifestyle, and some degree of profit sharing and progressive opportunities among workers. We favor ways of capitalizing the poor that do not increase dependency, including the use of revolving funds, multilateral funds, and food for work.

While professional pride may balk at the rough technology poor people can afford, we can learn a valuable lesson from Dr. Tom Dooley, who ran a simple clinic in Laos before he died of leukemia. "People accuse me of practicing nineteenth-century medicine," he said. "They are correct. I did practice nineteenth-century medicine, and this was just fine. Upon my departure, our indigenous personnel would practice eighteenth-century medicine. Good, this is progress, since most of the villagers live in the fifteenth century."[32]

At the same time, we must be aware that some poor farmers and businessmen have objected, "Don't feed us any more 'appropriate technology'! We want standard imports!" Why is this? Even though an imported tractor-drawn weeder may cost sixty times more than its animal-drawn alternative, the former may be desired because it carries more status. Often, too, the standard import is part of a more attractive retail package. The sales information about it may be more colorful. Importers may offer generous credit. Installment assistance and service and parts for repairs may be part of the deal. We who promote alternative technology, then, need to become more canny business operators.

As we adapt to the local economic situation, we may come to empathize with a strong felt need for political change—change that we may be able to facilitate.

Take the Bangladesh Rural Advancement Committee (BRAC, a group supported by Oxfam-America), as described by the Institute for Food and Development Policy.[33] In one village where BRAC has been working, 40 percent of the two thousand people were landless. Two percent of the population were rich landowners. But fallow, vacant land lay all around. This was the abandoned property of those who had fled to India during the 1971 war of liberation. Now it was government land, but the rich landowners used it for illegal grazing or cultivation.

BRAC taught the people to read. Armed with a new skill and with better articulated ideas about their situation, the poor people of one village formed the Rajhason Landless Cooperative Society. They started petitioning the government to grant them title to some of the abandoned land. Two years later, after unrelenting corporate pressure from the cooperative, the government ceded them sixty acres, which amounted to one and one half acres per family.

Then the local hassles began. The rich landowners were alarmed. They were losing illegal use of the abandoned land, and they were also losing their stranglehold on the poor laborers. They consequently incited other villagers to break the irrigation canal on which the cooperative's land depended, and they tried to block the cooperative from using the river. But they didn't try terribly hard, because they suspected that starting from scratch would prove too difficult for the farmers with no tools or capital.

"They'll be mortgaging their farms right back to us. Give them one season," they laughed to each other. Instead, the new farmers got a loan for equipment from BRAC at 12 percent interest instead of the 50 percent to 200 percent rates available from local moneylenders. At the end of the first season, in spite of bad harvest weather, the new farmers paid back the loan, plus the interest. Now the cooperative wants to extend their joint activities to fishing. And they are feeling adventuresome enough to take the initiative in seeking better health care and child care. They are even going out of their way to seek out family planning information.

Adapting economically may mean identifying with people's felt need for political change. In specific ways we can support their struggle for increasing their influence in the political processes that dominate them.

Beyond this are national and international political and economic structures. To affect international structures, Christians have bought shares in various transnational corporations, attended stockholders' meetings, and lobbied for specific changes in company policies. George Fuller reports that in 1979, three such resolutions for policy changes were presented. By 1980, twenty-five had been negotiated successfully with management. Many more were under consideration.[34] Other Christians in "primary donor" nations have joined forces to lobby their governments to seek justice and mercy through specific legislative action.

As for affecting national structures, foreign social workers have often argued that they dare not speak up for political change because they are "guests" of the government. On this point, Dick Dowsett, a missionary with the Overseas Missionary Fellowship, has commented:

> Missionaries normally keep quiet, concentrating on a pietistic type of salvation, quietening their conscience by saying, "We are guests here, we have no business to criticize." But when we behave like this we are *not* neutral, we are simply supporting the status quo. That is often a terrible thing to do, for Christianity is not the same as middle-class conservatism. Oh for a return of the spirit of prophecy to our ministries. Amos was told to go home to Judah or shut up. But he did not use the "guest" excuse.[35]

Adapting to local economic resources is one way to develop empathy. That is not unachievable; it is just costly. Thomas and Elizabeth Brewster have recently developed the concept of "bonding" with a culture, analogous to mother-infant bonding. They suggest four strategies essential to achieving such bonding:

(1) Be willing to live with a local family.

(2) Limit personal belongings (to twenty kilos in weight).

(3) Use only local public transportation.

(4) Expect to learn the language within relationships that one will be responsible for maintaining.[36]

These strategies apply equally to singles, couples, and families. They are just as necessary for those crossing ethnic boundaries within a nation as for those crossing oceans. The Brewsters rightly comment, "A willingness to accept these conditions tells a lot about an individual's attitude and flexibility"— and, we might add, a lot about an agency's priorities.

A Concluding Unscientific Postscript

Among the many considerations that give people pause before they rush headlong into a socioeconomic project, here are three special concerns that we must keep in mind when we deal with the ethos, the worldview, and the culture of people in many developing nations.

The Beam in Our Eye

"In many instances, demonic influence has wreaked havoc in [North American Indian] communities with alcoholism, drugs, despair, and suicide a tragic part of Indian life today. . . ." So runs a story in a current missions newsletter, typical of many reports. Is this a balanced view? What—or who—has precipitated the unleashing of this demonic chaos? Do those North Americans whose forebears immigrated to this country in recent history share any blame for the sense of loss among Indians today? If so, why blame only the devil?

In fact, the exploitative, aggressive practices of industrialized countries are part of the reason why populations of poor countries look at their "developers" with a jaded eye. "Development is now used in a pejorative sense . . . in Latin America. . . ." One reason for this is that development "has been frequently promoted by international organizations closely linked to groups and governments which control the world economy in such a way that the rich get richer while the poor get proportionately poorer."[37]

Transnational corporations are so enormous that they can keep a stranglehold on small nations. Unfortunately, they tend to emphasize cheap profits and united military defenses rather than good water, safe working conditions, profit sharing, increasing ownership of land for the landless, and justice for civil protesters. Corporations based in "developed" countries tend to press for unequal trade treaties. They often try to sqeeze out local entrepreneurs, patent-holders, trade unions, and even attempts at agricultural self-sufficiency. And they have been known to dump unsafe products on foreign markets.[38]

Private business is not alone in its assaults. Powerful governments behave similarly. "The United States does not have friends; she just has interests," John Foster Dulles once said. At best, in such a milieu, government and private development schemes have been viewed lukewarmly. "Developmentalism came to be synonymous with reformism and modernization, that is to say, synonymous with timid measures, really ineffective in the long run and counterproductive to achieving a real transformation."[39]

Unfortunately, those working in development may often neglect or avoid those very critiques that they ought to be making. An agency may well argue,

> We should immediately antagonize and alienate a significant part of our constituency if we came out asserting that the First World enriches itself at the expense of the Third World. Many people would simply stop supporting us financially. What is the use of having morally clean but financially empty hands?[40]

People in developing nations may be justly skeptical about our goodwill when private voluntary aid and missions giving from the U.S. total together only about $2,000 million per year at the same time that trade between developing and industrialized nations amounts to some $200,000 million annually. Those people in the industrialized nations speak about the ethics of spending; yet they never seem to examine the ethics of their massive earnings.[41] In general, those in the developing nations wish we would get the beam out of our own eye, so that we would be a less unbalanced partner.

People Are Not Problems

People resist approaches that categorize them solely as problems. "Why do magazines always write about us like we're drunks?" North American Indians exploded in a survey of articles about them. "Why do they always say we're poor?"[42] People may well have economic needs that social workers must tackle, but let us never see certain groups merely as objects needing help. Let us not see only their poverty. Even in the worst of conditions—amid squalor and disorganized families and drunkenness—there can still be family warmth and children's games and gaiety and dancing and loving sacrifice. The needy still have pride.

"There is absolutely no community spirit here," reported an article in a recent development agency magazine.

> The houses are scattered all over. Very few of the children attend school. There is no sanitary water supply and there are no toilets. There is no one to give health care and the people just don't seem to want to try to follow directions. We try to teach just simple things like hygiene . . . but often we are unsuccessful because of their tribal beliefs. They drink very little water because of the old belief that it would slow down a warrior chasing his enemy. Their lives are often ruled by spirits and there are many things that are taboo. Sometimes if someone dies or is sick during harvest time, they will completely abandon the crop because they think they may have offended the spirits. But we have been

patient and have started construction on the "bridge." The love of Christ and modern medicine have teamed up to span the river, but much more time and effort will be needed.

No doubt every fact in this article is true. But do the people described see themselves this way? The report was written about the broad-shouldered, self-assured Ifugao, who have molded the Philippine rice terraces for centuries, managing a breath-takingly complex irrigation system without outside help. Where in this assessment is there an appreciation of Ifugao culture? At the pragmatic level, how are Ifugao college graduates likely to react, should they read such an article?

People are not necessarily "culturally deprived" simply because they are economically poor. Rather, they suffer cultural deprivation when outsiders view their culture as something to be ashamed of. When this happens, apathy, chaos, and a loss of trust may develop. Shame *may* be based on a low economic standing, but it is not a natural outgrowth of it. When mass advertising, for example, nurtures the idea that there are equal opportunities for all and the idea that everyone *should* be rich, the clash of cold reality may well induce shame. But in the absence of that advertising—those external symbols that lead people to be ashamed of their restricted economic standing—there need be no shame. A member of a well-integrated mountain tribe with a life expectancy of forty-five may in fact be richer—culturally richer—than a slum garbage collecter with a life expectancy of fifty.

In our urgency to solve "the problem of poverty," do we keep in mind the crucial nature of pride in cultural traditions? Do we remember that the destruction of cultures in the name of economic advance has had tragic results, sometimes leading to the extinction of whole peoples? Or do we replace time-honored traditions with dehumanizing, robotlike work procedures? Do we trivialize indigenous art and artifacts, fostering instead assembly-line trinkets aimed at the U.S. market?

Why is it so easy to reduce people to problems? Part of the problem is simply culture shock. When one goes to a foreign culture a "hostility grows out of the genuine difficulty which the visitor experiences in the process of adjustment. There is maid trouble, shopping trouble, and the fact that the people in the host country are largely indifferent to all these troubles. They help, but they just don't understand your great concern over these difficulties. Therefore, they must be insensible and unsympathetic. . . ."[43] If, added to this, development workers emphasize human depravity instead of God's common grace, they may well tend to view people as problems to be solved, not bearers of that grace.

How often do we train cross-cultural workers to discipline themselves to ask affirmative questions about the culture, questions which will dig out treasures that will enrich them? How often do we make "bonding" with the local culture a top priority?

Let's remember that every culture is the lifeway of people made in the image of God, regardless of their standard of living. Most people with whom God has communicated throughout history have lived in cultures far different from ours. Was Noah literate? Did David believe in democracy? Did Mary have indoor plumbing? Probably no—yet their lives were as valid as ours. They dominated nature less. Fewer alternative products, customs, and ideas were available to them. But they experienced friendship, love, parenthood, creativity, learning, responsibility, choice, dignity, adventure, and a relationship to God. They had as many significant experiences as any modern Western person.[44]

As the Christian historian Herbert Butterfield has observed,

Each generation is . . . an end in itself, a world of people existing in their own right. . . . Every generation is equidistant from eternity. So the purpose of life is not in the far future, nor, as we so often imagine, around the next corner, but the whole of it is here and now, as fully as ever it will be on this planet. . . . (I do not know of any mundane fulness of life which we could pretend to possess and which was not open to people in the age of Isaiah or Plato, Dante or Shakespeare. . . . Each generation—indeed each individual—exists for the glory of God. . . .[45]

Contemplative Confronters

We North Americans seem to believe that progress, not frustration, is the last word. Any problem can be solved if we put enough effort into it. Yet people in poorer countries find us amazingly ignorant of the rest of the world, and correlate our optimism with our naiveté.

North Americans, and to a lesser extent social workers from other parts of the industrialized West, are ignorant in two ways. First, we tend to ignore the complexity of the variables present in a situation of potential change. We make decisions quickly. We consult largely in Western languages. We allow a significant percentage of the decision making to occur in home offices in Western countries. And we forget that our own motivations and assumptions add greatly to the complexity of unexamined, enigmatic variables. We favor a systems approach. We are goal oriented, and our progress toward the goals must be measurable. Imponderables do not fit our planning procedures—hence uncertainty, ambiguity, and paradoxes get screened out.

Such ignorance can be dangerous. A Japanese nuclear specialist argues that U.S. reluctance to admit uncertainty as a significant variable has in fact reduced our ability to guard against nuclear war. An Overseas Development Council publication observes that "many Americans are so locked into certain assumptions about charity that they fail to perceive that their very humanitarianism may have inhumane effects. A premium is still placed on good intentions, and the historical American can-do mentality takes over from there."[46]

Those who confront other cultures for the sake of changing them must also be contemplatives—humbly sensitive to the transcendence that largely eludes us, and to the paradoxes that so pervade our world. We are ignorant first of the complexity of the obstacles to changing the world. And second, we are ignorant of the ubiquitousness of recurring disasters. "People with more means," says a character in Oscar Lewis's *Children of Sanchez,* "can afford the luxury of allowing their sons to live in a world of fantasy, of only seeing the good side of life, of protecting them from bad companions and obscene language, of not hurting their sensibilities by witnessing scenes of brutality, of having all their expenses paid for them. But they live with their eyes closed and are naive in every sense of the word."[47]

Rather than expecting success, rather than smothering the poor with cheap cheerfulness, we may at times need to sit in silence with them, to empathize, to share our mutual lack of answers. When we can do no other, we must weep with those who weep. But then we may discover that sometimes a crisis is not a crisis, and a failure is not a failure. John Sommer says that "what might be seen by some outsiders as a disaster requiring external assistance may not be seen as a crisis at all by the local people."[48]

When we learn to see things through the eyes of others, we may get a better idea of what constitutes true failure. For us Westerners, goals are everything. But for people for whom doing is part of success, missing a final goal is not necessarily failure. When people compartmentalize less between process and achievement, meaningful process may be its own reward. If aid agencies were not always thinking about justifying themselves to their Western supporters, and if workers were sufficiently bonded with the receiving culture, we might be more open to partial successes, slow successes, and successes that are not easily quantifiable.

"Men of spiritual resources may not only redeem catastrophe, but turn it into a grand creative moment. . . . The rarest creative achievements of the mind must come from great internal pressure, and are born of a high degree of distress. In other words, the world is not merely to be enjoyed but is an arena for moral striving. . . . History is in the business of making personalities."[49] These personalities are to be conformed to the image of God. Let us fulfill the cultural mandate to this end, empowered by God's Spirit.

Notes

1. Eugene Nida, "Why Are Foreigners So Queer?: A Socio-Cultural Approach to Cultural Pluralism," *International Bulletin of Missionary Research,* July 1981, pp. 102-6.

2. John Gillin, "National and Cultural Values in the United States," *Social Forces* 34 (1955-56), pp. 107-13.

3. Charles Taber, "The Missionary Gap," *The Other Side,* August 1979.

4. Nida, "Why Are Foreigners So Queer?"

5. C. P. Snow, *The Two Cultures* (Cambridge: Cambridge University Press, 1964), p. 26.

6. Roy Rappaport, *Pigs for the Ancestors* (New Haven: Yale University Press, 1967), p. 6.

7. Clifford Geertz, "Thick Description: Toward an Interpretive Theory of Culture," in *The Interpretation of Cultures* (New York: Basic, 1973), pp. 4-5.

8. Alfonso Ortiz, *The Tewa World* (Chicago: University of Chicago Press, 1969), p. xvi.

9. David Kaplan and Robert Manners, *Culture Theory* (Englewood Cliffs, N.J.: Prentice-Hall, 1972), p. 159.

10. There is a yawning abyss between those who find conflict a catalyst for cataclysmic positive change, as do Marxist anthropologists, and those who see conflict as an escape valve that merely enables the system to let off steam without exploding. Does conflict contribute to change? Or to stability? Are systems in conflict moving directionally? Or are they in equilibrium? These are the questions over which anthropologists do battle.

In the final analysis, these alternative perspectives may be complementary. Marx zeroed in on the origins of conflict. Several factors exacerbate social tensions, he found. For example, if the distribution of scarce resources is increasingly unequal, conflict will mount. If workers become aware of their joint interests, conflict will mount. Such awareness springs in turn from certain prior conditions. If owners instigate disruptive social changes, they may alienate the workers. If the latter have access to communications media, they may develop systems by which to communicate their grievances to each other. Awareness will also be enhanced if the workers develop their own unifying set of beliefs. To do this, they must produce articulate ideological leaders and must evade the owners' propaganda. When they are aware of their joint interests, when they have organized leadership, when they are not convinced by the owners' propaganda, and when they view their deprivation as relative to the owners' standard of living, then workers will organize and initiate conflict.

Many of Marx's thoughts on the origins of conflict have enriched anthropological studies. But when he proceeds to the development of conflict, however, his propositions ring less true. For example, Marx contends that the most highly organized workers will engage in the most violent conflicts. But the history of union disputes shows that well-organized workers are often most amenable to negotiation. Rather it is the overwhelmingly but inarticulately frustrated who run amuck.

George Simml, who connects conflict with equilibrium, generates more significant questions on the development of social conflict. He argues, for example, that the more conflict is seen as a means to an end, the less likely it is to be violent. Likewise, frequent, low-intensity conflicts in a highly interdependent society will contribute to social integration in that they allow people to vent their hostilities, they give people a sense of control over their destinies, and they often lead in the end to needed incremental change through compromise.

For more information, see Karl Marx, *Das Kapital* and *The Communist Manifesto;* George Simml, *Conflict and the Web of Group Affiliations* (Glencoe, Ill.: Free Press, 1955); and Jonathan Turner, "The Conflict Heritage," in *The Structure of Sociological Theory* (Homewood, Ill.: Dorsey, 1978).

11. Miriam Adeney, *God's Foreign Policy* (Grand Rapids: Eerdmans, 1984), p. 108.

12. Jim Wallis, *The Call to Conversion* (San Francisco: Harper and Row, 1981).

13. H. Richard Niebuhr, quoting Tertullian, in *Christ and Culture* (New York: Harper and Row, 1951), p. 54.

14. Niebuhr, *Christ and Culture*, p. 66.

15. Ibid.

16. A. A. Stockdale, "God Left the Challenge in the Earth," unpublished paper.

17. Hans Rookmaaker, *Modern Art and the Death of a Culture* (London: Inter-Varsity Press, 1970), p. 36.

18. Erich Sauer, *The King of the Earth* (Grand Rapids: Eerdmans, 1962), p. 81.

19. Miriam Adeney, "Do Your Own Thing (As Long As You Do It Our Way)," *Christianity Today*, 4 July 1975, p. 12.

20. A. N. Triton, *Whose World?* (London: Inter-Varsity Press, 1970), pp. 86, 43.

21. Alexander Schmemann, "Solzhenitsyn," *Radix*, March 1974, p. 11.

22. Adeney, *God's Foreign Policy*, p. 108.

23. See ibid.

24. Anthony Campolo, "The Greening of Gulf and Western," *Eternity*, January 1981, p. 32.

25. Ian Bradley, *The Call to Seriousness: The Evangelical Impact on the Victorians* (New York: Macmillan, 1975), pp. 89, 81, 87, 93.

26. Bill Bentley, interviewed by John Alexander in "Growing Together: A Conversation with Seven Black Evangelicals," *The Other Side*, July-August 1975, p. 45.

27. Niebuhr, *Christ and Culture*, pp. 70-71.

28. Ibid., pp. 67-68.

29. Afif Tannous, *Extension Work Among the Arab Fellahin* (Washington, D.C.: Foreign Service Institute, Department of State, 1951).

30. Bruce Olson, *For This Cross I'll Kill You* (Carol Stream, Ill.: Creation House, 1973), pp. 136-50.

31. Juan Flavier, *Doctor in the Barrios* (Quezon City, Philippines: New Day Publishers, 1970), pp. 142-45.

32. Thomas Dooley, *The Edge of Tomorrow* (New York: Farrar, Straus, and Cudahy, 1958), p. 54.

33. Frances Moore Lappe, Joseph Collins, and David Kinley, *Aid as Obstacle: Twenty Questions about Our Foreign Aid and the Hungry* (San Francisco: Institute for Food and Development Policy, 1980), pp. 143-46.

34. George Fuller, "Making Business Behave," *Eternity*, May 1980, pp. 17-21.

35. Dick Dowsett, quoted in Michael Griffiths, *The Church and World Mission* (Grand Rapids: Zondervan, 1980), p. 101.

36. E. Thomas Brewster and Elizabeth Brewster, *Bonding and the Missionary Task* (Pasadena, Calif.: Lingua House, 1982), p. 14.

37. Gustavo Gutiérrez, *A Theology of Liberation* (Maryknoll, N.Y.: Orbis, 1973), p. 26.

38. See Adeney, *God's Foreign Policy*.

39. See Gutiérrez, *A Theology of Liberation*.

40. Jorgen Lissner, *The Politics of Altruism: A Study of the Political Behavior of Voluntary Development Agencies* (Geneva, Switzerland: Lutheran World Federation Department of Studies, 1977), p. 187.

41. David Beckmann, *Where Faith and Economics Meet: A Christian Critique* (Minneapolis: Augsburg, 1981), p. 99.

42. Miriam Adeney, "Magazine Coverage of American Indians," unpublished paper, 1968.

43. Kalervo Oberg, "Culture Shock: Adjustment to New Cultural Environments," *Practical Anthropology*, July-August 1960, pp. 177-82.

44. Adeney, *God's Foreign Policy*, p. 119.

45. Herbert Butterfield, *Christianity and History* (London: Fontana, 1957), pp. 89, 91.

46. John Sommer, *Beyond Charity: U.S. Voluntary Aid for a Changing Third World* (Washington, D.C.: Overseas Development Council, 1977), p. 146.

47. Oscar Lewis, *Children of Sanchez* (New York: Random House, 1961), pp. 38-39.

48. Sommer, *Beyond Charity*, p. 44.

49. Butterfield, *Christianity and History*, pp. 101-2.

Social Justice and Human Liberation

Robert W. Wall

Evangelicals understand faith and discipleship as personal and spiritual. This stems in part from the Reformation's protest against the abuses of the clergy, which led to the recovery of the biblical idea of the "priesthood of all believers." The gospel speaks to individual believers to proclaim good news to the needy and life to all those who live in the presence of death. The wisdom that liberates the individual—and through individuals our society—comes from a personal relationship with God through Christ and in his Spirit. Yet a relationship with God that is exclusively private hides the social contour of the gospel.[1] While we also accept the priesthood of all believers, without the balance of other biblical ideas that emphasize public forms of discipleship, the ideal of the Reformers can be institutionalized into an individualism perilously close to the old heresy of Gnosticism.

Gnostic religion deifies the individual through personal quests for spiritual knowledge. It rejects social concerns as unnecessary for spirituality and salvation—if not demonic. But the apostles rejected such a division of Christian life into personal and public spheres: Christ is Lord over both salvation and creation (Col. 1:15-20; the argument of Ephesians also supports this idea), and in the Christian proclamation neither can be separated from the other. God's justification of the church is attested by believers' private acts of piety (see, e.g., Matt. 6), but also by their public acts of mercy.[2]

The church in North America, however, has tended toward individualism and a consequent emphasis on individual piety. But prophetic voices within evangelical Christianity have recently called the North American church back to a more balanced form of discipleship. People like Ron Sider and Jim Wallis and ministries like World Concern, Evangelicals for Social Action, and Voice of Calvary Ministries have defined repentance as a corporate turning from public and systemic forms of evil.[3] This is not a denial of the need to exercise personal faith in God's gospel but rather a recognition that in authentic Christian life God's power and grace enter and transform both the personal and public aspects of a believer's existence.

Since the time of Christ, God has made available certain resources and instruments which, when humbly appropriated by the church, can reverse the

activity of the demonic dominion within human history. Thus when evangelicals attend discussions and demonstrations for human rights or for sociopolitical and economic justice, they come not as secular agents but as persons who
are convinced of the authority of God's word which announces freedom for the
oppressed and contentment for the impoverished. They come as a people empowered by God to act on behalf of the needy for Christ's sake.

Not everyone has heard or responded to this prophetic voice within the
evangelical church. As in the Israel of old, some resist the invitation to turn and
obey this word of God. Some continue to restrict God's gospel and his Spirit to
personal forms of transformation, while others continue to fight their battles on
other fronts. Part of the problem, we admit, is cultural: religious institutions
share in and are shaped by the ideologies and mythologies of the society in
which they exist.[4] The North American church, for example, is imbued with
the dominant, liberal myth of the self-sufficient individual.[5] This myth stifles
that part of the gospel which bids the church to engage in social forms of redemption—to help redeem individuals from their dependency upon self or
upon social institutions which are opposed to God, and to call them to an inter-
dependency with others, especially that found in the community of faith.

The diversity of opinion found within the church over these issues is
partly due to the diversity found within Scripture. The Bible never gives hard
and fast rules about how we must live. Yet it also grants no justification for absolutizing our own way of life over against that of others. We must resist the
rigidity of parochial interests, whether prophetic or establishment, and begin to
celebrate agendas different from our own which are nonetheless based upon
Scripture. We must appeal to different interpretations and definitions of Scripture and society as a way of bringing balance to our own points of view. We
must appeal to a biblical view of reality to check and correct our tendency to
shape our faith uncritically by engaging secular myths and ways of life. By so
doing, believers will recover different, heretofore unrecognized, aspects of the
same Christian gospel. We may still draw battle lines at different places from
other believers, but we will do so with the recognition that we all fight a common struggle against the powers and principalities of this evil age and that we
are all armed with a common authoritative biblical witness to God's salvation
in Christ.

The Starting Point: Interpreting the Bible on Its Own Terms

Our faith must always be transmitted through and evaluated by the Bible.
What the church identifies as important and true is measured by what the Bible
teaches. In an age of skepticism and agnosticism, the evangelical church must
stay loyal to the demands of the sacred texts for the life of God's people.

While the authority of the Bible remains a fundamental of evangelical
faith, the justifications for such a claim and the proper methods of interpreting
Scripture remain contested.[6] In recent years, a new discipline of biblical studies, "canonical criticism," has offered an important assessment of existing

methods of biblical interpretation along with a new hermeneutical program that takes seriously the principles of interpretation forwarded by the Bible itself.[7] Rather than conceiving a method of biblical hermeneutics based on Enlightenment historiography and modern literary criticism, we should study the Bible in the light of the clues it provides its readers. For example, the diverse character of the biblical witness to God's salvation in Israel and in Christ suggests a dynamic rather than a static method of relating Scripture to life. The Bible enshrines a diversity of God's revelation and its witnesses, different genres of literature, a multitude of problems facing multiform audiences, and differing accounts of how the gospel is to be understood and lived. This calls attention to a living God who goes on speaking to a living people in a living context.

The function of the Bible is thus to enable God and his people to converse, forging an ongoing, stable covenant in the midst of new concerns that might arise in any historical situation. The "scholastic" view of the Bible, which regards the sacred texts as a static word from which immutable and harmonized codes of right conduct and doctrine for every age are determined, is inconsistent with the true nature of biblical revelation. Likewise, the critical view, which tends to view the Bible as a document of past history instead of a book relevant for present faith, is also inadequate—it locks the Bible into the past and robs it of its dynamism and its canonicity.

A second clue for biblical hermeneutics gleaned from the Bible itself is the "inner dialectic," which seems to emerge between different biblical theologies and ethics.[8] Different perspectives, all within a common inspired canon, tend to balance if not correct an exclusive dependence upon a single account of the gospel, which often results in a distorted view of God and of his salvation. By attending to the whole canon, bringing different biblical theologies and ethics into "canonical conversations," such distortions are corrected and a fuller, more balanced understanding of biblical faith and life emerges. This intratextual dialectic becomes a paradigm that informs and guides the intraecclesiastical dialectic between different groups of believers. This assumes, of course, that the church universal identifies itself in the Bible and is shaped by reading it as an inspired and authoritative medium of God's word. In this sense, canonical conversations reflect conversations between believers in every age; the diversity found within the Bible is also found within the church of today.

We should hasten to argue that the kerygmatic unity found within the Bible, which centers on the recitation of God's gracious action in his Messiah, Jesus of Nazareth, and his people, Israel, is also the unity of faith found within the one holy and apostolic church. The diverse ways in which that unity is understood and applied by the biblical writers to their communities of faith resemble the diverse ways in which that unity continues to be understood and applied by the people of God in their own situations.

More importantly, the inspired diversity found within the church's canon becomes the authorized context within which the diversity found within the church is controlled and even brought into profitable dialogue. One ecclesiastical tradition embodying one biblical theology might help another tradition with another theological or ethical emphasis to "see" the fuller picture. Such discussions, rooted in the biblical word, are mutually informing if not self-correcting.

Actually, there are two different modes by which the Bible might be engaged in such conversations. These modes follow from two discrete functions the Bible has always assumed in the life of the believing community. First, the Bible is "Scripture"; that is, it transmits a sacred heritage that *informs* and that finally *forms* a way of being and a way of seeing that is uniquely Christian. Second, the Bible is "canon"; that is, it *evaluates* Christian formation, correcting what is not right and calling the church to repentance.[9]

Of crucial importance for the canonical critic is the canonical function of the Bible. The community adapts the Bible to its life in a "prophetic" manner, to correct it as well as to nurture it. As such, the various canonical conversations one can recover from the Bible, reflected in the different points of view one can discover in the church, are viewed as "self-correcting." Thus, even as the prophetic tradition of the Old Testament tends to correct the wisdom tradition and James tends to correct Paul in the New Testament, so also a prophetic theology within the church corrects a wisdom theology found there, and believers who emphasize the "merciful work" of James correct those modern-day Paulinists who over-emphasize "saving faith" to the exclusion of responsible actions of liberation. History teaches us that a truly biblical faith must be shaped by taking seriously what all of Scripture says. Any believer who excises a "canon within the Canon" runs the risk of distorting what is a diverse medium of revelation and the multivalent inspiration of it.

Defining Justice by the Canon

The biblical form of justice can be adequately defined only when we draw upon all that the Bible says about it. For example, the prophetic and wisdom traditions of the Old Testament, while both calling Israel to just conduct, provide different contours of this common concern. Both understood that Israel's survival as Israel, as the chosen people of God, required the righting of social wrongs. While sage and prophet defined Israel's social discourse along similar lines, their underlying theological conceptions differed markedly. In part this is due to wisdom's "royal" roots,[10] while the prophetic tradition tends to be antiroyal and is rooted rather in the Torah of Moses.[11] The sages were concerned primarily with proper social action within the existing hierarchy of power in society. The prophets, however, were primarily interested in Israel's *spiritual* rather than its social condition, in its obedience to Torah rather than in its relationship with the king.[12] Prophets railed against the king and against the nation's "royalist" theology when the king's civil religion, with its utilitarian concerns, led the people away from a dependence upon God and obedience to Torah.

The Prophet and Justice

To interpret the prophetic idea of justice, we must recall that Moses understood Israel in its covenant with God as a people whom God liberated from slavery to Egypt. This revelation of God's goodness in Israel's history obligated this people to a life that bore concrete witness to his transcendence (i.e., his nonhuman, nonworldly character): Israel was very different from other nations in life and faith in the very ways its God was different.

Israel's covenant obligation was to represent God, who is above history yet within history. Thus Israel's economics, politics, religious life, and social structures were to bear witness to God's character, which was disclosed in the Exodus events (including those events leading up to the Exodus that are enshrined in the patriarchal narratives of Genesis). The public form of justice championed by the prophets and envisaged in Torah came from beyond history; it was not managed or manipulated by human notions of fair play, but derived from the radical mercy of a liberating God.

More specifically, Torah's idea of social justice is framed by the principle of *jubilee* found in the Code of Holiness (Lev. 25; cf. Deut. 15).[13] The Hebrew word for jubilee, *yobel* (LXX, *aphesis*), means "release" and refers to the freeing of slaves and the restoring of property to jailed bankrupts demanded by the jubilee code's legislation. However, the prophets expanded the meaning of jubilee to include all who were oppressed by injustice, and jubilee became for them the model for the eschatological society.[14]

This prophetic view of social justice called into question those structures that kept peace by keeping marginal people marginal. Jubilee envisaged a society of "equal opportunity" in which all had sufficient opportunity and endowments to reach and retain equality with one another. Jubilee also viewed personal wealth as something to be recycled rather than hoarded, to be redistributed rather than retained. After all, Israel's liberation out of slavery was its own paradigm of monetary grace toward the unfortunate: even as a merciful God had compassion on an impoverished Israel, so now Israel is to have compassion on its impoverished.

Jubilee economics, then, is grounded in grace, not greed. The marketplace structures of liberated Israel exist to share possessions and to redistribute wealth to the impoverished in order to build a society that bears witness that God's mercy transforms all equally.

Social evil was symptomatic of the "real" disease, which was spiritual and not social.[15] Consequently the prophets' criticism of social injustice served a higher end than just to right social wrongs. The protest logically ended with a call to repent; or, later, the sentence of destruction or exile logically ended with the hope of restoration. The prophetic mission was *theocentric*. Likewise, our outrage against social injustice must fit into a larger, God-centered agenda that calls the nations back to their ruler.

Prophetic hermeneutics, best seen in the exilic prophets, emphasizes God's freedom to punish in order to transform his people. The power of renewal is finally placed outside of national and institutional efforts: with the nation of Israel now exiled, the hope of God's restoring grace could no longer be mediated by the monarchy nor by the cultus. Israel is left only with God, and with the Torah which tells the story of God's liberating grace and the stipulations of covenant with him.

The principle of prophetic jubilee is also at the center of Jesus' message.[16] It is clear from the Gospels that Jesus' messianic ministry fulfills the principle of jubilee. Further, the ethic of liberating mercy shapes the conditions of his discipleship.[17] Mercy is the dynamic of the disciples' life together (Luke 3:7-14; 10:25-37; 11:1-13; 14:1-14; cf. Acts 2:39-47; 4:32–5:12) and of their view of money and possessions (Luke 16:1-15; 18:18-30; and par.). The ministry of God's Christ inaugurates an age of mercy—of God's mercy, which fulfills through Christ the promises of salvation, and consequently of the church's mercy, which is to bear witness to God's triumph over evil and its various social and economic manifestations in the world.

Wisdom and Justice

While not a contradiction of the prophetic conception, the wisdom of ancient Israel emerges from different theological and sociological soil.[18] The sages of Israel construed God's revealed word as a natural "event." Since the created world embodies God's word, human observation and insight—humanity's experience and social discourse—constitute the resources of God's truth. While also collectors of "folk" wisdom, sages were often professional scholars assigned to the king's court to provide advice to the royal institutions of the nation. As such, the theological contour of wisdom retains an elitist, nationalistic view of God and society.[19]

This tendency is logical when one recalls the rather elitist and nationalistic elements found in the Davidic covenant. After all, there God's relationship is with a *national* Israel, and his rule and covenant blessings are mediated through the king. Since the kings were members of the affluent minority, a royal theology would tend to conceive of God and God's covenant with Israel "from the top down."

Even during the exile, the wealthy class viewed wisdom as containing God's promises for them. Attitudes found in Proverbs, for example, are consistent with those of any wealthy class: a special "duty" to provide for the poor (though much of this duty is merely to maintain the status quo); respect for authority and opposition to change (Prov. 14:35; 16:10); approval of wealth and the power it brings (Eccl. 10:19; Prov. 10:15; 18:23; 22:7); and tying relationships and honor to material security (Prov. 10:30-31; 14:20; 19:4). Affluence not only stabilizes society, it also brings personal contentment (Eccl. 5:18-19). No doubt the sages of Israel observed these dispositions in the wealthy and the opposite in the poor.

By appealing to a theology of experience, it was "theo-logical" to assume that God's blessing (as indicated by human contentment) was passed onto the upper classes. This same logic tended to construe economic justice as "just deserts"; that is, a certain social structure follows logically upon certain actions. A society that lives wisely will achieve for itself the good life for all.[20] If God created a world with certain built-in patterns that yield, when followed, the good life, then those who are wise enough to heed them will prosper. And, to turn it around, those who have not prospered must not have followed the dictates of wisdom—yet they too have gotten what they deserved. In this sense, justice is wisdom, and the just thing to do is what wisdom tells one to do.

Justice is also "fair play." Wisdom encourages an orderly society since its quest after the good life means not to mistreat the oppressed as others do (Prov. 1:3—*mesharim;* Job 31:21-22). While this form of social justice is not as revolutionary as the prophetic idea rooted in divine grace, it does envisage humanitarian ideals and does correlate with the sages' desire for a stable national life. (Yet this stability can be achieved within the status quo.) The nation (as well as family and business) will thrive as the "just deserts" of "fair play."

Wisdom theology is concerned with the *individual's* response rather than with that of the whole community, perhaps because the Davidic covenant, from which the royalistic tendencies of wisdom spring, is cast in rather personal terms (2 Sam. 7). Thus societies, or even their families, are viewed as collections of individuals, each of whom is responsible to be wise and so to enhance personal as well as social good. The just society is the net result of wise individuals who live fairly and so beget security and prosperity for all.

There is a strand of this theological tradition present in the early Christian evangelists, reinterpreted as a "wisdom Christology" in which Christ became the incarnation of the "wisdom from above."[21] In this sense, eschatological Israel devotes itself to Christ as God's heavenly wisdom and ensures for itself the good (and everlasting) life.[22]

It is not surprising that one would find a wisdom orientation in the latter books of the New Testament, which are concerned with the "institutional" church (see, e.g., 1 and 2 Tim. and Titus).[23] Paul's growing concern for the church's stability, for its integration within society (already reflected in Romans), and for "paying one's own way" in the world leads him to encourage institutional structures (e.g., church leadership, a community's written "tradition," apostolic memory, and "official" doctrine).

Application to the Church's Engagement with the World

Israel's kings, and the wise men who advised them, were primarily concerned with the nation's survival, given the possibility of military defeat and the grim memory of slavery. Wisdom, understood against this realpolitik, teaches how to survive and even prosper as a nation. In this sense, its theology is not for transformation but for the preservation of the national status quo. When these royal interests sought to preserve an evil status quo for the preservation of the nation, though, the prophets, as champions of Yahweh and of Yahweh's Torah, reacted in protest.

The tension between sage and prophet provides a biblical paradigm for the church. Even as biblical history moves from the reformation of the Mosaic covenant to the formation of a nation under the Davidic covenant, so also contemporary transformation must begin with the reforming word before moving into institutional forms that stabilize it in society. Further, even as the prophets constantly challenged those institutions that were corrupted by national (elite) self-interest, so also the church must allow its own prophets to redirect, if not replace, its institutional forms when the survival, status, and power of the institutional church replaces the glory of God as the primary goal. It is the prophetic Spirit who grants the discernment to correctly perceive what is wrong within, and it is the same Spirit who empowers courageous action to correct what is wrong. Both actions are mediated through the inspired Scripture which is useful for the Spirit's rebuke and correction of human failings.

The prophetic protest against the social evils promoted within Israel is rooted in the biblical idea of jubilee. It is a protest that moves from social criticism to spiritual reconciliation, from challenging systemic evils to encouraging national and individual repentance. But the historical manifestation of a true reconciliation between a people and its God and its repentance toward God is the dismantling of anything that marginalizes and oppresses people. Social criticism is that which identifies the failure of relationships and the need for reconciliation and repentance. In this sense, the call for justice is motivated by a desire for right relationships; justification means establishing peace between parties who are in conflict, whether socially or spiritually.

Prophets win no popularity contests; they are not favored in their own backyards. A message shaped by criticism and the need for repentance simply does not endure long. The established powers will not tolerate prophets because their criticism is against the very system the powers rule over and attempt to secure. Prophets were not anarchists; they, as well as the sage, worked for a synthesis of reform and form, although the sage emphasized form while the prophet emphasized reform.[24] The point is this: the church must realize that reform and the language of protest need concrete, institutional forms for the fruit of that reform to continue into the next generation. To continue the prophetic call, the work and the words of the prophets and the prophetic Messiah must be taken over and adapted by institutions (synagogue, church) that can work within the culture. The messianic reforms of Jesus were effectively spread from generation to generation, and from Palestine to the ends of the earth, but only within institutional forms.

The biblical idea of transformation includes both form and reform: the church must act wisely as an institution, and yet it must be critical of all that is wrong in a nation's life. Even within itself, the church must allow for new and reforming ideas. All too often the church engages new territory with cold and rigid methods. It evangelizes by ecclesiastical confessions which are proclaimed without adaptation and sensitivity to the new situation. Religious triumphalism, which imposes a vision without, without appropriate revision within, characterizes much of the church's efforts.

Yet to reform old methods by calling for a total change of existing national and ecclesiastical structures is also wrongheaded. Such anarchistic programs yield only chaos as the atmosphere for transformation. By offering reform as form, or form as reform, the church's work ends in failure. Transformation must flow from a open dialogue between those who work within institutions (pastors, teachers, bankers, government workers, relief and service agencies) and those prophets who call us to reform and revise our messages, methods, and institutions (liberation theologians, labor leaders, missionaries, development workers).

Such a dialogue will underscore two crucial elements of transformation that must be held in constructive tension. First, wisdom emphasizes the power of human insight and experience—concrete, realistic, and practical. It is a "realistic" view of life that promises just deserts for those who excel in fair play and follow the proverbial directives. The prophetic word is more "idealistic," calling for a view of life shaped by the undeserved blessings of God's grace and the ideals revealed through the Torah. A realistic view of things tends to lead to a championing of the status quo; it is concerned with "what is." An idealism empowered with the prospect of transformation, however, is concerned with what ought to be. An exclusive concern with realism leads to a characterization of change as a "real impossibility," whereas an exclusive concern with what ought to be and now is not leads to a naive assertion that change is a "simple possibility"—to use Niebuhr's phrases.[25] The church should embrace the ideals of biblical faith, but always with the shrewdness of serpents (Matt. 10:16).

Second, there is an important interplay between the individualism of wisdom and the communalism of the prophetic model. There are times when the reformer's agenda is too vague or too ambitious to work well; there are times when the prophetic word dismantles global problems with the global sweep of a simplistic idealism. Such pronouncements often fail to be implemented because they are too imprecise. Perhaps a reason why the sages addressed real problems with concrete advice is that their conceptual world emphasized an individual's responsibility and specific actions which must be assumed or avoided. Until the church concerns itself with individuals—until it has compassion on and takes responsibility for specific victims of greed and violence—our programs for social justice will not work. An intimate personal acquaintance with a person's problems, with his or her needs, and with the complexities of that particular situation of need insures appropriate motives and actions. Personal insight and experience molds the form of reform.

On the other hand, to allow personal ethics to elbow out social issues or to push for the self-centered gospel of a "quiet pietism" is to pander to the narcissism of the present age. By stressing community, the prophets take social justice beyond the self to include all those who are mistreated. The identification and elimination of global evils are the prophetic goals toward which the small, incremental, and wise steps of the church must continually move.

Defining Human Liberation by the Canon

Theological and humanistic definitions of human liberation proliferate. Humanistic definitions tend to emphasize the freedom of people to do certain things or the freedom from certain social hierarchies or cultural expectations. Under such a conception liberation can refer to any relaxation of legal principles that restrict people's rights.

Liberation theologies interpret God's involvement in and through the church as reversing, or liberating persons from, social—and, less often, spiritual—evils. In this sense, social justice and human liberation are two sides of the same coin: pursuing justice in society is allowing for God's justifying and liberating action in the world. But the use of such a conception of God's grace in missions demands a careful authorization from the Bible. It would seem that the church too easily buys into secular models of liberation (e.g., Marxist or capitalistic), clothes them in Christian rhetoric, and resells them as "biblical."

The starting point in any discussion of the biblical idea of human liberation is the jubilee of the Mosaic Code of Holiness and of Jesus' teaching (above). "Jubilee" means liberation and refers to the liberation of persons from social structures that oppress. In this sense, then, human liberation is the *product,* the concrete manifestation of those justifying *processes* that seek to right social wrongs. It should be stressed that in both the Mosaic legislation and the Messiah's teaching such reversals of human condition are evidences of God's mercy. Thus, whether we speak of social justification (a process) or of human liberation (its product), we must speak of it in terms of the gospel that envisages and empowers such actions.

The Manner of Human Liberation in the Book of Romans

Paul wrote Romans to reconcile households of Jewish and non-Jewish believers who for a variety of reasons were at odds with each other.[26] The failure of Roman believers to secure good relationships with each other jeopardized Paul's missionary work in the West.[27] More importantly for Paul, the divisions between various households of believers in Rome jeopardized the spiritual, if not also the political, well-being of the entire Roman church.[28]

Paul's primary concerns were religious and not social since his gospel locates the liberating righteousness of God *within* the community dependent upon Jesus' messianic work, and not in the rest of the world, which stands under God's curse. Nevertheless, from the account of Paul's ethic in Romans 12–13, we must assume that God's righteousness is demonstrated through the church's agency within and before a watching world. In this sense, the church's peace with God, which is a spiritual reality, is disclosed by its members' ability (provided by God's mercies) to live at peace with each other (see especially Rom. 14:1–15:13) and with the world, which is a social, or "public," reality.[29]

The manner in which relationships are conducted in public follows from the relationship that the community of faith has entered into with God. If a people depends upon the work of the Messiah Jesus, they have peace with God (Rom. 5:1); they boast in God rather than in themselves (Rom. 5:2-11). Reconciliation with God reverses interest in self and in "this evil age," which values self-interest rather than God's reign. The yield of this realignment is human freedom,[30] which Paul views holistically. Peace with God yields the capacity to hope in the face of personal trials; it yields freedom from the fear of death. God's justifying grace also yields freedom from sin, and consequently the freedom to serve the interests of God as God's servant. The reconciliation of persons, and the social transformation which results, follows a pattern of life that rejects evil and embraces righteousness.

Freedom from legalism is further evidence of God's liberating grace. While Paul's discussion of this in Romans 7-8 is often described in rather personal terms (e.g., Rom. 7:7-8:1),[31] his guiding principle has social implications: personal—and also corporate—transformation is possible only through the Spirit of our risen Lord.[32] Certainly, the Spirit's activity within the church is eschatological since final freedom from the legalisms that promote sin and death within the community is posited at Christ's return (Rom. 8:18-39). Yet the spiritual power of the age to come, which gives life to God's people, is *currently* available, and the eschatological fruit of God, such as reconciliation, is a *present* possibility.[33]

Once again we should emphasize that for Paul the gift of the Spirit whose power can transform human life is conditioned on a community's dependence upon the messianic work of Jesus rather than upon its own religious or moral merit. Human liberation, according to Paul, is the yield of human trust in God's Christ.

Human Liberation According to James

The New Testament letters can be divided into two broad groups—a collection of Paul's letters (Romans through Philemon) and another collection of non-Pauline letters (Hebrews through Jude). Paul's letters reflect the church's mission to the Gentiles, while the non-Pauline letters reflect the church's mission to the Jews.[34] Thus, while there is fundamental agreement between Paul and the non-Pauline writers of New Testament letters, their audiences and their theological and ethical emphases do differ.[35]

James, for example, retains a more conservative posture toward Jewish traditions than Paul does, which is appropriate for a leader of Palestinian-Jewish Christianity. His emphasis on Jewish wisdom (James 1:5-8, 13-21; 3:13-18; etc.), on the observance of the law (1:22–2:26, especially 2:10),[36] and on synagogal meeting (2:1-5) reflects clearly the "Jewishness" of Jamesian Christianity. To be sure, both James and Paul stress the saving mercies of God and the importance of Christ's return as the climax of salvation's history; and both understand human liberation as the result of the church's obedient response to God. Yet the two have different emphases which are, to use Paul Hanson's words, "indispensable sides of an essential polarity." We must resist those interpretations of James that try to bring him into line with Paul, for the letters of both, as they stand, are inspired by God and are equally authoritative for God's people. What James has to say about human liberation provides the church with an authority for a definition of liberation that is truly biblical, even though not Pauline.

James argues that human liberation is a matter not of pious words but of wise actions (1:26-27; 2:14-26); for him, true religion is characterized not merely by orthodoxy but also by orthopraxis. To act in a wise manner means to observe all of Torah,[37] for Torah reveals the mercies of God that liberate human beings.[38] Specifically, God is concerned with the poor who are exploited by the wealthy. Obedience to Torah, especially to its "royal" or central rule to love one's neighbor, insures that the needs of the least within the community will be met.

James 2:14-26 is one of the most contested passages in the New Testament. Whatever we might say about it, James's point is clear and is repeated several times: loyalty to God is disclosed in concrete acts ("works") that, in the large context, are in conformity to the revealed Torah. For James, faith alone is nothing more than a "religion of the mouth," a worthless religion (1:26) made up of pious confessions (2:18-20) and good intentions (2:14-17) that never truly puts into action God's demand to love.[39] Thus Abraham's justification (and Isaac's salvation!) was based on his hospitable deeds ("works"), which made clear and concrete his commitment to God (James 2:21-24).[40]

Paul sees human liberation as the product of God's justifying mercy which comes through faith in Christ. James understands human liberation as the product of works in conformation to God's Torah, which enshrines God's justifying mercy. For Paul, God's justice is found in the community that depends upon Jesus' messianic work, while for James God's justice is found in the community that obeys the "royal law."

Some attribute this "inspired polarity" to the historical division between the Jewish mission of James and the Gentile mission of Paul. Thus James "corrects" Paulinists who have wandered onto his territory and who have "corrupted" his Jewish converts.[41] While this is perhaps the case, this historical reconstruction of the differences between Paul and James tends to prevent us from reading *both* of them as contributors to an inspired canon. Both James's and Paul's writings are canonical—and thus authoritative for shaping Christian faith and life. Consequently, if a definition of human liberation is to be fully biblical, and in that sense "Christian," it must utilize the conceptions of both Paul and James without elevating one over the other or falsely harmonizing the two into a single account of God's will. A biblical faith is more dynamic: it appeals to one facet of the revelation to correct or balance any unhealthy dependency on another side of the whole reality. James corrects the modern-day Paulinists who overemphasize "faith alone," while Paul reminds those believers who reflect the James perspective that there is more to human liberation than merciful works.

Application to the Church's Engagement with the World

Evangelicals tend to speak of missions in exclusively evangelistic terms.[42] From this vantage point, humanity's liberation is the yield of personal faith in Christ. Transformation is the means to evangelize society, while evangelization is correspondingly the means to transform society. In other words, the end of transformation is actually evangelization, and transformation is best accomplished through evangelization. Human souls come before human society.[43] Right faith yields good deeds, it is said, and from that the inference is made that without justification there can be no liberation. Social justice is thus placed in the shadow of spiritual justification.

While the view that justice is a consequence of true justification is biblical, it takes only part of the biblical word (Paul) into consideration. As a result, matters of social conscience and human liberation are often demoted in importance: what finally matters is whether people are converted and baptized into the church. When confessions of orthodox faith supercede works of mercy, however, the resultant missiology comes dangerously close to the one James rebukes as worthless!

God calls the church to be the ongoing agent of his mercy in the world. God knew Abraham for his loving works and called him "friend" for that reason. Likewise, the church demonstrates its loyalty to God and its right relationship with him through Christ by its concern for the marginalized of the world. According to James, religious life is defined by social responsibility rather than by confessions of spiritual purity: true faith *is* works, evangelism *is* obedience to the law of love, simply because God makes his purposes clear through a life which transmits his mercy to those in need.

Programs for transformation should not consist of formulas that suggest that spiritual justification is the sole reason for and logical result of social justification. On the other hand, strategies that envisage a "social gospel" to the exclusion of spiritual formation also fail to hear the whole word. Together, spiritual and social formation are the twofold goal of mission, and each must be given its own integrity and importance. To the extent that the church remains imbalanced on one side or the other, it must repent by hearing that word, from either Paul or James, which calls it back to a balanced perspective.

Neither Paul nor James misplaces God's transforming grace; their versions of the gospel do, however, emphasize different aspects of it. Paul emphasizes the *mythos*—the verbal narrative, or the story—of God's justifying action through Christ, which continues to shape our identity as Christians. And James emphasizes the *ethos* of God's word—the demands that obligate our obedient actions in response to the revelation of God's triumph over evil.[44]

Paul's emphasis corrects those who depend too much upon human effort *(ethos)* and deny the power of God's participating grace in social justification. These believers tend toward a functional agnosticism and toward a legalism that leads to feelings of insecurity and blunted expectations. Human liberation must be seen as good news rather than as bad news, as possibility rather than as impossibility. Without the hope that springs from our ongoing participation in God's eschatological triumph, and that is stripped by insecurity and diminishing expectations, there is no motive to work for the good of others. There is left only the preoccupation with one's self in the present moment.

James's stress upon human responsibility *(ethos)* moves us in a different direction. The history of the Protestant church is a short history of Pauline Christianity. One of the most common distortions one finds among Protestants is a dependency upon "right faith," to the neglect of "right action." Unlike Catholics, who are more sacramental, Protestants relate all things to their confessions of orthodox doctrine: one is simply not a believer unless one confesses the truth of specific teachings. This is a tacit reflection of Paul's emphasis on *mythos*—on the content of God's good news—and is typically underscored by the denial of "works righteousness" as contrary to the gospel. As a result, various strains in Protestant Christianity have moved dangerously close to the heresy of antinomianism (the belief that under grace the moral law is of no obligation) and to a cheapening of God's grace, which not only saves but also empowers merciful actions in the world.

While it is, of course, important to stress sound doctrine, to deemphasize or even to deny good works as a Christian's obligation is itself a denial of God's triumph over all forms of evil. For a missiology to demote social forms of transformation to a secondary station is against a biblical understanding of human liberation. To this point, Paul's emphasis on *mythos* and his denial of Torah's efficacy is balanced by James's emphasis on *ethos* and his affirmation of Torah's efficacy for the social good.

The tension between James and Paul remains an "indispensable polarity" for the church, inspired by God to bring about the necessary balance between right faith (orthodoxy) and right action (orthopraxis), between faith in and obedience to God, between God's forgiveness and human repentance as necessary elements of Christian formation, and between theological respectability and moral responsibility. Discussions between those who fall on different sides of this polarity will be useful only if each listens to the other under the aegis of the Spirit as the conduit of a correcting word from God. God's will may very well be for the debate, if it results in the repentance and redemption of all those involved.

An Exhortation

Christianity is a biblical religion. That is, the church's self-understanding must always be shaped by its conversation with the Bible. It is only within a biblical context that the church learns what it means to be the church and to do as it ought. Yet Christianity is a religion of the world as well. The church is also shaped by its ongoing conversations with others, believers or not, who are engaged in the common task of developing the resources to liberate people from evil. Rather than reject out of hand what non-Christian agencies are doing, we must call upon them and learn from them so that together we can champion the common task.[45]

The church must take on its distinctive and powerful role in reversing injustice and bringing human liberation into history. God's Spirit is ours! Our minds and hearts have been renewed to think God's thoughts and to have his compassion for the downtrodden. We alone are empowered to act upon what we know is for God and for his creation. Thus it is left to the people of God to lead the fight for freedom from sin, in both its spiritual and its social forms.[46]

Notes

1. Jim Wallis in *Agenda for Biblical People* (New York: Harper and Row, 1976), pp. 47-50, argues that the evangelical emphasis on the personal and spiritual has shaped a religion preoccupied with "selfhood." While all religious traditions debate "meanings," perhaps this individualistic orientation of the evangelical tradition lends itself to the rich diversity one finds therein. Virtually every crucial theological point is contested among evangelicals; the "fundamentals" such as saving faith, biblical authority, the lordship of Christ, and the elements of the gospel receive varying emphases and definitions in the various confessions and groups that make up the evangelical church. See William J. Abraham's book *The Coming Great Revival* (New York: Harper and Row, 1984) for this point.

2. Whereas Matthew's Sermon on the Mount tends to emphasize the personal and the spiritual, Luke's Sermon on the Plain tends to emphasize the public and social sides of the community of true disciples. Notice, for instance, the differences between the Beatitudes of Matthew (5:3, 6) and of Luke (6:20-21), differences that reflect the different emphases of the two inspired evangelists. See Eugene Lemcio's treatment of this point in "The Gospels and Canonical Criticism," *Biblical Theology Bulletin* 11 (1981): 117-19.

3. See Stephen C. Mott's summary of "systemic evil" in "Biblical Faith and the Reality of Social Evil," *Christian Scholar's Review* 9 (1980): 225-40. Mott's later *Biblical Ethics and Social Change* (New York: Oxford University Press, 1982) extends his argument to clarify the social and political aspects of both evil and redemption. It should be noted, as Donald Dayton has shown in his *Discovering an Evangelical Heritage* (New York: Harper and Row, 1976), that social activism has always been a crucial part of the evangelical tradition but was truncated during the modernist-fundamentalist controversy following the Civil War in America.

4. Peter Berger shows in *The Sacred Canopy* (Garden City, N.Y.: Doubleday, 1967) how cultural myths shape religious and institutional perspectives.

5. Christopher Lasch argues convincingly in *The Culture of Narcissism* (New York: Norton, 1978) that the founding and generating mythology of North American life is individualism.

6. David Kelsey contends that the terms one employs in arguing for biblical authority are interrelated: all are linked to the way one understands revelation. See his *Uses of Scripture in Recent Theology* (Philadelphia: Fortress, 1975).

7. For an introduction to canonical criticism, see James A. Sanders, "The Bible as Canon," *Christian Century* 98 (2 December 1982): 1250-55.

8. See my article "Introduction: New Testament Ethics," *Horizons in Biblical Theology* 5, no. 2 (1983): 49-94; see also Paul D. Hanson, *The Diversity of Scripture* (Philadelphia: Fortress, 1980).

9. Note the language of 2 Tim. 3:16: "All scripture is inspired by God and profitable for teaching, for reproof, for correction, and for training in righteousness...." The first and last operations (teaching and training in righteousness) reflect the *scriptural* function of the

Bible, while the middle two operations (reproving and correcting) reflect its *canonical* function. Because canonical critics are concerned with the *idea* of canonicity—with the formation of the Bible to *measure* Christian faith and life—they emphasize the Bible's usefulness to evaluate, to correct, and to change the way the church understands itself.

10. There is a growing literature that traces wisdom to the courts of Israel's kings. For a popular treatment of this idea, see Walter Brueggemann, *In Man We Trust* (Atlanta: John Knox, 1972).

11. See Brueggemann's "Trajectories in OT Literature and the Sociology of Ancient Israel," *Journal of Biblical Literature* 98 (1979): 161-85; for the prophetic side of the biblical drama, see also his popular treatment, *The Prophetic Imagination* (Philadelphia: Fortress, 1980).

12. See James Barr, "The Bible as a Political Document," *Bulletin of the John Rylands University Library* 62 (1980): 268-89.

13. The jubilee motif has been given contemporary treatment in such popular magazines as *Sojourners, Christianity and Crisis,* and *The Other Side*. Ron Sider's *Rich Christians in an Age of Hunger* (Downers Grove, Ill.: Inter-Varsity, 1977) introduced a wide evangelical audience to the motif.

14. Robert North's important *Sociology of the Biblical Jubilee* (Rome: Pontifical Biblical Institute, 1954) shows how the biblical jubilee was reinterpreted in Second Temple Judaism as the sociology of the messianic age. This shaped early Christianity's understanding of the kingdom of God as an egalitarian theocracy.

15. Claus Westermann uses the categories "diagnosis" and "prognosis" to explain the prophet's two tasks. Social criticism diagnosed the problem; it identified symptoms of the disease. The real problem was spiritual, however, and the remedy was repentance and observance of the law, which, according to the prophetic prognosis, would result in healing. See *A Thousand Years as a Day* (Philadelphia: Fortress, 1962).

16. This is especially evident in Luke's Gospel (4:16-30). See the development of this theme by Robert Sloan, *The Favorable Year of the Lord* (Austin: Schola, 1977). See also the study by Sharon Ringe, *Jesus, Liberation, and the Biblical Jubilee* (Philadelphia: Fortress, 1985), who extends the theme into the Synoptic Gospels.

17. See Luke 6:36 (in context), which becomes the central demand of Jesus' entire discipleship ministry as recorded in Luke's "special section," 9:51–19:27.

18. Wisdom is contained in the books of Proverbs, Job, Ecclesiastes, Daniel, some Psalms, and portions of the books of Kings and Chronicles.

19. See Bruce Malchow, "Social Justice in Wisdom Literature," *Biblical Theology Bulletin* 12 (1982); but note Roland Murphy's caution in *Wisdom Literature,* The Forms of the Old Testament Literature (Grand Rapids: Eerdmans, 1981), p. 3. Robert Gordis has commented on the sages' social elitism in his "Social Background of Wisdom Literature," *Hebrew Union College Annual* 19 (1944): 77-118; yet this was not a part of a specific agenda, but was reflected in a general way to the audience.

20. See Brueggemann, *In Man We Trust,* pp. 14-17.

21. This is especially true of Matthew's Gospel—11:29; 12:42; 13:54; cf. 1 Cor. 1:30. Jack Suggs, *Wisdom, Christology, and Law in Matthew's Gospel* (Cambridge: Harvard University Press, 1970), develops the idea that Matthew identifies Christ as Wisdom. Paul S. Minear, *To Heal and to Reveal: The Prophetic Vocation According to Luke* (New York: Seabury, 1976), recovers the prophetic contour within the Synoptic traditions (esp. Luke). This tension between the wisdom and the prophetic traditions, enshrined within the Hebrew Scriptures, can be recovered within the New Testament, especially in the Gospels. In this sense, Jesus, as the Word of God, like God's revelation in Israel, is the fulfillment of both the sage's wisdom and the prophet's oracles. Likewise, those who follow after Jesus as his disciples must continue to embody the conversation between wisdom and prophecy.

22. The book of James revolutionizes wisdom by infusing it with a prophetic character so that the wisdom from above (1:5-8, 13-21; 3:13-18), which helps the community endure to the end (1:2-4; 5:7-9), bids the community toward a jubilary conception of life (1:9-11) with its emphasis on antimaterialism (4:1–5:1) and mutuality (1:22–3:18).

23. Bengt Holmberg has appealed (not uncritically) to the sociology of authority developed by the German sociologist Max Weber in interpreting the development of Paul's conception of authority from a view that sees authority in charismatic-apostolic structures to a view that sees authority more in institutional structures. Without developing the parallels found in the Pastoral Epistles (which are not Pauline, according to Holmberg), he describes a sort of institutionalism which is very much at home with the sage's commitments to societal stability and the authority of society's secular institutions—political, economic, and familial. See Holmberg, *Paul and Power* (Philadelphia: Fortress, 1978).

24. Paul D. Hanson, *The Diversity of Scripture* (Philadelphia: Fortress, 1980), pp. 18-36, suggests that the Old Testament debate between kings and prophets over Israel's security represents "indispensable sides of an essential polarity." I accept this summary but resignify it as a polarity that is also "self-correcting," with one side balancing the other.

25. Reinhold Niebuhr, *An Integration of Christian Ethics* (London: SCM, 1936), pp. 113-45.

26. Perhaps the best introduction to the problematic "Romans occasion" is the collection of essays edited by Karl Donfried, *The Romans Debate* (Minneapolis: Augsburg, 1977). For a broader discussion of Paul's theology of reconciliation, see Ralph Martin, *Reconciliation: A Study of Paul's Theology* (Atlanta: John Knox, 1981). My own treatment of Romans, and specifically of the Romans occasion, can be seen in my forthcoming commentary, to be published in book and on cassette by Word Books in Waco, Texas.

27. See Robert Jewett, "Romans as an Ambassadorial Letter," *Interpretation* 36 (1982): 5-20.

28. See Paul S. Minear, *The Obedience of Faith* (Naperville, Ill.: Allenson, 1971).

29. Note the way in which Paul introduces his moral teaching, or paraenesis, in Rom. 12:1: "Present your bodies as a living sacrifice. . . ." The life that demonstrates God's mercies is "bodily" and "living"; i.e., it is a public act of worship, with consequences for how church members live together (12:3-8; 14:1–15:13) and for how the church relates to outsiders (12:9-21), to civil authority (13:1-7), and to the neighbor (13:8-10).

30. Freedom *(Freiheit)* is Ernst Käsemann's term in *Commentary on Romans* (Grand Rapids: Eerdmans, 1980), pp. 131ff. For Paul, peace with God yields "freedom" from death (Rom. 5), sin (Rom. 6), and legalism (Rom. 7–8), which makes reconciliation between persons possible.

31. I do not believe that Paul is describing a "Christian" experience here; rather, the moral frustration he describes in the first person is clearly parallel to his prior description of sexual and social vices in Rom. 1:26-31. It is that sort of conflict that manifests God's curse, from which the believing community has already been liberated by its faith in Christ. The believing community has been liberated from the legalism that is promoted by an emphasis solely on the observance on the law. Thus what Paul describes in Rom. 7:7–8:1 is the manner of life that results when the believer attempts to observe the law during the new age, which is ruled over by the Spirit of life in the risen Christ, whose aegis yields life and not death (or moral frustration) according to Rom. 8:2.

32. The result (and intent) of this transformation is that we might "bear fruit for God" (Rom. 7:4) and that we might live "in newness of life" (Rom. 6:4). Such catchphrases draw the reader's attention to a new age, introduced by the messianic work of Jesus, with which the community must identify if transformation is to be possible.

33. See Rom. 8:2-17. See also Gal. 5:22-23, which indicates that a human community truly shaped by the Spirit will bear the fruit of God's love, which is profoundly ethical and social.

34. The *theological* distinctiveness of these two missions of early Christianity is ordained by God, according to Acts 15 and Gal. 2:1-10.

35. See my article "Introduction: New Testament Ethics." For treatment of Paul and James, see my article "The Liberated Legalist," *Christian Century* 100 (28 September 1983): 848-49.

36. For James, it is the observance of the law that "liberates" (1:25; 2:12).

37. Note James's tripartite summary of wisdom in 1:19: "Let every man be quick to hear, slow to speak, slow to anger." To be wise is to be "quick to hear"; yet this must always be followed by a readiness to do—see James 1:22-2:26.

38. The phrase "law of liberty," which is found in James 1:25 and 2:12, is eschatological in the sense that God uses Torah to judge the community's fitness for entering into his blessings (1:25; cf. 1:4, 12), presumably at the Lord's parousia (5:7-9). Those who act mercifully toward the poor, by obeying the law of love, are liberated unto eternal life (see the "crown of life" in 1:12). The kingdom of God is "already but not yet." That is, while perfection of the godly must await the final day, there are still immediate blessings. In a paradoxical sense, the eschatological liberation of those who live according to Torah has its immediate fruit in the liberation of the impoverished from their difficult circumstances (cf. 2:5-8, 14-17). Obedience to Torah liberates in two senses, then: on the coming Day of the Lord it will liberate the observant doer from eternal death unto eternal life, and in the here and now it liberates the poor from their present difficulties.

39. The "accepted" religion (i.e., the religion that is eschatologically fit) is characterized by observance of both the social and spiritual contours of Torah—see James 1:27; cf. 2:8-11.

40. See Roy Bowen Ward, "The Works of Abraham: James 2:14-26," *Harvard Theological Review* 61 (1968): 283-90, who identifies the Jewish tradition behind this account of Abraham. It is not Abraham's faith in God, as disclosed by his willingness to offer up his son as a sacrifice, that "justifies" him in God's sight; the passage clearly speaks of "works" and not a single "work." Rather, Abraham's justification, which God makes clear during the sacrifice of Isaac, is based upon his earlier hospitality shown to the three men in Gen. 18. Again, Abraham becomes the exemplar, as God's friend (James 2:23), of neighborly love, and he is justified on that basis. Likewise, the community's faith is recognized by God because they, like Abraham, love their neighbors (or, in the context of James, because they care for the community's poor).

41. This belief is reflected in James Dunn's *Unity and Diversity in the New Testament* (Philadelphia: Westminster, 1977), pp. 251-57.

42. The statements coming out of the Consultation on World Evangelism at Pattaya in 1980 reflect this tendency. See Darrell Whiteman's review, "Special Report from COWE," *Catalyst* 10 (1980): 284-87.

43. This perspective is authorized by the Pauline emphasis that follows.

44. For the ideas of *mythos* and *ethos* in Pauline writings, see James A. Sanders, "Torah and Paul," in *God's Christ and His People: Festschrift in Honor of Nils Dahl*, ed. J. Jervell and W. A. Meeks (New York: Universitetsforlaget [Columbia University Press], 1977), pp. 132-40.

45. For a missiology that marries a critical anthropology and evangelical theology, see Charles Kraft's excellent article "Can Anthropological Insight Assist Evangelical Theology?" *Christian Scholar's Review* 7 (1979): 165-202.

46. Chris Sugden comments in a personal letter: "A Christian plan for the world church to participate as a global body to achieve justice in every place, needs the insights and encouragements—even rebukes—of Christians outside of North America and Europe, to address some of the injustices and brokenness in society in the other Two Thirds of the World, which Christians here may be blind to. Christians from nations which in former decades have been overtly imperialistic, and continue to be so in more covert ways even

today, need to learn from partnership with people from Two Thirds World nations how the resources of the West may be most acceptably received and shared by those struggling for Christ's kingdom in the economically poorer nations of the world."

God's Intention for the World

Vinay Samuel and Chris Sugden

Introduction

God's intention for the world, set forth already in creation, reaches its ultimate consummation in the return of Jesus Christ and the future he will bring to the world. The theme that relates God's intention in creation to its final fulfillment is the kingdom of God, which will be completed with the establishment of a new heaven and a new earth in which the righteousness of God will reign through the lordship of Christ. God has not become inactive in this interim period between creation and consummation, however, so we must ask how his ultimate intention for the world—the consummated kingdom—relates to his intention for the world today, for the church, for human society, and for the historical process *before* the final consummation.

God's Action in History

How does the Bible relate God's work in bringing the final consummation to his work in human history? God's call to and covenant with Abraham, the Exodus, and the settlement of Canaan were each part of a historical project. Through the nation Israel and its society and laws, and through the blessing and punishment that followed obedience and disobedience, God revealed himself, his character, and his purpose to the world. The nation of Israel, its laws, and its history were God's light to the nations (Gen. 17:6; Isa. 42:6; 49:6), and so we should see God's relationship with his people Israel as a model for his intentions for all of human society.

The Old Testament makes no separation between religious history and the rest of history, between a people's relationship with God and its participation in human society, or between God's work among his own people and among other peoples. We know that God initiated the history of the Israelites and made his covenant with them, but his control over Israel is not fundamentally different from his control over the history of other nations—the Bible states that he also directed the history of the Philistines and the Syrians (Amos

9:7). While his work among his own people and that among other peoples are distinct and not to be confused, they are always integrally related.

For example, God does not always refer to his people in ways that distinguish them from other peoples—he uses the same words to refer to both. In the Psalms the Hebrew word *am* (simply, people) is used to refer to the people of Israel, but not exclusively so. The word does not designate *God's* people, for other nations may also be designated by the word *am* in this sense, as in Psalm 18:43: "Thou didst deliver me from strife with the peoples; thou didst make me the head of the nations; people whom I had not known served me."

In Genesis 10, where we read of the establishment of nations from the generations of the sons of Noah, we should not view the designation "nation" as somehow distinct from the designation "people." One must not think that "nation" simply refers to those groups that are estranged from God while "people" refers to those in a relationship with him (the people of God). Psalm 82:8 declares that "to thee belong all the nations"—*Lagoyyim*, whether estranged or not. In Psalm 87, where the Lord calls out the register of the peoples *(ammim)*, he includes Rahab (Egypt), Babylon, Philistia, Tyre, and Ethiopia, even though these were referred to as nations in Genesis 10. And within a single psalm, Psalm 102:15, 21-22, the terms "nations" and "peoples" are synonymous. Kenneth Cracknell concludes that English translations of the Bible are "misleading" in drawing a distinction between Israel as a people and others as nations.[1] While the focus is on Israel as God's chosen people, the terms "people" and "nations" are used interchangeably.

An examination of Old Testament covenants shows that the covenant with Abraham (Gen. 15:1-6; 17:1-21) did not abrogate those with Adam (Gen. 1:26-31) and Noah (Gen. 6:18; 9:11, 16), which were general covenants with all nations. Moreover, the covenant with Noah was not somehow incomplete—it too was a covenant of both preservation and redemption.[2] By choosing Abraham to be the father of multitudes, God did not cut himself off from the rest of humanity. In fact, the prophets insisted that any covenant with Israel was for universal benefit and significance, not exclusive blessing (Isa. 42:6; Jer. 4:2; Ps. 67). God's covenant with Abraham was particular, but again not exclusive—it took its place alongside the other covenants.

The Old Testament looks forward to Egypt and Assyria being God's people along with Israel: "In that day Israel will be the third with Egypt and Assyria, a blessing in the midst of the earth, whom the Lord of hosts has blessed, saying, 'Blessed be Egypt my people, and Assyria the work of my hands, and Israel my heritage'" (Isa. 19:24-25). God makes plain that he will not gather the people of other nations merely as subsidiaries of Israel, but as themselves under the lordship of the Messiah. Egypt will not have to join Israel to become God's people but can maintain its identity. This is not to deny that Israel is distinct from other nations, that it does have a special covenant, and that it is already God's people; but it is important to note that God never intends by this to exclude others from being his people, unmediated by the work of Israel.

The Millennial Vision in Scripture:
The Prophetic and Apocalyptic Traditions

God's activity is part of human history and calls for a human response. In the Old Testament the prophets of Israel focused sharply on this relationship and demanded that Israel respond to God. They interpreted the events of the past, called for obedience in the present, and announced hope for the future. Important to them was the meaning, not just the events, of life. To prophesy was in itself an act of demonstrating life's meaning—not only to explain, but also to call, to invite, and to condemn.[3] The prophets made no separation between religious and political history, nor between facts and their interpretation. They were convinced that God is in charge—not only of the history of his people but of all history.

In prophecy, God was active in speaking directly to his people in the present. Immediate events were decisive in that the prophets interpreted them as foreshadowing the impending end. They then related the end in turn back to the present in an attempt to motivate obedience to God. This was never a simple task, however, because it was not always apparent how God was acting in history, how his people were to respond to him and his promises, and how they could fulfill his purpose. Perhaps even more distressing, it was not always clear that God actually was in charge of history, that he really did care for his people, and that he would maintain his covenants with them. When this was unclear, God's people sometimes questioned his justice, and this doubt sometimes found its way into the Bible—in Job, for example. But God always answered his beloved people with the assertion that he was still in control, despite any appearances to the contrary.

After the fall of Jerusalem and the exile, Israel experienced a series of defeats in its attempts to rebuild the nation in obedience to what it saw as God's will. This time, however, there were no assurances that God was in charge. The heavens answered Israel's prayers with a deafening and unending silence. Prophecy faded away.

Had God really abandoned history? Apocalyptic literature, including Daniel and Zechariah in the Old Testament and the extracanonical books of Enoch and Maccabees, arose in an attempt to answer the question. It reasoned that God had acted in the past and therefore would act in the future. In an effort to appear to speak with greater validity, apocalyptic literature often put present events into the mouths of past figures as prophecy, thus "foretelling" events that had in fact already occurred. As all that was "foretold" had come to pass, so the next event, the end, would come as foretold. The essence of the teaching was vindication for God's people and judgment on his and their enemies. As for the present, God had abandoned it.[4] The apocalyptic writers posited the end only on the basis of past prophecy; they no longer claimed to see God's action in the present and could give their contemporaries no advice other than to wait.

In apocalyptic, any meaning was to be found behind and beyond history, not in God's activity within present human existence. God was no longer seen as an actor on stage; he was behind the scenes where the real decisions that mattered took place. It no longer made any sense for the Israelites to beg God to defeat their enemies and so prove that he was Lord. It did not make sense to pray to God to send fire from heaven to prove to the unbelievers that he was the true God, as Elijah did. It did not make sense because Israel no longer believed that God was active in their lives and history. Further, they did not see in present events the image of the end. In fact, the present really did not have any meaning in the life of Israel. True, it would eventually be invested with meaning, but that would happen only in the end, in the final conclusion: God's victory over all evil people and powers, and the establishment of his reign of peace with justice. The only relation that this end ever had to present events was that it brought the present to a conclusion. The line between the present and the end had no significance in itself: it merely led up to the end.

Though such a view of history may seem terribly pessimistic, it was in fact a great foundation for faith. Any present setbacks could be turned aside with the assurance that things would change in the future. The pagan empires could win all the battles, but Israel could live in the knowledge that they would not conquer in the end. Evil could take over the world, but it would be defeated finally. There was no need for despair or fatalism because God would win in the end. Meanwhile, his people must remain faithful and loyal to him and must patiently endure.

Is apocalyptic a retreat from history? Richard Bauckham suggests that it did not begin with the idea that God cannot act in history but with the observation of God's relative absence from history since the fall of Jerusalem.[5] Although apocalyptists were negative about this period, they did not view history in general in such a negative light.[6] In fact, their belief and desire was just the contrary; they longed for God to intervene on behalf of the faithful and expected that he would vindicate his people and his justice on the stage of history, by transcending it. So they spoke of a "new creation": they affirmed the prophetic faith in their declaration that though God was now absent, he would eventually return in a total transformation of history.

Israel, then, no longer needed to look for daily evidence that God was in control, that virtue was rewarded and vice punished. But as things seemed only to worsen and suggest the absence of God, the Israelites began to wonder how God would win. Some attempted to resolve this problem by proposing that God was indeed active in the world in the exercise of his judgment, that God's activity was in allowing evil to pervade the world, and that he exercises his judgment by allowing it to bring destruction to the world and its inhabitants.

The New Testament Perspective

The New Testament does not share this negative evaluation of history because in Jesus Christ the expectations of the apocalyptic tradition began to be fulfilled. The coming of Jesus showed that God *was* active in the world, and even more, that he was active not only to judge but also to save, to establish his victory, to bring the firstfruits of the final destruction of evil, and to introduce his kingdom to bind the strong man and set the captives free. In Jesus the kingdom was like the mustard seed growing: its ultimate power and influence were out of all proportion to its beginnings. The kingdom was to be conceived as a present reality attacking evil, driving out demons, healing the sick, and forging new relationships of trust between alienated groups. Jesus also affirmed the apocalyptic tradition in speaking of the consummation of the kingdom as a future event that would include the vindication of his mission and the judgment of those who rejected it. The kingdom knows no final consummation in this world as it stands. It did not take its origins in this world, nor is it bound by the limitations of what is possible in it.[7] So pervasive is the disease of sin that the final consummation of the kingdom can mean nothing less than a new heaven and a new earth.

The hope in the triumph of the kingdom at the end is validated by the resurrection of Jesus. Thus Christians in New Testament times and ever since then have believed that what can be tasted now of the kingdom is but the firstfruits of the final harvest. The final harvest is not yet, but the fruits are apparent now. In the struggle against the dominion of evil, in the fruits of judgment and redemption, New Testament Christians experienced the true shalom, the true peace, that one day would prevail everywhere. They knew that not only did present events image the end but also that in Christ they tasted a firstfruit of the final end event.

Paul's letters stress that in Christ the dividing wall between Jews and Gentiles is broken down and that one new humanity is *already* formed (Eph. 2:11-12; Gal. 3:23-29; Rom. 15:7). One significance of Pentecost was that the Holy Spirit was poured out on *all* nations (Acts 2:7-8, 17; 10:47). While God made it clear that his message and promise were for all people, Paul still had to resist those who attempted to argue that God's Spirit was mediated only by the nation of Israel (Gal. 3:1-9). He asserted that all the nations receive the Spirit through their faith; and the Gentiles are inserted in the olive tree of Israel through Christ the Messiah (Rom. 11:17-27; Eph. 2:11-13). Israel's obstruction of God's purposes and his plans for the nation did not totally thwart God's intentions; he was able to fulfill them through other means related to but not dependent on Israel (Rom. 11:25-27). The great vision of the end sees all the nations bringing glory and honor into the new Jerusalem (Rev. 21:24-27).

Does the presence of the kingdom through Christ and its triumph at his return cancel the significance of the history of the Old Testament and of present history? In order to answer these questions it is critical to understand the relation between the history of Israel and the history of other nations. In the Old Testament, the history of Israel was demonstrably God's history. Divine and human activity were integrated as God ruled over and interacted with his people. It is clear that we can draw some distinctions between the story of God and his people on the one hand and the story of God and other nations on the other. But at the same time we must challenge, as the prophets always did, any *separation* between God's relationship with Israel and his relation with other peoples. Both relationships took place within *one* history, and there was always interaction between the two. God was equally concerned with all nations. His people were blessed in order that they might be a blessing to other nations, which God also used and for which he also had a purpose. This concern and purpose was not denied but was confirmed as the Gentiles entered the new Israel proclaimed by Jesus.

The invitation to the Gentiles took place despite their histories. That is, even though the Gentiles were "aliens from the commonwealth of Israel" and entrance into the people of God was not a logical or necessary outcome of their history, they were invited nonetheless. And they came with their histories as nations intact, for they were not considered agglomerations of private and separate individuals but rather public, corporate bodies. As nations, they will lay the tribute of all of their members at the feet of Jesus, while the Jews also keep their national identity within the new Israel.

The new Israel affirms the ethnic identity of the Gentile Christians without dispensing with the old Israel. The old Israel will one day enter into the full inheritance of God's promises, but these promises are not exclusive. The Gentiles will enjoy those promises as well, because what in the Old Testament was particular to God's relationship with the old Israel is in the New Testament opened by Christ to all peoples. The Gentiles enter into covenant history and share the final fulfillment with the remnant of the old Israel as they bring their histories, the wealth of the nations, as tribute to the feet of Jesus.

We must never equate this covenant history with some sort of spiritual history. To say that when the Gentiles entered the church God was no longer concerned with their history in human society but only with their spiritual history, as some would do, is not at all biblical. The New Testament never spiritualized or individualized history. When the Gentiles entered the church they were incorporated into the people of God and took the history of Israel and the Messiah as theirs also, not as a replacement for but as an addition to their own national history.[8] So the history of Israel was the history of God's promise to all the nations, and the promise to Abraham was likewise a promise for blessing to all peoples.[9] Now in Christ all nations must relate their own histories to Israel's history and must incorporate themselves into it.[10] All nations must be grafted into the olive tree of Israel to participate in the blessings of redemption vouchsafed to it and through it. For Paul, the faithfulness of God in keeping his promises to Israel is the key issue on which the certainty of faith depends. If God does not keep his promises to Israel, how can he be trusted to keep his promises to anyone? Consequently, the final salvation of Israel (Rom. 9–11) is central to the argument of Paul's letter to the Romans: "The consummation cannot come unless Israel is saved."[11]

God's faithfulness depends on the fulfillment of his promises to Israel and, by implication, the promises to the other nations as well. The double historical reference into which all Gentile Christians are called to enter is crucial.

The temptation is to neglect it and opt for a monohistorical approach. Some Indian Christians, for example, in seeking an authentic identity, tend to take their Indian history as an absolute and see the Old Testament as a mere example, as only a pattern for how God may act in Indian history. If we absolutize our own history in this way, however, we lock ourselves into the ghetto of an ethnocentric church that has no necessary relationships with other "churches" as part of the body of Christ. It would be sufficient unto itself in terms of its own historical identity and self-understanding, but it would not meet the demands of Christ. No matter what nationality we may be, the Old Testament does not say to us "this is akin to how God acted in your history" but rather "this *is* your history." Old Testament history is a formative part of all Christian history,[12] and so we might say that all Christians participate in two histories—both Judeo-Christian and ethnic. The former is a history for all nations, the bearer of God's promise to the world, and it is only when we see this in balance with a particular ethnic history that we can truly understand the nature of the church.

Evangelicals sometimes fall into one of two traps here. Either they so identify with the new Israel that they forget about their own national history and lose their context in concrete existence, or they make the history of the new Israel subordinate to their own history and produce a national religion. Both the tendency to allow Jewish Christian history to obliterate all other history and the temptation to ignore it are monohistorical. The solution is, as always, to return to Jesus Christ. If we take him seriously, we will recognize that we do live within two histories, neither of which denies the other. Indeed, we cannot live a fully human existence wholly within one to the exclusion of the other. This dual history is united under the umbrella of the kingdom of God, which fulfills God's promise to the nations mediated through the history of his people. People from all races with their histories find their fulfillment in the consummated kingdom, when the wealth of the nations is brought into the new Jerusalem.

With a heritage of hundreds of years of Christian history, the Western church has tended to neglect the task of relating God's particular activity in the history of his church and his people to his more general activity in all human society. The Western church has tended to see Western cultural history and Christian history as one and the same, and it has consequently lost at times the ability to distinguish Christianity from non-Christian civil religion. In the Two Thirds World it is much more difficult to do this simply because Christianity has not been a formative cultural and historical force here as it has been in the West—the situation here is more akin to that in Europe before Christianity became the dominant and accepted religion. Christianity in the Two Thirds World does not have the inertia that it has in the First World, and consequently believers here are constantly seeking to define for the first time the place Christianity must play within and in distinction to culture. The situation in the non-Western world makes it impossible for believers to accept unthinkingly Western ideas about the relation of God's activity among his people to that throughout history—even if those ideas are valid in the context of the West.

The history of mission in Africa, Asia, and Latin America has often been written as if it were little more than the expansion of the Protestant churches of Europe and America. African churches have been pushed to perceive their histories as part of Western Christianity and to submerge their relationship to their own African histories. As we mentioned before, a biblical perspective encourages us to relate the history of Africa to that of Israel, and to draw the continuity between God's action in Israelite and African history. African churches are unified with Western churches not in their acceptance of Western forms of Christianity but in their acceptance along with the churches of the West of the entire stream of Judeo-Christian history—even as they retain their own cultural history. This process is crucial for the discovery of African, Asian, or Latin American Christian identity.[13] We shall see that it is also crucial for accounting for the influence our historical and cultural contexts have on the way we perceive God at work in history.

The Messiah and History

Jesus the Messiah is the fulcrum on which the continuity and discontinuity of the Old and New Testaments turns. As David Bosch writes, "'Geographically' Jesus journeys to the temple, to Jerusalem and his death; 'theologically' he is bound for the nations. In the final analysis he himself would take the place of Jerusalem and the temple (John 2:19-21). As the 'New Jerusalem' he himself becomes the place of encounter with the nations."[14] Thus Jesus is not the Messiah of Israel alone, or of the new Israel alone. His kingdom is not to be identified with the church. Much more than that, it is the establishment of God's rule over the cosmos, the whole creation (Eph. 1:21-22). Even though the church is a sign of God's rule, his plan to govern all things established in the Old Testament is not fulfilled in the church alone. Its fulfillment is a universal one, as his rule extends over all creation and all nations. God's present activity in the world, in part demonstrated by his care for the church, gives us reason to see his kingdom building activity in the history of all the nations and human society.

The sense that history was now the scene of God's activity impelled the mission of the New Testament Christians and marked them off from other groups who still believed that God had deserted history. David Bosch writes that

> if the present is empty, as the Pharisees, Essenes, and Zealots believed, then you can only flee into the memory of a glorious past recorded in codes (Pharisees), or you can with folded arms sit and wait for God's vengeance upon your enemies (Essenes), or you can play God yourself by violently liquidating the empty present, thus trying to make the utopian future a present reality (Zealots), or you can enter into an uncomfortable compromise with the status quo (Sadducees). But if the present is filled; . . . if "the kingdom of God has already come upon you" (Luke 11:20) . . . those who partake of this new history . . . can only let themselves be taken along by Christ into the future, not as

soldiers fighting in the vanguard, but as "captives in Christ's triumphal procession" (2 Cor. 2:14).[15]

Some views of the relation between the kingdom and history make a sharp distinction between the mission of Jesus and that of his church. Some theologians believe that early Christians and Jesus himself thought that the apocalypse was imminent. But when the expected apocalypse did not come, the church found itself with a task unforeseen by Jesus. Arthur Johnston took such a position in 1982 when he wrote that there is "a basic discontinuity between the Old and New Testaments, and the kingdom mission of Jesus is largely unrelated to the visible church which possesses an interim mission until the restoration of the historical Israel by the second coming of Jesus."[16]

For Johnston, "the kingdom of God was present in a unique way in history by the incarnation," and this is not continued in the mission of the church and present historical experience.[17] If this view of the discontinuity of Jesus' mission with that of the church is correct, then history would once again be empty: it could not be filled with the presence of the kingdom as the Gospels record. Bosch notes, however, that this position is made untenable by certain pivotal events in New Testament times. The resurrection of Christ and the coming of the Holy Spirit assured the early Christians that the present was still filled with the power and activity of God. These events prevented them from attempting either to retreat into the golden past of the unrepeatable experience of Jesus' ministry or to escape into another world with eyes only on the parousia. God made it clear to his people that they were irrevocably involved with the world and therefore with mission, so it made sense to live—still within this world—according to the standards of the "coming age."[18]

Does our refusal to segregate God's work among his own and other peoples into "sacred" and "secular" history mean that we deny any difference between special revelation and general revelation? God works in many different ways in different histories, but always with the same goal. If we used a distinction between sacred and secular history to define the difference between special revelation and general revelation we would be assuming that God's special revelation is confined to his activities with either Israel or the church. Such an assumption is not biblical. In the Bible God used historical events at Sodom and Gomorrah, Nineveh, Babylon, Assyria, and Rome to reveal himself. His special revelation does not create a sacred history of his own. God identifies certain normal human histories as revelatory of himself in a special, privileged, and authoritative way. He reveals himself in all history, but some revelation is special in that it helps us to understand that historical revelation and see it more clearly. Although it was directed to Israel and the church and was proclaimed by them, special revelation is never confined to them—it does not create a sacred history in contradistinction to profane history. To separate sacred from profane history and to state that special revelation is the only place that God acts is to propose that God has a plan for one people that is wholly different from his plan for the rest of humanity.

While it is true that the destiny of the nations in God's purpose is linked with that of Israel (Rom. 9–11), we must emphasize again that it is not mediated through that people. Instead, all nations have equal access to God through the Messiah, who is Lord of both Israel and the nations. We cannot state that God's activity with Israel is revelation while that with the other nations is mere providence. There is no such distinction between revelation and the rest of history, because God was involved with Israel, Assyria, and Philistia all at once, in both their political and religious histories, and he will rule them all directly through his Messiah.

The Millennial Vision in Relation to Creation and Fall

Obviously the kingdom is not yet, however. It is not complete; evil still exerts its power in the world; and humans are still fallen from the position of honor granted them at the creation. How does God deal with the fall of humanity and the power of evil? Is it merely wishful thinking to believe that he is still at work in human history to restore humanity to the stewardship of creation? Not at all. The New Testament tells us that God's activity in history is now focused on the Messiah to whom Israel and the nations owe allegiance. God *is* back on the stage of history in Jesus Christ, in the Holy Spirit, and in the church. The rift between sacred and profane history is healed. God does not deny that the struggle continues, that his people are still awaiting the final victory, but at the same time he proclaims that victory has already begun—in our world—in Christ the Messiah. In the process of judgment and redemption, God has already established the foundations of his kingdom.

God's activity in the world provokes ever more virulent opposition from the forces of antichrist and evil as they see the hour of their banishment coming. The devil roams around "like a roaring lion, seeking some one to devour" (1 Pet. 5:8), and Paul warns of "the prince of the power of the air, the spirit that is now at work in the sons of disobedience" (Eph. 2:2). How do we reconcile this with his affirmation that Christ now rules above all heavenly rulers, authorities, powers, and dominions (Eph. 1:21)? It may be helpful to say that Christ is center stage while the lion roars offstage trying to get on. Christ has become the central element of history, and Satan has been thrown aside. Though we may not see Christ at center stage, we know from the Scriptures that he is there. The New Testament confirms that Jesus, not Caesar, is Lord of history, a confession by the power of the Holy Spirit (1 Cor. 12:3). If we only let Christ be de jure and not de facto ruler now, it may be that we are looking too much at the problems of the context and taking the roar of the lion for substance. Those problems are only evidence of the lion's roar and not of his rule. This is the paradox of the kingdom: the devil still roars even while Christ is already Lord.

After the Resurrection, the disciples asked Jesus whether he would "at this time restore the kingdom to Israel" (Acts 1:6-7). He answered them and said, "It is not for you to know times or seasons which the Father has fixed by his own authority. But you shall receive power when the Holy Spirit has come upon you; and you shall be my witnesses in Jerusalem and in all Judea and Samaria and to the end of the earth" (Acts 1:7-8). His answer was not an evasion, nor an indication that he was not invested by God with dominion over the world. Rather, it was an attempt to change the disciples' expectations for the kingdom of God. The disciples thought that the kingdom would consist in the restoration of the Davidic kingdom to Israel. Jesus' reply was that his kingdom was not an ethnic kingdom, limited in scope, but the rule of the Lord extended "to the end of the earth." He promised that the Holy Spirit would come so that the disciples would witness to that kingdom and its presence in Judea, Samaria, and the end of the earth.

Different biblical traditions about the fulfillment of God's work in the world are in tension with each other. Prophetic themes stress God's action within history that leads to a final consummation. These themes do not necessarily tie God to historical processes but see his activity as charging history with significance. Apocalyptic themes on the other hand stress God's work behind the scenes, so to speak, in another realm beyond human history. What we experience in this world are consequences of decisions and activities that take place elsewhere. While neither tradition is wrong, neither tells the whole story; and to concentrate on one to the exclusion of the other can lead to an inaccurate view of the way God really acts. An overemphasis on the prophetic tradition can produce the optimistic idea that history holds God within its process and keeps him ever present. On the other hand, an overemphasis on apocalyptic can lead to a very pessimistic view of the present—and of the future until the eschaton. Apocalyptic can become so concerned with God's judgment and so taken up with a higher realm that it reduces this world to a mere waiting room for the end to come. Our job is to be aware of this tension between valid biblical themes and to show what both traditions at their best are trying to affirm.

In our analysis of the relation of the kingdom of God to the historical process, as elsewhere, we must be careful to keep these two traditions in balance. If we do not, we may fall into a view that is overly pessimistic—for example, the view that the historical process is in a continual state of deterioration that will continue until some future time when God will intervene to bring dramatic and final change. According to this view, the world today bears few signs of the kingdom—and to know the kingdom as it is represented in the world now is not to know it as it will be. The real kingdom is a new heaven wholly beyond our knowledge. What matters is the arrival of this kingdom, and consequently everything else becomes a lesser concern.

The Activity of God in History

Those who hold this view affirm God's work in human history only when his sovereignty, grace, and perfection can be clearly seen: in experiences of new birth, deliverance, or guidance. For the rest, they consider God to be absent; and they hold that God excludes humans from participating in his kingdom work. By instituting the kingdom in the incarnation of Christ, they say, God seemed to say that those who hope to contribute to this divine-human work must follow Christ's example of perfection. But God does not ask us to model ourselves on Jesus' divine nature. Rather, we are to focus on his mission, with all its ambiguities, misunderstandings, and apparent imperfections. Jesus knows that we will all fail him in the end, but that does not mean that we cannot participate with him in the building of the kingdom. Indeed, he chose to include among his disciples a leader who denied him—not to mention a traitor who handed him over to those who would kill him. Jesus knows that we are children of Adam; but through our adoption as sons and daughters, through our union with the New Adam, we are called to take part in his mission. Though the church often seems rife with quarrels, disagreements, and backslidings, it is still through this body—Christ's body—that his mission is continued in history, guided by the Holy Spirit. In this mission God, by his sovereignty, grace, and perfection, takes and uses our human imperfections and ambiguities to fulfill his purpose.

The Perfect and the Imperfect

To assume that everything "spiritual" must be perfect is to imply that an experience of redemption cannot be mingled with imperfection. However, the Scriptures do not imply that redeemed people will be perfect in the world. God will judge our response to him: have we built with gold, silver, wood, grass, or straw on the foundation of Christ (1 Cor. 3:10-15)? We cannot take salvation for granted; the parables of the talents and the separation of sheep and goats and the teaching on grace, sin, and righteousness (Rom. 5–7) all show that God will judge our response to his gifts. So redemption is not a mystical experience that is perfect and cannot be removed. Instead, it comes only in a relationship of forgiveness, love, and obedience to God that is subject to his judgment.

We cannot separate our spiritual experiences or our relationship with God from our life in the world and our human relationships. The individual is called as God forms a community and a people.[19] His forgiveness depends on our forgiveness of others (Matt. 18:35): if we do not love our brother we cannot love God (1 John 4:12, 20), and we forfeit our inheritance. Love of God and love of neighbor explain each other and give the meaning of the law.[20] No law of God enjoins us to relate to him independently of a relationship with other people.[21] His laws demand rather that we live in union with other people even as we live in union with him. Life in union with Christ is life in union with others in Christ (Gal. 3:26-28).

This union is made visible in the world in the church, where true relationships in Christ are characterized by love, forgiveness, compassion, generosity, and patience. These values are "heavenly" in contrast to "earthly," because they will last (Col. 3:1-17). Even though these relationships are imperfect and will be judged, God can still use them in their present state to mediate his redemption and demonstrate his concern for us. God's grace in redemption takes these imperfect human relationships, redeems them, and uses them in care and love. Relationships redeemed in the church will be fully transformed only when the bride is reunited with the bridegroom; but now, while we are still in this world, these relationships are a real experience of the future kingdom. Heavenly values of the kingdom are shown in earthly bonds—between husband and wife, parent and child, and master and slave (Col. 3:18-22).

Heaven and Earth

Just as imperfect relationships in the church can provide some real experience of the kingdom, other imperfect experiences in society outside the church can also demonstrate some signs of the kingdom.[22] "If the kingdom is limited to the spiritual relation of men to God," writes George Eldon Ladd, "the consummation of the kingdom would be achieved by the final inclusion of all men in the kingdom when every last individual on earth has accepted God's rule."[23] To view the kingdom as wholly spiritual is to separate what God has joined together in his creation. As Andrew Lincoln points out, heaven and earth must not be separated, for they are one structure in God's creation.[24] Not only were both created by the same God, but both were affected by the Fall: "For in him all the fulness of God was pleased to dwell, and through him to reconcile to himself all things, whether on earth or in heaven, making peace by the blood of his cross" (Col. 1:19-20). The heavenly world is populated now by spiritual forces of wickedness that believers are to fight against (Eph. 3:10; 6:12). Heaven too is involved in the battles of the present age, and war in heaven will go on until victory brings in the fullness of the new age with its reconciled cosmos. "Above all," Lincoln writes, "heaven and earth are shown to be inseparably connected by the redemption which God has accomplished in Christ"[25] (cf. Col. 1:19-20; Eph. 1:9-10, 22ff.; 4:10). The important point is that heaven is not the place of perfection that will one day replace earth. Heaven is not set over against earth. Both form one structure of created reality, partake in the results of human sin, and will experience redemption in Christ.

Humanity can respond in two different ways to what God has made. "The sinful response brought about disunity in the cosmos, and this direction of disobedience can be called 'earthly.' . . . In Philippians 3:19 and Colossians 3:2, 5, 'earthly' is contrasted to heavenly and takes on the connotation of sinful, with the earth being viewed as the primary setting of fallen creation."[26] In Colossians, the things of the earth include the practices of the old human nature (3:5-9), the indulgence of the flesh (2:23), and life in the world with its bondage to elemental spirits (2:20). The direction of obedience, exemplified by the obedience of Christ (Rom. 5:19), is linked with the heavenly (1 Cor. 15:47). Insofar as believers continue to live in Christ in response to God's offer of salvation, they are blessed with spiritual blessings in the heavenly places (Eph. 1:3), can be called "heavenly" themselves (1 Cor. 15:48), and are encouraged to seek the things that are above (Col. 3:1).

Now in union with Christ we experience the substantial restoration of the unity of the whole cosmos, which expresses the restoration of all things under the rule of God. Lincoln adds that

> because they belong to Christ, all things belong to believers, including the world (1 Cor. 3:22). Colossians demonstrates that it is because believers participate in the triumph of the exalted Christ over the powers that they have been set free to use this world and its structures. . . . Since their Lord is in heaven their life is to be governed by the heavenly commonwealth (Phil. 3:20). . . . Paul does not believe that real life is in this other world and that as a consequence life on earth has relatively little significance (Col. 3). . . . The apostle can insist both on the necessity of heavenly-mindedness and on the fulness he expects to see in the personal, domestic, communal and social aspects of Christian living. The quality of the concentration on the things above where Christ is will ensure that the present sphere of his rule will not remain simply in heaven but will be demonstrated in the lives of his people on earth.[27]

When Paul writes of the heavenly things, he is expressing humanity's restored relationship of obedience to and reconciliation with the Creator, which is part of the total reconciliation of the whole creation. He is describing a relationship with God that embraces and affects life in both this world and the next. He is not speaking of a sphere of existence that sometime in the future will invade this world but of a relationship with God that is both possible now and will last forever. This relationship is expressed in a lifestyle that gives precedence to the values that Jesus demonstrated in his life and taught in the Sermon on the Mount. God vindicated these values, the ethics of the kingdom, in the Resurrection, and he promises they will last forever.

The Conscious Confession of Christ

To limit God's work to an inner, individual experience and to relate only our spiritual life to the future kingdom is to assert that we experience now a lesser Christ than the one who does and will reign in glory. This "two kingdoms view"—the kingdom of the world as wholly separate from the kingdom of God—falls down on its Christology and thus its doctrine of God by suggesting that what we experience of Christ and his kingdom now is but a pale imitation that has little continuity with the future reality. The kingdom, as it exists even now, is not an individual spiritual entity. It is corporate, and it permeates with its influence all of historical life. There are many activities, structures, and movements in the world that already share in God's saving work by his grace. God's salvation has redeemed the human race, broken the power of evil, and created a new humanity—already, though the process is not yet complete. The world is already changed by Christ's victory on the cross and the Resurrection, which exalts him as Lord of all.

One need not submit personally to the lordship of Christ to be able to experience this grace and this transformation in one's life. For example, in India many women who do not confess Christ may experience the fruit of the king-

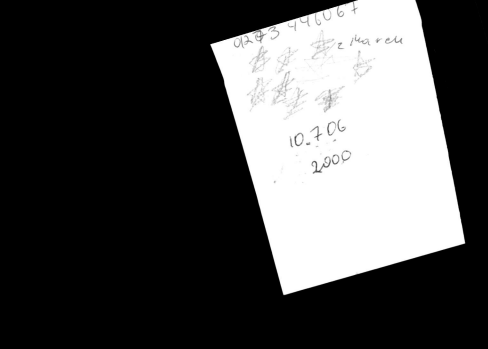

dom in the transformation of their status in society. Yet this transformation is still part of God's work of breaking down the dividing wall of hostility between separated groups, of creating in himself one new humanity in Christ in which there is neither male nor female. God has used the church in India in its witness to Christ to change the status of women and other oppressed groups in society. Those who benefit from this work live transformed lives to some extent—they are no longer the same people they would have been. Transformation is not salvation, though. Those who do not confess Christ are not saved by the kingdom in this world; only obedience to and faith in the King can provide salvation.[28] But even without that confession of faith, many still participate in the transformation that the kingdom brings. Christ healed ten lepers, all of whom participated in the blessings of the kingdom; yet only one demonstrated any faith and returned to thank him (Luke 17:11-19).

In the confession of Jesus as Lord, which is the heart of the kingdom experience inspired by the Holy Spirit, there is freedom for Christ's lordship to operate, to be expressed, and to be experienced in its fullness. On the other hand, Christ's lordship may be evident in many other areas of life—in the struggle for economic justice, for example—though it cannot be confined to any one of them. The Holy Spirit's activity of applying the lordship of Christ may begin with economic justice, but it breaks through to infuse all of life with the lordship of Christ so that all people will profess his name and bow to him as Lord of all.

The Spiritualization of History

Because God desires to rule over history in this world, we have to seek a statement of the relation of the kingdom to history that does not spiritualize history or relegate it to insignificance. The spiritualization of history is a fundamentally Hindu idea, based on a monistic view of the cosmos in which the only reality is God. Everything else, including humanity, is nonreality or illusion until it achieves the desired goal of union with God. History, too, is unreality, and thus God cannot be experienced within history. Consequently, any desire to approach God must be furthered by the denial of history in the attempt to depart the plane of unreality for that of reality. The Hindu desire is to spiritualize history and make it and human life ahistorical (in the Western sense) and mythological. God and human history are and remain separate.

Any attempt to spiritualize the history of Jesus and the kingdom—isolating it from the Old Testament, from secular society, or from the church—by creating a "sacred" history devalues human history because it is regarded as no longer truly real. This sacred history then becomes ever more divorced from humanity, and Jesus himself becomes a wholly mythological character akin to the deities of Hinduism. As David Jenkins writes, "If worshippers of God do not really believe that he is to be encountered in and through the actualities of daily living and contemporary history, then he is indeed merely a cultic object sustained by a 'myth' which works effectively only as long as the myth dominates culture, but which is simply a mere story maintained by 'believers' against the realities of the world, once culture changes."[29]

Those who affirm that only Jesus and his kingdom are truly real remove him from ordinary history, spiritualize his history, and so make him a "myth." By asserting that Jesus and his kingdom are truly real by virtue of being removed from ordinary history, they directly deny the message of the Bible, which states that the "Word became flesh" and "in him dwelt the fulness of God bodily."[30]

It is interesting to note that when this "mythologized" Jesus is the subject of evangelical preaching in India, he elicits little response. For the Hindus he is little different from the thirty-three million other gods in their pantheon, so they place him there along with the rest. But when Christians proclaim that Jesus and the kingdom are at work now, in human history, through healing miracles, social change, and social development then there is significant response.[31]

The anthropologist Paul Hiebert suggests there are three levels in anyone's worldview. First is the level of cosmic gods and forces that are involved in the origin of the universe and are at the heart of the questions that permeate all of life: What happens at death? What is our fate and destiny? The second level is concerned with intermediate forces—demons, witches, and saints. The third level is the level of interaction between persons and of interaction between people and nature through science. The second level—the level of the intermediate powers and forces—is very powerful among poor communities whose life is often dominated by religion.[32] No area of life is secular in the strictest sense; all things are under the control and influence of these intermediate powers. People in these cultures see life as a constant interaction between the human and the level just above. Though this level may be considered the domain of forces both good and evil, in many cultures it is dominated by the evil forces. Day to day life is then lived in fear. People attempt to manipulate these forces to their benefit or to propitiate them when they have been offended. Sin, as a rebellion against the cosmic God above all, has little significance.[33]

In Christian mission, it is necessary that the rule of the one true God be proclaimed in all areas and levels of life. If God is proclaimed as being high above the world and human concerns, those to whom the mission is directed may hold on to their existing beliefs about intermediate deities and the need to propitiate them to get pragmatic results in the healing of worldly ills. For example, Christian mission has often preached a cosmic God and practiced medical science for healing. But if the level of principalities and powers is not addressed adequately, if God is not continually proclaimed as the author of all healing, then the new believers may ascribe that healing to the influence of those intermediary deities. As far as they are concerned, the propitiation of a local deity or demon to heal a sick child does not contradict at all adherence to the transcendent God of Christianity.

Both the process of demythologization advocated by some Christians and the spiritualization of history practiced by others demonstrate the effects of the Enlightenment on Christian mission worldwide. The first proposes that the supernatural cannot be real simply because science and rationality can tell us nothing about it. The only reality there is is the cosmos, which we must deal with as we can. The second process, the spiritualization of history, states on the contrary that a supernatural God is real but the world is not. Each process results in a secularism that denies the interaction of God with human history.

To push God out of our human history is to accept the rise of paganization and totalitarianism. It also turns realism about human sin into pessimism about the human condition. Jenkins states that

> a properly Christian doctrine of sin must be placed firmly within a Christian understanding of creation and redemption. We are to perceive what sin is in relation to the Glory of God, his commitment to the fulfillment of creation and saving work in Christ to redeem, restore and sum up all things. Realism concerning evil distortion and failure is demanded but pessimism is exorcized. Pessimism arises out of the basic theological mistake of pushing God out of history and out of the mistake in discipleship which will not share in God's risk of getting close to men and women in their actual struggles, sufferings and hopes.[34]

How Far Is the Kingdom Continuous with History?

The biblical understanding of the new earth depends on the belief in God's continuing action in the world. An indispensable part of the new reality, of the new order, is a consummated and perfected human history. The work of God in creation, and the work of humanity as his steward in history, will be taken up and completed in the new earth. Furthermore, the Old Testament clearly proclaims that our earth, not some other place, is to be the site of the consummation of history. Because Christ affirmed the continuity of the Old Testament and the New, we as his followers must include in our eschatology the hope of the transformed earth. The New Testament continues the Old Testament view of one history by universalizing the history of Israel and making it the olive tree into which all Gentile nations are grafted in order to participate in redemption.

While we may see this earth as the site for the future consummation, what continuity is there in the New Testament between present history and the kingdom? We have seen the dangers of asserting that there is none: religion becomes otherworldly and believers seek either merely to endure or to escape this world. But does this allow us to move in the opposite direction to say that certain historical events have some sort of "kingdom value"? Do historical happenings help to bring the kingdom that God prepares and will establish in the parousia? In discussing this question, José Míguez Bonino argues that we must seek an answer in terms of causality. He fears that too often the desire to protect God's initiative—and the fear of claiming initiative for ourselves—reduces our view of historical action to a minimum. We may see in history images that remind us of the kingdom, but we do not claim that they have any actual significance for its coming among us. This fear of regarding any human action as an activity of the kingdom means that historical action of both right and left are equally valuable—or invaluable—as far as the coming of the kingdom is concerned. Neither is effective, we might say, so there is nothing to distinguish between them.

Is there some way for us to move beyond this fear while still recognizing the danger of absolutizing our human action? Can we map out a conception of the relationship between the kingdom of God and human history that is biblical and that enables us to commit ourselves to pragmatic action in history as a project of the coming kingdom?[35]

Key to a biblical answer is the resurrection of the body. The body is resurrected so that who we are in our present historical life will be recognizable in the next. Our identities as physical human beings are vitally important in the coming kingdom. Yet at the same time, we will be totally transformed—not to disfigure or weaken our bodily life, but to fulfill and perfect it by eliminating all corruptibility and weakness. This is in great contrast to Eastern mysticism. God does not propose to "rescue" our spiritual elements from the bodily experience and personal identity of physical life. Rather, in the resurrection of the body God proclaims the total redemption of humanity, the fulfillment of bodily life cleansed from self-deception and self-seeking (Matt. 22:29-32; Phil. 3:20-21; 1 John 3:2; Rev. 7:13-17).

According to Paul, what we do in our bodies in everyday life is vitally important. We will be perfected only after our resurrection. Yet before that we are to live in Christ; that is, we are to mirror his bodily perfection, putting off all things of the flesh and donning the fruits of the Spirit, above all "love, which binds everything together in perfect harmony" (Col. 3:14). We must attempt to model the life of the kingdom within the structures of history, as masters, slaves, wives, husbands, parents, and children (Col. 3–4). Because Christ has risen and brought in a new realm of love, deeds of love bear the marks of the new age and will find lasting fulfillment when that age is fully with us at the return of Christ.

This new age does not deny history but eliminates its corruption, frustration, and sin in order to bring to fulfillment the communal life of humanity. Any deed in any sphere of life, be it social, political, economic, or religious, will remain if it is marked by the love of the new order. This fulfillment is not a matter of gradual evolution, however. We do not see in society a continual progression to a state of perfection. The pathway by which history finds its consummation in the kingdom is paved with suffering, conflict, and judgment. The kingdom at its consummation will redeem and transform deeds of love done in history. Though these deeds will be fulfilled only in the total transformation at the return of Christ, now in the present they are not mere reflections or foreshadowings of the kingdom within history but the actual presence and operation of the kingdom already begun, however imperfect and partial. The kingdom is present now, but its fulfillment is still not yet.

Protests against expressions such as "building the kingdom" are valid as a protection against a naive optimism and as a validation of the sovereignty of the divine initiative. But they are usually cast in an unbiblical view of God as a preprogrammed force who produces certain events like the Incarnation and the return of Christ without reference to what is going on in human history. We must remember that God is also active *within* our history—he does not just impinge on it at widely separated intervals—and he calls us to act with him. So the parables that serve to illuminate the growth of the kingdom, those of the sower, the mustard seed, and the leaven, for example, have biblical and theological warrant.

If we adopt this perspective, the main question is not the whereabouts or signs of the kingdom in today's history, but, "How can I take part in, express, and produce the quality of personal and corporate life that will be fulfilled in God's kingdom?" Such action will involve both proclamation and deeds. Both the announcement of the kingdom and action in keeping with its quality are eschatologically significant, and neither can be reduced to the other. There is a tension between them, between what names this future and what corresponds to its reality, that cannot be reduced this side of the full realization of the kingdom. To avoid absolutizing any of our human action in the name of the kingdom, we must have recourse neither to idealism nor divine politics, but to the best human politics possible—and that will always be open to debate.

The Christian faith stimulates us to look for the actualization of the kingdom in history in terms of justice, equal access to the creation that God intended for all, and the creation of human community through love, worship, work, and play. In the light of the present and coming kingdom, Christians can invest their lives in the building of a historical order in the certainty that neither they nor their efforts are meaningless or lost. The confession of the resurrection of believers is not a selfish desire for immortality, a recompense for sufferings, or a wish-fulfillment, but rather the affirmation of the triumph of God's love, of the fulfillment of humanity's stewardship of creation, and of the vindication of all struggles against evil.[36]

The Option of Suffering

In seeking options for historical engagement, the clear Christian option set forth in the Scriptures demands a life of suffering. In his life, on the cross, and in his resurrection, Jesus' suffering was God's way of bringing change and God's instrument of redemption. While salvation comes only through Christ's suffering, as we share in that suffering we may serve as vehicles of God's change and reconciliation in the world. But this is not to say that we must idealize suffering. Indeed, nothing indicates more clearly the imperfection and corruption of human society than the sufferings we experience as its members and the persecution we endure as the church. The New Testament does not regard these sufferings as apocalyptic messianic woes that have to be endured before the end comes. Instead, the presence of the kingdom in history impels Christians to address the injustices caused by humanity and, as far as possible, to remove the sicknesses of the sick and the poverty of the poor.

Views that see the presence of suffering as confirmation that this world is bound for destruction tend to cut off any impulse toward addressing personal and social evil. By no means is all suffering to be endured as we await the final consummation. Some suffering will be irremovable, such as deformities, psychological hurts, and incurable diseases. But we can only identify the irremovable ones in the process of trying to remove them. Far from being an experience of imperfection and evil that cuts us off from the love of God (see Rom. 8, esp. vv. 38-39), suffering is experienced with Christ (Phil. 3:10-11); it is a channel of his resurrection life (2 Cor. 4:7-18); and it is the means of overcoming the powers of evil (Rev. 12:11). Sufferings in union with Christ are by God's grace both a real *experience* of redemption and a *means* of redemption.

Jesus changed history through his suffering—much more than through his miracles, which stood as signs of the presence of the kingdom. His message was "Take up your cross and follow me." In response to that, the church's witness to redemption must not be to escape from the world, nor to resort to an isolated mystical experience that cannot be touched by the world and suffering. Rather, believers must attempt to witness in the sufferings involved in living out redemption. Redemption, then, can be a present reality; it can be mingled with imperfection and known in imperfect suffering relationships. It can even mediate redemption to others.

The experience of suffering always reminds us that the kingdom cannot be consummated in this world as it stands, nor even in the perfection of the "spiritual." We know this because the consummation promises a world from which all suffering has been removed (Rev. 21). The continuing experience of suffering in this world thus prevents us from the triumphalism of both "super-spirituality" and utopian expectations.

Suffering implies and presupposes conflict: it resides in injustice, and we bring it on ourselves as we challenge those situations of injustice and so unearth the conflict within them. Yet such sufferings are "in Christ." God is at work in them bringing his change to the heart of their imperfection. As we engage in the struggle for justice, as we undergo suffering for God's sake, we are not constructing the kingdom of God here on earth by seeking to create perfect structures and model situations that can be proclaimed "foretastes of heaven." The sign of Christian development and social change is not the New Jerusalem but the cross.

The struggle may make us weary, but the suffering of the cross is victory, not defeat. Bound up in this suffering is the reality of the Resurrection and its promise of life (2 Cor. 4). While the Resurrection does not promise that the angels will come to open our prison gates in a miraculous deliverance, it is a sign that all suffering is to be borne in the promise of ultimate vindication and triumph. Such experiences of suffering and resurrection in the conflict involved in social change are, in their ambiguities and imperfections, true experiences of the kingdom of God at work in human history.

It is not easy to see God at work in the midst of suffering and conflict. It is not always easy for those who suffer to feel his presence. It is easier to say that he is not at work here now but that he will triumph over suffering sometime in the future. We are tempted to project all change into the future, to wait passively for God's powerful solution, and in the meantime to rejoice in the "spiritual" aspect of "heaven" here. Isn't it easier to see blessings and success as signs of belonging to that final kingdom? Isn't it easier to see demonstrations of the kingdom's presence in miracles and other events beyond our control? Isn't it easier to identify right entirely with our cause and to go forward in an uncompromising crusade? It is much more difficult to see God at work in suffering, in a situation that is ambiguous and provisional because of our involvement. Yet we have the promise that just because God is in it this work is not ultimately futile.

Our survey of the relationship between the kingdom and history shows that our vision of the future molds and determines the content of our mission. Our different contexts and commitments in the world give different emphases and meanings to the same biblical material. Our vision of the future sometimes leads us either to put God's spiritual work in a plane wholly and eternally above history or to see the kingdom restricted to certain actions within history. Some put the spiritual above the historical and others seem to lose sight of the spiritual completely and find the kingdom wholly of the world.

Perhaps it is best to view the kingdom as a higher plane that intersects the imperfections of the historical order. The ambiguities and provisionalities of history do not stop God acting through them; yet we cannot absolutize these imperfections and sufferings because we know that there is much more to this plane than what intersects our history. This higher plane of the kingdom gives meaning and hope to the impermanence of history without making it permanent. It affirms the reality of our personal relationship with God and our future glorious inheritance and consummation in the future. It reminds us of the personal dimension of history and of the incompleteness of the historical experience. By establishing the presence of his kingdom not just in the church but in history, God commits himself to work through history to bring change, the results of which will be incorporated into his future kingdom. With this assurance, the option for involvement in society is chiefly one of suffering to bring change.

We are not simply following a predetermined countdown to a final destruction. However ominous the signs of the times, they are not just of judgment and destruction. The judgment of the old age is always in conjunction with the foundation of the new age that breaks into it. The interim and imperfect nature of our work in the world is not a mark of the corruption of a world that will be destroyed but a sign of the new day to come, an indication of the new earth prepared for us by God that is already active within imperfect human history and will one day come in all its glory.

This view of the future saves us from both unalloyed optimism and unrelieved pessimism. Our works of reconciliation will all be judged and found

lacking. But ⌐
will n⌐

⌐ough the sieve of God's judgment and grace, they
⌐ingdom. Historical events do not make up the
⌐: they are provisional. The world situation that
⌐ renewed and perfected by God. Our view of
⌐neither a utopian dream nor a mere holding
come. We should see ourselves as going
⌐orld, caring for his property with the aid
⌐ arrival when he will evaluate and per-

⌐pment

⌐ be able to detect where God works and involves him-
⌐⌐ities of human history? One clear guideline is where we see
⌐⌐ the kingdom replacing values not of God in persons, movements,
⌐⌐uctures. God is thus at work in every corner of the world and history.

Where we see *human dignity* being affirmed and people discovering a sense of self-worth, self-acceptance, and a sense of having something to contribute to the world and others, there God is at work.

Where we see that people have the *freedom* to act according to their conscience without threat from others who control their actions and thus their attitudes, there God is at work.

Where people are able to make their own contribution to the life of society, especially in *participation in decisions* that affect them in the family, in the community, in religious matters, and in political structures, there God is at work.

Where people can live in *hope*, a sense that it is possible and worthwhile to plan for the future, where they can experience the *respect* of the community, and where there is *sharing* that enhances, not reduces, the humanity of the community, there God is at work.

Where people are committed to the *struggle against evil and injustice*, and where there is a sense of *equity*, there God is at work.

Where women, the weak, and the handicapped find roles that give them dignity and *equality*, and where their needs get priority and power is shared to benefit all and dehumanize none, there God is at work.

Where we find a *sense of God's presence*, a *recognition of the power of evil* without and within, and true *humility* about the limitations of our knowledge in the face of God's wisdom, there God is at work.

We should also look for God's work and influence as people make decisions, share information, help each other in emergencies, look for and work at jobs, attend social functions, direct the course of their families, help the underprivileged and marginalized, use resources, and worship. We should see the expression of God's work in social and family structures, in the political and government sphere, and in religious institutions. The temptation is to see God at work only in values, but he also works to transform structures to promote the values of the kingdom. While it is possible to be content with the expression of the values of the kingdom in the lives of individuals or small groups, if these values do not find structural expression they cannot bring lasting change. So development work must also focus on structures, both to transform them and to bring to light those that already reflect the values of the kingdom.

APPENDIX

The Vision of the Kingdom in the History of the Church

A strong tradition in the early church (linked with Montanus, Tertullian, and Irenaeus) stressed that Christ would come to reign on this earth. But from the time of Constantine to that of Augustine, this vision was progressively spiritualized. Gradually, many came to believe that the kingdom of God was a matter of faith that had nothing to do with society. They believed that God's activity and kingdom were locked in the church. Closely related to this was the acceptance of the church by some of the later emperors of the Roman Empire. The culture of the late empire and afterwards became identified as Christian and was considered to be superior to all others. This decisively changed the mission of the church. Christianity was originally an outsider religion: it had worked among people who had no place in society, it was despised itself, and it had taken other religions seriously. But now Christianity had become an insider religion—the religion in power.[1]

The Reformers protested against equating the kingdom of God with the divinized authoritarian institution of the church. Protestants saw God at work outside and beyond the structures of the church. Anabaptists saw him as judging both the world and the institutional church. And Lutherans detached God's work in the church from that outside it: within the church Christians were judged by the laws of God, but outside the church they could take part in society as ordinary citizens, according to the laws of the land and the demands of society, not as church members. Calvin focused on the current rule of the ascended Christ over the whole of human history. He did not believe that secular bodies were necessarily in opposition to the spiritual kingdom nor separate from it, rather that they were complementary—"that a public form of religion might exist among Christians and humanity among men." He saw the kingdom of God as penetrating and transforming the political realm, and he believed that to be involved in this process, to be involved in the political realm, was part of the witness and mission of the church.

The European Enlightenment secularized God's work in the world and the coming of the kingdom. Even while many Enlightenment thinkers denied the direct action of God in the world, they still tried to maintain the idea of the coming kingdom—*a* coming kingdom—that would bring perfection to the world after a long period of progress. They tried to remove the promise of the kingdom from the church and to wrest its ultimate fulfillment from a far-off transhistorical future because they wanted the new age of humanity to take place in the here and now, or at least in a historical time in direct continuity with the present. Kant sought in human reason and moral strength a basis for continuity between human history and the kingdom of God. It was on this rock that the Enlightenment tradition was to founder, for it proved too optimistic about the goodness of human reason and the altruism of human moral choice.

The child of this tradition was the social gospel movement in the United States. This saw God working as a spirit in history directing it towards its final goal, an idea in consonance with the evolutionary optimism and the doctrine of progress of the day. But not all its supporters saw the coming of the kingdom as the inevitable result of uninterrupted human progress. Some believed that humanity could never perfect itself, so they tried to reserve the initiative in bringing the kingdom for the divine and to maintain an awareness of the power of evil over humanity. A major question about others in the social gospel tradition, however, is whether they saw the kingdom as the result of human historical processes, which may have been under the control of God, or whether they even saw the kingdom as a wholly human construct.

The first expression of the vision of the kingdom in the United States was permeated by an optimism similar to that of the social gospel. Up to the time of the Civil War, many people believed that the kingdom would be established on earth before the return of Christ. The great outburst of revival and mission, the sense of destiny about the growth of the United States, and the apocalyptic terrors of the French Revolution and Napoleonic Wars were all taken as signs of the approaching end. In Britain, by contrast, upper-class Christians who feared the loss of their privileges by revolts among the lower orders took the French Revolution as a sign of approaching catastrophe. Drawing from the same signs on which the North Americans based their optimism, they pessimistically believed that the kingdom would not be established before Christ returned.

This latter view—that only Christ could bring in the kingdom—came to dominate evangelical circles as the nineteenth century progressed. Slowly there took place what Timothy Smith and David Moberg call the Great Reversal: the social concern of evangelicals in the nineteenth century gave way to a distinct antipathy to social involvement by evangelicals in the twentieth century. Moberg traces this change to a way of interpreting the Bible that precluded guidance for social concern and to a preoccupation with the supernatural facets of faith that, in combination with a pessimistic vision of the future, cut off this world from the other.[2]

Moberg also links this reversal with the shifting social basis of the evangelical community. Old cultural values of the frontier did not fit the inner city, and evangelicals withdrew to the suburbs. I. J. Rennie noted some of the social factors surrounding the two kingdoms view: "Following the Civil War in America, things instead of getting better were continually getting worse. This brought about increasing disillusionment and pessimism, which seriously undermined the . . . optimistic outlook for spiritual and cultural progress of society."[3] In addition, "the cataclysmic events at the turn of the nineteenth century" and "two world wars in the twentieth" contributed greatly to the rapid spread of the two kingdoms view. Its "apocalyptic assumptions" give it "a special appeal . . . in times of great crisis and distress."

The tension between prophetic and apocalyptic traditions of eschatology runs throughout Christian history. There is also tension between the desire to make the kingdom relevant to all history, and the conflicting desire to root it in the experience of the church. Obviously, how one resolves this tension has a direct influence on what one believes to be the proper relation of the church and society and the kingdom and history. Believers' views are also influenced by the cultural values of their time and their relationship to the cultural mainstream. For example, when the church settled into society under Constantine, it took on a spiritualized vision of the future. Socially marginalized people are sometimes drawn to revolutionary apocalypticism and the hope it provides for a radically changed future. In the social and cultural optimism of early America many saw the French Revolution as a sign of the fulfillment of the kingdom; but in Britain the upper classes viewed it as a threat[4] and a sign of the deterioration that would continue until the return of Christ.

While the two kingdoms view expects the world to get worse and worse, holding out little hope for human reform, those who hold such a view often (but by no means always) resist change and strongly support existing structures and patterns of life. For them, the more the present is radically separated from the future hope, the more the existing order loses realistic reference points for criticism—and the less reason there is to worry about change. Any social or political option is equally good or bad. When Christians lose hope about the efficacy—or necessity—of action in history, they merely reproduce the dominant cultural values of their society. Some supported Hitler in the Third Reich, and some support today's oppressive regimes.

While in the twentieth century many see the kingdom as an escape from a doomed history, in the nineteenth century, by contrast, evolutionary optimism reigned and the hope of the kingdom was identified with the doctrine of progress by those whose experience of the world was of situations that were getting better and better. Though both views claim to take the Bible literally, they each lack a sound method of interpretation. Many who hold limited views of the kingdom are socially concerned, but on the face of it their views are not theologically integrated. The internal logic of the two kingdoms view cannot criticize or direct Christian social responsibility. Adherents who want to demonstrate Christian faith in a socially responsible way must do so in obedience to other scriptural themes such as the love commandment, not in response to the demands of the kingdom.

But social action, to make the impact the kingdom demands, must be motivated by a kingdom vision of God's intention for society, history, and the world—not just by a desire to show the fruits of our spirituality. There are two poles to Christian social involvement: personal obedience to God and God's activity and purpose for all history. Those who take the first pole alone, who see their relationship to God as a wholly personal matter, do not orient social action within the historical context of God's plan. They may address the needs of communities and even the problems of structures, but they are not motivated then by the God of history. We must heed the warning of Christian leaders in Marxist countries who point out that social action without a Christian vision of the kingdom will give place in the end to the Marxist alternative, which is rooted in a vision of history. Furthermore, Christian social action, which is based on a vision of the kingdom that sees the present only in negative terms, is not as effective as it could be.

The close link between historical context and views on eschatology does not mean that we must try to—or can—divorce ourselves from our context to get an objective, neutral, biblical view. Nor should we regard most eschatology since New Testament times as declensions from an obvious and clear biblical position on the matter. Each was a pilgrimage to discover the meaning of the biblical material in the readers' own context. Each has a claim to be rooted in the biblical tension between different qualities of the kingdom. Yet although there is no one viewpoint from which to judge all the various views, this does not mean that all views are equally valid.

The main evangelical view today has its roots in the premillennial tradition of the nineteenth century. It strongly distinguishes between the consummated kingdom and present experience. No experience of the kingdom now can connect with the consummated kingdom or share any of its qualities. All that we can know of the future in the present is spiritual and limited to the church. Any material dimension of the kingdom that seems to be revealed in the biblical records is therefore not part of the human task in history but is to be isolated in the mission of Jesus, which was unique, or to be located in the millennial future. We have already examined in the main article above some of the theological questions and practical consequences that this view raises.

God's Work outside the Church

One further question, however, is whether the kingdom's connection with this world is limited to the church or whether it has to do with the whole of human history. What is the future of God's work outside the church? Some describe this as the work of God's left hand and believe it is not connected with his work within the church. The kingdom, in their view, is manifest in history only in the church, in the spiritual realm. Such a view, however, demands certain untenable theological assumptions, so we must examine the possibility and the nature of God's work outside the church, and its relationship with the presence and consummation of the kingdom.

Can we use the term *redemption* for God's activity outside the church? If we define redemption as God's activity in fulfilling his intention for the world, the focal point of which is the lordship of Christ in the present working toward the consummation of his purpose, then we can see some evidence of redemption outside the church. Within this overarching understanding of redemption, one may speak of the experience of regeneration, forgiveness, and new life. But the experience of regeneration itself cannot be the defining category for redemption. The defining category can only be Jesus' lordship, not the individual experience of that.

The church's own experience of redemption is based on the lordship of Christ over creation. Jesus as the resurrected Lord is exalted now as Lord over all creation, from which he derives his lordship over the church. Paul writes that God "has put all things under his feet and has made him the head over all things for the church, which is his body, the fulness of him who fills all in all (Eph. 1:22-23). God has given Christ full authority in heaven and earth, that is, throughout the unified creation (Matt. 28:18). So we may boldly pray, "Thy kingdom come, thy will be done on *earth* as in heaven"—and not just "in the church as in heaven." David Bosch notes in this context that "the Kingdom comes wherever Jesus overcomes the evil one. This happens (or ought to happen) in fullest measure in the church. But it also happens in society."[5]

According to Alfred Krass, the rediscovery of a vision of the future that affirmed Christ's present lordship in the world came in the struggle of the German churches with Hitler, for Nazism challenged all that the Reformed tradition had stood for. The issue was joined, according to W. A. Visser't Hooft, with the Barmen Declaration of 1933: "In the light of the Kingship of Christ, it is a priori to be explained that the state stands under the Lordship of Christ, all power has been given to him."[6] Krass adds that "Reformed theologians had been tempted to operate with a 'history of salvation' separate from the natural order, but they discovered under pressure that 'the New Testament does not know a general providence apart from the history of salvation. . . .' When Hitler sought to turn the course of world history against what the church knew was God's plan, the church was pushed to exercise its proper, positive, prophetic vocation, to speak out on behalf of all efforts contributing to the intra-historical realization of God's promises."[7]

After this experience, the Netherlands Reformed Church published "Foundation and Perspectives of Confession" in 1950 and 1954. It stated "We can take our place in history without fear. History is the total event, directed from Christ's first coming toward his second coming. . . . History manifests itself in a series of crises. There is no evolution, but a continuing advance of Christ's work and consequently an increasing raging of anti-Christian forces."[8]

One author of this document was Hendrikus Berkhof, who held the tension between the kingdom's work both beyond and within history. "The kingdom of God," he wrote,

> is the work of God himself. This is the truth of the orthodox position. The error is to believe that it must therefore be sudden, even entirely from without. God is active in the world. The kingdom of God grows. This is the truth of the liberal position. The error is to believe that it is therefore man's labour, and that it is identical with moral and social progress. . . .
>
> In the struggle for a genuine human existence, for the deliverance of the suffering, for the elevation of the underdeveloped, for the redemption of the

captives, for the settlement of race and class differences, for opposition to chaos, crime, suffering, sickness and ignorance . . . an activity is taking place throughout the world to the honour of Christ. It is sometimes performed by people who know and desire it; it is more often performed by those who have no concern for it, but whose labour proves that Christ truly received—in full objectivity—all power on earth.

He concludes: "The new world does not fall into the old like a bomb, nor does it take the place of the old which is destroyed, but is born through the old in which it had been active."[9]

The kingdom does not act only in the church. The church always exists in a historical context, and there is thus much interaction between the two.[10] Sometimes the church interacts with secular history almost "unintentionally," as when converted individuals cause positive change in society merely by example. At other times the interaction is more overt and intentional. The influences of the church may be tragic, as in the case of the Crusades and the Inquisition, or it may be creditable, as in the vast expansion of the church in parallel with the growth of mercantile colonialism. Even when the church is faithless to its inheritance, God can work through and around it to spread the gospel outside its original confines. This only supports our contention that the experience of redemption cannot be limited to the action and body of the church.

The Fear of Absolutization

In a justified effort to maintain the sovereignty of God, some are afraid to identify any historical project with the kingdom of God. To stop us from identifying our own projects with the work of the kingdom, they prefer to see history only as an image, foreshadowing, or reflection of the kingdom. Westerners are particularly sensitive to anything that seems to make history absolute, in part, we think, because they live against a background of movements and institutions that tried to do just that. Many of them believe that liberation theologians have fallen into the trap of identifying acts of liberation with the bringing of the kingdom, for liberation theologians are in dialogue with Marxism, which represents an absolutist tradition.

Oddly enough, both those who attack Marxism and the Marxists themselves—both those who spiritualize the significance of history and those who endorse life in this world completely—are children of the Enlightenment. This tradition attempted to bring religion into the realm of rational discourse and scientific examination. Some reacted against Enlightenment thinking merely by denying the validity of reason and science in this field—they spiritualized religion and history. If history is not really "real" they can only turn their eyes to the transcendent. But the religion they find there is not grounded in any sort of concrete reality, and the life of the world is left devoid of any Christian perspective and influence. The Marxist tradition, on the other hand, accepted the critique of the Enlightenment that made human experience and reason absolute. Human experience and reason are in turn directed by the collective life of classes and the means of production. The only arena for the fulfillment of human aspirations is within earthly history understood as a conflict between classes.

The social gospel of the nineteenth century was also a child of the Enlightenment, which, as we noted, was an attempt in part to make real the Christian millennial vision of the world. The social gospel movement sought to reclaim this heritage for Christianity. So we can represent these offspring of the Enlightenment as follows.

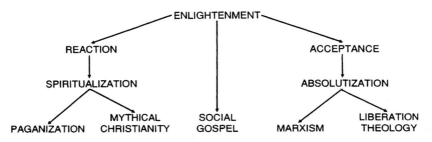

We must beware of both spiritualizing and absolutizing history, and of the fear of doing so, as we seek an open space for other options for Christian historical engagement.

Western theologians are particularly sensitive to anything that seems to absolutize history. The West experienced the growth of freedom and human rights only through desacralizing institutions that tried to make history absolute. The early church condemned the emperor cult and replaced it with prayer on the emperor's behalf, so setting a limit to his power. In the Reformation, freedom got a boost through the desacralization of political orders. These orders gained strength even as the church lost it, but they were restricted to serving the welfare of the people, not providing salvation. In the English-speaking world, Puritanism replaced the divine right of kings, a sacred institution, with a constitution or political contract, a wholly secular institution. Demands for freedom of religion and conscience led to demands for free assembly, freedom of the press, and civil liberties. Jürgen Moltmann concludes that in the long run this is to the benefit of Christianity, which indeed must stay on the path of secularizing, desacralizing, and democratizing political rule if it wants to keep true to its faith and hope.[11]

The experience of the Two Thirds World is somewhat different. In Asia there is little absolutization of history because the predominant view is that history is unreal. The only reality recognized is the transcendent—God—but God can never be experienced in history and there is little chance of seeing him at work there. There is in Asia, then, much less hope—or even concern—for history than there is in the West. But when Asians are converted to Christianity, the news they hear is good news indeed. They are only too glad to see and know of God at work in history because that restores meaning to what they see around them; there is now reason to work for the betterment of society because not only is God here but he is working for the same things that they are. This is a great revelation for non-Westerners because their society is not based on Christian assumptions of justice and rights, as much of the West is at this point, but instead on the naked exercise of power in relationships at all levels. In this context, to see God at work for justice in their own situation is their great desire.

One's context always shapes one's response to God's work in history. When Europeans hear theologians from the Two Thirds World speaking enthusiastically about God bringing the mighty low, they fear that those theologians have absolutized history and lost sight of the transcendent. And when those from the Two Thirds World hear the warnings from the West about absolutization, they fear that the Westerners have spiritualized history and have lost sight of the importance of this world—something that those in the Two Thirds World know well from their own context.

Obviously we must keep a partnership and balance between these two perspectives. To make any category absolute is the wrong road. Neither justice through social action nor a faith that looks only to the transcendent can be absolute. To absolutize or spiritualize is to ask for a perfect new earth or a perfect new birth here. It is to demand that whatever God does now must be perfect, complete, and final. David Jenkins writes that "idolatry has always been a besetting sin which leads again and again to dreadful destructions and inhumanities. Idols are not always just false gods. They may be the promotion by absolutization of a provisional and ambiguous good to the level of a god, and this particularly in politics." He concludes that "to redeem and renew the distortions and destructions arising from false absolutizations of valuable insights, we need a clear worship of the Presence, Power and Promise who relativizes every human activity and every created fact. We also need the hope that comes from beyond us and makes provisional every definition we make or every expectation we entertain."[12]

That we reject absolutization does not mean that we deny God's present work in bringing either the new birth or the new earth. We should not let the fear of absolutization blind us to seeing where God is at work in the imperfect and ambiguous. The reaction of spiritualization and the fear of absolutization can so convince people that they will never see God at work in history that it becomes a self-fulfilling prophecy. Such paralysis may be infecting many Western Christians. They do not expect to see God at work in normal human history but look for him only in the supernormal dimension of healing and tongues. What they are left with is a God-of-the-gaps: a God defined by humanity that can exist only in the few gaps between the areas from which the Western worldview has "conclusively" eliminated him. In the Two Thirds World, believers are more ready to see God at work in human history, which may also be a self-fulfilling prophecy.

Notes to God's Intention for the World

1. Kenneth Cracknell, "God and the Nations," in *Dialogue in Community*, ed. C. D. Jathanna (Mangalore: Karnataka Theological Research Institute, 1982), pp. 2-3.

2. See Karl Barth, *Church Dogmatics* (Edinburgh: T. & T. Clark, 1956), IV, 1, pp. 26ff.

3. See José Míguez Bonino, *Revolutionary Theology Comes of Age* (London: SPCK, 1975), pp. 134-35.

4. See Stephen Travis's discussion of this in *Christian Hope and the Future* (Downers Grove, Ill.: Inter-Varsity Press, 1980).

5. See Richard Bauckham, "The Rise of Apocalyptic," *Themelios*, vol. 3, no. 2, pp. 19-23. See also K. Koch, *The Rediscovery of Apocalyptic* (London: Allenson, 1970; Naperville, Ill.: Allenson, 1972), pp. 28-33.

6. Bauckham argues that Daniel's four world empires embrace only the period after the fall of Jerusalem, not the whole of history. And, since temporal dualism did not arise until the first century A.D., apocalyptic did not begin from a dualistic dogma but from an experience of history. See also Travis, *Christian Hope*, pp. 37-38.

7. Vinay Samuel and Chris Sugden, "Evangelism and Social Responsibility: A Biblical Study on Priorities," a paper presented at the Consultation on the Relationship Between Evangelism and Social Responsibility (CRESR), held in Grand Rapids in 1982, and published in *In Word and Deed*, ed. Bruce J. Nicholls (Exeter: Paternoster, 1985; Grand Rapids: Eerdmans, 1986).

8. See Bonino, *Revolutionary Theology Comes of Age*, pp. 135-36.

9. David Bosch notes that "the history of Israel is a continuation of God's dealings with the nations. Precisely as the elect, the patriarch, and with him Israel, is called into the world of the nations." *Witness to the World* (Atlanta: John Knox; London: Marshall, Morgan & Scott, 1980), pp. 61-62.

10. Andrew Walls of Aberdeen University emphasizes this.

11. J. Christiaan Beker, *Paul the Apostle* (Edinburgh: T. & T. Clark; Philadelphia: Fortress, 1980), p. 337.

12. The tendency here to absolutize Indian history arises from an evolutionary understanding of history that rejects the authority of biblical revelation.

13. The necessity of this process was affirmed by the First Conference of Evangelical Mission Theologians from the Two Thirds World, held in Bangkok in March 1982. Papers from this conference were published in *Sharing Jesus in the Two Thirds World* (Bangalore: Partnership in Mission—Asia, P.O. Box 544, Bangalore-5, 1983; Grand Rapids: Eerdmans, 1984).

14. On this see Bosch, *Witness to the World*, p. 63.

15. Ibid., pp. 64-65.

16. This quote is from the manuscript of "The Kingdom in Relation to the Church and the World," a paper presented by Arthur P. Johnston at the Consultation on the Relationship between Evangelism and Social Responsibility. This paper was later revised and published in *In Word and Deed*, ed. Bruce Nicholls, but without the section containing the quote.

17. Ibid. See Nicholls, *In Word and Deed*, p. 117.

18. See Bosch, *Witness to the World*, pp. 65-66.

19. See G. E. Wright, *The Biblical Doctrine of Man in Society* (London: SCM, 1954), pp. 18-19.

20. See Victor Paul Furnish, *The Love Command in the New Testament* (London: SCM, 1973), ch. 1.

21. See Vinay Samuel and Chris Sugden, "Evangelism and Social Responsibility," pp. 193ff.

22. See further Jürgen Moltmann, *The Church in the Power of the Spirit* (London: SCM; New York: Harper & Row, 1977), p. 196.

23. George Eldon Ladd, *Jesus and the Kingdom* (New York: Harper and Row, 1964; London: SPCK, 1966), p. 179. This book has been revised and updated and is now published under the title *The Presence of the Future* (Grand Rapids: Eerdmans, 1980).

24. Andrew Lincoln, *Paradise Now and Not Yet* (New York: Cambridge University Press, 1981), pp. 191-92.

25. Ibid., p. 192.

26. Ibid.

27. Ibid., p. 193.

28. See John Howard Yoder, *The Politics of Jesus* (Grand Rapids: Eerdmans, 1972).

29. David Jenkins, "Doctrines which Drive One to Politics," in *Christian Faith and Political Hopes*, ed. Haddon Willmer (London: Epworth, 1979), p. 145.

30. Many Christians affirm the Incarnation in theory—that the Word became flesh—but still maintain in practice a docetic soteriology. They betray their similarity to the Docetists—early Christian heretics who proposed that Christ only *seemed* to have a human body and to die on the cross—in that even as they pay lip service to the idea of God become man they hold to a salvation out of the world and out of history, which maintains the removal of God from the world.

31. For case studies that demonstrate the importance that preaching the historical Jesus has for social development projects, consult the following: (for Bombay and Madras) Graham Houghton and Ezra Sargunam, "The Role of Theological Education in Church Planting Among the Urban Poor," *TRACI Journal* 19 (April 1981); (for Jamkhed) Vinay Samuel and Chris Sugden, "Dialogue with Other Religions—An Evangelical View," in *Sharing Jesus in the Two Thirds World* (Bangalore: Partnership in Mission—Asia, 1983; Grand Rapids: Eerdmans, 1984); and (for Bangalore) Vinay Samuel and Chris Sugden, eds., *Evangelism and the Poor—A Third World Study Guide*, rev. ed. (Bangalore: Partnership in Mission—Asia, 1983).

32. See Paul Hiebert, "Folk Religion in Andhra Pradesh: Some Missiological Implications," in *Evangelism and the Poor—A Third World Study Guide*, ed. Vinay Samuel and Chris Sugden, rev. ed. (Bangalore: Partnership in Mission—Asia, 1983).

33. We contend that the effects of the Fall are seen predominantly at the second level, which controls and deforms humanity. The effects of the atonement and resurrection of Christ also have their most significant impact at this level, leading captivity captive.

34. Jenkins, "Doctrines which Drive One to Politics," p. 149.

35. See Bonino, *Revolutionary Theology Comes of Age*, pp. 139-40.

36. Ibid., pp. 140-42, 152.

Notes to the Appendix

1. See Arthur P. Johnston, "The Kingdom in Relation to the Church and the World," the manuscript of a paper presented at the Consultation on the Relationship between Evangelism and Social Responsibility, p. 18. This paper was later revised and published in *In Word and Deed*, ed. Bruce Nicholls (Exeter: Paternoster, 1985; Grand Rapids: Eerdmans, 1986).

2. See David Moberg, *The Great Reversal* (Philadelphia: Lippincott, 1973), p. 33.

3. I. J. Rennie, "Nineteenth Century Roots," in *Handbook of Biblical Prophecy*, ed. Carl E. Amerding and W. Ward Gasque (Grand Rapids: Baker, 1980), p. 44.

4. D. N. Hempton formulates this conclusion about the situation in England in an unpublished paper, *"Evangelicalism and Eschatology,"* University of St. Andrews, Scotland, 1977, pp. 15-16.

5. David Bosch, *Witness to the World* (Atlanta: John Knox; London: Marshall, Morgan & Scott, 1980), p. 209.

6. W. A. Visser't Hooft, *The Kingship of Christ,* The Stone Lectures, Princeton University, 1947 (New York: Harper, 1948), p. 136.

7. Alfred Krass, *Five Lanterns at Sundown* (Grand Rapids: Eerdmans, 1978), p. 140.

8. Quoted in ibid., pp. 142-43.

9. Hendrikus Berkhof, *Christ the Meaning of History* (Richmond: John Knox, 1966), pp. 169, 173.

10. See José Míguez Bonino, *Revolutionary Theology Comes of Age* (London: SPCK, 1975), p. 137.

11. Jürgen Moltmann, *The Church in the Power of the Spirit* (London: SCM; New York: Harper & Row, 1977), p. 179.

12. David Jenkins, "Doctrines which Drive One to Politics," in *Christian Faith and Political Hopes,* ed. Haddon Willmer (London: Epworth, 1979), p. 153.

Development and Eschatology

Maurice Sinclair

Introduction: Toward a Biblical Wholeness

That development and eschatology should have been so rarely considered together reveals a weakness in Western culture and Western theology: impressively specialized as they are, they are yet fragmented and compartmentalized. When we are challenged by the poverty in the world around us, we try to respond through certain development "imperatives" to safeguard the rights and opportunities of the deprived. Yet when we formulate our theories and imperatives of development, our assumptions about what the future should be is not often checked against God's plan for the future. In this, development workers often lag behind those involved in evangelism: Christian development workers are less likely to have their minds upon the imminent return of his Lord than are their evangelist colleagues who proclaim the urgency of repentance.

To such a separation of interests one might be tempted to respond: So what? As long as some Christians are concerned about some of these matters at least some of the time, isn't that enough? It seems, however, that God will not allow us to remain complacent in our specializations. Both evangelism and development in their current practice meet some apparently intractible difficulties and impenetrable barriers. But these "impenetrable" barriers can in fact be opened if we bring evangelism with its emphasis on eschatology back into dialogue with development. The difficulties in each separate field are in fact intertwined; they may be resolved when we apply the insights of both simultaneously.

My purpose then is to contribute to the task of bringing development and eschatology together into a biblical whole. The Mataco Indian believers in the Paraguayan Chaco, with whom I am privileged to work, hold a unified view of things, wonderfully held together by the Father God in whom they focus a robust and practical faith. That they come to terms so well with the here and now makes it easier rather than harder for them to anticipate the hereafter. Even within a temporal compass, they very naturally and biblically recognized the lordship of Christ over the affairs of the church and the village alike.

Whether or not our "village" is built of adobe bricks or glass and steel, we should seek to learn from the biblical insights and the coherent understanding of our Mataco brothers. For them, there is only one universe of experience, and God is at the center of it. Following their lead, we should seek to avoid a false separation between the secular and the sacred, and thus remove one of the obstacles now preventing relating development to eschatology.

Just as the Mataco see the universe as unified, they would also never divide the scriptural revelation: the Bible is one. Even though we may detect differences or tensions between prophecy and apocalyptic, between Proverbs and Ecclesiastes, or between various New Testament passages that speak of the kingdom yet to come and the kingdom already here, we must creatively and coherently hold them all together. I would hope that the kind of coherence we are struggling to express might be intelligible to all our fellow Christians. If it really is biblical, they should be able to see how it affects them and how they relate to it. Our biblical message should give direction and provide a wholesome corrective to present life in the world, but it should also create expectancy and be full of promise. It should be something the Holy Spirit can take, in order to spur people into action.

Our consultation on a Christian response to human need reflects a theological tendency—a kind of evangelical radicalism. We agree about the need for "contextualization"; we want our evangelism to be "holistic"; and we are anxious that our theological reflection should stem from and lead back into a genuine "praxis." For specialists within our in-group this is excellent, but for those outside it is obscure. Our words do not communicate anything to outsiders. Who would write "evangelical radical" across his tee shirt? Who could fit "contextualization" into a chorus beat? Our language betrays us; we have allowed a distance to grow between the theologian and the believer. Once we have worked out between us how eschatology relates to development, then we need God's grace to tell others how it does so—with words of simplicity and power.

Development and Eschatology within a Historical Context

I remember being taught in the late 1950s that, with the technology already then in our grasp, it would have been possible to provide abundant food supplies for the existing world population, and that, by bringing all available agricultural land into production, it would have proved possible to feed a population many times larger still. With such a prospect in mind, development was conceived as the widespread application of the productive technology already in the possession of the Western nations. Their prosperity relative to the rest of the world was interpreted as ample proof of the vastly greater productive potential created by that technology. Through development, many thought, the great blessing could be multiplied and shared.

And so development has become a key word and a priority concern in the world. However, even in the optimistic fifties and sixties, it was evident that worldwide prosperity could not come from technological development alone. Obviously choices needed to be made regarding the distribution of resources within and between nations. All that has happened in the subsequent years suggests that these choices have mostly reflected a less than enlightened self-interest: social ethics have not matched scientific technology. And now there is even cause for a weakening of confidence in the technology itself. Many of its modern applications are wasteful of limited resources, environmentally harmful, and dehumanizing. Modern communities are being compared critically and unfavorably with primitive or traditional communities.

If it is true that both locally and globally the development certainties of the earlier postwar years are being shaken, what can be said of the certainties of previous ages? Wasn't fertility the central concern of the people in the fertile crescent thousands of years ago? Their religion was geared to the increase of their crops, their livestock, and their descendants. Who among the dwellers in Mesopotamia or Canaan would have questioned that fertility was what life was all about? For them this all-important factor determined survival and indicated prosperity; it made all the difference between life and death, enjoyment and misery.

Somewhat later, the fertility and prosperity of the Greco-Roman civilization gave its more privileged sons more time to sit and think. Surely reason, not fertility, they thought, must be the golden thread giving meaning to life.

The dark ages intervened. To grow crops for a feudal lord must have seemed a tolerable price to pay for his protection against marauding bands. It isn't likely that there were debates on the merits of feudalism in the baronial halls. The important thing was to submit to the system, not to question it. There were rivals to be subdued and battles to be won.

In the end the battles concentrated power in fewer hands. Under these barons a new power group arose and with it a new preoccupation and certainty. The merchant class flourished, not only through the protection of the medieval kings, but even more through the scientific revolution.

So our sketch has taken us full circle: we are returning to the certainties of our own day. If we are Westerners, our grandfathers will have talked about progress and civilization, but behind these ideals has been the march of capitalistic and technological development. The tendency to identify progress and civilizational advance with this technology is surely irresistible. We can certainly question technology and the effects it has on our lives, but can we truly and effectively distance ourselves from it? Why, even the men in the Kremlin are trapped in the dependency it brings!

I am convinced that Scripture, not Marxist analysis, provides the profoundest commentary and most searching criticism of the particular kind of development that dominates our modern world. Scripture speaks of creativity, vice-regency, and stewardship, rather than of development. God made Adam to be a gardener-prince: his attempt with Eve to usurp the throne upset his gardening as well as his governing.

Having placed before us God's original intention for humanity—its freely submissive and cooperative partnership in the ongoing creation—Scripture then traces the successive and drastic consequences of the human failure to cooperate with God and others and of the mistaken human bid for independence. In the striving for scarce resources some snatch more while others secure much less. Injustice breeds envy and vanity and it all the while destroys community. Yet the ruthless who "gain the whole world" discover that their glittering prize lacks solid worth. They live in the shadow of death.

The Old and New Testament thus expose every false hope of fallen humanity. If the root of our problem is disobedience, how can some imagine that the manipulation of the sources of fertility can secure their welfare? Such a cult that seeks only to increase the amount of technological products in the world leads only to frustration and perversity. Independent human-centered reason rates no higher in the biblical estimate. "God made foolish the wisdom of the world." Nor would Paul have encouraged the medievals to seek in the protection of their feudal lords their worldly satisfaction. His criticism of our modern assumptions and our modern false hopes would have been equally severe. One can imagine Paul being less than impressed by our scientific technologies and our capitalist economies upon which so many build their hopes. For, unless humankind reckons with its greatest ill, it cannot realize its greatest good. Without a renewed opportunity for stewardship in a redeemed creation, human development must remain fatally flawed.

God's biblical revelation is more than a profound and critical commentary on human society, however. It reveals a passionate struggle as well as deep criticism. Not only are false hopes exposed but true hope breaks in.

Abraham hoped against hope. His own infertility mocked him, but in response to the stirring of God's Spirit, he reached out to a hope beyond fertility, to a blessing in which every family of the earth would share. Abraham was taught a contrasting way of secure relationship. He became God's friend.

The free trusting relationship remained very vulnerable in the fallen world. The chosen tribe, which expressed this new quality only in part, found itself engulfed in Egypt by oppressive forces. Moses challenged these forces as God inspired him to inspire hope among the despairing slaves. God's chosen leader then forged a national community and pointed its members to the Lord who had acted in grace toward them, who required of them obedience to a law of liberty, and who offered them a homeland and a better country.

Once the nation was formed and the promised land occupied, a new dimension to the struggle emerged. As well as being threatened by violent external forces, God's community became subject to destructive influences from within. In the face of this internal threat, the historic task of the prophets was to resist the reassertion of the fertility cult and to preserve the way of responsive relationship with God and among the people. The struggle between the ideal relationship and actual compromise was unrelenting. On balance the nation disobeyed the message of the prophets and consequently suffered division, conquest, deportation, and dispersion. A remnant was gathered and returned from exile, but its enclave around Jerusalem was darkly overshadowed by pagan superpowers. Once more God's people found themselves a conquered people. Threatened once again by despair and extinction, the prophets pointed to a brilliant prospect: a new king, a new law, a new land, a new community, and a new creation.

When the time had fully come and God's moment of intervention had arrived, the faithful successors of Abraham, Moses, and the prophets were few in number and small in influence. True, a young north-country girl was willing to bear the baby king, but his advent and his method of establishing his kingdom was a source of stumbling to his own Jewish people and seemed a mere foolishness to the civilization that surrounded them. What a strange intervention this was! Could the rise and fall of a messianic pretender from Nazareth herald the transcendent and decisive Day of the Lord? In fact, Christ did not rise to fall, but fell to rise. God's servant was vindicated. God's invading kingdom was already here.

God's invasion was thus secured through a bridgehead, quite unpredictable to human intelligence. The subsequent advance of his kingdom has been characterized by a baffling mixture of human weakness and divine power. Because of human participation, its advance has been erratic. The church has at different times misunderstood, perverted, forgotten, but also remembered and heroically obeyed its Great Commission. Consciously or unconsciously, the church has had to incarnate the gospel, but in so doing it has often compromised or even betrayed it. Feudal tribalism reerected barriers between Christian groups that should have been enjoying and expressing their oneness in Christ. The doctrine of merit obscured the doctrine of grace. Enlightenment reason ultimately made no more sense of the cross than Greek reason had before. Scientific humanism appeared to banish God, even from the perimeter of the universe. Violence—the very antithesis of both the creative relationship to which Abraham was first called and the wider reconciliation made possible through Jesus—has fluctuated at scandalously high levels throughout the gospel age. Sometimes it has been used against the church, but much worse, it has also been used in the name of the church. Now nuclear violence threatens to engulf Christians and non-Christians alike.

When the Old Testament saints were tempted to despair because of corruption within Israel and destruction from without, they needed the apocalyptic message. The same has been true for Christians in later ages. The erratic advance of the gospel has taken place under the looming prospect of an impending crisis. On the one hand Scripture speaks of mounting opposition to the church, of natural and political traumas and of widespread apostasy. Yet on the other hand there is always promised the evangelization of the nations.

Indeed, against a background of external opposition and internal failure, God's initiative in his mission has never been totally frustrated. While the frontiers and the centers of missionary advance have continually shifted, the momentum has never been completely lost. The appalling weight of spiritual and physical distress in the world today must remove any trace of complacency from the missionary church, but the church can still look forward to new gains: to old Israel's recognition of her Messiah and to further miraculous signs of his kingdom of healing and peace. The ultimate crisis will be heralded by heavenly portents and then the Son of Man will appear upon the clouds of glory.

At this point history flows into eternity. George Knight in *A Christian Theology of the Old Testament* notes that Israel was unique among the nations in looking both back into its history and forward into the eternity of the future.

> It was natural for them to do so, because they alone believed in the "living" God. Before Israel was, God is. Thus after Israel is, God will be. Again, since Israel as a people was created by God for his own ends, and Israel's history has a purpose running through it, then Israel's history must have an End to which it is moving, as well as a point from which it began. Moreover, since God had set Israel within a universe which he had created in the beginning, then that universe too must have an End. On the other hand, the End to which the whole OT is looking forward, emphasis upon which is such a dominant note within it, is not merely and only the historical last moment in a series of historical moments; it is also and primarily the *meaning* of the whole.

In this way Israel discovered meaning in history: God guaranteed Israel's significance. But, as we know from Israel's canonical writings, the people of God did not isolate their history from that of any other people. Thus for us too, with this meaningful coherent biblical framework, there should be no question of dividing history or marginalizing vast tracts of it.

I have already attempted to describe my impression and understanding of the outline of history. Human rebellion against God and attempts at self-sufficiency mark the one persistently negative historical trend. God's redemptive purpose marks the one positive movement in history. To the degree that there has been submission and response to the Redeemer, there has been enrichment of relationships, growth of community, and a different handling of the other sources of power. But still, at many points in history, the negative has threatened to destroy the positive and chaos has threatened to engulf community.

It is at one such moment in history, when this threat is again gathering strength, that we are living our lives. Both salvation and judgment appear closer than we first believed.

Directed by a Divine Wisdom

Living as we do at a time of deepening crisis, there is a special urgency that we be able to summon adequate resources of wisdom. But just when this is most crucially important, it is also most exceptionally difficult. Turbulence increases confusion. Even so, we were right to read our biblical historical map and attempt to plot our position on it. In our study the sharp lines of good and evil are obscured on the one hand by repeated compromise with sin on the part of God's people, and on the other by the creation virtues retained by those who profess no allegiance to the Creator. All the more reason then to ask for wisdom to discern the good and perfect way of God.

Biblical wisdom is not like Greek wisdom: it is not abstract, academic, dualistic, and elitist. Biblical wisdom is concerned with daily living and is learned in the experiences of daily life. It informs and guides the making of workable plans and even inspires appropriate technology (see Isa. 28:23-29). It is competent to deal with the immediate things and the ultimate things as well. The key to its versatility and authority is that it is centered upon the Creator who is at work redemptively in his creation.

God, as he is revealed in Christ, is the source of wisdom. Christ *is* our wisdom. Acknowledgment and respect for God are thus the beginning of wisdom for his creatures. Thus true wisdom cannot be separated from dependence upon God; without God we have only foolishness.

With the help of God's wisdom we are freed from pessimism in a darkened period of history. Regrettably, eschatological theories seem to have been influenced by reaction to world trends as much as by discernment of the Spirit of wisdom. For example, pessimistic premillennialism appears to underestimate the good things that God is prepared to do in the present age. A biblically balanced wisdom, in contrast, increases our anticipation of the good that God will do; it also gives us the strength to endure what Satan will do. Thus a balanced biblical wisdom encompasses both vision and realism. It guides a widespread transformation of society radiating from a revived and vigorous church.

In observing the scope of biblical wisdom, we have already noted that it includes very practical things within its area of concern. Nothing is too big or too small to be shaped and directed by wisdom: development is no exception to this rule. Wisdom provides the means to discern the true qualities of a developed society. Wisdom also helps to define the goal of social transformation: what sort of society are we trying to create? A biblically based development or social transformation should reflect the characteristics of the messianic kingdom of wisdom and peace.

Notice that these familiar characteristics interact in a dynamic way, because they are energized by God's Spirit:

> The Spirit is poured upon us from on high, and the wilderness becomes a fruitful field, and the fruitful field is deemed a forest. Then justice will dwell in the wilderness, and righteousness abide in the fruitful field. And the effect of righteousness will be peace, and the result of righteousness, quietness and trust for ever. My people will abide in a peaceful habitation, in secure dwellings, and in quiet resting places. (Isa. 32:15-18)

We should therefore look for spiritual renewal, social justice, material productivity, and peaceful settlement together and not separately. If we add to our vision of social transformation the prophecies of swords beaten into ploughshares and the leopard lying down with the kid, then we can include disarmament and ecological harmony in our list of fruits of the transformed earth.

Furthermore, the hills will break forth into singing, the trees will clap their hands, thanksgiving and the voice of song will be heard in the reclaimed desert. The renewal of society will evoke worship in the Spirit.

How can we wisely apply this sunlit vision to the urban decay, rural poverty, and international tension of the world we live in? We obviously need to interiorize and appropriate for ourselves the values of the messianic society. We then need to distinguish these values from any conflicting vision of prosperity. For instance, the modest extent of distributed ownership suggested by "every man under his vine and under his fig tree" is very different both from unbridled capitalism and totalitarian communism. But how do you bridle capitalism, especially in relation to land tenure, something that has a particularly important bearing on development? In his study *Land and Power in South America* Sven Lindquist points out that the owner of a large estate is often in effect shopkeeper, policeman, member of parliament, and judge, as well as employer and landlord to his workers. Such a concentration of power can easily be abused. A biblical wisdom would seek a more equal sharing of power, as well as a fairer distribution of wealth. But how do we do this?

The difficulty of distributing power, land, or wealth by whatever means highlights another point. The messianic society is not the utopian society, but neither is progress toward it impossible. The biblical vision can neither be dismissed as unworkable nor be implemented mechanically or ideologically. While a political system and a framework of laws can help or hinder compassion, a hallmark of the messianic society, they cannot of themselves generate it. Even so, the political and legal options cannot be a matter of indifference. The better option needs to be identified through consecrated and rigorous examination.

The failure of the church in relation to the world raises a question that cannot be postponed further. Is God's wise purpose for the church the same as his purpose for the world, or indeed for the whole creation? Does God have a plan for the secular world that is wider than, different from, or even unrelated to his plan for the church? In response I will make just three comments. First, a recurring summary of God's purpose presented in Scripture is: "I will be your God and you shall be my people." That this declaration stands alone does not of course preclude any other purpose that God may have for his creation. It is, however, a prominent and even central biblical statement.

Second, the epistle to the Ephesians speaks of God's purpose in universal and cosmic terms: "a plan for the fulness of time, to unite all things in Christ, things in heaven and things on earth." It is "according to the eternal purpose," Paul affirms, "that *through the church* the manifold wisdom of God might now be made known to the principalities and powers in the heavenly places." More remarkable still, the apostle declares that "God has put all things under Christ's feet and has made him head over all things *for the church*."

Third, if God's purpose has to do with unity and community, then both relate essentially and necessarily to himself. He is the Father, "from whom every family in heaven and earth is named." Community cut off from the father of community can only wither.

I conclude therefore that God's redemptive purpose for secular society must at its heart involve a restoration of our relationship with God as our Father. Restoration of community without renewal of this fundamental relationship would seem in the final analysis impossible. God sets before his small but faithful Philadelphian church an open door. His purpose for the vast world outside that open door is not unrelated to his purpose for the little congregation. It is a creative purpose and an evangelical purpose. A biblical balance and wisdom keep us from restricting God's plan to the confines of an institutional church; at the same time they also prevent us from wrongly separating his purpose for the world from the community of the redeemed, both actual and potential. God-informed wisdom thus defines the good into which society should be transformed. It correctly relates God's wide purpose to his concentrated purpose in the community of the church.

Wisdom has many more tasks besides. It must evaluate different expressions of human culture and in so doing separate their creative and destructive elements. There would sometimes appear to be a serious lack of wisdom in the way Christians of different traditions make their estimates. Radicals recognize the evil powers in Latin American culture only in relation to its oppressive capitalism. Reactionaries recognize Satan only in the oppressive spiritism. Has the Devil outwitted both Christian extremes? Clearly we need some balance here.

Finally, wisdom must relate the temporal to the eternal. The nineteenth-century Christian may have been acutely aware of the eternal plight of human beings but much less sensitive to their temporal condition. The burden of Christian conscience in our own time is likely to have an exactly opposite bias. The correction of these imbalances surely involves sympathy toward all human anguish—both of the materially deprived and of the spiritually alienated. Wisdom helps us learn this double sympathy, but it also leads us to attempt some differentiation of values. Paul does not hesitate to advise the Colossians: "Set your minds on things that are above, not on things that are on earth." Paul's faith here is a pilgrim faith; his roots and his ambitions are transferred to the new creation (as yet invisible) and rest more lightly (though still responsibly) in the old. In the last days, as the crises that surround us intensify, Christians must seek ever more wisdom to apply our scarce resources to the most urgent goals.

Expanded by Substantial Hope

Jeremiah, the prophet of doom, learned to call God "Thou Hope of Israel." He had been taught, through the loneliness of his ministry, how precious a thing it is to enjoy personal communion with his Lord. Even more remarkably, in the midst of apostasy, judgment, and disaster, he gained a vision of hope.

This brings us back to the similar state of our own position in history. We live at a time of impending judgment. We face the incomprehensible succession of calamities that the writer of Revelation wept over: war, genocide, scarcity, natural disaster, persecution, and death. These recur in history to such a degree as to threaten its meaning.

Yet this is also a time of hope. Now, "the Lamb who was slain" can break open the seals of significance. Clearly, however, this biblical hope is vastly different from other optimistic philosophies and ideologies; it is the only true ground for our lives. If we leave our theory and practice of development with their underlying assumptions of progress or evolution unchallenged, then we are indulging in false hope. Development must be chastened and corrected by God's judgment if it is to relate positively to the coming kingdom.

It is not enough, however, to mark the distinctiveness of biblical hope. We must also celebrate its greatness. Hope from God bursts our circle of experience wide open, and it promises us "what eye has not seen" and what "has not entered the heart of man." Hope is fulfilled in the new, perfectly integrated creation. Humanity's sphere, earth, loses its distance from the angelic sphere, heaven. All God's reconciled and obedient creatures enjoy his immediate presence and are bathed in the light of his glory.

I write this not on a day when the trumpets are sounding or when Christ is coming publicly to announce the new age, but on a day when the newspapers feature the corpses of Palestinians massacred in West Beirut. How can we focus at the same time on both the horrors of the immediate present and also the glories of the ultimate future? We must remember that against all appearances our present hope is securely anchored in eternity (Heb. 6:19). This is of course a resurrection hope. Because of this, death is not a full stop but a colon: what comes after it amplifies and explains what has gone before. There is a transformation but also a continuity. The individual who has been raised is not some other person but the same person.

Resurrection is always more than an individual affair, however. As George Knight states, "the hope which Israel entertained was the hope of resurrection not merely of some in Israel, or even of all mankind, but the hope of a final consummation of a resurrection of all creation." This being so, there will be a continuity of existence on a scale perhaps rarely considered. We are so conditioned by transience that we may be surprised at the extent of the continuity of the resurrection, by the permanence of creation. It may be helpful to think of continuity and even discontinuity in terms of God's memory. What the eternal God remembers must have a place in eternity, but what he forgets will pass away. He graciously chooses to forget the sins of the redeemed, but he remembers every good, and even every apparently neutral, detail in his creation (see, e.g., Matt. 10:30). God's good creation will most assuredly be renewed. I would conclude that the things we humans create in agreement with God's creativity will also be renewed and will also gain an eternal significance. "The kings of the earth shall bring their glory" (Rev. 21:24), "preserving in the new order," as Bruce Milne says, "all that has been true and righteous and God honouring in the old." This truth greatly increases the value and meaning of all that we do in harmony with our Creator; in that respect it enhances development also.

If the scale of the future resurrection widens our hope, then the fact of achieved resurrection intensifies our hope. Christ's resurrection anticipates the general resurrection and is of a piece with it. Christ's miracles are signs of the resurrection kingdom and, as such, signs of hope. When Jesus promised that his followers would do "greater works," he was surely asserting that these signs of hope would continue and even increase. To be effective signs, their character must reflect the qualities of the eternal kingdom. Even development that only imperfectly represents the kingdom of peace serves to announce that kingdom and helps, though fractionally, to usher it in.

Hope beyond history is boundless and exulting; it surveys a glorious prospect. Hope within history can hold the line in the most desperate battle, and with the aid of the hope beyond history it is always ready to advance. This positive hope was expressed by the Puritans, whose vision was enlarged by the promises of Scripture. In particular they were looking for the conversion of the Jews and the widespread acceptance of the gospel among all nations. They also believed that spiritual renewal would penetrate society, that the salt would preserve the perishable, and that the leaven would raise the lump.

Hope needs to work its good work in the modern church. Meanwhile advice given by John Calvin to a different generation speaks to us still: "Let us hope boldly, then, more than we can understand; Our Lord will still surpass our opinion and our hope."

Applied through a Vigorous Mission

All things biblical have a dynamic quality. Biblical wisdom does even more than identify good and worthwhile goals; it provides ways and means of achieving them. This wisdom is inspirational and so is biblical hope.

Let's go further and say that biblical renewal ignites an explosion of creativity. The new experience of God's power makes the impossible seem possible. The healing of the cross cuts people free from the old morbidity. Sharpened faculties excitedly explore a world newly transparent to the glories of its Creator. Perhaps *explosion* in this context is a misleading word, though. It rightly gives the impression of a great release of power, but it also suggests its rapid dissipation. Christian action in the world could more accurately be described as an even burning that continues to release its power and light over time.

In Scripture hope is suggestively linked with patience and is significantly associated with love. With this in mind, it is clear that one form that Christian action must take in the world is patient building—an unspectacular brick by brick, inch by inch process. One more pastoral visit, one more mother and baby clinic, one more cooperative decision hammered out, one more sack of potatoes sold, one more broken pane of glass repaired. Let us never lose sight of the ultimate significance of such gradual action. While "one more" may seem only an inconsequential increment more, and while daily tasks may seem dwarfed into insignificance by the vast scale of what needs to be achieved, these small actions are nonetheless the building blocks of God's dwelling. Such patient building is adaptive and ingenious. It takes notice of the cultural and political contours of the terrain. It doesn't bring in an ideological bulldozer to lay it all flat.

It may be worth adding the point that this patient building is not to be limited to Christian action at a local level only. Tackling global issues requires the same undespairing patience. A letter to a member of parliament and a signature on a petition may seem only tiny drops in a vast ocean, but true Christian hope cannot be paralyzed by these comparisons.

This constructive drudgery of biblical action in the world—this patient building—is a necessary contribution but, by itself, not a sufficient one. While this building adds gradually to the powers of growth, we also need some action that will multiply the powers of growth.

I find in the letter of James an arresting statement that indicates what this fruitful kind of action may be: "The harvest of righteousness is sown in peace by those who make peace." I personally find it very helpful to think of biblically informed and Spirit-inspired action in the world as the sowing of peace, an activity that relates especially to evangelism and community education. What is sown might be a spoken word, a written word, or an incarnate word. If, in whatever way, it mediates the life-giving Word, then its potential is vastly greater than its initial size or importance may suggest. Currently many of us place great emphasis on political and economic structures in the quest for social transformation. According to this thinking, bad structures are closely identified with oppression and good structures promise liberation. But granted that structures are by no means neutral in their effects, doesn't this approach attribute to them a dynamism in their nature that they do not possess? Therefore, when we seek to sow peace in the world, let us remember that both capitalistic and socialistic systems may prove stony soil and that the true life of peace is in the seed.

Sowing as used in the Bible serves as a metaphor not only for the multiplication of the powers of growth but also as a metaphor for wholly new life growing out of death. The seed that falls into the ground and dies speaks primarily of Christ and his cross, but it also gives meaning to the suffering and apparent failure of those who act in Christ's name—it lets us know that all is not in vain.

The Bible tells us not only about the seed that dies and eventually bears fruit but also about the seed that is never buried; instead it falls on the hard pathway and is devoured by voracious birds. The reference here, according to the Gospel interpretation, is to satanic interference. Both sowing and building are peaceful occupations, but it is scarcely possible to make peace with Satan, the enemy of all good. The Old Testament picture of building with sword in hand (Neh. 4:13-18) may help here. Peaceful building and sowing must be accompanied by dogged fighting.

The controversy about violence and which weapons are legitimate in this warfare is well rehearsed. Could I plead for the recognition, however, that evil powers possess individual people as well as political systems. Exorcism, prevailing prayer, testimony prompted by the Holy Spirit, identification with the defenseless—these are all the normal ingredients of the Christian struggle. True it is that the struggle often appears to be at "the last ditch."

Yet whether the struggle is at the last ditch or on the point of some great victory, it must be consistently pursued alongside building and sowing as part of the necessary human action in response to God's redemptive purpose. Repentance and faith are written across God's plans for the restoration of all his children. The actors with a positive role in the redemptive transformation of society are those who are Christian believers and those who are in the process of coming to faith.

I would like to identify holistic evangelism with human action in response to the eschatological vision. By definition, this kind of gospeling brings together the spoken *message* of hope, the compassionate *actions* of hope, the selfless *service* of the needy, and the Christian *nurturing* of the reborn. If Christian participation in development does not adequately relate to the messianic kingdom, it will share the frustration and failure of all development apart from Christ. Approaches such as "people participation," though excellent in themselves, can never compensate on their own for their lack of reconciliation with Christ the Redeemer. Development is not advanced by abbreviating the gospel to its this-worldly dimension alone; and neither is discipling advanced by abbreviating the gospel to its otherworldly dimension alone. It is not a true evangelism that shows little care for social misery and that relies too much on the word pronounced from afar and too little on the word that lives and suffers alongside those who need both to hear and see it.

As a staff member of a missionary organization, I have to say that such organizations share the blame for abbreviating the full mission task. Half are dedicated to discipling, with a nodding assent to social action; and half are committed to relief and development, with an anxious thought spared for the issues of eternity. It is often economic pressures that force us into these divergent groupings, but the net result is that none of us bears witness as we should to the totality of mission.

What is needed then is a high view of mission, a passionate commitment to its advance, and a structuring that unites rather than divides its temporal and eternal goals. In a world in which three thousand million people make no Christian profession, the size and urgency of the eternal issue may daunt believers; but they must realize that no other human agency except the church will bring the good news of eternal life in Christ to these masses. In the face of the corresponding weight of temporal need and physical distress, the church must be careful not to underestimate its responsibility. Governments and government agencies are effectively ignoring some of the most serious global issues. Their bland response to the report of the Brandt Commission betrays their refusal to commit themselves to any undertaking on the behalf of the poor that they deem politically inexpedient and costly. That must never be the response of the church. We, who have pioneered hospitals and schools, will have to take entirely new and major social initiatives. Who else will care for the needs of the millions on the margins of society? Because secular education has other priorities, why should we not found open universities of Christian education to begin to equip people to tackle global issues such as these?

To talk in ambitious terms about what the church must and might do smacks somewhat of triumphalism. We need to keep returning to the gradualism of the "building," the "sowing," and the "fighting." But humble steps do not preclude a giant stride. The powerful Spirit of God may yet provoke that burst of creativity and compassion that could bring temporal as well as eternal hope to the world.

Evangelism and Social Transformation

Tite Tienou

Introduction

We live in a time of inflation. Besides the monetary kind, there is an inflation of words and meetings. Just as the things we buy cost more and more money, all these words and meetings take up more and more of our time. For many of us, the temptation is great to call for a moratorium: let us stop talking and start doing! We feel this temptation particularly in the area of evangelism and social concerns.

Those who participated in the International Congress on World Evangelization in Lausanne in 1974 paid a great deal of honest attention to this matter, and since then evangelicals have been called to reflect on the issue and also to act appropriately. One concrete accomplishment of the conference at Lausanne was the Lausanne Covenant, which deals directly with "the nature of evangelism" and "Christian social responsibility." The covenant states that

> to evangelize is to spread the good news that Jesus Christ died for our sins and was raised from the dead according to the Scriptures, and that as the reigning Lord he now offers the forgiveness of sins and the liberating gift of the Spirit to all who repent and believe.... The results of evangelism include obedience to Christ, incorporation into His church, and responsible service in the world....[1]
>
> Although reconciliation with man is not reconciliation with God, nor is social action evangelism, nor is political liberation salvation, nevertheless we affirm that evangelism and socio-political involvement are both part of our Christian duty.... When people receive Christ they are born again into His kingdom and must seek not only to exhibit, but also to spread, righteousness in the midst of an unrighteous world. The salvation we claim should be transforming us in the totality of our personal and social responsibilities.[2]

But while the covenant obviously advocates a link between evangelism and social transformation—following the belief of Christians throughout the ages that the results of evangelism should be "translated" into society—it does not clarify the nature of that link.

In June 1982, another consultation was held, the Consultation on the Relationship between Evangelism and Social Responsibility, held in Grand Rapids, Michigan. From this conference came the Grand Rapids Report, a joint publication of the Lausanne Committee for World Evangelization and the World Evangelical Fellowship. As is clear from the name of the consultation, a primary aim of the meetings in Grand Rapids was to clarify what was left unclear in Lausanne—to formulate an evangelical understanding of the link between evangelism and social responsibility.

Because a contemporary evangelical response cannot be clarified without an understanding of what has gone before, the authors of the report give, in the fourth section, an outline of the historical understanding of the relationship between evangelism and social action.[3] They then discuss three ways in which Christians can be involved in social action as an adjunct to the task of evangelism. First of all, social action is the natural outgrowth of the conversion to faith in Christ: as "a consequence of evangelism . . . God brings people to new birth, and their new life manifests itself in the service of others." Second, social action can also further the cause of evangelism: it can serve as "a bridge to evangelism. It can break down prejudice and suspicion, open closed doors, and gain a hearing for the Gospel." And third, social action can serve as a partner to evangelism: the two must work hand in hand to further true transformation in the mission of God.[4]

The Social Implications of Evangelism

This brief background provides the perspective necessary for several more comments on evangelism and social transformation. We should never act as if we were the first to discover that evangelism and social transformation each draw on and have implications for the other. I noted earlier that Christians throughout history have believed that the results of evangelism should be translated into the life of society. And we know that long before the Christian era, the Old Testament proclaimed God's great concern with the social life of his people Israel.

John the Baptist, whom we might call the first evangelist, preached the gospel in terms of social implications. His was a spiritual ministry: "preaching a baptism of repentance for the forgiveness of sins" (Luke 3:3). But it was also a social ministry: the salvation of God will be shown to society in social terms. This is why Luke, after describing this spiritual ministry, quotes from Isaiah (Luke 3:4-6). The paths made straight, the valleys filled, the mountains brought low, the crooked made straight, and the rough ways made smooth all speak of the restoration of justice in the land, a concrete, social implication of the preaching of the gospel. That is the salvation of God. John emphasized that repentance is made real by the fruits it bears. Forgiveness is not just a way of "escaping the wrath to come." Nor does it allow one to escape the world here and now. Every forgiven person has the responsibility to "bear fruits that befit repentance," for "every tree . . . that does not bear good fruit is cut down and thrown into the fire" (Luke 3:8-9).

On seeing the necessity for repentance and the implications of the failure to repent, people ask "What shall we do?" (Luke 3:10). John's reply has two integral parts. There must be "repentance for the forgiveness of sins," but this is always coupled with the demand for "fruits" or concrete signs of transformation. Repentant and forgiven people should be merciful and kind to those in need around them (Luke 3:11). They should show the change wrought in them by righting the specific wrongs of which they had been guilty: tax collectors should not collect more than their due, and soldiers should not extort money or accuse others falsely (Luke 3:12-14).

John the Baptist was by no means the only one who preached the social implications of God's good news. The same ideas run throughout the whole New Testament. Whether people are intuitively aware of what is demanded of them, like Zacchaeus (Luke 19), or whether they have to be admonished by an apostle (see the explicit words at Phil. 4:8 and 2 Thess. 3:10-13), the teaching is clear: evangelism aims for total transformation, personal and social. Justice in society and the land is a natural and necessary result of spiritual transformation.

Forgiveness and Personal and Social Sins

It is just as difficult to separate personal from social sins as it is to discriminate between the so-called private and public life of a person. Everything we do has social implications: the sin that takes root inside of us reveals itself outwardly. Jesus uses the same metaphor used by John the Baptist when he says that a tree is known by its fruit. But while John spoke of the fruits of repentance, which are good deeds, Jesus extends the metaphor to include the fruits of evil as well. James too describes the process of our sinfulness when he says that desire is born in the heart. "Then desire when it has conceived gives birth to sin; and sin when it is full-grown brings forth death" (James 1:15). The message is the same: sin germinates inside, infects the person, and spills over to others.

Nowhere is sin shown as both personal and corporate as clearly as in the story of Achan (Josh. 7). His hidden disobedience is Israel's unfaithfulness, and it thus is reason enough for God's anger to reach the entire nation. Peace and harmony can be reestablished within Israel and between God and Israel only by removing the evil one from the people's midst. This is entirely in keeping with the oft-repeated command, "You shall purge the evil from the midst of you" (see Deut. 22-24). In New Testament times, too, personal sin was able to infect the community. The sin of Ananias and Sapphira was certainly personal; yet they had to die so as to purge the evil from the congregation (Acts 5). Again, Paul's amazement at the Corinthian church's tolerance of immorality (1 Cor. 5:2) shows that the Bible has no category for personal sin without a social dimension. The sin of a few members is always the concern of the entire congregation. They should have removed the evildoer from their midst because by tolerating the sin they too shared in it and in its consequences.

It is nearly impossible for Christians to agree on the nature of the "social sins" of their immediate contexts. It is even more difficult when the social sins are global in their impact. But the biblical data warrant the definition of social sins as any action or thought that violates the rights of others to the good that they are entitled to. My social sins are those things that I do, or my indifference to wrong, that reduces someone else's dignity before God. If I am transformed through an encounter with God and forgiven of my sins, my highest priority should then be to restore others—those whom I have wronged myself and also any others who have been wronged—to their full dignity by proclaiming the gospel and promoting justice in society.

Thus forgiveness too has both personal and social dimensions. As we turn to the living God we are not instantly made aware of all of our sins. Instead, as we continue to progress in the Christian way we continue to be made aware of our sins and we should continue to repent. Forgiveness can only follow this realization that we continue in our sins, even when we desire not to. So forgiveness cannot be privatized and interiorized: it has social effects. It must show that as we continue to sin we also continue to try to heal the wounds created by our wrongs. Christ's death and resurrection bring forgiveness of both personal and social sins, but in both cases we have to show evidence by our fruits that we have truly repented and have experienced salvation and forgiveness.

The Proclamation of the Gospel

At the very heart of social transformation is the proclamation of the gospel. Proclamation, of course, is a matter of both word and deed. Precisely because they believed the gospel to be relevant and true, the messengers of God's good news have almost always been concerned with bringing justice to the land. Thus the aim of the good news, as both God and his people speak it, is to call people to reconciliation with God through Christ, which demands both repentance and action. Reconciliation with the God of justice will often result in a dissatisfaction with the status quo. Though we know that full justice and redemption are not possible in this world, our reconciliation with God is sufficient ground for challenging the status quo to promote the good of neighbor, community, and world. Far from being merely a promise of "pie in the sky by and by," this is a recognition that as long as we live in this world we cannot but concern ourselves with the affairs of society.

The Social Effects of the Proclamation of the Gospel

The very presence of the church in society is the beginning of social transformation: a move toward justice. The church is the light and salt of the earth. The community of disciples is a sign of the righteous kingdom of God in this world of unrighteousness. But the church in this world has not always lived up to its responsibilities and its own proclamation. It has not always been an agent of social transformation. In many places, in fact, churches are agents of repression, and those who profess themselves to be Christians show themselves to be no more, or even less, moral than non-Christians. But when the church is truly salt and light, then its fruits can be seen by all. The social effects of its gospel proclamation do not depend on its numerical strength but spring forth from the quality of its life, and its refusal to be monopolized by any part of society proves to all this is the true community of the ruler of the universe.

We all know that a perfect community is impossible on this earth before the return of the Lord. Corruption and all forms of wickedness are rampant even in countries that are filled with Evangelical Christians witnessing to Christ. But let this not be cause for us to resign ourselves to the triumph of evil, or, even worse, to a "Christian" promotion of evil. Rather this should be cause for us to renew our efforts, for our proclamation of the gospel will not bring transformation to society if people do not see that transformation bearing fruit first in the community of faith (see Phil. 4:8 and 1 Tim. 3).

Conclusion

Evangelism and social transformation are two sides of the same coin. While there can be social transformation apart from evangelism, there is normally no evangelism that does not result in social transformation. Social transformation is part of the message of and a natural outgrowth of evangelism. And it is a mark of the truth of the witness, for it will likely not take place through a dead evangelism: evangelism will likely not result in social transformation unless the church and the Christian community witness by their lifestyles that they have already been transformed. If we really mean business, let us deflate our empty words and inflate our actions: let us "bear fruits that befit repentance" and work for justice in the land.

Notes

1. See the Lausanne Covenant (Lausanne Committee for World Evangelization, 1974), paragraph 4. The covenant has been published in many places; see, for one instance, John Stott, *The Lausanne Covenant: An Exposition and Commentary* (Minneapolis: World Wide Publications, 1974).

2. Lausanne Covenant, paragraph 5.

3. "Evangelism and Social Responsibility: An Evangelical Commitment," the Grand Rapids Report (from the Consultation on the Relationship between Evangelism and Social Responsibility held in Grand Rapids in 1982), Lausanne Occasional Papers no. 21 (Lausanne Committee for World Evangelization, 1982), section 4, paragraph (a).

4. "Evangelism and Social Responsibility," section 4, paragraph (c).

Toward Evangelism in Context

David J. Bosch

Transformation involves much more than just outward or superficial change; it is more accurately a change in the very nature and character of something.[1] To characterize a particular sort of transformation, social transformation, and then to link it with evangelism is to suggest that there is an intimate relationship between evangelism and change in the nature and character—the very fabric—of society.

The Early Church: Evangelism from the Periphery

Transformation has been a part of the Christian mission and influence in society right from the beginning. In a society described as "macabre, lost in despair, perversion, and superstition,"[2] Christian communities emerged as something entirely new in the populous and far-flung Roman Empire. A tiny minority, they shone "as lights in the world," as communities of "children of God without blemish in the midst of a crooked and perverse generation" (Phil. 2:15).

The early church was on the periphery of society. It found many of its earliest adherents among slaves, women, and foreigners—people who had no special influence on the shape of society. It was held in contempt by the reigning philosophical and religious systems.[3] And everywhere in the early years it had to struggle against overwhelming odds under frequent persecution. So Christians did not expect to transform the social fabric of a powerful empire. It was hard enough even to hold their own. Yet although the Christian influence in society in those early years of persecution was subtle and often unrecognized, it was to provide a true transformation over the next two millennia.

Christianity began by preaching and practicing the "gospel of love and charity,"[4] which included almsgiving and care for widows, orphans, slaves, travelers, the sick, the imprisoned, and the poor. Over the course of the centuries this practical charity led to the universal health services and education that we now take for granted. Thus the Christian faith became a leaven in society: women eventually gained greater status, and even slavery succumbed in the end. That this took almost nineteen centuries was not because the gospel was unclear on its attitude toward slavery but because Christians had hardened their hearts to God's will and brought blindness upon themselves.

The Church without Privileges

The socially transforming dimension of the early church's evangelism was unintentional or at least indirect. Though many Christians sought to right wrongs where they could, to confront the structures of society head-on would have been impossible because those who shaped society did not share the Christians' presuppositions. We may note several modern parallels—in China, some other Communist countries, and some Muslim ones as well—in which the church may operate as an almost-silent antibody, unobtrusively undermining the status quo and always keeping alive the smoldering wick of hope.[5] The church prepares for a new role in a changed future society. This is the church without privileges.

In such situations, the kind of evangelism that has developed in the Western world during the past two centuries is unworkable. This evangelism requires the open proclamation of the message of God, but in many of the societies where the church is without privileges this is simply impossible. For example, Father Jean Kermarrec, a Roman Catholic missionary in South Vietnam, described how he prepared his congregation for Christian life and witness under a Vietcong takeover.[6] Foreseeing that the Vietcong would destroy all visible vestiges of the church, he and his parishioners themselves deliberately destroyed their chapels, church buildings, crucifixes, lists of names, prayer books, crosses, church bells, rosaries, pictures, altars, and cassocks. Though his church could no longer exist as a visible and public community, he taught his people that all the signs of the church could still survive invisibly where believers live, work, weep, and bleed.

All peripheral, exterior, and incidental things were to fall away. Even an invisible way of crossing oneself was to be adopted. "A drop of Christ's blood drops on my forehead. It enlightens my thoughts and I say, 'In the Name of the Father.' That drop of blood trickles down to my heart to kindle love, also for my enemy; I continue, 'In the Name of the Son.' It goes from my heart to both my shoulders to give them strength to carry their cross. I conclude: 'and in the Name of the Holy Spirit.'" In this way, Father Kermarrec prepared his flock for life in the desert, where they would have only an invisible shepherd to guide them. Evangelism has not ceased in such situations. It differs radically from Western radio and television evangelism, from evangelistic crusades and so on, but it is genuine evangelism nonetheless. Indeed, silent witness may be more eloquent in certain circumstances than amplified rhetoric.

Until well into the twentieth century, most churches occupied a privileged sector of public life in which they had freedom of action and belief. But now, many churches have lost those privileges; they can no longer take for granted that they will be promoted or even protected by society. When a church loses its props and privileges through social circumstances beyond its control, it faces two temptations. It may either withdraw into a ghetto for self-preservation, or it may seek to become the official religious arm of the new regime, thus regaining a position of semi-establishment.

It is difficult to remain a church without privileges for long. It is easier to fall prey to one of the two temptations, to sell out to expediency or to power, both of which are concessions and adaptations to the world. The challenge is to go on operating as an antibody, silently dissenting from the values of the world and challenging society, becoming a consistent sign of hope not only to Christians but also to those outside the church.

Even the threat of martyrdom cannot succeed in wiping out that hope, and consequently it has never been one of the greater threats to the church's survival. As Tertullian of North Africa wrote to persecutors of Christians in the third century, "You achieve nothing by your ever more refined techniques of cruelty; they become simply the bait that entices people to the church. As often as you mow us down, we multiply; the blood of the martyrs is the seed of the church."

We do not know how the church's situation may change in coming decades. But one major task in some parts of the world will undoubtedly be to teach our Christian communities, not how to speak, but how to be silent effectively. That is, we must teach Christians how they may be effective in evangelism by not speaking, by remaining silent and yet proclaiming through their actions and attitudes the hope they have inside them. Just because a church has lost its privileged status in society does not mean that it has lost its ability to witness. In fact, in times of persecution and suffering the real issues become crystal clear. But when the church is a privileged partner in society the issues become blurred and the essence of the gospel is watered down. Thus the church in the catacombs is truer to the name church than the church in the palaces and the houses of parliament is.

Let no one think that we should masochistically work for or even desire persecution. Far from it! But we should take the church without privileges as our point of reference to help us define what the real issues are. The New Testament church was one such church without privileges, and unless we recognize this practically we may fall into the trap of seeing it in terms of our own society and molding it in our minds into the form of our own church which is tolerated, or perhaps even valued, as a (somewhat boring) aspect of public life.

Our Eschatologies

The main area of difference among evangelicals about the relation of evangelism and social responsibility lies in the area of eschatology.[7] Some Christians have taken the view that the kingdom of God is an entirely future reality and that the supreme task of any Christian is to do his or her share so that others may be saved eternally. A saved person may indeed have some responsibilities in the world, including in the area of justice, but these responsibilities are merely the *result* of the fact that he or she is now saved eternally.[8] To expect salvation only from the future, however, is essentially pre-Christian, for this understanding of eschatology is closer to Jewish apocalyptic than to the spirit of the New Testament. A pessimistic view of history is essential to this kind of eschatology: the world is evil and the present is empty. The past is a golden era for which people yearn nostalgically and which will be superseded in a future that will bear no relationship to the dreary present. Evil and injustice are thus to be tolerated now since they show the lateness of the hour and are signs of Christ's imminent return.

Although there certainly is a future component to salvation, a true Christian eschatology cannot relegate all of salvation to the future. Christ has cleft that future in two and has made part of it already real and present. Because in Christ the forces of the coming age have flowed into the present, we cannot proclaim merely a future salvation. Our evangelism must take account that we live on the basis of the salvation that is "already," en route to that which is still "not yet."[9]

The early Christians based their belief that the future has invaded the present on two events: the resurrection of Christ and the coming of the Spirit. These two events were experienced in the New Testament as the firstfruits of the harvest and the guarantee of what is to come, that is, the Resurrection and the events of Pentecost were a first installment and the promise of a full settlement (see 1 Cor. 15:20, 23; 2 Cor. 1:22; 5:5; Eph. 1:14). Their message was that the old order has passed, and the new has already begun (2 Cor. 5:17). The Resurrection and the presence of the Spirit were clear signs to the early Christians that it made sense to live *already* according to the standards of the coming age. The new creation is "promised in Christ, pledged in his resurrection, present in foretaste through the Spirit."[10]

Our Understanding of Salvation

For many of us, salvation is purely personal and religious. It is a reality now for individual souls who are saved from the world, like survivors rescued from a sinking ship. We hold on to one another in an uncomfortable little lifeboat, with no relation to the sea around us other than searching it for other survivors who could be saved from the perils of the sea. This approach, in its depiction of salvation as a rescue *from* the world, falls short in its understanding of sin and salvation.[11] In the Bible, salvation is intimately related to creation: it cannot be isolated from "secular" history, because it is always aimed at overcoming sin, which (whether personal or structural) is the great disorder within this world that tries to frustrate the work of God. Salvation, then, is a sort of re-creation that regains control of God's great plan.[12]

Sin and evil bring sickness of mind and body, demon-possession, lack of love for God, wrong words and deeds and the absence of right ones, loveless self-righteousness in the pious, hypocrisy in ecclesiastics, maintenance of special class privileges, abuse of authority, unjust distribution of the burden of taxation, exploitation of the masses, selfishness, and self-destruction. But Jesus came to reverse all this evil and its further evil effects. In Luke 4 he quoted from the prophecy of Isaiah (61:1-2) and proclaimed that he had come to fulfill it. In doing so he gave us, as E. Stanley Jones said, the agenda for evangelism. Even as he did, we are to preach "good news to the poor (that is, the economically disinherited) . . . release to the captives (the socially and politically disinherited) . . . [and] recovering of sight to the blind (the physically disinherited)." We are "to set at liberty those who are oppressed (the morally and spiritually disinherited) . . . [and] to proclaim the acceptable year of the Lord (a new beginning on a world scale)."[13]

In the Old Testament, the reversal of such personal and structural maladies is all wrapped up in the concept of *shalom,* or peace; in the New Testament the corresponding concept is God's *basileia,* his kingdom. God offers his people new life, both now and in eternity, and he gives the assurance that salvation will culminate in the fullness of the kingdom: a wholly new order of life characterized by love, freedom, justice, and peace.

To offer the assurance of personal salvation in Christ is therefore only part of evangelism. If this part is seen as the whole, the gospel is dissociated from the world and the incarnation of Christian faith is denied. The gospel so proclaimed then contains "an other-worldly kingdom, a private, inwardly limited Spirit, a pocket God, a spiritualized Bible, and an escapist church. . . . Such a gospel makes possible the 'conversion' of men and women without [their] having to make any drastic changes in their life-style and value-systems."[14] On the other hand, we know all good structural changes taken together fall short of the kingdom. So even if a vision of the heavenly polis (Augustine's City of God) demands us to include politics and structures in our understanding of salvation, we know that we cannot wholly succeed and that those structures are doomed to decay and dissolution.

For this reason we will show no *ultimate* concern for them, perishable as they are.[15] We know that the new order announced by the gospel will not be exhausted by historical structures. We must never replace the hope of a new creation with the hope of an earthly utopia. And our discussion of salvation must never focus exclusively on social salvation, since that would leave untouched the personal root of sin.[16] Our concept of salvation must include both the personal spiritual aspect and also the social concrete aspect, and it must emphasize neither to the detriment of the other. We must reject a gospel that is ultimately spiritualized to such an extent that it does not touch reality, but also one that has been secularized to the point that there is no call to repentance and no relationship with God above.

Present Ideas of Evangelism

Against the background of what has been said so far, we may now examine various views on evangelism, particularly as it relates to social transformation. Some people evangelize for the sake of the expansion of their own church—even when it comes at the expense of other churches. They see the church (or perhaps *their* church) as a divine institution, franchised by God, to whom "customers" are supposed to come. It is true that evangelism and the recruitment of church members may be inseparable, but they are also distinct.[17] If we see this, we will be saved from false triumphalism (believing that the numerical growth of our church is a direct result of our "effective" evangelism) and from defeatism (believing that absence of numerical growth proves the absence of genuine evangelism).

Others confuse a "prophetic"[18] or "holistic"[19] ministry with evangelism. Principalities and powers, societies and nations can be challenged through the church's prophetic ministry, which is thus valuable, but they cannot *as such* repent and come to faith. This is not always realized in some ecumenical and Roman Catholic circles, in which "evangelism" can become an umbrella for the entire Christian ministry.[20] I do not deny that authentic evangelism has profound significance for development, liberation, justice, and peace, but this does not mean that one can turn it around and claim that these activities of social relief can somehow together constitute the comprehensive concept of evangelism.

Many have also mixed up the idea of evangelism with their own Western cultural molds.[21] Some outstanding exemplars of the faith have contributed unwittingly to this tendency. Jonathan Edwards sought the direct and succinct articulation of the gospel; George Whitefield sought its persuasive communication; John Wesley desired the effective nurture of new disciples; and Charles Finney discussed the evocation of personal response with immediacy. However, these exemplars were often transplanted to our own time without appropriate historical and theological judgment. This produced an understanding of evangelism which was, in many respects, culturally determined—and determined by a culture that is no more. This kind of evangelism leads to an alienation from the world. It preaches an over-personalized gospel wedded to the idol of success. It imposes a psychological cum spiritual crisis that does little to address the more basic challenge of discipleship. Under the pressure of the consumer culture it offers the gospel as an inducement and packages salvation as a marketable asset.

Any evangelism reflects the church as it functions in its surrounding culture: "a place where fellowship can be sought and found, where emotional and spiritual needs can be met, where moral standards can be affirmed, and where God can be worshipped."[22] The three understandings of evangelism discussed above, however—that which focuses on the numerical growth of the church, that which confuses prophetic ministry with evangelism, and that which demands that the evangelized accept Western forms of belief—not only reflect but are made subservient to culture. But the church, to be true to its being, must counteract the values of the culture. It must not become subordinate to its context, but yet its message must always be relevant in the context: it must be a model of "authentic contextualization." It must preach a gospel that *judges*, but not necessarily condemns, everything in the context in which it operates, pointing it beyond itself. It must not—as the types of evangelism we have looked at above do—compromise the message of the gospel as it seeks to be relevant to the context.

Contextual Evangelism: The Purpose

What are the features of an authentically contextual evangelism? Much current evangelism fosters pious self-centeredness or egocentrism. It occupies itself with the self-seeking, narcissistic pursuit of personal fulfillment. The new convert expects the church to be a social agency for the relief of painful disappointment, the suppression of uncomprehended fears, and the blanketing of uncomfortable memories as well as awkward expectations. Evangelism in our world can also often operate as an insurance policy that offers a guaranteed safe passage to the next life with a minimum of hazards en route.

In both definitions, whether a psychological panacea or a seat on the train to the hereafter, evangelism fosters a self-serving mindset in church members.[23] Now it is true that Christ gives peace of mind and eternal life to all who come to him. That is part of the gospel's very bedrock. This assurance must always go hand in hand with a firm understanding of why Christ saves us, however. What is it that he saves for *for?* What is the purpose of evangelizing people, of calling them to repentance and faith? Much of modern evangelism has tended to neglect these questions, focusing only on the assurance of salvation. Christian teaching, as Karl Barth shows,[24] has tended to regard the church as a kind of institute of salvation and to view Christians as enjoying an indescribably magnificent private good fortune.[25]

The terrible danger in this view is that eventually Christ may be downgraded to little more than the dispenser and distributor of special blessings.[26] People who come to the church then become concerned chiefly with the saving of their souls or with their experiences of grace and salvation—in short, only with establishing their personal relationship with God.[27] This whole understanding of becoming and being a Christian is self-centered, however, and thus is quite unbiblical. The personal enjoyment of salvation nowhere becomes the theme of biblical conversion stories: not in the case of those who listened to John the Baptist (Luke 3:10-14), nor of Zacchaeus or the Philippian jailer.[28]

Enjoying salvation is not wrong, unimportant, or unbiblical (see Col. 3:15; 1 Tim. 6:12; Heb. 9:15; 1 Pet. 5:10; Rev. 19:9); but it is incidental and secondary.[29] People receive it without expecting or seeking it. What makes people Christian is not primarily their personal experience of grace and redemption but their *ministry*. Indeed, the new Christian receives forgiveness, justification, and sanctification *in order to* become a servant.[30] Being called by God to faith in Christ means simultaneously being commissioned by God to perform a task in the world. If we play down this dimension in our evangelistic outreach, we are offering cheap grace.

Contextual Evangelism: Making Disciples

Authentic evangelism is also disciple making. But there is disagreement about what disciple making entails. Donald McGavran argues that "to disciple" means to lead non-Christians to a first commitment to Christ.[31] This must be followed by a second, more progressive and more comprehensive, stage, which he calls "perfecting." This two-part mission—discipling, which means evangelizing, and its necessary sequel, perfecting—finds expression in the words of the Great Commission: "Go therefore and make disciples of all nations . . . teaching them to observe all that I have commanded you" (Matt. 28:19-20). In some circles the distinction between discipling and perfecting has been described in another way: as that between the "evangelistic mandate" and the "cultural mandate."[32]

But it is wrong to define discipling or the evangelistic mandate so narrowly.[33] The distinction between the two (in spite of any help it might give us in the area of conceptualizing, that is, dealing in universals as mental concepts only)[34] puts asunder what God has joined together. As it gives priority to the evangelistic mandate, it tends to make the cultural one optional. In the Great Commission, however, the participial phrase "teaching them to observe all that I have commanded you" is to be understood as explicating the imperative "Go . . . and make disciples."[35] People are made disciples by learning *to follow* Jesus, that is, by learning *to do* what he has commanded.

This concept of being a disciple and evangelizing others was a big change in the religious thought world of Jesus' time. While in contemporary Judaism the disciples of the Jewish rabbis had their legitimation from the Torah and adherence to the Law, Jesus took the place of Torah and expected his disciples to renounce everything for his sake alone. Moreover, while in Judaism a disciple or follower of a rabbi could aspire to gain some position of status, to become a rabbi himself, following Jesus was never the start of a promising career: discipleship was and is *in itself* the fulfillment of life's destiny. Indeed, to be a disciple of Jesus was to be his servant: his disciples did not merely listen to him, they obeyed him. While a rabbi's disciples did not share his destiny, Jesus' disciples will because they are all called to *follow* him. "If any man would come after me, let him deny himself and take up his cross and follow me" (Matt. 16:24). To follow Jesus means not merely to pass on his teachings to others or to become faithful trustees of his insights but to be his obedient witness, his "martyr."

It is in this demanding way that we must obey the command, "make disciples!" People become disciples by being incorporated into the church (as we work in "baptizing them") and by obeying Jesus (as they learn to "observe all that I have commanded you"). Jesus' commandments in Matthew's Gospel can be summed up in the twin demand: seek justice and love one another and your God.[36]

Love manifests itself in righteousness or justice. Most English Bibles translate the Greek word *diakaiosyne* as "righteousness," which is a moral or spiritual quality we receive from God. But this word also has references to concrete action and may also be translated as "justice." In this sense it refers to the way we behave toward our fellows and seek for them that for which they have a right. Thus in Matthew we read that the justice of the disciples ought to surpass that of the Pharisees (5:20), who did not follow the way of justice shown by John the Baptist (21:31-32). Those who hunger and thirst to see that justice is done will be satisfied (5:6); those who suffer persecution for the sake of justice will be blessed (5:10); and only when our minds are set on God's kingdom and his justice will all the rest be given to us as well (6:33).[37]

The central aim of the Great Commission is making disciples, which includes simultaneously practicing love and righteousness, that is, upholding justice.[38] The tendency to narrow mission down to personal, inward, spiritual, and heavenly concerns makes a travesty of the gospel; yet this tendency is not far from much of modern evangelism. In the minds of some foreign mission administrators, "the church exists for the purpose of worship, communion, spiritual growth, and evangelistic witness. . . . Preach the gospel, win the lost, and social ills will gradually vanish as the number of believers in society increases."[39] But as we have seen, such interpretations distort the gospel. Falsely, such evangelism teaches that pious individuals who have a personal experience of Christ automatically get involved in changing society. Christ teaches otherwise! When he talks about making disciples, especially in Matthew's Gospel, he means commitment to both the King and his kingdom, to both righteousness and justice.

The concepts of discipleship, the present and future existence of the kingdom, and the call to righteousness and justice are like plaited strands in the fabric of the first Gospel. We cannot declare that any one element is primary, the others secondary; any one to be the root, the others the fruit. To do so is to deny the mission entrusted to us by Christ. T. K. Thomas of India cries bitterly, "We have freedom in many Asian countries to preach the gospel, to speak in tongues, to conduct healing ministries . . . as long as the gospel we preach does not disturb, the tongues do not make sense, [and] the healing does not extend to the diseases of the body politic."[40] Is this evangelism? It may be the very opposite.[41]

Contextual Evangelism: The Evangelists

We now see that to evangelize is not only to invite people to accept Jesus as Savior, but also to tell them what following him implies.[42] This does *not* mean that the gospel is superseded by the Law. When we challenge people to consider the cost of discipleship, we do it because the kingdom *has already come* in Christ. On the basis of what God has done and still does, we offer them new life, we give an authoritative word of hope, and we announce the new age. Response to evangelism overflows from recognition of the kingdom's reality.

This is why it makes little sense to say that evangelism is only a verbal ministry. Even the verb *euangelizomai,* to evangelize, can scarcely be taken to refer exclusively to verbal activity.[43] For Paul, evangelism was a way of life that involved his total being.

Word and deed are not opposites in the Bible as they are in Western thinking. In the gospel the word and the deed come together; the "Word became flesh." The deed without the word is dumb, the word without the deed empty. The words interpret the deeds and the deeds validate the words.[44] We see in the concept of the martyr this continuing union of word and deed. The Greek word *martyria* originally meant witness; yet in the course of history it came to acquire the meaning of martyrdom: to prove by one's deeds, even unto death, the validity of the words professed in the witness. This surely has a bearing on evangelism now. Even as believers from the beginning have sealed their words with their suffering, so should we, as evangelists for Christ, seal our own witness to others with deeds, even to the point of suffering for the truth.

The disciples recognized the risen Christ by the scars on his body, not by some demonstration of earthly power. The Galatians believed because branded on Paul's body they recognized the marks of Jesus (Gal. 6:17). In the same way, we, who as disciples are not greater than our master, cannot win people to him by might. Yet our evangelism can become credible when those outsiders see our scars.

Expectant Evangelism

Max Warren coined the expression "expectant evangelism" a long time ago.[45] To evangelize expectantly is to prepare for the end by getting involved in the here and now. The world may be enemy-occupied territory, but the enemy has no property rights. He is a thief and a liar. Our responsibility is to be good stewards of the King.[46] We may not be indifferent to the way the world is governed, nor to endemic injustice. Salvation in Christ has to be realized in the world now, even as he is still and will always be present among us as a consequence of his coming, death, and resurrection.[47]

Notes

1. To transform, dictionaries say, is "to change in character or condition," "to alter in function or nature." The noun *transformation* then refers to the action of bringing about such a change. The Greek-derived synonym of this Latin-based word is *metamorphosis.*

2. Gerhard Rosenkranz, *Die christliche Mission: Geschichte und Theologie* (Munich: Christian Kaiser, 1977), p. 71.

3. Celsus, the second-century Platonist, wrote the first but by no means the last notable attack on Christianity. See his *True Discourse* (c. A.D. 178).

4. Adolf von Harnack, *The Mission and Expansion of Christianity in the First Three Centuries* (New York: Harper, 1961). Harnack describes the witness of love and charity on pp. 147-98.

5. For an account of the life and witness of some early Christian communities in the People's Republic of China, see D. Vaughan Rees, *The "Jesus Family" in Communist*

China (Exeter: Paternoster, 1959). A more recent account can be found in Raymond Fung, *Households of God on China's Soil* (Geneva: World Council of Churches, 1982).

6. Jean Kermarrec, "Auf dem Wege zur schweigenden Kirche" (On the way to the silent church), *Die Katholischen Missionen* 95 (March-April 1976): 45-48.

7. See my paper "In Search of a New Evangelical Understanding," prepared for the Consultation on the Relationship between Evangelism and Social Responsibility, Grand Rapids, 1982, and published in *In Word and Deed,* ed. Bruce J. Nicholls (Exeter: Paternoster, 1985; Grand Rapids, Eerdmans, 1986), pp. 63-64.

8. Extreme examples of such Christian apocalypticism range from the followers of Montanus in the second century to the Millerites in North America and the Mennonites in Russia in the nineteenth century.

9. See my book *Witness to the World* (Atlanta: John Knox; London: Marshall, Morgan & Scott, 1980), pp. 64-65.

10. Lesslie Newbigin, "Cross-Currents in Ecumenical and Evangelical Understandings of Mission," *International Bulletin of Missionary Research* 6 (October 1982): 149.

11. The view that sees sin as purely personal and salvation as escape from the world is closer to Greek and Hindu thinking than to the message of the Bible. For the Greeks, *sōtēria* (from which we derive the English *soteriology*) meant being saved *from* physical life: salvation from the burdens of material existence. In the Hindu scriptures, "the real human person *(purusha)* is found by stripping away all the 'sheaths' *(upadhis)* that constitute one's visible, contingent, historical being as part of the ever-circling wheel of nature *(samsara).* In . . . contrast to this, the Bible always sees the human person . . . as a living body-soul . . . ; continued existence as a disembodied soul is something not to be desired but to be feared with loathing. The New Testament is true to its Old Testament basis when it speaks of salvation not in terms of disembodied survival, but in terms of the resurrection of the body, a new creation and a heavenly city." See Newbigin, "Cross-Currents," p. 149.

12. See Orlando E. Costas, *Christ Outside the Gate: Mission Beyond Christendom* (Maryknoll, N.Y.: Orbis, 1982), p. 27.

13. The "agenda" is from E. Stanley Jones, quoted by Virginia Ramey Mollenkott in her article "New Age Evangelism," *International Review of Mission,* January 1983, 32-40.

14. Costas, *Christ Outside the Gate,* p. 26.

15. Newbigin, "Cross-Currents," p. 149.

16. Costas, *Christ Outside the Gate,* p. 26.

17. See David Lowes Watson, "The Church as Journalist: Evangelism in the Context of the Local Church in the United States," *International Review of Mission* 285 (January 1983): 71-73.

18. It is not very helpful to use the term "prophetic evangelism" introduced by David Lowes Watson and others (see Watson, "Evangelism: A Disciplinary Approach," *International Bulletin of Missionary Research* 7 [January 1983]: 7), particularly if it is the task of such "evangelism" to unmask the principalities and powers, stand up to them, outlast them, and care for their victims (see in this context Mollencott's quote of G. W. Webber in her "New Age Evangelism," p. 40). That this kind of ministry is legitimate is incontestable, but it is not *evangelism.* Neither is it evangelism to "call . . . societies and nations to repentance and conversion" (Watson, "Evangelism: A Disciplinary Approach," p. 7).

19. On holistic ministry see Newbigin, "Cross-Currents," p. 149.

20. Note, for example, John Walsh's statement: "The church is in the process of reaffirming this most important scriptural insight when it states that human development, liberation, justice and peace are *integral* parts of the ministry of evangelization." See Walsh, *Evangelization and Justice: New Insights for Christian Ministry* (Maryknoll, N.Y.: Orbis, 1982), p. 92.

21. David Lowes Watson reminds us that evangelism as practiced in many parts of the American church has a long pedigree in the Augustinian piety that has motivated Prot-

estant missions since the eighteenth century. See his discussion in "The Church as Journalist," pp. 57-74.

22. Ibid., p. 72.

23. Pastors "find themselves trapped in the role of personal priest to people who feel they are paying for a service and are entitled to it." Ibid., p. 73.

24. This section of my paper draws on Karl Barth's penetrating excursus in *Church Dogmatics* (Edinburgh: T. & T. Clark, 1962), IV, 3, pp. 561-614.

25. Ibid., p. 567.

26. Ibid., pp. 595-96.

27. Ibid., p. 572.

28. Ibid.

29. Ibid., p. 593; see also p. 572.

30. Ibid., p. 593.

31. In his argument McGavran refers to the imperative "make disciples" in Matt. 28:19. The verb form used there, *mathēteuo*, is also used in three other places in the New Testament: Matt. 13:52; Matt. 27:57; and Acts 14:21.

32. See C. Peter Wagner, *Church Growth and the Whole Gospel* (San Francisco: Harper and Row, 1981), pp. 190-93. In a recent response to an article by Lesslie Newbigin, Wagner explains the difference between the evangelistic and the cultural mandate as follows: "The goal of evangelism is the conversion of sinners, saving souls, making disciples. . . . The goal of social ministry is to make people healthier, wealthier, less oppressed and less oppressing, more peaceful, fairer, more just, liberated, enjoying shalom, more secure." See Wagner's article in the *International Bulletin of Missionary Research* 6 (October 1982): 153.

33. McGavran and Wagner are among many who are too narrow in their view of discipling. See the works of Wagner cited in note 29.

34. See the article of Tito Paredes in this volume, "Culture and Social Change," note 48.

35. See my article "The Structure of Mission: An Exposition of Matthew 28:16-20," in Wilbert Shenk, ed., *Exploring Church Growth* (Grand Rapids: Eerdmans, 1983), pp. 218-48.

36. *Love* is the key word in the six powerful antitheses of the Sermon on the Mount (Matt. 5:21-47) and in the twin commandments of Matt. 22:34-40.

37. We are to understand all the cited references to righteousness/justice in Matthew in both a *moral* and a *religious* sense. Waldron Scott rightly says that disciple making involves more than was commonly assumed in evangelical circles. He adds: "One must understand discipleship in order to make disciples, and discipleship is not fully biblical apart from a commitment to social justice. . . . To be a disciple is to be committed to the King and his kingdom of just relationships." See Scott, *Bring Forth Justice* (Grand Rapids: Eerdmans, 1980), p. xvi.

38. Harold Lindsell is in error when he says, "The mission of the church is pre-eminently spiritual—that is, its major concern revolves around the non-material aspects of life." See Lindsell, quoted in Scott, *Bring Forth Justice*, p. 94.

39. This is Scott's summary of the opinions of twenty-four North American executives of mission work in Latin America. Only two of them recognized any relationship between evangelism and social justice; the remaining twenty-two discerned no link at all. One view that Scott reported is that "the growing churches in Latin America are those that minister most to the soul and least to the body." See Scott, *Bring Forth Justice*, p. 157.

40. T. K. Thomas, quoted in ibid., p. 156.

41. "Where . . . the church invites men and women to take refuge in the name of Jesus without . . . challenge to the dominion of evil, then it becomes a countersign, and the more successful it is in increasing its membership, the more it becomes a sign against the

192 / David J. Bosch

sovereignty of God. An 'evangelism' that seeks to evade this challenge and this conflict, which—for example—welcomes a brutal tyranny because it allows free entry for missionaries . . . becomes a sign against the gospel of the kingdom." Newbigin, "Cross-Currents," p. 148.

42. "In issuing the gospel invitation we have no liberty to conceal the cost of discipleship." See the Lausanne Covenant (Lausanne Committee for World Evangelization, 1974), paragraph 4.

43. Richard B. Cook has illustrated this point with particular reference to the epistle to the Galatians. See his article "Paul the Organizer," *Missiology* 9 (October 1981): 490-94.

44. Newbigin, "Cross-Currents," pp. 146-49.

45. The expression was coined by Max Warren in *The Truth of Vision* (London and Edinburgh: Canterbury Press, 1948); see pp. 132-45.

46. We affirm the kingdom as the only absolute in history. As we witness to the gospel of present salvation and future hope, we "identify with the awesome birthpangs of God's new creation." Watson, "Evangelism: A Disciplinary Approach," pp. 6-9.

47. "Preparation for the 'end', which is the triumph of God in history, involves taking history seriously as the sphere within which moral issues are real. Preparation consists in such a demonstration by the Christian church of the rightness of the righteousness of God that the world cannot gainsay the witness, although it may refuse to repent because of it. The 'end' comes when the rightness of this demonstration is vindicated by the establishment of the reign of God." "If the temporal order cannot see the vindication of God then His experiment with time has been a failure." Warren, *The Truth of Vision*, pp. 132, 135.

Compassion and Social Reform: Jesus the Troublemaker

Vishal Mangalwadi

Compassion for the suffering individual and concern for the glory of God were undoubtedly the prime motives of Christ's service. But if compassion had meant for Christ merely what most Christians understand by it today, then he would never have been killed. He would have been a fit candidate for a Nobel Prize, not the cross.

Christ's compassion was a prophetic compassion. It was much more than a gut-level reaction—as we would respond to pictures of starving children. Rather it was a compassion that grew out of a prophetic insight into the social and theological *causes* of suffering. Thus in his response Jesus went to the root of human misery and dealt with it directly. Here in this essay I will look at three facets of Christ's compassion and service that led to his death. In an earlier age, when Protestants still believed in social protest, such a discussion would have been redundant. But today? Well, we have drifted so far from our biblical and historical heritage that this may seem "too radical" to some people.

Service: Stirring the Stagnant Pool

We read in John 5 that Jesus healed a lame man who had been sick thirty-eight years. The man lay near the pool of Bethzatha, or Bethesda, in Jerusalem. When the waters of the pool were stirred, therapeutic powers went into action and the sick who entered the water were healed. This was not superstition but something the man had witnessed for decades. If he had not seen the powers of those waters, he would not have stayed there for all those years. He was sick, and the treatment was free and in sight; yet he could not get it. Why not? He explained to Jesus that he did not have anyone who would put him into the water when it was stirred. No one cared for him.

Jesus cared, though. He told him to pick up his pallet and walk. "At once the man was healed, and he took up his pallet and walked" (John 5:9). But this day was the Sabbath. In Israel, you could forget whether it was Tuesday or Thursday, but no one ever forgot when it was the Sabbath. The society was so well organized that in no time the authorities knew that this unknown man had dared to break the Sabbath rule: he had picked up his pallet and was walking. They began an inquiry on the spot. Did such efficiency reveal the beauty of that society? No. An establishment that had not cared for a man for thirty-eight years was now instant in caring for its own inhuman rules. I find it hard to believe that the authorities were so keen to enforce the Sabbath legislation because they wanted to please God. I am more inclined to think that their real interest was to impose a fine and collect a little extra revenue! The sick man complained to Jesus that his problem was that the Jewish society had no compassion. It had not even bothered to enforce a basic etiquette of civilized behavior—first come first served. The powerful came late but got healed first.

It was not by mistake that Jesus asked this powerless man to challenge an inhuman society by a deliberate act of defiance of its rules. God had provided the stirred-up pool to heal this man, and he might have been healed long before with the help of others. It was really the social pool of a stagnant, selfish society that needed to be stirred up for the healing of men like him. That was precisely what Jesus did. He not only healed the man but also asked him to break the Sabbath rule which led to an attempt by the establishment on Jesus' life (John 5:18).

Does the healing ministry of the church today, even its community health work, lead to such retaliation from society? No, because our service does not touch the real issue at all, the real ills in society. Many sick men, women, and children die daily in villages and slums around the world, not because treatment is unavailable or expensive, but simply because no one cares to take it to them. In some of the villages in my district, young women die during childbirth simply because every year their villages are marooned for three months during the monsoon. Our society builds overpasses on the streets in Delhi because the elite cannot stop for two minutes at red lights, but we are not bothered about those who have no access to any medical treatment for three months almost every year.

The establishment in India plans to hold the Olympic games and to have color television; it has the resources and the ability to send up satellites; but it does not take simple sanitation to the dying destitute in its slums. The church says it cares; yet so often it does not dare to expose the selfishness of the elite which is the real cause of hundreds of basic diseases which should have been wiped out by now, if only clean water, hygienic sanitation, adequate nutrition, health education, and immunization were made available to the poor masses. The technology and financial resources are available in abundance for taking these services to the rural poor. Yet they starve, suffer, and die because the powerful have other priorities. Christ's mercy did not touch an individual alone. It also sought to touch the heart of a society and to awaken its sleeping conscience. It troubled the stagnant waters which brought about a torrent of retaliation from the vested interests.

Service: A Judgment of a Blind Society

Again on a Sabbath day, when he knew that it would be seen as a deliberate defiance of the establishment, Jesus spat on the ground, made mud with the spit, and then used it to open the eyes of a beggar who was born blind. Jesus did not portray himself as a "servant." He said, "For judgment I came into this world, that those who do not see may see, and that those who see may become blind" (John 9:39). Jesus said this partly in response to his disciples, who had asked him, "Rabbi, who sinned, this man or his parents, that he was born blind?" (John 9:2). Their question seems to have hurt Jesus. It is hard to believe that the disciples were asking a sincere question about the cause of an inexplicable suffering. Certainly Jesus did not think that they had a profound philosophical interest in the problem of suffering that deserved an answer. Perhaps the disciples were really asking, "Rabbi, could you kindly give us some good rationale to justify our indifference to the suffering of this man?"

True, the man was born blind. But did he have to be a beggar? True, both he and his parents were sinners. But was Israel justified in ignoring the fact that he was also a human being made in the image of God, worthy of love and care? At heart he was begging neither because he was blind nor because he was a sinner but because Israel was blind to the fact that he was an image-bearer of God, the crown of God's creation. He was a beggar because Israel had sinned by not caring for him. Instead of seeing their own sinful indifference, the disciples were more keen on finding out his sin and that of his parents.

The incident in John 5 was not an isolated happening. It was part of Christ's pattern. On that occasion Jesus had simply asked the sick man to break the Sabbath law. Then in chapter 9 he did it himself. He did not need to spit on the ground and make mud with the spit in order to heal the blind man; he especially did not have to do it on the Sabbath, when he knew that it would be seen as a deliberate act of defiance of the establishment's laws. Yet he did it nonetheless. It was a deliberate provocation of the establishment. Then Jesus asked the blind man to break the law as well: "Go, wash in the pool of Siloam" (John 9:7). Jesus did not need to do this to heal the blind man, but healing was not the only objective of his service. Christ's objectives included publicly exposing and condemning the blindness of the self-righteous establishment. Had not God commanded Israel in the Old Testament to have mercy on its poor? If Israel was righteous and obedient, why did this man have to beg on the streets in order to live?

Civil disobedience is a deliberate and courageous act of a reformer to expose and condemn the institutionalized evils of his or her day. That is what Jesus was doing. And the establishment was blind enough to be thus exposed. Instead of containing Christ's service by patronizing it, they condemned the healing of a blind man, simply because it was done on a Sabbath day. They excommunicated the man from the synagogue and thereby further exposed their own blindness. The world was thus able to see that a mighty prophet had arisen among them who could open the eyes of a man born blind; yet the establishment could see nothing more than the violation of its own petty rules. Its values, ideals, attitudes, and priorities all stood exposed and condemned. The world could see that the rulers did not care for their people but that Christ did. The sheep could see that Jesus was their true shepherd who dared to stand against the wolves who only pretended to be their custodians.

Jesus made the formerly blind man pay a heavy price for his healing. Because the man chose to speak the truth he was excommunicated from the synagogue. No doubt he would have been welcomed into the community of Christ's disciples, which would lessen the impact of his social ostracism. Yet his excommunication must have helped many sincere Jews make up their minds against their own rulers whose blindness had been exposed and judged.

Such service that judges the world is not pleasant. The authorities not only excommunicated the healed man, they also made it known that Jesus was persona non grata. Whoever professed that Jesus was the Christ would also be excommunicated. It became ever harder to associate with Jesus; even being seen around him could lead one into trouble.

From 1973 to April 1983, I served the rural poor in Chhatarpur district of Madhya Pradesh with a community called the Association for Comprehensive Rural Assistance (ACRA). We have been involved in service that stirs the social pool and judges the blindness of the establishment. When you judge the world, the world retaliates by judging you. During May 1982, thirty of us were arrested on four separate occasions, because we not only served the victims of a hail storm but also through our service exposed the insensitivity of the politicians toward the victims of the storm. The politicians not only had us arrested, they also tried to have me murdered. The superintendent of police himself threatened to have me murdered. Many Christian leaders were frightened and disassociated themselves from me.

Such service hurts. It makes you lose friends. They choose not to associate with you, lest they too get into trouble. Yet one has to decide whether to walk in the footsteps of the Master and serve the oppressed, or to live to please one's friends. Jesus' mercy did not touch a blind beggar alone. How many blind could he heal in three years anyway? How many blind can the church today heal through its hospitals and eye clinics? We must have compassion for the individual sufferers, of course, but we must also understand that the beggars beg not because they are blind but because the society in which they live is itself blind to their needs. The blind can be happy and fulfilled if their society cares for them.

Our mercy must not merely open the eyes of the blind man but must also reach out to restore the sight of a blind society. Karl Marx rightly understood that true compassion calls for dealing with the social context that makes human beings miserable. This is a biblical understanding of compassion. Marx defeated his own purposes, however, by trying to build a case for compassion on atheistic premises. If individual human beings are merely the product of random chance in an impersonal universe, then there is no meaning in caring for them, especially when they are too weak and powerless to be of any use to others. But if humans are created beings, then they are special to the Creator. If they are created as the image-bearers of the Creator himself, they are even more special. And if they are to relate to the Creator in an intimate, personal relationship and to carry out his will for him in this world, then they are very special indeed. That is how Jesus saw the blind beggar: he is blind so "that the works of God might be made manifest in him" (John 9:3). And this is why God calls us to have compassion on others: so that his will may be done.

A great composer would not have a single note in his music that had no relevance. A great artist would not have a hue on her canvas that had no significance. A great architect would not have a stone in his building that was not a purposeful part of the design. A great poet will not have a word in her poem that has no meaning. If the universe is indeed the work of a great designer, no individual is meaningless, insignificant, or useless to the designer. Because an "unknown" blind beggar is special to God, we must have compassion for him individually. This compassion must be visible in specific acts of mercy, but it must also go deep enough to create a society that can see that the beggar is a special person to God, a person who should not be allowed to destroy his self-respect by begging. The beggar should not have to live an insecure, hand-to-mouth existence until one day he falls sick, becomes too weak to beg, and rots by the roadside to be eaten by beasts, birds, and worms.

If a society cannot see that a blind beggar is a special person, then it is itself blind to truth. If it does not acknowledge its blindness, then it is hypocritical, self-righteous, and sinful. In that case, our compassion—Christ's compassion—for the beggar must lead us to prophetically expose and condemn the blindness of society, as well as to build a more humane and compassionate counterculture within this society.

Service: An Alternative Power for Social Change

It is not enough to stir a society or judge a blind establishment. If the leadership does not repent, if it does not decide to fulfill its responsibility, then it becomes our task to seek to provide an alternative. Servanthood is the biblical means of acquiring power to lead. If it becomes known, however, that the purpose of our service is to change the status quo, to change the leadership, we often run into trouble. The Jewish authorities made the final decision to kill Jesus after he had raised Lazarus from the dead (see John 11) and began to be seen as a shepherd, Messiah, and king.

Jesus loved Lazarus and his sisters, Mary and Martha, who had sent word to him that his beloved friend was sick. Jesus could have healed him by a word spoken then and there and spared Mary and Martha much agony. But his healing ministry had purposes other than just the healing of bodily ills. So Jesus waited outside Bethany until Lazarus died. He waited until the Jews in Jerusalem had heard of the death and had assembled in Bethany to comfort Mary and Martha. Then, in front of a crowd, Jesus displayed his love for the dead man and his sisters. He displayed sorrow and anger at sickness and death, which caused such anguish to his beloved. He displayed his unique relationship with God his Father, and then he displayed his authority and power to give life to the dead.

This display of love, sorrow, anger, and power was not hypocritical but a means of exhibiting who he really was, so that people could make an intelligent choice for or against him. Jesus' prayer in John 11:41-42 makes it abundantly clear that even though he could have healed Lazarus or raised him from the dead without exhibiting who he was, he now felt it necessary that the world see his heart, his being, and his power.

The miracle had the intended effect: many people came to believe in Jesus (John 12:11). Their decision to accept Jesus was an automatic rejection of the establishment, for Jesus provided an alternative to Israel. The Jewish establishment was in alliance with the exploitative Roman regime (John 19:15). It existed because it not only allowed but also helped Rome to continue its exploitation of the people. The chief priests of the Jews knew that if Jesus were allowed to extend his influence over the people, a new center of mass power would be created that would be in the interest of the common people. They also knew that Rome would not tolerate a new power center that defended the interests of the people. They believed that it was inevitable that "the Romans will come and destroy both our holy place and our nation" (John 11:48). In the view of the local authorities, then, the Shepherd had to be eliminated to save the nation (John 11:49-50). Their rationale was that slavery was better than destruction.

Thus we see that Jesus' healing ministry was intended not only to heal but also to build up a following, just as his preaching aimed not just at educating but also at drawing out a wholehearted dedication to following him. The separation of evangelism and church planting in the Western world has created a mentality among Christians all over the world that leads to preaching and serving but not to building up a following. Because of this mentality, many people cannot even see in the gospel the obvious fact that Jesus was building up a disciple-based movement through his teaching, preaching, and healing.

A fresh look at the Gospels, however, will convince one that Jesus carefully built a large following that was not just another religious sect but an alternative center of power in Israel. It was a threat to the status quo not only naturally but also intentionally, because it was the very antithesis of all that the establishment stood for.

First of all, this alternative center of power was a *moral force* in contrast to the immoral Jewish establishment. Jesus not only healed people but called them to "sin no more" (John 5:14). He called his disciples to righteousness that "exceeds that of the scribes and Pharisees" (Matt. 5:20).

Second, this new power was a *social force* that stood for the smallest of the small in contrast to the establishment, which protected the interests of the powerful exploiters such as the traders in the temple whom Jesus called "robbers" (Mark 11:15-18). Jesus called his followers to serve "the least of these my brethren"—the naked, the sick, the homeless, and the imprisoned (see Matt. 25:31-46).

And third, this alternative power was a *courageous force*. It required a determination to stand for the protection of the harassed and helpless sheep to the point of laying down one's own life as Jesus did (John 10:1-18). This was in contrast to the attitude of the Jewish establishment, which was concerned primarily with its own safety and well-being and which in the face of the Roman threat was prepared to sacrifice the interests of the common people (John 11:45-48).

Jesus intentionally built up his following, his church, as a power structure to withstand the mighty forces of destruction and death. Christ said to Peter, "You are Peter, and on this rock I will build my church, and the powers of death shall not prevail against it" (Matt. 16:18). The destructive forces of death will fight against Christ's new society but will not prevail against it. The church is meant to stand against the forces of oppression and death because Christ gave it the mandate to feed his lambs and to tend his sheep (John 21:15-16). In an unjust, oppressive society, when a group stands up for the littlest of lambs, it necessarily stands up against the mighty vested interests that grow fat on the flesh of the lambs.

Jesus and his new community were naturally and intentionally a threat to the establishment. When he set his course to go to Jerusalem and precipitate a face-to-face confrontation, the establishment had to choose between the status quo and its own survival on the one hand and an immense sociopolitical change and transfer of power to another group on the other.

This is not the Jesus taught by many Sunday schools, the Jesus who confines himself to changing human hearts. Rather, the Jesus of the Gospels aimed at changing both human hearts and human society. He prepared shepherds to replace wolves as leaders of the lambs of Israel. He verbalized his intentions explicitly a number of times. For example, in the parable of the vineyard left in charge of tenants (Matt. 21:33-46), Jesus makes it clear that the chief priests to whom he was speaking had rejected the kingdom and would bear the consequences. "The kingdom of God will be taken away from you and given to a nation producing the fruits of it" (Matt. 21:43). Here was an explicit statement of a radical social transformation, of a change of political power. The Jews understood it and tried to arrest Jesus on the spot, but they were afraid of the crowds, who considered him to be a prophet (Matt. 21:46). Jesus announced his intention of a social change to the establishment itself after he had carefully built up his mass support. Even though the wise men had announced Jesus' kingship at his birth and John the Baptist had announced some of the changes that he was to bring about, Jesus did not assert his power immediately. He asserted his royal authority over Zion through the dramatic events of his triumphal entry into Jerusalem on Palm Sunday, only after the raising of Lazarus, which had created excitement among the masses.

The power instituted by Christ was not an accident of service—it never is. In India today, the church has no real competitor in the field of service; yet it continues to be powerless because our service is very different from Christ's. He consciously cultivated a mass following. He was a man of the masses and built up by his service a mass following. Just look at his strategy following the raising of Lazarus in John's Gospel (John 11:54–12:33).

First, he brought a dead man back to life. He allowed the story of the raising of Lazarus to spread to the point of ringing alarm bells in the establishment (John 11:45-53). Then he hid in the desert town of Ephraim (11:54). This was the time of the Passover festival, and there were great crowds of people in Jerusalem who naturally gossiped about him (11:55-57). After he had become the hot topic of debate, he came back to the home of Lazarus in Bethany, just outside Jerusalem. The word spread in Jerusalem and crowds flocked to Bethany to see not only Jesus but also Lazarus, whom he had raised from the dead (12:1-11). Then, when a large enough crowd had gathered, all excited about Jesus, he asked for a colt and allowed his disciples to organize a procession. They all marched into Jerusalem, shouting slogans and proclaiming him to be the king of Israel. The entire city was stirred up, until the authorities took notice and said to each other, "You see that you can do nothing; look, the world has gone after him" (John 12:19).

As a result, the Jews decided to kill both Jesus and Lazarus (John 12:9-11). Christ knew that this would be the consequence of what he was doing, but he had no choice. The establishment had refused to repent; it had refused to believe the truth and had decided to continue in its evil ways. Either Jesus had to give up his call for repentance and change or he had to precipitate a confrontation to give a last opportunity to the establishment either to repent or to kill him. Jesus was prepared to pay the price of such a confrontation.

Jesus did not heal the lame and the blind men and raise Lazarus from the dead merely to make them live comfortably. He was paying the price for the world, and his followers had to pay the same price. But paying this price was his glory: he accepted his death as a criminal because it would end as his glory. He carefully chose the time and manner of his own death so that his cause would receive the maximum benefit from his crucifixion.

Jesus did not cultivate a mass following to gain a selfish crown. At the beginning of his ministry he refused the crown that Satan offered to him (Matt. 4:8-10). He refused to have the kingdom for himself. Rather he wanted the kingdom for the poor (Matt. 5:3; Luke 6:20), the sorrowful (Matt. 5:4), and the meek (Matt. 5:5). When the poorer masses saw him as their Messiah and began to follow him, the Jewish authorities naturally felt the status quo threatened. When even the Greeks came looking for Jesus, he immediately preceived what the Jewish authorities had perceived—that the whole world was following him and that he thus had to be eliminated. His crucifixion, not international recognition, was his real glory—his laying down his life for the poor of his nation, the harassed and helpless sheep.

Jesus' service gave him a mass following that in turn gave him power. This seriously threatened the establishment and meant death, which was the final proof of whether he was really serving others or only himself. An all-out love for God and for one's neighbors has to be tested, and Jesus was prepared to be tested by fire.

When people are so committed to changing the unjust social structures in favor of the enslaved, exploited, and oppressed that they will lay down their lives for the cause, they are bound to create ripples in history that never cease.

Neither the Jews nor the Romans killed Jesus in order to make him a sin-offering. The *historical* cause of his death was that he was a serious trouble-maker as far as the establishment was concerned. Their charge against him was that he had claimed to be the legitimate king of the Jews, which meant that their rule was illegitimate.

Yet this is not to say that the *theological* meaning of the cross—that Jesus died for the sins of humanity—is in any way false, less true, or historically un-true.

As Jesus hung on the cross of Calvary, it was literally the sin of the world that was hanging there at that moment of history. Whether or not they were Christ's followers, the people who saw the crucifixion, who saw him die, saw that it was not the justice but the injustice of humanity that was carried out that day. In Christ's arrest, trial, and crucifixion, the sin of humanity was more than visible. Disobedience of God, rejection of the truth, cruelty, lies, hate, greed, vested interests, oppression, exploitation, abuse of power, deliberate choice of evil—all were there on the cross for everyone to see, hear, and feel. That is why the Bible's statement that Jesus became the sin of the world is not theological mumbo-jumbo but a statement of historical fact. It was not Jesus who was judged on that cross but the sin of humanity; this sin was condemned in history on that day.

The eyewitnesses, such as the dying thief, could see that humanity's evil was hanging on Jesus' cross. Since Jesus loved sinners so much that he became the sin of the world himself on the cross, God now decreed, as the Bible testi-fies, that all human beings can find forgiveness for their sins through faith in the death of Christ as the final and complete sin-offering. But those who do not personally accept the death of Christ as a means of salvation from sin cannot be saved. They will themselves have to take the full consequences of their sin before a perfectly holy God. Many people find it hard to accept that the sacri-fice of Jesus on the cross is the only means of finding forgiveness for one's sins. But who else ever became sin for the world? In the whole of human his-tory, Jesus is the only one who took all the sins of humanity upon himself.

The Jews did not crucify Jesus to make him a sin-offering for the world, but since Jesus became sin on the cross by his own choice, God has now de-clared that "there is no other name under heaven given among men by which we must be saved" (Acts 4:12). Indeed, the New Testament focuses on the theological meaning of the cross—Jesus the Savior from sin—far more than it focuses on the historical meaning of the cross—Jesus the troublemaker. One of the reasons for this is that the historical meaning of the cross was obvious to the contemporaries of the New Testament writers, whereas the theological mean-ing needed exposition, defense, and practical application.

We can ignore the theological meaning of the cross only at an eternal cost to ourselves. But the current assumption that the historical meaning of the cross is irrelevant is equally mistaken. Jesus not only carried his cross, he asked his disciples to carry their crosses too. We cannot be disciples of Christ unless we take up our crosses and follow him (Luke 9:23).

What does it really mean to carry one's cross? Punishment by hanging on a cross was the weapon Rome used to perpetuate its reign of terror. Those condemned to die had to carry their own cross to the public place where they were to be crucified. When Jesus asked his disciples to carry their own crosses he was asking them to fight Rome with its own weapons instead of trying to fight it with swords.

Mahatma Gandhi well understood and imitated Christ on this point. While there were many Indians who wanted to fight British colonialism with guns and bombs, Gandhi asked his followers to fill the British jails and to submit to British beatings and bullets. When the British threw Gandhi in jail, it was not he who was judged and condemned but they themselves. When they beat and killed peaceful protesters, they in fact destroyed their own kingdom. That is what Jesus invited his disciples to do. To "take up your cross" means to become a rebel, to fight a corrupt establishment with its own weapons, to be a troublemaker, and to take the consequences of those actions.

Historically, the cross was the strategy of Christ and his followers in their battle against the powers, principalities, and rulers of a dark age. Today, in many countries of the world where evil, corruption, and tyranny reign, heaping untold miseries on the weak and the poor, Christ calls his disciples to a practical compassion for the sheep. He calls his followers to take up their cross and to follow him in the path of service, protest, and confrontation.

One whose perception of Christianity is conditioned by the contemporary image of the church is very likely to dismiss my interpretation of the historical meaning of the cross as a heresy. But Gamaliel, a respected Jewish rabbi who watched Jesus and his cross-bearing community closely and sympathetically, saw them as well-intentioned political rebels. He naturally classed the apostles with Theudas and Judas the Galilean who "also" led revolts against Rome. The entire Jewish Sanhedrin—both critics and sympathizers of the apostles—agreed with Gamaliel's perception of the church as a band of rebels (Acts 5:33-40).

Through his service, Jesus deliberately became a champion of the masses. But this does not mean that he went after cheap popularity with the masses. He demanded costly discipleship, not cheap fanaticism. Only by creating disciples who are prepared to care for the sheep at the cost of their own lives can we hope to stand up against the powers of death. The Lord Jesus created a mass following, a power base, to affect structures that kept the blind man a beggar.

Our service today lacks power, either because it is marked by self-love or because the compassion behind it does not include understanding of the social roots of human misery and gives no answer to them. But if we choose to live for others in such a way that we are willing to lay down our lives for them, we will produce fruit for God because we will have power. This will bring honor to God and to us through the cross.

A Story from Indian Church History

Indian society has gone through enormous change and improvement during the past two hundred years. Many forget that this social change was a process initiated by Christian missionaries who understood that Christian compassion called for a crusade against those social institutions and practices that oppress and dehumanize. The battles against sati, caste, child marriage, female infanticide, bonded agricultural labor, drunkenness, opium addiction, and other social evils were generally initiated and led by the missionaries and only taken up by Hindu reformers later. However, we must admit with shame that when the reform began to touch the most serious evil of colonialism itself, the church backed out of the reform, leaving the leadership in non-Christian hands. Nevertheless, there is much we can learn from the early missionaries. One good example was the missionary crusade against the exploitation of forced laborers by the planters of indigo, a plant from which dye is made, in Bengal.

After indigo growing ceased to be very profitable in the West Indies and America, many European planters came to Bengal and joined Indian landlords in the indigo plantations. They leased or bought large estates and rented them out to Indian peasants for cultivation. They gave the peasants initial loans, which eventually landed the peasants and their children in virtual slavery. According to the terms of the loan and cultivation rights, the peasants had to grow a fixed quantity of indigo for their landlords' factories, whether or not that left them able to grow any food for themselves. For decades, during which the cost of other agricultural produce doubled or tripled, the price of indigo was kept fixed. Consequently, production cost was often higher than the selling price. This perpetually kept the peasants on the point of starvation. Those who protested were often kidnapped, locked up, and beaten by the musclemen of the landlords. Many in the police force and the judiciary were bought off with bribes, and honest officers and magistrates could do little because no peasant dared to witness against a landlord or his musclemen. It was a reign of terror.

Cruel as they were, the European landlords were a great help to the missionaries whenever they went on their preaching excursions among the peasants. But when the missionaries heard the peasants' tales of woe, they realized that these people with empty bellies could not possibly pay attention to the gospel. Even if they could hear the message, they would not accept its truth as long as the missionaries were patronized by their oppressors, the landlords.

The Reverend F. Schurr, a Church Missionary Society missionary, was among those deeply grieved by the cruelties of the indigo planters. Like Moses, he chose to reject the patronage of the masters in order to participate in the sufferings of the peasants. Furthermore, he exposed to others the cruelties of the planters' system when he read, at the conference of Bengal missionaries in

Calcutta in September 1855, a paper entitled "On the Influence of the System of Indigo Planting on the Spread of Christianity."

This sparked a great controversy. Initially, some missionaries opposed the idea of getting involved, but gradually as the facts became known most joined in the battle. The Hindu intelligentsia and the secular press also played helpful roles. Eventually a powerful appeal was made to the government to appoint a commission of inquiry and to change the system of forced labor. The planters predictably fought back, accusing the missionaries of leaving religious matters and meddling in political and secular affairs, thus creating class conflict. The government sided with the planters and turned down the appeal for a commission of inquiry without even giving a reason.

The missionaries were infuriated and brought the matter up in the British Parliament and aroused public opinion in both Britain and Bengal. They were aided in this by art and drama. The Reverend James Long, another Church Missionary Society missionary, translated, published, and distributed a Bengali drama, *Mirror of Indigo,* which was a satire on the indigo growing system, portraying its effects on a laborer's family.

In response, a libel case was initiated against Long for his actions, and he was eventually imprisoned for his service on behalf of the oppressed. Here was service that stirred up a society, exposed and condemned the cruelty of a blind establishment and brought cross, power, and honor to Christian servants. An Australian historian, G. A. Oddie, wrote thus about the results of Long's imprisonment:

> Long's apparent willingness to suffer for the sake of others and in the cause of peace with justice for the ryots [peasants] of lower Bengal, his lack of bitterness and self-regard and his cheerful acceptance of what he believed was an inescapable duty made a profound impression. Indeed, his attitude and stand on the indigo issue probably did more to commend his faith than any amount of preaching could ever have accomplished and, at least for the time being, affected Hindu and other non-Christian perceptions of Christianity. It reinforced the impression created by the missionaries' earlier participation in the indigo controversy that they totally rejected the racial arrogance of fellow Europeans and were not "partakers of other men's sins." "The Rev. J. Long," wrote the editor of the *Indian Mirror,* "has acted manfully and precisely in the manner a *true* Christian missionary should have done when placed under the same circumstances." Dr. Kay of the S.P.G. [Society for the Propagation of the Gospel] who visited Long in prison remarked on the tone of vernacular newspapers and quoted one as saying that, "if this be Christianity, then we wish Christianity would spread all over the country." Duff, Wylie, Stuart and others believed that Long's imprisonment was creating "a very favourable impression for Christian missions," and catechists informed Long that as a result of his imprisonment "people have listened . . . more willingly to their preaching."[1]

No doubt some will argue that Long lived in British India and thus was able to speak boldly against "his own system." Modern missionaries in India are prohibited from such interference. It may be true that as guests they do not have the right to interfere with the Indian socioeconomic system. But the problem comes when the missionaries (and even Indian church leaders) prohibit Indian Christians from involvement in such daring acts of compassion. They keep the Indian church away from the mainstream of national life, and prevent us Indian Christians from cultivating the feeling that this is "our system" and that we have not only the right but also the responsibility to love it and make it just.

Note

1. See G. A. Odie's assessment of the results of Long's imprisonment in his study *Social Protest in India: British Protestant Missionaries and Social Reforms, 1850–1900* (New Delhi, Manohar Publications, 1979), p. 192.

Mercy and Social Transformation

Waldron Scott

Introduction

Mercy is one of the great words of the Bible, extraordinarily rich in its implications. Twice our Lord challenged his critics to "go and learn what this means, 'I desire mercy, and not sacrifice'" (Matt. 9:13; 12:7; cf. Hos. 6:6). Without doubt, to "learn mercy" is to intuit the very nature of God and to grasp the essence of the gospel.

What then is mercy? It is kindness, or compassion, or pity extended by one person to another in his or her power, even though the other has no claim on that kindness and can be expected to give no requital. Mercy is the disposition to forgive or to show kindness when severity is merited or expected.

Understood this way, mercy is primarily an attribute of God, "who is rich in mercy" (Eph. 2:4). Because God is full of mercy, Jesus commands us to be merciful also (Luke 6:36). And, as R. E. C. Browne points out, to be merciful is to lead a style of life that makes both extending mercy and receiving mercy possible.[1] "Blessed are the merciful, for they shall obtain mercy" (Matt. 5:7).

We can trace the core of mercy back to the Hebrew word *hesed*, which appears about 250 times in the Old Testament. *Hesed* denotes God's faithfulness to his own gracious relationship with Israel despite Israel's unworthiness and defection. *Hesed* is variously translated into English as kindness, lovingkindness, steadfast love, and goodness. Its range of meaning also includes the concept of solidarity.[2] The Septuagint translates *hesed* into Greek as *eleos*, which is then carried into the New Testament where we translate it "mercy."

Compassion has to do with suffering together, with participation in suffering. Compassion is that feeling or emotion experienced when one is *moved* by the suffering or distress of another: "He had compassion for them, because they were harassed and helpless" (Matt. 9:36). More importantly, it is the emotion one experiences when one is moved to action *by the desire to relieve* that suffering: "And he had compassion on them, and healed their sick" (Matt. 14:14). It is a sign of weakness when compassion is merely sentimental or ostentatious.

The antithesis of compassion is indifference, aloofness, and unconcern. The antithesis of mercy is vengeance, indifference, retribution, and punishment.

With all this in mind, it would appear that when we speak of mercy and social transformation we are referring primarily to *acts* of mercy and compassion toward suffering fellow creatures who are not immediately positioned to return the favor. The merciful or compassionate one is precisely what the apostle Paul refers to in Romans 12:8: "he who gives aid, with zeal; he who does *acts of mercy*, with cheerfulness." Such acts of mercy, especially when offered in the face of contrary social mores, are valid proof of neighbor-love, as the story of the Good Samaritan makes clear. Jesus concluded that story by asking, "Which of these three, do you think, proved neighbor to the man who fell among the robbers?" When the lawyer replied, "the one who showed mercy on him," Jesus told him to "go and do likewise" (Luke 10:36-37).

When acts of mercy are rendered with some degree of organized, systematic intent, and especially when they are rendered as some sort of corporate endeavor, they are better described as *ministries* of mercy. Such ministries of mercy may be aimed at (or may simply result in) radical social transformation—a more or less complete change in the character and condition of a society. Since this is the case, we should address the following questions as the main subjects of our inquiry:

To what extent over the past two thousand years have Christian ministries of mercy induced social transformation, radical or otherwise?

Should Christian ministries of mercy aim directly at social transformation? Or do they indirectly, yet inevitably, transform social values and structures?

What is the relationship in our day between modern ministries of mercy and the often desperate struggle for social justice throughout the world?

Should the churches delegate their ministries of mercy to parachurch agencies? Or to secular governments?

What role do indigenous ministries of mercy have to play in social transformation?

Ministries of Mercy in Early Christian History

The earliest Christians were challenged as individuals to perform deeds of mercy as opportunities arose. "If a brother or sister is ill-clad and in lack of daily food, and one of you says to them, 'Go in peace, be warmed and filled,' without giving them the things needed for the body, what does it profit?" (James 2:15-16). The early disciples thus showed true mercy and compassion. Peter, who had no silver or gold on his person, gave a crippled beggar what he did have: the gift of health (Acts 3:6). Tabitha (Dorcas) is cited as an early disciple "full of good works and acts of charity" (Acts 9:36). Paul, in an illuminative situation, was deeply grieved[3] at the sight of an exploited slave girl and healed her (Acts 16:16-18).

Summing up his own ministry, Paul argued that he had labored partly in order to be in a position to help others. "I coveted no one's silver or gold or apparel. You yourselves know that these hands ministered to my necessities, and to those who are with me. In all things I have shown you that by so toiling one must help the weak, remembering the words of the Lord Jesus, how he said 'It is more blessed to give than to receive'" (Acts 20:33-35). Paul challenged new converts to follow his example. "Let the thief no longer steal, but rather let him labor, doing honest work with his hands, so that he may be able to give to those in need" (Eph. 4:28).

Generally speaking, however, the New Testament sees the ministry of mercy not only as an individual obligation, but as a corporate endeavor of the church, to be carried out first of all within the church itself. "So then, as we have opportunity, let us do good to all men, and especially to those who are of the household of faith" (Gal. 6:10). Thus members of the first Christian congregation "sold their possessions and goods and distributed them to all, as any had need" (Acts 2:45).

Again, when it became apparent that widows were being overlooked in the daily distribution of food and other necessities, the church at Jerusalem acted to relieve their need and to ensure that a repetition would not occur (Acts 6:1-6). In due course the care of widows was institutionalized by the early church (1 Tim. 5:3-16).

When Agabus predicted the widespread famine that in fact occurred during the reign of Claudius, the church at Antioch acted immediately. "And the disciples determined, every one according to his ability, to send relief to the brethren who lived in Judea" (Acts 11:29). As time went on, and the faith spread, spontaneous response evolved into something more systematic (1 Cor. 16:1-4). An important part of this more systematic approach was instruction: "let our people learn to apply themselves to good deeds, so as to help cases of urgent need, and not to be unfruitful" (Titus 3:14). This same concern for the well-being of others in need is elaborated in the letters of Clement, bishop of Rome around A.D. 95, and in the *Didache ton Dodeka Apostolon* (The Teachings of the Twelve Apostles), which was composed sometime between A.D. 70 and 200 and reflects the life of the church of the time.

As the church spread through the Roman Empire its ministries of mercy underwent considerable development. Social relief became a monopoly of the church in Rome and Alexandria, where it was manifested in distributions to the poor and in the establishment and upkeep of hospitals, orphanages, and homes for the aged. By the fourth century the church was also bringing relief to people whom inflation had plunged into distress.

Post-Constantinian churches spent great sums (for their endowments were growing enormously) on the work of ransoming captives. St. Ambrose proposed selling the precious vessels on the altars of his church in Milan to do just that. He declared, "There is one incentive which must impel us all to charity; it is pity for the misery of our neighbors and the desire to alleviate it, with all the means that lie in our power, and more besides."[4]

Julian the Apostate, pagan emperor at Constantinople during the fourth century, witnessed the impact of the church's ministries of mercy and was deeply challenged. Speaking of Christianity as atheism because it denied the pagan pantheon, he asked "Can we not see that what has contributed most to the development of atheism is its humanity towards strangers, its thoughtfulness towards everyone, even its care of the dead?"

The apostle Paul believed the gospel was given to the Gentiles in part to provoke the Jews to a kind of spiritual jealousy (Rom. 11:11-14). In like manner we see reflected in Julian's complaint the way in which Christian ministries of mercy gradually evoked a new set of values within the Greco-Roman world and, eventually, a thoroughgoing social transformation.[5]

In spite of what we have just noted, however, it can hardly be maintained that the early Christians deliberately attempted to restructure the empire. Instead, during the first two centuries when Christians constituted a small minority, their concern was to shape a new community motivated by compassion and characterized by communal justice. Still later, when Christians had become a majority of the population of the empire, one might have thought that the church would undertake the systematic restructuring of society. But the emergence of monasticism precluded this. Nevertheless, a social transformation most certainly occurred over a period of five centuries, and in this transformation corporate Christian ministries of mercy, wittingly or unwittingly, played a decisive role.

Ministries of Mercy during the Middle Ages

Among the barbaric tribes in Europe during the Middle Ages (roughly A.D. 500–1500), charitable institutions were introduced by missionaries who established convents, which were expected to exercise hospitality to strangers and to give help to the poor. A church synod at Aix in A.D. 815 ordered that an infirmary be built near each church and in every convent. Some time earlier Charlemagne had established privileged charitable institutions in order that strangers, pilgrims, and paupers be taken care of. In the 1200s Louis IX entrusted the Knights of St. Lazarus with the care of lepers, and in England the century before, King Stephen and others had established houses for lepers.

In the midst of all this institutional expression of Christian compassion, certain individuals stand out. St. Francis of Assisi kissed the hands of leprosy victims, and Queen Matilda of England washed their feet. This kind of intimate contact, then as now, in some parts of the world, communicated God's care and compassion to a people cruelly stigmatized by society.

At the time of the Byzantine-Persian wars of the seventh century, the Catholic patriarch of Alexandria was John the Almsgiver. A devout layman whose wife and children had died, he lived austerely, devoting the revenues of his see chiefly to the poor and to refugees. Throughout the eastern part of the church during this period monasteries were generally associated with philanthropic enterprises and had hospices for the aged and the poor and hospitals for the care of the sick.

Toward the end of the Middle Ages, during the turbulent fourteenth century, Catherine of Siena, a "practical mystic," gave herself to the service of the poor and the sick, even during an epidemic of the Black Death. She also concerned herself with politics, however. She endeavored to heal chronic feuds among prominent families in Siena, and she urged Pope Gregory XI, then engaged in war, to make peace, even if it cost him his worldly goods. She had a profound influence upon her generation.

During the fifteenth century Girolamo Savonarola became the most famous man of his time and the most influential personage in the city-state of Florence. He preached judgment and pled with the citizens of Florence to accept Christ as their king. He exhorted his hearers to give to the poor everything beyond their barest needs. Florence was transformed. But when Savanarola began to speak against the pope the tide turned against him: ultimately he was arrested, condemned, and hanged, and his body burned.

Monasticism and the papacy were the two decisive institutions in the society of the Middle Ages in the West. When a monk became pope, the two came together. Gregory the Great (A.D. 590–604) was one such person. As pope he continued the austere simplicity of monastic life, and at the same time he excelled in charity.[6] He fed the hungry from his own frugal table; he intervened continually in favor of injured widows and orphans; he redeemed slaves and captives and sanctioned the sale of consecrated vessels for charity; and he made efforts (though in vain) to check the slave-trade.

Gregory the Great represents the best in medieval charity. Yet he was a strong believer in the efficacy of almsgiving to gain merit. The more alms the better, both for one's own salvation and for the relief of departed relatives and friends. This idea, as the historian Philip Schaff notes, ruled supreme in Europe during the Middle Ages. At the height of the period many people gave and ministered no longer for the sake of helping and serving the poor in Christ but ultimately to obtain for themselves and their loved ones release from purgatory. To a great extent, then, poverty was not alleviated but actually fostered. Walter Rauschenbusch, the great advocate of the so-called "social gospel," agrees with this judgment.

> For sheer willingness to give, modern Christianity cannot match its beneficence with ascetic Christianity.[7] But this giving is not essentially a social conflict with the moral evils of pauperism, but a religious conflict with the moral evil of the love of property. The aim was not primarily to lift the poor recipient to social health, but to discipline the soul of the giver. . . . The desire to discipline the soul and the desire to win merit united in making men give large amounts to charity, but they also vitiated the social effectiveness of the giving. . . . The poor, through whom this virtue was acquired, were "the treasure of the Church," part of its equipment, a kind of gymnastic apparatus on which the givers increased their moral muscle.[8]

In contrast, others assert that during the Middle Ages the church effected a complete revolution in morals by regarding the poor as the special representatives of Jesus Christ, thus making the love of Christ, rather than the love of humanity, the principle of charity. Some would say that for the first time in the history of humankind thousands of men and women were inspired to devote their entire lives to the single object of assuaging the sufferings of humanity, covering Europe with countless institutions of mercy unknown to the pagan world.[9]

Surveying this medieval period Kenneth Scott Latourette concludes that "little thought appears to be given to remedying the conditions which gave rise to poverty and illness. The majority accepted as inevitable a social and economic order in which poor existed, and attempts at public hygiene were usually rudimentary or entirely absent."[10]

Ministries of Mercy after the Reformation

The German historian Gerhard Uhlhorn notes that the first effect of the Protestant Reformation on charity was a decline in giving. In large measure this was a reaction against the unbiblical motives for almsgiving that had come to dominate the late Middle Ages. Moreover, as Latourette perceptively observes, Protestantism, by its rejection of monasticism, deprived itself of the organizations through which ministries of mercy had long expressed themselves.

In due course, however, Protestantism developed its own agencies for the care of the destitute. For example, the Pietist movement created the famous orphanage at Halle. While Pietists, and Lutherans in general, concentrated on measures of relief, Calvinists tended more toward seeking the reformation of social structures. In Scotland John Knox advocated the idea that those unable to work should be supported out of public funds, that all those able to work should be compelled to do so, that every child should be given an opportunity for education, and that each promising student should have a way open to the university.

Wesleyans did not set out to effect basic changes in society, though John Wesley himself worked strenuously to relieve poverty and started missions among prisoners. One of his warm friends, John Howard, later became an outstanding pioneer in prison reform.[11] Wesley was also a pioneer in the antislavery movement and persistently contended against such evils as bribery and corruption in politics, smuggling, and plundering wrecked ships. Wesley's followers worked against those social ills that exploited one group to the benefit of another. Quakers, meanwhile, pioneered in advocating the equality of women with men, the abolition of slavery, and the humane treatment of the insane and the criminal.

The impulse that led Christians to respond to the plight of sufferers first with direct measures of relief then with efforts to reform social structures reached its zenith in the nineteenth century. It is simply not possible in the short confines of this paper to list, much less describe, the multitudinous ministries of mercy that evolved into programs of social reform. From the Inner Mission in Germany came schools for infants and cripples, rescue homes, clubs for apprentices, and campaigns against beggary, drunkenness, and prostitution. Kaiserswerth, an obscure village on the Rhine that became a major training center for philanthropy, provided the vision and example—as well as the training—for Florence Nightingale. Out of her memorable service in the Crimean War came schools that created the modern nursing profession. In England the evangelical Earl of Shaftesbury was the prime mover in legislation that improved treatment of the insane, brought better conditions for laborers in mills and factories, barred boys under the age of thirteen and women from the mines, protected chimney sweeps, and improved housing conditions. At the same time, the earl promoted a variety of missionary endeavors overseas.

A famous evangelical, William Wilberforce, led the successful campaign to abolish slavery throughout the British Empire. In the United States revivals led by Charles Finney fed antislavery impulses that strengthened the movement for emancipation. Jonathan Blanchard, founding president of Wheaton College, Illinois, was a renowned abolitionist. Another evangelical abolitionist, A. J. Gordon, founder of what developed into Gordon College and Gordon-Conwell Theological Seminary, advocated the "complete enfranchisement" of women "and their entrance into every political and social privilege enjoyed by men."[12] Walter Rauschenbusch, pastor to a working-class German Baptist congregation on the border of Hell's Kitchen in New York City, became the prophet of the emerging "social gospel," claiming that "if Jesus stood today amid our modern life, with the outlook on the condition of all humanity which observation and travel and the press would spread before him, and with the same heart of divine humanity beating in him, he would create a new apostolate to meet the new needs in a new harvestime of history."[13]

The nineteenth century was of course the great century of missionary advance. And it was in the mission fields that Christians, time and time again, were led from isolated acts of mercy into dramatic programs for social reform, often in confrontation with imperial authorities in their home countries as well as local authorities in the colonies.[14] Vishal Mangalwadi notes that "the battles against sati [immolation of widows], caste, child marriage, female infanticide, bonded agricultural labor, drunkenness, opium addiction, and other social evils were generally initiated and led by the missionaries and only taken up by Hindu reformers later." It was the missionaries "who understood that Christ's compassion called for a crusade against those social institutions and practices that oppress and dehumanize."[15]

Ministries of Mercy Today

With twenty centuries of tradition behind us it is not surprising that Christian compassion is expressed today in a multitude of forms. But it is the parachurch agencies, especially the newer relief and development agencies, that dominate the twentieth-century scene, exemplifying all the strengths and weaknesses of modern Christian charity.

Relief is big business—startlingly so. In 1979 five of the larger North American relief agencies reported a combined income approaching $125 million.[16] Such bigness represents power and raises serious questions with which we must grapple.

Bigness can be a blessing. The good work being done today by parachurch agencies specializing in relief, development, and health activities is too well publicized to require documentation in this paper. But unfortunately, large-scale relief agencies have sometimes misused their power—they have gained through their size the ability to affect social life for the worse.

Relief organizations commonly exercise three types of power: the power of finances, the power of expertise, and the power of organization.[17] Parachurch agencies are often in a position to wield all three unilaterally, sometimes insensitively. Indian mission executive Theodore Williams reminds us that "it is not the fulfillment of programmes but the fulfilling of human relationships that matter. If we ride roughshod over the feelings of people and have no time for individuals, under the guise of carrying out projects and programmes for God, our mission has no credibility."[18] Christ provides the model for such service devoted to individuals. He never sought to bring relief through domination. Indeed, it was prophesied of him that "he will not break a bruised reed or quench a smoldering wick, till he brings justice to victory" (Matt. 12:20). Jesus also instructed his disciples to follow the same course: "You know that those who are supposed to rule over the Gentiles lord it over them, and their great men exercise authority over them. But it shall not be so among you" (Mark 10:42-43).

Alongside this impulse to ride roughshod over those to whom we minister is an equally devastating tendency to co-opt the best leadership of the national churches in order to achieve parachurch agency objectives. This free-wheeling entrepreneurial spirit merely perpetuates the worldly values of our era. It works against the kingdom while purporting to extend it.[19]

A third area of concern relates to politics. Most evangelical ministries of mercy claim to be apolitical. This of course is an absurdity. We may not be consciously political, but in fact our relationships with governments—or, alternatively, our identification with oppressed communities within a nation—are political stances. *Newsweek* magazine quotes a World Vision staff member as saying, "We do our best not to offend the government. If we offend the government, we're gone."[20] The problem is, however, that many of these governments are committed to the preservation of an unjust status quo. What is the proper stance of a ministry of mercy then?

Summation: A Way Forward

Guatemala provides a provocative case study for seeking a forward course. Evangelicals have been preaching the gospel and patiently planting churches in Guatemala for a century, but it is generally agreed that the current and most impressive wave of church growth has occurred during the past six or seven years. In the aftermath of the 1976 earthquake that killed more than twenty thousand people and reduced hundreds of villages to rubble, North American relief agencies came to the rescue. That they made mistakes cannot be denied; yet their overall impact was perceived by the populace as positive. As a result, tens of thousands embraced the gospel, for evangelical relief agencies were prominent among the plethora of agencies that descended upon the country. Today it is estimated that 22 percent of the population is identified with the evangelical movement.

Among these recent converts is General Efrain Rios Montt, Guatemala's former president. The general mounted a powerful and apparently effective counteroffensive against communist-supported insurgents and justified it on biblical grounds. Evangelical leaders in Guatemala were reported to be supporting the general with enthusiasm.[21] It is quite clear that Guatemala is in the process of social transformation, stimulated in part by evangelical relief agencies. Whether that transformation will result in a better life for the country's masses or whether it will aid only the middle class is still very much open to question though.

While international evangelical relief agencies in Guatemala are not aiming directly at social transformation, an indigenous ministry in India, the Jamkhed Comprehensive Rural Development Project, has such transformation as its primary thrust, as can be seen in its use of the words *comprehensive* and *development*. This project, encompassing about two hundred villages of Maharashtra State in India, is spearheaded by two dedicated physicians, Raja Arole and his wife Maybelle Arole. The Aroles are motivated by a combination of compassion and justice. Their initial thrust into the area was designed as a ministry of mercy: relief of leprosy sufferers, the living dead. Their specialized training qualified them to offer four-dimensional healing—physical, spiritual, social, and vocational—to villagers burdened with a disease notorious for its devastating impact on individuals and communities.

Had they accomplished only this they would have earned the undying gratitude of their patients. But the Aroles' vision was much greater. They saw leprosy sufferers in the total context of rural life in India today. Consequently they developed leprosy care as an integral facet of a larger primary health care program, in line with the World Health Organization's declared objective of "health for all by the year 2000." But health, of course, is not merely a matter of medicine. The Aroles recognized from the start the relationship between primary health care and the economic realities of Indian village life. Soon they were involved in well-digging, the introduction of new crops and appropriate technology, the establishment of agricultural cooperatives and revolving loan schemes, and numerous other ventures.

Even this was seen in its larger context. The Aroles undertook an intensive, long-term educational, or conscientizing, effort. Women began to understand the extent to which they were dehumanized by male domination. All the poor began to comprehend the measure by which they were being exploited and permanently marginalized by rapacious landlords. Entire villages were taught to insist on their rights in the face of pervasive corruption by petty government bureaucrats.

At a still deeper level, as the message of Jesus was introduced, villagers experienced victory over the fear of spirits that was, in fact, the source of their lifelong bondage to disease and sickness. Little by little the kingdom of God has invaded a portion of Maharashtra State, transforming the quality of life of the poorest of the poor for whom Christ died and rose again. The Aroles avoid the term "anonymous Christians"; yet they assert that the Hindu villagers know full well it is Jesus, working through those who minister in his name, who has effected this transformation.

Two questions emerge from the Jamkhed experience, however. The first has to do with the project's relations with the national and state governments of India. Jamkhed has become a recognized model of rural development. The Aroles were honored by the government and served on the advisory council for health of former prime minister Indira Gandhi, of whom they have spoken favorably. Taking into consideration the skepticism with which many evangelical leaders, both Indian and foreign, regarded the record of Mrs. Gandhi's government on human rights and other values, it is not unreasonable to ask whether the Aroles were co-opted, and perhaps domesticated, by their government.

The second question that emerges relates to the church. To date, the Aroles, devout Christians, have studiously avoided inviting the church—the church of North India specifically—to join in the Jamkhed experiment. They are convinced that church involvement at this stage would spell disaster, for they are convinced that church leaders lack understanding of the overall process of development. This may be true, but is it right?

We have seen how, during the European Middle Ages, ministries of mercy were divorced from local parishes and made the exclusive activity of the church hierarchy. Is there not something fundamentally askew in our own day when ministries of mercy appear to be delegated either to high-powered parachurch agencies or, as in the case of Jamkhed, to independent indigenous organizations?

As a result of this study, superficial and truncated as it may be, I have reached some tentative conclusions. Let me couch them in the form of theses.

Ministries of mercy are both an individual and corporate expression of the Spirit of Christ.

Ministries of mercy motivated by Christian compassion have their own validity whether or not they aim at social transformation, and whether or not individual conversion or church growth is an immediate outcome.

Ministries of mercy, holistically understood in the context of the biblical demand for justice, can be instruments in God's hand to directly effect radical social transformation, including spiritual conversion in line with kingdom values.

Ministries of mercy wrongly motivated by the lust to exercise power or inadequately understood in terms of their social implications have the potential to sabotage the kingdom of God.

Ministries of mercy, whether domestic or foreign, are easily and unwittingly co-opted by ungodly principalities and powers. This must be guarded against.

Ministries of mercy, while necessarily functioning as specialized endeavors, ought to be the natural expression of the body of Christ in its congregational incarnations, and as such accountable to it.

Ministries of mercy, to accomplish the above, should devote a significant portion of their time, energy, and money to dialogue with the churches in order to achieve a higher level of church/parachurch interdependence.

Notes

1. See R. E. C. Brown, "Mercy," in *Dictionary of Christian Ethics,* ed. John Mac-Quarrie (Philadelphia: Westminster Press, 1967), p. 213.

2. See *The Illustrated Bible Dictionary,* ed. J. D. Douglas (Wheaton: InterVarsity/Tyndale, 1980), 2: 982.

3. This is one of those rare instances when the King James Version, with its translation "grieved," more accurately expresses the original Greek than does the Revised Standard Version, with "annoyed."

4. Ambrose, quoted in H. Daniel-Rops, *The Church of Apostles and Martyrs* (New York: Dutton, 1960), p. 575. For the historical sketches that follow I draw upon Daniel-Rops; Philip Schaff, *History of the Christian Church* (Grand Rapids: Eerdmans, 1960); Kenneth Scott Latourette, *A History of Christianity* (1953; New York: Harper and Row, 1975); and Latourette, *A History of the Expansion of Christianity* (1937; Grand Rapids: Zondervan, 1970). All of these rely in some measure on G. Uhlhorn's pioneering study, *Die christliche Liebesthätigkeit* (Stuttgart, 1882–1890).

5. For a more extended discussion of these early ministries of mercy and their impact on the social structures of the Roman Empire see Latourette, *Expansion,* 1: 265ff.

6. *Charity* derives from the Latin *caritas,* which originally denoted dearness or costliness and assumed in the church in the Middle Ages the more significant meaning of benevolence, especially to the poor and suffering. *Caritas* is the equivalent of our "acts of mercy."

7. The reference here is to the medieval church.

8. Walter Rauschenbusch, *Christianity and the Social Crisis,* ed. Robert D. Cross (New York: Harper Torchbooks, 1964), pp. 168–69.

9. See W. D. H. Lecky, *History of European Morals* (New York: Appleton, 1884), 2: 79ff.

10. Latourette, *Expansion,* 2: 366.

11. Howard later lost his life while traveling in Russia, searching for ways to prevent the spread of the plague.

12. Donald W. Dayton, *Discovering an Evangelical Heritage* (New York: Harper and Row, 1976), p. 93.

13. Rauschenbusch, quoted in Ronald C. White, Jr., and C. Howard Hopkins, *The Social Gospel* (Philadelphia: Temple University Press, 1976), p. 43.

14. See James S. Dennis, *Christian Mission and Social Progress,* 3 vols. (New York: Revell, 1897–1906).

15. See Vishal Mangalwadi's essay in this volume, "Compassion and Social Reform: Jesus the Troublemaker," p. 193.

16. Samuel Wilson, ed., *Mission Handbook,* 12th ed. (Monrovia, Calif.: MARC, 1979), p. 56.

17. See Donald B. Kraybill, *The Upside Down Kingdom* (Scottdale, Pa.: Herald, 1978), pp. 262, 283ff.

18. Theodore Williams, "The Servant Image," *AIM,* September 1980, p. 20.

19. See my essay, "The Fullness of Mission," in *Witnessing to the Kingdom: Melbourne and Beyond,* ed. Gerald H. Anderson (Maryknoll, N.Y.: Orbis, 1982), p. 53.

20. *Newsweek,* 29 November 1982, p. 62.

21. Wade Coggins, "Guatemala Report," unpublished memo (Washington, D.C.: EFMA, 3 January 1983).

Justice, Freedom, and Social Transformation

Chavannes Jeune

Introduction

There is a saying in Haiti: "When God made the world he did a good job, but he forgot one thing—to distribute the wealth evenly."

As never before, humanity today confronts the stark reality of abject poverty in the midst of plenty. One quarter of the world's population is in unprecedented affluence, while the rest is condemned to absolute poverty. Eight hundred million people are destitute, their lives at the mercy of malnutrition, disease, illiteracy, unemployment, low income, inadequate shelter, and high birth rates. In Haiti, some 40 percent of the six million people fall into this category, scratching out a meager living through subsistence farming. The gap between rich and poor widens as the standard of living of the rich minority steadily increases. While millions in the world starve to death each year, 40 percent of the population of the United States is overweight. Thirty percent of the world's population eats 75 percent of the world's protein. Nine hundred million people in the world subsist on less than seventy-five dollars a year, while in the United States a family that earns fifteen thousand dollars a year is officially classified as on the edge of poverty. One-third to one-half of humankind lives without access to health services of any kind. The rich third of the population of the world claims 87 percent of the world's total Gross National Product, while the poor two-thirds is left with the remaining 13 percent.

How can we understand these contradictions and overcome them? I intend to discuss some of the mechanisms that perpetuate injustice and inequality, then analyze some fundamental questions on the role of the church in the process of liberation, the fight against poverty, and the struggle for justice. As a member of the church and a citizen of the Third World—indeed, of Haiti, the poorest country of the Western hemisphere—I am qualified by my own personal experience to offer some thoughts—and prescriptions—about the church and justice, freedom, and social transformation.

Since 1977 I have devoted my life to working very closely with poor people in grass-roots community organizations, adult education, cooperatives, leadership training, and other activities. I have found that poverty is not an accident. It is fundamental to a world of abundance in which many are poor *in order that* a few others may stay rich. Injustice, exploitation, and oppression are created and sustained by the rich and powerful. As such, they seem to be problems too big to tackle; but tackling them is precisely part of the historical purpose of the church. The gospel has always dealt with social and economic structures that oppress people. It includes proclaiming "release to the captives and . . . liberty [to] those who are oppressed" (Luke 4:18).

Mechanisms of Injustice

When we speak of poverty we are not dealing primarily with conditions of scarcity but rather with fundamental questions of power, control, and distribution. The Uruguayan theologian, philosopher, and sociologist Julio de Santa Ana says:

> The suffering of the poor is not . . . limited to material needs (scarcity of goods, lack of basic health care services, lack of job opportunities, inadequate school facilities, etc.). Their life is also characterized by dependency and oppression. They have very little opportunity for their own decision-making to shape their lives. What and when they eat, where and when they work, what wages they should receive and what price they should pay, where and how they should live, how many children they should have and how to bring them up, what they say and how they should say it, even when they should laugh and when they should cry and how—all these things and many other aspects of life are determined or conditioned by the economic system, political power and religious sanctions controlled by the rich, the powerful and the influential.[1]

Thus certain relationships in society—those to do with ownership and power, whether social, racial, economic, cultural, or political—are responsible for perpetuating poverty. Bound up in these relationships are also social structures that foster injustice and inequality between the powerful and powerless, rich and poor, beneficiaries and victims.

Injustice and oppression have been reinforced during the last twenty-five years by the expansion of capitalism. Private ownership of land and its resources, of the means of production, and of high technology has provided for some the necessary power to own and control the very lives of other human beings. Capitalism and the system of private ownership as it is practiced in the twentieth century has resulted in every conceivable kind of oppression and dehumanization: slavery, racism, economic exploitation, dependency, and other social evils. It has also given some nations the idea that they have the right to cross geographical boundaries and, in the name of civilization, to colonize and govern other peoples while exploiting their human and natural resources. International corporations are typical of the foreign capitalistic forces that join together with those within a nation to oppress the poor and concentrate economic and technological power in the hands of a few. All of them claim to bring capital and technology to the countries where they operate, creating employment and income. But their primary motive is to take advantage of cheap labor and to profit from it, all the while wielding control over world trade and prices.

One word for the poor in the Indonesian language is literally translated "they who are not"—not "they who *have* not," but "they who *are* not." This is the linguistic expression of their state of exclusion, both from possession and also from being fully human. It is a vivid way of describing the ever-growing *marginalization* of the poor in the economic, social, political, and even religious life of their communities. While it is no secret that poor countries are excluded from the affairs of the world, even within poor societies there is the same stratification. The poorest of the poor are excluded even from such benefits and opportunities as are available to poor communities. They do not count in the affairs of the life of the community and play no part in its decision making. They are considered ignorant and worthless and are treated as outcasts—as nonhumans.

There are individuals, groups, governments, churches, and voluntary agencies who, with the support of well-intentioned people, have tried genuinely to do their best for the poor and oppressed. But often they look on the poor as mere objects of charity: as passive recipients of their goodwill. Their efforts have mainly been *for* the poor and seldom *with* the poor. These efforts fail to reverse the marginalization of the poor, for they fail to involve them as important agents in their own situation. The poor strive to be treated as subjects rather than mere objects, as having the potential to change their own situation and society as a whole. The last two decades of intensive development efforts in the Third World prove that conditions of the poor cannot and will not be solved by others doing things for them or by handouts. The nature of structural poverty demands that we tackle its root causes rather than just its effects.

The period of true colonialism is over. Yet the lust for economic gain that drove much colonialism still finds expression through political power, which dominates weak nations and lets loose oppression to preserve and perpetuate the system that works for the exclusive benefit of the few. National elites and international oppressive forces make every effort to keep the system working for their benefit, so keeping the poor where they are. As a necessary measure to maintain prevailing patterns of domination at home and abroad, the dictatorial and authoritarian regimes in Asia, Latin America, and Africa tend to institutionalize their violation of human rights.

A new mechanism of injustice and oppression is *thought control*, which is intimately linked with this century's developments in the technology of communications. At one time it was technologically impossible for a traditional dictatorship to compel acceptance of its dogma, to enforce constant and enthusiastic adoration, and to successfully demand that the news media and cultural and educational institutions reinforce its control and permeate every facet of existence with the cult of the dictator himself. Now, through communications techniques, the majority of Third World leaders maintain absolute thought control. They control what the people can know and learn and so they deprive them of independent choice and judgment.

The rich countries deprive the Third World of its professionals. For example, in 1970, 11,236 university graduates emigrated from underdeveloped countries to the United States. Doctors, scientists, and artists take their skills to affluent countries, where they often serve at lower wages than their counterparts. Over 30 percent of all Haitian doctors now practice in Canada, leaving only one doctor for every ten thousand people in Haiti. All these professionals would have been of great help to the poor in their home countries who paid for their training, but they drain away to the rich countries.

The church in many parts of the world identifies with the social, economic, and political system that is founded on and propagates the dominance of the few over the many. This practice often degenerates into what many have called a civil religion, which blesses the status quo instead of calling it into question. Civil religion is amoral and has little capacity to bring a word of judgment or correction to the social order. Its function is to provide religious justification for the social order, to serve as the ideological glue that holds the society together in consensus and conformity.

Freedom and Social Justice in the Bible

The Bible is full of teachings about social justice, freedom, and transformation. These are not to be relegated to the past, for they continue to speak to us today to help us understand God's desire and plan for his people.

The principle that the earth is the Lord's, and that we are only stewards of it and its resources, is the premise for the Jewish tradition of the *jubilee year* (Lev. 25:10-12). God's intentions for his people were not only religious and political, but also social and economic. He instituted the jubilee year in order to create a new social and economic order. God wanted the poor and the oppressed to be given a new opportunity to help themselves, so he founded the jubilee as a year in which land and wealth were redistributed; thus it served to make it difficult for a few to accumulate and hold wealth at the expense of the many.

Questions of wealth, poverty, and social justice are central in the ministry of the prophets. Isaiah says that God delights in the day of fasting, the day acceptable to the Lord, which means breaking the yoke of oppression, treating fairly those who work for us and giving them what they earn, sharing our bread with the hungry, bringing the homeless poor into our houses, and clothing those who are without (Isa. 58:5-7). Amos claims that not only does God delight in such acts of social justice but our relationship with him depends on it. Our worship and praise are not acceptable to God unless we "let justice roll down like waters, and righteousness like an everflowing stream" (Amos 5:24). Jeremiah, Hosea, and Micah all rebuked oppressive affluence and exploitative power and demanded economic and political justice for the poor, the exploited, the oppressed, the defeated, the defenseless, the weak, and the alien.

Jesus begins his ministry by asserting that he will continue the Old Testament concern for the poor and the oppressed. As he quotes from Isaiah 61:1-2, he identifies his mission as that foretold by the prophet: he has been anointed by the Spirit to preach good news to the poor, to proclaim release to the captives and recovery of sight to the blind, to set at liberty those who are oppressed, and to proclaim the acceptable year of the Lord (Luke 4:16-21). We must continue Jesus' deep involvement and close identification with those that society considers worthless. He tells us that our profession of love for God will be tested by our actions in feeding the hungry, clothing the naked, caring for the homeless, and ministering to the practical needs of the afflicted (Matt. 25:31-46). Moreover, our responsibility to our neighbor extends to anyone in need, even those we might have considered our enemies, as the parable of the Good Samaritan shows. Our responsibility leaps over human barriers of race and class, at the personal cost of time, money, and danger (Luke 10:30-37). His concern for the poor, the sick, the outcast, the downtrodden, and the ignorant brings social revolution.

The common life and sharing were distinguishing marks of the early church (Acts 4:32-35; 2 Cor. 8:1-5). The early Christians saw that nothing was their private property and that resources were to be shared and freely given for the good of the body rather than for any individual advantage. They founded a whole new system of distribution that included each person in a process of giving and receiving according to ability and need.

Practical Implications for the Church

If it is truly to become a viable and dynamic agent in the glorious new day that God has promised us, the church cannot choose to play it safe by adopting policies of neutrality. Even more, it must not ally itself with the powerful when the well-being of the poor is at stake. The principles of the jubilee, the words of the prophets, the life of Jesus, and the witness of the early church all challenge us to participate in the suffering of the community of the poor, the disinherited, the victimized, the outcast, and the broken-hearted. As the custodian of the message of the gospel, the church cannot remain uninvolved and indifferent. It is impelled to side with the poor instead of the forces in society that create oppression, dehumanization, marginalization, paternalism, tyranny, capitalism, and poverty. To respond to these challenges, several tasks face the church.

Major injustices in all sectors of life are widespread, if we consider the fair and equitable distribution of services and resources to be a benchmark of what is socially just. The causes are deeply embedded in society's social, economic, and political structures. Consequently, attempts to root them out often involve direct confrontation with the centers of worldly power. This directly challenges the church to denounce injustices, recognizing that silence in the face of oppression speaks even louder than words. The church must preach a full gospel that allows no separation between the spiritual and physical needs of humanity. The mission of the church is thus threefold: first, to plead the cause of the poor, defending the weak and helping the helpless (Prov. 22:22; Ps. 12:5; 10:17-18); second, to stand for equality and social justice (Prov. 14:21; Ps. 41:1); and third, to institute structures that will create a just and more equitable distribution of wealth (Lev. 25:28).

Ignorance may be the number one ally of those seeking to maintain the imbalance between the urban and the rural church, the rich and the poor, the powerful and the powerless. The church has a great deal to do here. We must not only promote education but also orient it to our neighbor in a spirit of love, service, and dedication. We must be concerned for whole persons in their biological and physical, social and economic development. The church must educate its own members to hold to the precepts of respect, justice, and human dignity and to beware of seeing the individual as a mere object, case study, or experimental material. The church should enable its members to take part in government-run public services: to be active, like Daniel and Joseph, in public processes encouraging humanization and justice. Church youths should be reminded of social service and humanitarian vocations that should be undertaken in a spirit of self-denial and dedication to one's neighbor. The church should work for the just distribution of resources to ensure that the marginalized strata of society have equal access to them. This is God's will, for he gives preference to the poor and forsaken.

Over the past two decades Christian organizations have initiated development projects in the Third World that have received substantial support from donor agencies in developed countries in the West. These programs were expected to become self-supporting and to provide examples of the self-reliance and successful participation of Third World peoples. Instead, most of them became new institutions depending largely on outside funds. They also became symbols of power and patronage or instruments for creating a new elite. That seems to be the tragedy of many Third World countries so far.

Self-reliant development concentrates on people and requires structural change in society. This is possible if policies of social justice are followed. When people receive a fair share of social production, they are motivated in turn to contribute a fair share to the social effort. Instead of the rich getting richer and the poor poorer, there must be a reduction of inequalities, a better sharing of economic, social, and political power between the privileged few and the underprivileged majority. So the church is not to join the existing status quo. Its mission is to be always on the move, to get people serving, to act as a prophet in the midst of an unjust society. It is always to be in the breach, defending the rights of the oppressed.

An Integrated Development Program

This is the experience of the Integrated Rural Development program of the Baptist Mission in South-West Haiti. Two hundred and seventy churches associated with the Baptist Mission in South-West Haiti span the entire south-west peninsula. Yet forty years of successful gospel proclamation did not change the people's physical situation. The churches' attitude to the poor had long been paternalistic, until they finally realized that they could not remain passive before the social and economic challenges. Then, in August 1979, pastors, missionaries, and lay people met to analyze the church's situation in Haitian society. In order to enable the churches to play a major role as agents of change, to demonstrate as well as to proclaim the gospel, they decided to start a program of Integrated Rural Development.

By motivating village people too powerless to speak up for themselves, the program seeks to bring the poor to a new awareness of their condition. It helps them struggle for a better life by means of development programs that stem from and are carried out by the local community. These give the people a sense of dignity, achievement, and hope.

Motivators in the program seek to motivate the villagers to action rather than directing them to do something. The motivators' primary aim is just to be with the people, sharing their everyday lives and winning their confidence. They motivate the villagers to reflect on their situation, to ask questions not asked before, to define their needs, and to establish a list of priorities. So begins a common search for a constructive program of self-development. For example, in 1982 our motivators persuaded farmers in one community in southwest Haiti to take their coffee crop directly to market, bypassing the middlemen. By selling their coffee beans directly to the buyers in Port au Prince, they increased their profits two and a half times. They are now forming a cooperative so as to take even greater control of their own lives and economic future.

These motivators often deal with the questions of injustice, exploitation, capitalism, and oppression. As a result of this interaction, development activities are planned and carried out by the people themselves. Health care programs are implemented with the people participating in decisions; local leaders are trained; agricultural cooperatives are organized for economic production; and most importantly, the liberating gospel of Christ gains deeper meaning for the people. The church program no longer manifests paternalism but rather gives a proclamation that helps people to better understand how to reaffirm their deep convictions and values.

Service

In the struggle for justice, the church is challenged to join hands with the poor, the hungry, and the oppressed. It can do so only by its tradition of service, the central theme of biblical thought: "You shall love the Lord your God with all your heart, and with all your soul, and with all your mind. . . . And . . . you shall love your neighbor as yourself" (Matt. 22:37, 39). Service stimulates reflection, draws Christians from different cultures together, and helps us discover the Lord in each of our neighbors.

The church's ministry of service promotes humanity, enabling it to develop its full creative potential. In choosing to serve the poorest, most marginal sectors of society, this ministry seeks to redeem both the oppressed and the oppressor. This aim excludes all paternalistic, charitable attitudes that belittle the human personality. It requires Christian organizations in more affluent countries to give Christians in poorer areas "equal justice" in the use of the resources of their nations. In true partnership, we must join hands north and south, east and west to change those systems that oppress the poor and rob people of their dignity and freedom.

Stewardship

The church and Christian organizations are responsible for managing the resources available for ministry according to moral standards and in such a way as to respond to the felt needs of the most marginal, nondeveloped segment of society. We are called to follow the doctrine of "active redistribution," that is, we must actively redistribute all of our time, talents, and resources to make the greatest possible impact on seeking the kingdom of God in our world.

When people followed Jesus, their decision always altered their lifestyles and radically changed the way they used their time and resources. Peter and Andrew left their boats to follow Jesus. Matthew resigned his job. Zacchaeus and Nicodemus gave up their relationships with the power structures of their society. Those who work in development need to experience a similar turnabout: they need to demonstrate in their own lives more responsible lifestyles, and they need to challenge their constituents to live more justly. Indeed, those who choose to follow Jesus must not rationalize away his radical expectations in relation to their own lives of affluence. They must not adopt a "fractional" view of stewardship that gives to God only a fraction of their money, time, and talents while reserving the rest all for themselves.

This whole-life approach to stewardship would allow every single member of the church and Christian organizations to start using the global resources of God more intentionally and equitably and to examine personal lifestyles for wasted resources that could be invested in the kingdom. The church must provide leadership by example and action in the biblical struggle for justice, freedom, and social transformation.

Note

1. Julio de Santa Ana, introduction to *Towards a Church of the Poor,* ed. Julio de Santa Ana (Geneva: World Council of Churches, 1979), p. xvii.

The Genesis of Human Needs

Samuel Baah

In the beginning, God made the provisions necessary to meet human needs. He created the Garden of Eden with the amenities of food, shelter, and security. God then gave the command that brought man and woman into being, blessed them with dominion over the earth and fellowship with their Creator, and bid them to be fruitful and multiply, to fill the earth and subdue it.

Satan's ploy was to make it seem plausible for humans to be independent and undying. This brought about their insubordination to God, their fall, and their final ejection from Eden. Under the circumstances, God's response showed mercy, compassion, and continued loving concern for humanity. Although he put them under an unpleasant curse to work hard and maintain themselves, he allowed almost all the systems of support that he had created to continue unchanged.

Since that time, humans have seen at different times in history God's active involvement in their affairs: we have never been left on our own. Whatever one may think the world to be, the fact remains that the earth has always been the sphere of human habitation, and it has always supplied our needs and material resources. Yet every epoch of civilization has found us struggling and laboring to meet our needs for food, clothing, shelter, and security. We have strived to have dominion over the earth and to subdue it, to appropriate our blessings and to multiply them, but we have failed in the area of fellowship with our Creator.

The apostle Paul said to the Athenians that God "made from one every nation of men to live on all the face of the earth, having determined allotted periods and the boundaries of their habitation, that they should seek God, in the hope that they might feel after him and find him" (Acts 17:26-27). People have always called on the name of the Lord, but he sees that their imaginations are continually evil, and none can qualify on their own merits for his favor. So God's program to redeem us to a state of eternal glory shows his concern and compassion for us. He has continually watched over us and has involved himself in our affairs (Heb. 1:1-2)—for this we must be thankful.

God made a covenant with Abraham and maintained it by manifesting his grace to Abraham's descendents. Then God shaped the destiny of the world by giving us a new covenant in Jesus. Through Christ's coming, death, and resurrection, God has stamped his authority on the world. The Word (the eternal Son) became flesh. By the agency of the flesh, where God was incarnate in Jesus Christ, the Word consummated the triumph of the cross.

The body must be supported in a manner consonant with God's creative command that all people should live fruitful lives. To gain insight into what this command means in the world today, we should consult the examples of Moses and Jesus, since their ministries were directed toward and solved both spiritual and physical needs. The Great Commission is a demand to meet needs of all sorts: we have to work in a way that brings material as well as spiritual improvement to society. The church, as colaborer with God in resuscitating the divine economy, must radiate more than just spiritual power.

The Example of Moses: Zeal for the Nation

Moses was born into the Hebrew nation, and even though he was raised by a daughter of the Egyptian Pharaoh, he remained preoccupied with zeal for his nation, with the desire to free his people from the misery of serfdom. The Hebrews were dehumanized by bearing the burden of Egypt's economic development and the responsibility for providing social amenities for the Egyptian people. At the same time, they also gradually lost their own indigenous culture.

One day Moses saw one of the Egyptian taskmasters beating a Hebrew worker. Filled with the desire to mete out justice for his people, he killed the Egyptian and buried the body. When Pharaoh heard of this, he in turn sought to kill Moses, who was then forced to flee into the desert. Moses went to live in Midian and eventually became a shepherd in the wilderness of Sinai; yet he still remained occupied with the fate of his people.

Once when Moses had led his flocks across the desert to Horeb, the mountain of God, an astonishing scene arrested him: a bush that was burning but was not consumed. "I will turn aside and see this great sight," he decided— and the die was cast. The voice of God, the clarion call to duty, sounded with miracles and wonders in accompaniment. By these events, God confirmed to Moses one great fact: that he really did call things into being merely by the word of his mouth. He proclaimed that he did care for his people in Egypt— that suffering and oppression were against his plan for them—and so he sent Moses to Pharaoh to bring Israel out of Egypt. Moses then grew noble in God's service and distinguished himself by his humble response to human need. Through Moses' service God brought both physical and spiritual deliverance to the Israelites.

When Moses responded to the call of God in the burning bush and gave himself over to his service, he became the model for all those who seek to respond to the call of the Great Commission to meet the spiritual and physical needs of their fellow human beings. "By faith Moses, when he was grown up, refused to be called the son of Pharaoh's daughter, choosing rather to share illtreatment with the people of God than to enjoy the fleeting pleasures of sin. He considered abuse suffered for the Christ greater wealth than the treasures of Egypt, for he looked to the reward" (Heb. 11:24-26).

The Example of Jesus: The Gospel of the Kingdom

Jesus inaugurated the gospel of the kingdom at the synagogue in Nazareth. When he stood up to read he was given the book of Isaiah, and he read: "The Spirit of the Lord is upon me, because he has anointed me to preach good news to the poor. He has sent me to proclaim release to the captives and recovering of sight to the blind, to set at liberty those who are oppressed, to proclaim the acceptable year of the Lord." Then Jesus declared: "Today this scripture has been fulfilled in your hearing" (Luke 4:18-19, 21; cf. Isa. 61:1-2).

Jesus followed his words with actions and deeds. He left Nazareth and went to Capernaum, preaching "Repent, for the kingdom of heaven is at hand." He proclaimed the gospel of the kingdom, teaching his chosen disciples and healing all manner of sickness and disease among the people. His nobility was recognized promptly because of his exceptional public service. His was a kingdom mission of compassion, social justice, and liberation from both spiritual and physical poverty—from broken-heartedness, captivity, blindness, and bruises. His mission proclaimed the true interpretation and application of the word of God.

Jesus emphasized the purpose of God in the creative goals of the kingdom—and also in the costs and compensations of trying to carry them out for God's sake (see Matt. 10:16-42). The paramount concern of the church was to preach the gospel of the kingdom so that it invaded the whole earth. One of the best ways to proclaim this gospel was to seek justice and righteousness: "Seek first his kingdom and his righteousness, and all these things shall be yours as well" (Matt. 6:33). God has said of the patriarch Abraham: "I have chosen him, that he may charge his children and his household after him to keep the way of the Lord by doing righteousness and justice; so that the Lord may bring to Abraham what he has promised him" (Gen. 18:19). To achieve the objectives set by God, the church in response to human need should always program its actions according to Christ's keynote address at Nazareth, which reveals the biblical foundation for seeking and promoting justice, freedom, development, social transformation, and social responsibility.

Creative Power Poured Out for the Church

After Jesus' ascension, the Holy Spirit was poured out to fulfill two promises: "I will build my church, and the powers of death shall not prevail against it," and "I will give you the keys of the kingdom of heaven, and whatever you bind on earth shall be bound in heaven, and whatever you loose on earth shall be loosed in heaven" (Matt. 16:18-19). These passages suggest that the church has God-given power to promote a better life by better programs for the future. Nowhere in the world can the intention of the church to further the kingdom through the gospel be overcome. The opposition may prove to be stiff, but the trump card is always held by Christ.

With the help of God's creative and guiding power the early church developed the community of goods—a system with the means to meet both the spiritual and the physical needs of the church's members (Acts 4:32). Though only a small group, the church still had the message and authority to transform the social and cultural systems of Jerusalem and Samaria, indeed, of the whole world. By meeting the challenge of its mandate, the church sees economic well-being follow for the people.

Making people disciples meets their spiritual and physical needs. The task of evangelism and conversion enlarges the spiritual and social responsibilities of the church. It is especially here that the power of love and compassion ought to be exercised, that members of the church should model themselves after Christ. It was in the midst of evangelism, while preaching to the crowds, that Jesus saw the people as sheep without a shepherd. He was moved with compassion; and, having ministered to their spiritual needs, he ministered also to their physical needs—he fed them (Mark 6:34-44).

Today there are many sheep without a shepherd. The church has to have a realistic plan to contain human hurts such as hunger, misery, slum-dwelling, spiritual and physical illness, oppression, exploitation, and the lack of the basic necessities of life. Christian businessmen, for example, should give constant consideration to the human needs of the church and should take account of the necessity of transforming social, economic, and cultural conditions. The church should begin its program of reform by endeavoring to model the unity of the Spirit in the bond of peace. There is one body, one Spirit, and a calling to one hope. There is one Lord, one faith, one baptism, and one God and Father of all, who is above all, through all, and in (us) all. Believers must love God and his Christ above all.

Passing through the preliminaries of hearing the gospel, repenting, and being converted, a person is baptized and prayed over to receive the Holy Spirit. Birth precipitates growth in mental and physical development. "And Jesus increased in wisdom and in stature, and in favor with God and man" (Luke 2:52).[1] Any person in quest of fellowship with God must mirror the growth of Christ and must develop mental creativity. "If any of you lacks wisdom," says James, "let him ask God, who gives to all men generously . . . , and it will be given him" (James 1:5). If the patience of the church is to be rewarded, if the church is to have its perfect work accomplished, its members need wisdom. For as individual church members grow in wisdom, stature, and favor with God and other human beings, so also may the structures of the society of which they are part be transformed, becoming imbued with wisdom, stature, and favor.

Social Transformation

The message of the church rings clear: "Serve the purpose of God." Gradually but meticulously, God builds his kingdom. "Of his own will he brought us forth by the word of truth that we should be a kind of first fruits of his creatures" (James 1:18). Still, we deceive ourselves about the efficacy of our own human work. In Ghana, for instance, there is a very high concentration of churches; yet corruption and all forms of evil are still prevalent. This incongruity obtains in many countries, and it reveals that we have not yet fulfilled God's purpose that we should "be doers of the word, and not hearers only" (James 1:22). If the church is to set in motion social transformation in our advanced scientific and technological world, it needs much more than mere intellect—it needs the dynamic of the Holy Spirit.

For Paul, the power of the Holy Spirit alone was necessary and sufficient to impel him to his ministry: "But when he who had set me apart before I was born, and had called me through his grace, was pleased to reveal his Son to me, in order that I might preach him among the Gentiles, I did not confer with flesh and blood" (Gal. 1:15-16). While Paul did not need to consult others, but was driven by the Spirit to action, many of us today still deceive ourselves and remain hearers only. Many intellectuals in the Third World are churchgoers; many professionals and privileged people hold respectable positions; yet their lifestyles, conduct, and behavior leave much to be desired. For this reason, all of us, as members of God's one holy church, have the task and responsibility to encourage each other—and so ourselves—to move beyond words to action to further God's plan for the world.

Jesus did not seek to alleviate the sufferings of the people by delving into Old Testament theology. Rather, in pursuing the will and righteousness of God (John 5:30), he went about actually *doing* good (Matt. 4:23; Acts 10:38). Many of his actions broke down the theological barriers of his time (John 9:16),[2] because God's compassion (Ps. 86:15; 111:4; 112:4; 145:8) knows no barriers (cf. Rom. 9:15). This compassion was the key to Christ's action (Matt. 14:14; 15:32): he had compassion on the blind (Matt. 20:34), the demon-possessed (Luke 9:42), the leper (Mark 1:41), the bereaved (Luke 7:3), the dead (John 11:35, 38), the sinful (Rom. 5:8), the lost (Matt. 9:36; Mark 6:34), and the spiritually dead (Eph. 2:1, 4-5). Indeed, Christ identified—as we also should do (see Heb. 10:33b-34)—with any form of misfortune ending in wretchedness and degradation: "Come to me, all who labor and are heavy laden, and I will give you rest" (Matt. 11:28).

The compassion of the Son of God did not stop at feelings and words, however (see 1 John 3:18). It created positive action in self-sacrifice: a consistent, practical ministry to meet the needs of everyone that Christ encountered. In the Good Samaritan (Luke 10:33) we see exemplified this prime characteristic of Christ, that he addressed himself to every situation that came his way, and that the neighbor to whom one owes service is not limited to family, friends, or countrymen but includes every other human being, even enemies.

Christ's creative compassion sparked spiritual and social transformation. The church today has to rekindle its creative power to carry on that responsibility. Now, as we have put our hands to the plough (Luke 9:62), we must look ahead, and we must work hard by faith as never before. Before Jesus returns, we must work for righteous government that rules in love (Rom. 13:4a; cf. 1 John 3:16), justice (Rom. 13:3b, 4b), and equity (Rom. 13:3a; cf. Gal. 5:23b), and that provides for all (Rom. 13:6-7a; cf. 1 John 3:17). We must work for the transposition of all humanity into God's better, global kingdom.

The Kingdom of God

The kingdom of God, according to Scripture, has been prepared from the foundation of the world (Matt. 25:34). Flesh and blood or fallen human nature cannot inherit the kingdom; false professors of Christ and followers of Antichrist cannot enter it. "Not every one who says to me, 'Lord, Lord,' shall enter the kingdom of heaven," warns Jesus, "but he who does the will of my Father who is in heaven" (Matt. 7:21).

Many Christians are heading for disappointment. Vigorous and persistent evangelical preaching is still necessary. For the church to step up evangelism is good, but it is best by far for the church to support evangelism through practical social service, as Christ did. "Faith by itself, if it has no works, is dead," declared James (2:17). "What does it profit, my brethren, if a man says he has faith but has not works? Can his faith save him? If a brother or sister is ill-clad and in lack of daily food, and one of you says to them, 'Go in peace, be warmed and filled,' without giving them the things needed for the body, what does it profit?" (James 2:14-16).

All of us, as brothers and sisters in both developed and developing nations, are the children of God created in his image and likeness. Paul says of our Lord Jesus Christ that "though he was rich, yet for your sake he became poor, so that by his poverty you might become rich" (2 Cor. 8:9). And even though not all people can be made materially rich, all people, through the blessings of Christ, have the right to—and should be enabled to—live in dignity as children of one Father.

Now let my Christian brothers and sisters in the developed countries, who are well informed about the degradation and injustices suffered by Third World countries and by the underprivileged everywhere, let them develop an evangelization strategy that does not disregard the troubles of others. The gospel message, the mandate of the Great Commission, must be carried to the doors of Western governments, multinational corporations, and the privileged class.

How are we going to go about making this, and the dignity of all, a reality? The church, as God's umpire on earth, must play the leading role. In Christ Jesus, God gives the church the mandate to bring the triumph of righteousness:

righteousness exalts a nation and its people. The Great Commandment and the Great Commission are explicit on this vital issue: the church must demonstrate concern for the liberation and salvation of humanity for the sake of Jesus Christ. In very concrete terms of restoration, Isaiah identifies such a dedication to righteousness and the right exercise of justice as natural consequences of authentic conversion: "Your people will rebuild the ancient ruins and will raise up the age-old foundations; you will be called Repairer of Broken Walls, Restorer of Streets with Dwellings" (Isa. 58:12, NIV).

Before Isaiah, Moses spoke of God's provision for human need in the desert: "I have led you forty years in the wilderness; your clothes have not worn out upon you, and your sandals have not worn off your feet" (Deut. 29:5). What God was able to do for forty years he is still able to do and in fact is now coming to do. God's provision for his people in the desert and the restoration of the city foretold by Isaiah are examples of the providing care and renewal that will be present in the coming kingdom. The church is daily praying for the kingdom to come, and we believe that the Father will bring it in its fullness according to his will and timing.

Carrying Out Christian Justice

"The Lord is not slow about his promise as some count slowness," Peter reminds us. Rather, he "is forbearing toward you, not wishing that any should perish, but that all should reach repentance" (2 Pet. 3:9). It is important that the Lord's forbearance be reciprocated with repentance. The kind of conversion that is needed now is typified by the repentance and confession of Zacchaeus, who cried out: "Behold, Lord, the half of my goods I give to the poor; and if I have defrauded any one of anything, I restore it fourfold" (Luke 19:8). This sort of confession is marked by a willingness to *act*. If Western nations claim to be Christian, and if privileged people make the same confession, then they should at the same time be more Christlike in their actions on behalf of the oppressed. Jesus said: "By this all men will know that you are my disciples, if you have love for one another" (John 13:35). "Give, and it will be given to you" (Luke 6:38).

It is now prudent, and also required by the demands of Christian love, for the developed nations and their industrialists to give freely of the kind of technology that fits the immediate priorities of the Third World: namely, food, clothing, and shelter. The fair distribution of modern technology could be a meaningful contribution to the process of eliminating world poverty. If those in the developed countries do what must be done to preserve life, they shall receive "abundant life" in good measure. The Western nations should apply wisdom and understanding in the spirit of Christian social justice to ease global tension. By transferring needed help, they will win the renewed friendship and confidence of struggling developing countries. Furthermore, if the task of disciple making is to succeed, evangelization must be accompanied by the material development of the society.

Jesus said that "a disciple is not above his teacher" (Matt. 10:24; Luke 6:40). If the church takes this Scripture as the basis of its mediation, if it truly allows Christ to be its leader and guide in the world, it will be in a better position to initiate a meaningful dialogue between the superpowers. This will reduce East-West tension and will take away tactics accompanying the Cold War that serve to destabilize Third World nations. If the church follows this policy and exemplifies Christ's mediation and liberation, it will make efficient use of a God-given tool for disciple making and will carry out a mission for social justice and transformation.[3]

Notes

1. See Robert Moffitt's essay in this volume, "The Local Church and Development," for his argument from Luke 2:52.

2. See Vishal Mangalwadi's article in this volume, "Compassion and Social Reform: Jesus the Troublemaker," for his argument from John 9.

3. This paper was prepared for the consultation, but the author was unable to attend to present it.

The Local Church and Development

Robert Moffitt

Before I begin, I would like to set the groundwork for my discussion. First of all, in this paper I am writing to the local, evangelical church in the West. Many of the principles I discuss here are applicable to the local church in the Third World and local churches of nonevangelical persuasions, but I place my emphasis and choose my examples in the hopes of providing helpful responses to some of the problems facing especially the Western evangelical church, the church of my spiritual heritage. And second, I should note that I use the words *development* and *mission* interchangeably—especially after the first section where I try to show why I believe they are one and the same. For overseas missions I use the plural *missions*.

What Is Development?

Development from Luke's Perspective

A little noticed verse of Luke has become full of implications for me as I have struggled with the meaning of development: "And Jesus increased in wisdom and in stature, and in favor with God and man" (Luke 2:52). I think this verse is an excellent place to begin a study of the biblical view of development, for it gives us three keys to understanding. First, it talks about the development of a model person—the person Jesus. How Jesus grew, how he developed, is at the very least instructive for our understanding. Second, the verse reveals that God had a purpose for Jesus to fulfill. There is an obvious connection between the development of Jesus as a person and his fulfilling the purpose for which God sent him into the world. If Jesus is our model, certainly his development sets a model for ours. Third, as we consider the development of communities and then of societies, we must consider the development of their primary units—individual persons. Jesus was an individual. He lived in a family, in a community, and in a society. God's plan for Jesus' development as an individual would not be inconsistent with his plans for the development of Jesus' family, community, or society.

Luke mentions four areas in which Jesus developed: wisdom, stature, favor with God, and favor with man. If we were to translate these four areas into contemporary equivalents, we might say that Christ showed mental development, physical development, spiritual development, and social development.

Jesus' Development Covers Human Development

As I examine these four categories, I have difficulty thinking of any human need not covered. The need to observe, remember, integrate, analyze, and make wise decisions is covered under mental development—wisdom. Physical needs such as food, shelter, exercise, and a healthy physical environment are covered by physical development—stature. The need to develop, nurture, and maintain a vertical relationship with our Creator is covered under spiritual development—favor with God. And the need to develop, nurture, and maintain horizontal relationships with other individuals and groups is covered under social development—favor with man.

Development toward a Purpose

God's purpose for Jesus was kingdom related. Jesus' principal message was the kingdom of God, and his life was a foretaste of the kingdom, He died and rose so that human beings can share in that kingdom; and now, through individual believers and through his church, Jesus is advancing God's kingdom and moving it toward its fulfillment.

God's purpose for us is also kingdom related. Scripture tells us that ultimately God's purpose is that man "will be rescued from the tyranny of change and decay, and have *his* share in that magnificent liberty which can only belong to the children of God!" (Rom. 8:21, Phillips, emphasis mine). But what about the intervening time? Scripture describes God's purpose for us by saying that we are to love and honor our creator. "You shall love the Lord your God with all your heart, and with all your soul, and with all your mind. This is the great and first commandment" (Matt. 22:37).

God's purpose is that redeemed human beings demonstrate, as Jesus did, the wonderful nature of God's plans for our future. His purpose is that the redeemed tell the unredeemed the good news about, and recruit them into, his kingdom: "Go into all the world and preach the gospel to the whole creation" (Mark 16:15).

If these are God's purposes for humanity, then growth into God's purpose is the highest view of human development. Biblically based development is thus any movement of individuals or groups in the mental, physical, spiritual, and social arenas toward God's present and future purposes for us.

The Secular View Is Limited

This biblically based definition goes beyond the more commonly held contemporary view in which the focus of development is primarily material and social. It is understandable, however, that secular development agencies such as CARE, USAID, and OXFAM have this more limited perspective. (See note 1 of the appendix to this chapter below; see also Tom Sine's essay in this volume.)

A Christian Heresy—A Dichotomized Perspective

The church cannot stop with the secular perspective; yet it has unfortunately been heavily influenced by Enlightenment thinking. While Western Christians understand the human need for growth in physical, social, and spiritual areas, they have often accommodated the influence of the Enlightenment by separating physical and social from spiritual development. Unfortunately, this dichotomy is not limited to the church in the West. Third World churches have been influenced by Western missions even when a dichotomized perspective is not indigenous.

This dualism is heresy because it creates and supports an unbiblical dichotomy. Jesus and the writers of Scripture do not separate human developmental needs in this dualistic manner. Jesus' answer to the question "Teacher, which is the great commandment in the law?" (Matt. 22:36) tells us that human completeness is found in responding to spiritual, social, and physical needs *together*. The prophet Isaiah also ties the human relationship to God and his response to human need tightly together in Isaiah 58. The apostle James, probably the most pointed of biblical writers in integrating the physical and spiritual, says that "faith by itself, if it has no works, is dead" (James 2:17). It is thus safe to say that the Bible integrates what the Enlightenment separates and that it allows no room for a "Christian dualism" in which all the elements are there but separated.

A consequence of Christian dualism is the division it creates in the ministry arms of the church. It permits churches and overseas missions agencies, sometimes smugly, to see their calling as *either* relief and development *or* evangelism and discipleship. It thus underlies the great debate between liberal and conservative churches over the social gospel. It encourages the sin of pride in Christian liberals who are involved in a primary ministry to physical needs, and at the same time it causes conflict by leading Christians of a conservative persuasion to criticize liberals who pay little attention to evangelism.

At best, a dualistic view is unhelpful to the mission of the church. At worst, it turns men and women away from God's purposes for their development and thus diminishes and discredits the kingdom of God.

A Unified Definition of Development

Our definition of development, then, must unite what the Enlightenment began to separate and what many churches continue to keep apart. We will therefore define development as *every biblically based activity of the body of Christ, his church, that assists in bringing human beings toward the place of complete reconciliation with God and complete reconciliation with their fellows and their environment.* Activities that produce this reconciliation include the whole range of spiritual, social, and physical ministries, including specific ministry areas like evangelism, discipleship, teaching for literacy, medicine, community health, community development, relief, agriculture, church planting, and worship.

God does call different individuals and organizations to minister with emphasis in one or more specific areas of development—of mission. But that emphasis is to be seen as an essential part of a unified mission, not as better or more important than other facets of ministry. Further, no single aspect of ministry, such as evangelism, is meant to stand alone. Unless a given ministry emphasis fits into a plan for complete growth—unless people can be helped to develop in all areas of God's purposes for them—growth will be lopsided, incomplete, even abortive. (See note 2 of the appendix below.)

Implications for the Local Church

Development Is the Church's Mission

What are the implications of this definition of development for the local church? The first is that development *is* the mission of the local church. It is nothing less than the obedient response of the church to both the Great Commandment and the Great Commission. This definition of development is thus a view of holistic ministry.

Disobedience to the Mandates Leads to Serious Consequences

The consequences of disobedience to the mandates of the Great Commission and to those of the Great Commandment are both frightening, though disobedience to the spiritual ministry mandate brings different consequences from disobedience to the physical/social ministry mandate. For example, when Paul was addressing the elders of the church at Ephesus (Acts 20:24-37), he said that because he had been faithful in sharing the gospel of the grace of God (that is, because he had been obedient to the Great Commission) he was innocent of the blood of all men. If he had disobeyed his commission, he would have been guilty of the blood of those to whom God led him but with whom he did not share the gospel. The entire church then and today has the same commission. While we are not responsible for the consequences of sharing the gospel—for the growth of the kingdom—we are nonetheless responsible for sharing it.

But what if we are not obedient in ministering to the social and physical needs of others? The consequences are different and at a personal level substantially more grave. James says that faith without works is dead (James 2:17). And, all through the Gospels Jesus relates belonging to him to obeying him. Perhaps one of the most convicting passages is his message in Luke 6:20-49, where he tells us how we are to relate to and serve our fellow human beings. He concludes with an illustration of one who hears and obeys and one who hears but does not obey: the prognosis for the one who does not obey is disaster. Similarly in John 14, Jesus several times says that to be his disciple is to keep his commandments (vv. 12, 15, 21).

In light of these passages, lack of obedience in the area of social and physical ministry calls into question the very existence of a vertical relationship with God. Could we even say that it may be possible to be a Christian and neglect spiritual ministry but impossible to be a Christian and neglect social and physical ministries? I will not try to answer this question, but its consideration should be sobering. (See note 3 of the appendix below.)

Ministry Can Be Focused but Not Exclusive

If the individual Christian does not have an option of *exclusive* ministry to a particular ministry focus (to either evangelism or relief), then by implication the same is true for the local church or parachurch agency.

The key word in this statement is "exclusive." God gives individuals, organizations, and local churches different gifts and opportunities of service. But these special gifts in no way exempt them from obedience to the two broad areas of ministry. For example, I believe God has gifted and called me to a primary focus of ministry to social and physical needs. Further, I feel quite awkward in some areas of spiritual ministry. I get tongue-tied when I am involved in personal evangelism. But I have not been exempted as a consequence of that from the demands of obedience to the spiritual ministry implications of the Great Commission. Every opportunity God presents to my primary ministry to social and physical needs is also an opportunity to share the content of the gospel. If I am personally unable to spiritually minister because of a language barrier or some other obstacle, I have the obligation, out of obedience, to do whatever is reasonable (to arrange for an interpreter, for example) to ensure that the gospel is communicated.

The same is true in a spiritual ministry. If God has called a local church to a primary ministry of evangelism, that church must also at the same time take advantage, either directly or in collaboration with others, of every opportunity to minister to the social and physical needs of those being evangelized.

Steps of Application

How can the local church best achieve a balance between the social and the spiritual ministries? I suggest at least six initial steps.

1. Develop a sound understanding of and teaching about the biblical principles of a balanced ministry.

2. Examine the assumptions and practices of the church's past and present involvement in overseas missions activity for a balanced ministry.

3. Examine assumptions and practices of denominational mission boards, mission societies, or relief and development agencies that the local church supports or with which the local church cooperates to see if they are consistent with a balanced ministry. For example, don't take for granted that the relief and development organization your church supports also has a passion to see its work integrally tied to evangelism and discipleship. Check it out. If it does not, stop supporting it and tell why.

4. If the local church's development activities and relationships with missionaries, agencies, and societies are not consistent with biblical principles of balanced ministry, initiate a plan to correct the inconsistencies. If those in-

dividuals or agencies being supported by the local church are not willing to change, then adjustment of the local church's support for them is in order.

5. Make sure that your church's ministry emphasis fits into a total development strategy. Your church may not be able to change outside agencies, but it should be able to correct itself.

6. Remember that the objective of all mission is to minister to people in such a way that they will develop in every area of God's purpose for them.

A Global Development Strategy for the Local Church

I believe there is also a geographic implication for ministry in Jesus' statement to the apostles in Acts 1:8: "and you shall be my witnesses in Jerusalem and in all Judea and Samaria and to the end of the earth." Is it not likely that Christ wanted each local expression of his church to demonstrate as far as is possible God's geographically balanced concern for all humanity? If so, each local church—especially affluent Western churches—can minister to its own local "Jerusalem," as well as to "Judea," to "Samaria," and to "the end of the earth."

Of course most local churches, even the massive congregations of our era, cannot simultaneously engage in all development ministries in all parts of the earth. But I believe that the local church, if it can, *should* be engaged in *all* major categories of mission in *all* parts of the world.

The practical consequences of this commission are as follows: The church must minister in its home community, its "Jerusalem." Most of the church's resources are targeted here. The church should also minister, if possible, through missionaries or missions agencies to people of other countries. The types of ministry usually express the orientation of the local church. This ministry represents the local church's "remotest part of the earth." And the church should further minister to areas near home—for example, to the inner city or to the American Indians or to migrants or to refugees. This represents the local church's "Judea and Samaria."

A Litany of Problems

This strategy has some positive elements, but the manner in which it is carried out often leaves much to be desired. I see the major problems as follows:

1. There is skimpy awareness of the biblical nature of, or the mandate for, balanced ministry.

2. The investment of local church resources in global missions is uninformed, haphazard, and often not directed into the best channels.

3. Some ministries, especially those away from home, are merely the easiest way out for the supporting church. Instead of getting directly involved, the church hires others—missionaries and relief and development agencies—to do the work on behalf of it.

4. There is very little accountability between the church and those who represent it on its missions programs. The local church is often so ill-informed that even if it knew the facts of problems on the field, it would not know how to evaluate or respond to them.

5. There is very little personal contact between the local church members and the church's missions representatives (missionaries or overseas missions agencies), let alone between the church members and the people being ministered to.

6. Church support for missions programs is primarily financial. The local church members get the feeling that the appropriate response to the mandates of the Great Commandment and the Great Commission is to throw money at the world's problems.

7. Support for missions is shotgun rather than rifled. It is broadcast in insignificant amounts to many different targets rather than being focused in a few areas with enough investment both to make a difference and to encourage accountability.

8. Missions agencies, or relief and development agencies, often actually inhibit genuine accountability and meaningful personal relationships between the local church and the mission endeavor. Because those in the agencies are the experts and specialize in offering their services, the local church sees little need to develop its own expertise or global missions strategy.

9. It is not clear that a biblical basis exists for parallel mission structures, such as separate church missions boards and relief and development agencies, which do mission or development on behalf of the church. There is a biblical basis, however, of people-to-people and church-to-church mission and development activities.

10. Overseas missions in the local church often become the responsibility of a missions committee rather than of the entire church. Instead of being a catalyst to involve the entire congregation, the missions committee is a bottleneck.

11. Overseas missions are viewed by church leadership as secondary, as a threat to meeting other financial needs.

12. One of the most appealing dimensions of the kingdom in a world split by economic and racial enmity is that in Christ we become one. There are exciting possibilities of getting significant numbers of members of the local church directly involved in partnership ministries with believers of local churches in the Third World, or in the local churches in "Judea." But with the one-way funnel effect of traditional overseas missions structures, this opportunity is severely diminished.

A Problem of Delegation

All the problems listed above are related, some more closely than others, to an overall spiritual problem that pervades the local church in the West and the whole of our Western industrialized societies. If we focus on correcting this root problem, many of the problems addressed above will tend to solve themselves.

This spiritual problem is the tendency to delegate our responsibility for ministry to others. We have an unfounded belief, or hope, that professionals can solve our spiritual and social problems. Yes, professionals should and generally do have greater knowledge and technical expertise than laypersons. But wisdom is more important in spiritual and social problem solving than either knowledge or technical expertise, and many nonexpert members of the local church possess wisdom in good measure. (See note 4 of the appendix below.) Professionals as such have never been, nor ever will be, able to provide solutions simply on the basis of their expertise to human problems—including the problem of mobilizing the local church for its mandate of world missions. (See note 5 of the appendix below.)

A New Role for the Professional

Obviously the task is difficult and complex. Furthermore, we have gone about it in the wrong way: we have delegated the primary responsibility for being "the light of the world," "the salt of the earth," and "the firstfruits of the kingdom" to professionals rather than keeping it where it belongs—with the laity. But the solution is not to get rid of professionals. Untrained and poorly guided laity will not only get hurt themselves, but their mistakes can discourage others who would otherwise engage in the difficult task of direct ministry. It is not that professionals are not needed. They are. Far more can be accomplished, however, if professionals are primarily enablers and not doers. Thus we should first of all change the professionals' role: they should become teachers, catalysts, and facilitators. And second, we should insist that the laity accept their own responsibility for direct ministry.

This is not a new idea. Jesus spent almost three years teaching twelve men to minister. He taught by example, and he taught well enough that after three years he was able to send eleven of them out into direct ministry—to carry on the work he had started (John 20:21).

Paul understood this principle well. As he said to Timothy, "what you have heard from me before many witnesses entrust to faithful men who will be able to teach others also" (2 Tim. 2:2). Paul went from community to community, teaching, preparing, establishing churches, and then moving on. But in moving on he continued to encourage, to teach, and to facilitate, even though he did *not* often reinvolve himself in direct ministry in these communities.

Why should the pattern be any different with the local church today?

A Strategy for Direct Involvement on a Global Level

Laity should be involved in ministry in the most direct way possible. It is the laity's birthright, which carries with it certain responsibilities. It is not difficult to see how direct lay involvement can work in ministries in "Jerusalem," and perhaps in those in "Judea and Samaria" as well. But how can direct lay action work in "the end of the earth"? Let me suggest how.

1. Church leaders must make a preliminary decision to involve the laity of the local church directly in the implementation of the church's global mission.

2. The church must select from its members those who will lead the related research and planning efforts.

3. The selected leaders must then engage in a program of research and study. First, they should study the Scriptures to discern the missions mandate of the church. Second, they should review and analyze the relevant literature from overseas missions agencies and missions boards. (Most missions organizations will be biased toward traditional strategies, but, when requesting information, the local church members should explain their interests and intentions. There are often forward-thinking professionals in missions organizations who can be of great help in directing one to relevant materials.) And third, the elected leaders should enroll in short mission training courses such as those offered by the Missionary Internship Training Program of Farmington, Michigan, or the Center for World Mission in Pasadena, California. The focus of the course work should be practical and hands-on rather than theoretical.

4. The leaders should then design a study program for church membership on the basis of their research and study. That research should also be combined with consultations from mission and education experts. The result should be a curriculum of study materials to provide a survey of the problems and possible ways forward.

At a minimum, the curriculum should include (a) inductive Bible study of the believers' global mandate for balanced missions; (b) cross cultural communication; (c) inductive Bible study of development; and (d) review of biblically sound development case studies.

Each content area should contain at least two, but no more than four sessions of one to two hours in length.

The studies should be practical and related to the church's existing missions programs.

The curriculum should also include all age groups—to the extent possible.

5. The chosen leaders should then begin to train others for subleadership positions and they in turn should begin to train the laity. Trainers should go through all the materials and experiences through which they will take the laity *before* they teach the lay course.

6. At the same time, committees of the membership should be examining current mission strategies. On the basis of this examination, these committees should recommend changes of existing mission strategies and should begin to recommend wholly new strategies.

Possible recommendations may include the following:

(a) reordering financial support priorities, including the possible deletion of some projects;

(b) reducing the number of missionaries but increasing the support for those remaining;

(c) increasing the percentage of the church budget given to global missions;

(d) taking on the major portion or even all of the support—including the project costs—of the remaining missionaries;

(e) dividing the congregation into units—each unit being responsible for the full support of a given missions project. Each section of the congregation should have maximum contact with the missionary and the missionary's mission project(s);

(f) examining the possibility of establishing partnerships with churches in the Third World and sending a delegation to potential partners to explore the dimensions of that partnership;

(g) initiating pastoral exchange, student exchange, or delegation exchange with a partnering church in the Third World;

(h) ensuring that all missions efforts, wherever possible, are part of a balanced development strategy;

(i) encouraging members to discover their own personal global missions involvement and then providing them the technical assistance they need to implement their vision;

(j) encouraging members, especially young people and retired people, to consider full-time missions;

(k) providing in-church discipleship and internship programs for members who feel God's call on them for world missions;

(l) making missions the central activity of the church in both statement and practice;

(m) making long-term investments in partnership with Christians in the Third World;

(n) beginning to prepare the hearts and minds of very small children for a lifetime of commitment to the global advancement of the kingdom of God;

(o) making the local church its own mission-sending agency (this can of course be done in cooperation with established agencies and boards if they are willing);

(p) setting up programs that will allow local churches to learn from and receive from partners in the Third World; and

(q) developing and implementing an accountability procedure for each missions effort.

7. Once recommendations have been made it is time to implement them. For each recommendation adopted, the congregation should set measurable goals and a time frame in which they should be reevaluated or achieved. To aid in this, the church may want to retain professional counsel where needed. The church should always strive to involve a maximum number of its members in decisions in order to develop sense of community ownership of the conclusions.

8. Finally, the church should evaluate progress in accordance with the guidelines outlined above. It should then readjust to the findings and if neces-

sary begin a round of new recommendations. Overall evaluation should occur at least once every six months.

Models

I would like to suggest two models of direct involvement. These models should be viewed as a place to begin rather than a place to end—models to work from rather than models to work toward. The first model is of a partnership between a local church or similar group in the Third World and a local church in North America. The second model is of two Christian families—one in the Third World and one in North America, both of them acting in cooperation with their local churches.

A Model of Two Churches in Partnership

A partnership of two churches may begin when a denominational overseas missions board or other agency, such as a relief or development organization, contacts representatives of a Third World country's national church leadership. They in turn refer the agency to a local, grassroots church—the initiating partner. This church should be in or near a community where there is spiritual and physical need. Further, this church should have a vision for ministering to the community and should also be willing to be involved in a partnership with a local church from the more developed world—the responding partner. Together they should possess the necessary leadership and human and physical resources to carry out a joint and balanced ministry to the initiating partner's community.

The initiating partner then introduces the agency to the leaders of the potential development community—the community in which the initiating partner is ministering. Together the agency and initiating partner assess this community's appropriateness as the site of development projects.

The agency then assists the initiating partner and the development community in preparing a preliminary project proposal. The proposal should detail (1) the resources the initiating partner and the development community can give to meeting the priority needs; (2) the resources they need from the responding partner; and (3) a strategy for jointly meeting the priority needs.

The agency then goes to the more developed world to find a local church interested in becoming the responding partner for this partnership.

Representatives from the potential responding partner are led by the agency on a reconnaissance visit to the initiating partner and development community. During a short visit, the members of both partners get to know each other. They carefully define the detail and timing of the proposed project and the roles of each partner.

Upon returning home, the representatives of the responding partner relate their experiences to their home church or group and make a recommendation regarding the advisability of the partnership. If the potential responding partner agrees to a partnership, they commit themselves to a short-range immediate project (the project to meet the priority need described above) but remain open to the possibility of a long-term relationship.

Once the commitment is made, the initiating partner and the responding partner each select one or more project coordinating team members to (1) coordinate the partnership, (2) facilitate communication between the partners, and (3) assist the development community in long-range community development planning. If the partners are unable to identify appropriate individuals for this position, the agency can supply personnel who will be supported by both partners. The agency is responsible for training the coordinating team members.

After training by the agency, the coordinating team members move into the development community to prepare for the first project. The team serves under the direct supervision of the initiating partner and the indirect supervision of the agency.

Both partners now begin an orientation program, facilitated by the agency, in order to prepare them for the first project of the partnership. During this first project stage, volunteer teams from both partners can be engaged where appropriate.

Upon completion of this short-term project, the coordinating team settles into the target community so as to build relationships with the people and to develop a long-range comprehensive community development proposal.

The entire process is directly linked to or under the direction of the initiating partner, which ensures that the development community interprets these activities as an expression of God's love. The initiating partner "buys" the opportunities presented by the social and physical ministries to evangelize and disciple the development community.

As soon as is feasible, the agency withdraws from a formal relationship with both partners but remains available for consultation. The relationship between the two partnering churches continues.

The Model of Two Families in Partnership

Suppose a family in a local North American church would like to become responding partners with Third World believers who want to join with them for a ministry project in their country.

The steps such a family would follow are similar to those previously outlined for partner churches but are less complex. For example, the North American family would be linked during its vacation with a Christian Third World family. Together they would adopt a third family—perhaps a homeless refugee family. The three families together could build a house for the refugee family. The church of the North American family might cover the initial cost of the materials (which may be only a fraction of the cost of building a home in the more industrialized world), but the house would not be a gift. The mortgage would be paid off through an interest-free or low-interest loan. Any proceeds from the loan could then be used to create a revolving loan fund for other homeless families.

There are many other possible models of how people can become directly involved in development, but these two help to illustrate the possibilities.

Can It Work?

For more than a decade I was a community developer. I helped lay people catch a vision of what they could do to meet the needs of delinquent young people, and I helped develop support systems to train and support lay volunteers as they took responsibility for helping delinquent youths, their families, and their communities address the conditions that produced delinquent behavior. The successes God allowed me to see as people got directly involved in solving their own problems were an important element in allowing me to believe that people of the local church can become successfully and directly involved in missions.

I have also helped design and coordinate a village adoption between a Christian high school in Ohio and the village of Caballona, a needy community of sugar cane cutters in the Dominican Republic.

Anna, a young mother in Caballona, wrote a letter requesting help for her village. She wrote of no food and bad water. In a neighboring village more than two dozen children had recently died, probably of water-borne dysentery that their malnourished bodies were too weak to fight. Anna wanted to help her own village stave off such occurrences. I visited the village and asked for a meeting to determine priority needs and ways to meet those needs. The people expressed a willingness to enter into a partnership with a group of Christians from the United States if a group could be found there that would link up with them in securing adequate food and clean water.

In the meantime, God had touched the heart of Carl, an administrator at a Christian high school in Ohio. Carl wanted to celebrate the school's anniversary somehow out of the ordinary—without the traditional self-serving fund raising event. Instead, he wanted a project to demonstrate the school's thankfulness for God's blessing—a project that would do something for someone else. I suggested that his school adopt a village, Anna's village. The school accepted the challenge, and a miracle began.

Carl and I had our initial phone conversation in January 1981. By August an amazing and exciting string of events had occurred:

The students of the school held a car wash through which they raised approximately $60,000.

Thirty students and twenty parents and faculty were screened and trained; they then went on a three-week work project in Caballona.

Twenty Dominican young people from local churches volunteered and were trained to join the team of fifty Americans.

Thirty-two acres of land were bought at a very low cost from a sympathetic Christian. The land, only one kilometer from the village, was to be used for growing crops and as the location of a new community development center.

The villagers dug a large pond to raise fish for protein and helped prepare the land for the arrival of the work teams.

During the three-week project a transformation took place on the thirty-two acres: the teams installed a water cistern; they fenced the front acreage; they built a road into the property; and they dug the foundations and then constructed a house for volunteer staff and a community center for meetings and training.

On the last day of the work project the student workers, both American and Dominican, landscaped the property with twenty-five coconut palm trees donated by a Dominican army colonel who had become enthusiastic about the project.

Two of the Christian school teachers began to consider committing their lives to full-time missions. They both later enrolled in training.

Several young Dominican students decided they wanted to commit their lives to helping their people in full-time ministry.

A visiting U.S. businessman was so touched by what he saw that he and his wife decided to sponsor a mobile medical van for medically needy villages like Caballona.

A young Dominican volunteer gave one year of his life to serve the people of Caballona without salary. At this writing he is planning to give a second year.

One of the Dominican students was invited and accepted the invitation to come to the Ohio high school as an exchange student.

One Ohio couple decided that when their youngest child finished high school they would consider giving all their time to this type of ministry.

The relationship between the school and the village has continued, and the school has sent other teams both to Caballona and a second needy village.

What made a Christian school in a small Ohio town (which was in the midst of an economic recession) respond with such vigor? Spiritually, of course, God's Holy Spirit led and blessed. Sociologically, the sense of project ownership and direct participation on both sides prompted all participants to make a maximum investment of creativity, time, effort, and finances. Normally, churches and groups like this high school raise money and give it to a missions agency that helps needy people in unknown villages somewhere in the remote parts of the world. But by doing so, of course, they lose the aspect of direct involvement.

This only illustrates what can happen when God's people catch their *own* vision for mission—for the development of people whom God is inviting into his kingdom. The task before us is far too vast to be accomplished through the professional pastor, missionary, or relief and development agency. If the people of God's church are unleashed and aided in their ministry by professionals who would train, support, encourage, facilitate, and enable them, I believe we can accomplish things beyond our dreams.

APPENDIX

Note 1: What Is Development?

Too many Westerners, including Christians, think that development is helping the less fortunate in the Third World to become "like us." It is easy to see why we should think this way; for we in the West think of ourselves as successful, as developed, and as a model for those who have problems with their economies, with population control, with their political systems, and with their health care networks—all problems that we don't have, at least to the degree to which they seem to exist in the Third World.

But is it at all correct to place ourselves in the role of the model? In the first place, by whose standards are we successful? Is God more pleased with our lifestyles, politics, and value systems than he is with their equivalents in the Third World? True, we are materially better off than those in the Third World, and true, most in the Third World would gladly share our material abundance. But are we happier? Do we have closer families, better social systems? Do we care more for each other? Are we closer to God? Is our society closer to what God means societies to be?

We have to ask *why* we want others to become like us. Do we want them to become like us because we think that in the process they will have more of what God intended for them? Or is our reason simply because it gratifies our egos when we are the model? Or is it because we like the feeling of control when we are the teachers? Or perhaps it is because we would feel safer in a hostile world if there were more societies like ours.

Note 2: How Do People Know?

"How do the people of your community know that God loves them when they look at you?" This is one of the questions I ask representatives of local churches when I travel in the Third World. The question is just as relevant to the church in the West. Are we adequately showing the love of God in our lives? What is the church doing to demonstrate God's invitation to the people of the secular community to take on citizenship in his kingdom? For too many the sad answer is very little.

Some try by providing an inviting model of loving relationships that are a direct result of God's love for the members of his church—and of course of his love for all humankind. Others joyfully and corporately celebrate their faith. Still other churches show people in their community that God loves them by telling them so. They proclaim the good news of redemption and reconciliation. There are other churches that demonstrate God's love by ministering to the physical and social needs of their community.

All of these methods of demonstrating God's love are good and necessary. But they lack the wholeness of the biblical mandate for expressing God's love in our world. Any church that focuses on just a few of the biblical means for witness while excluding other parts of the whole will miss both the joy of service and the potential for a much more significant impact for the kingdom of God in the community.

Note 3: Compassion and Enlightened Self-Interest

I think there are two other reasons besides obedience to God's mandates for the church to be involved in balanced ministry. The first is compassion. When Jesus approached the city of Jerusalem during his triumphal entry, he had compassion on the city and its people—he wept (Luke 19:41)—because he knew what would happen to them. Paul had so much compassion for his people, the Jews, that he was willing to be himself separated from Christ for the sake of their salvation (Rom. 9:3). Our God is a compassionate God. His Son Jesus Christ demonstrated that compassion time and time again.

In our lives we should reflect the compassion of God. God has placed the Western church in a unique position in history: not only do we *know* about the physical and spiritual needs of people around the world, we have also been entrusted with the ability to *do* something about it. No people in human history have had such easy access to resources and such an incredible opportunity for mobility.

The second reason is enlightened self-interest. The church cannot give without receiving more than it gave. This is a principle of the king, and it is at exact odds with the world's wisdom. As a matter of fact, it is only as we give away what we have been given that we possess it at all. This is why Jesus said that those who would keep their lives should give them away (Matt. 10:39; 16:25). I think it is a safe implication that Jesus was talking not only about life proper but also about many of the things that fill our lives—including possessions and talents.

There is another side to the coin. If we keep our treasures to ourselves, we reveal how much we love them. But the love of possessions is the path away from God. For example, in Luke 12:16-21 Jesus told the parable of the rich man who had prepared for retirement and was ready to enjoy his ease. That very night he lost everything he had. In another example, Jesus told of the beggar Lazarus and the rich man who wouldn't share his wealth (Luke 16:19-31). At death the rich man lost everything, including eternal life.

So to hold or to keep is to lose, while to give is to gain. I wonder how many churches have lost for eternity the resources they have kept for themselves—that they have put into beautiful buildings and sophisticated programming—when they could have invested them in the kingdom's bank.

That we will be held accountable is certain. But just "giving it away" is not the only aspect of handling our gifts and our resources for which we are accountable. Even if we do not use our gifts on ourselves, we will still be evaluated on the wisdom of our use of them. In the kingdom parable of the talents Jesus makes it clear that the master's reward for good stewardship is related to the soundness of the investment (Matt. 25:14-30). The church has a responsibility, like a wise financial investor, to study kingdom investment opportunities and then to put the resources that God has placed in its stewardship to good use.

However, if God places a pressing need in the church's path, the church is not excused from meeting that need simply by its desire to make a better "investment" of its resources. The Good Samaritan may have been able to make "better use" of his time and money, but Jesus honored him because he responded compassionately to the need that God placed before him: he had the opportunity and the ability and he made good on it.

Note 4: Knowledge vs. Wisdom

Let me illustrate the difference between knowledge and wisdom with an example from my work in community development. In an urban slum of a large city there was a serious delinquency problem. Years before, the area that was now a slum had been a stable blue collar neighborhood of single houses, detached garages, and green lawns. Garbage trucks went weekly through the alleys of the neighborhood to pick up trash. In those times there was tangible community pride and spirit. But in later years the alleys became clogged with trash, and the people could no longer use their garages.

Young people began to use the empty garages as their clubhouses and then later as their private domain for all kinds of illegal and immoral activities. Crime in the neighborhood became so serious that the residents became afraid to leave their homes. After many requests for help, the city council hired professional urban planners to study the problem and make recommendations for change. Months later the planners presented the council with a multimillion dollar plan that included youth and recreation centers, better street lighting, renovated school curricula, and other progressive but expensive programming. As a final step to accepting the program, the council members took the plan to neighborhood residents to discuss it and get their response.

What stopped the professional plan was a visit at the home of an old woman. After being told of the plan she was asked for her evaluation. She said that she had lived there for many years and had watched the neighborhood turn into a slum. It started turning into a slum, she said, when the potholes in the alleys got so big that the garbage trucks wouldn't go through. When they didn't come, the trash started to pile up and people couldn't get into the alley to park their cars in their garages. "We asked the city to fix the alleys, but it didn't. The kids started to use the garages for doing what they wanted. That's when the problems started. Now, if it was me, I would fix the alleys and start picking up the trash." The old woman wasn't a professional, but she had the wisdom needed to solve a serious social problem—a solution that had evaded the knowledgeable and skilled urban planners.

Note 5: Rural Porches and Urban Boxes

How has our society come to the point at which it now delegates to professionals its own responsibility for containing and solving human problems? I think we can illustrate the changes in society with a conceptual model I call "Rural Porches and Urban Boxes." In the past, most of our society lived in relatively small towns or rural communities. Those who remember those days will remember spending much time on their front porches, visiting with and looking out for their neighbors. When there was a community problem, the people in the community would often spontaneously and voluntarily respond with help. For example, if a neighbor's house was being vandalized, people would get off their own porches and go to help. They took personal responsibility by intervening in the crisis they observed—even though the crisis did not directly affect them.

Now we don't spend so much time on our porches. Now we tend to live in a series of isolated urban boxes. We come home to our house box, turn on an electric box and watch the world through a glass screen, where we see our communities' social problems pass in review. We may have personally passed by the problems earlier in the day in our box with wheels, but there is precious little encouragement for direct citizen involvement in seeking solutions to those problems. As a consequence, people in New York City, who are just like us, look out of their apartment windows and watch a girl on the street below being murdered—but don't get involved.

In the rural porches environment, people are visible. There is a sense of belonging. The community and its people are predictable. As a consequence, there is a sense of security. People are willing to take responsibility for the community problems they see. They then have a tendency to volunteer spontaneously to meet community needs—the needs of themselves and their neighbors. As they volunteer, the people become significant to the ongoing life of the community. Being significant gives a feeling of importance and pride in the community, and consequently the people are willing to get even more deeply involved.

The opposite tends to happen in our urban box environment. People not only feel but are quasi-anonymous. As a consequence, they can easily avoid getting involved in community problems—no one will know the difference. People thus tend to be alienated from one another. There develops a sense of unpredictability about life: people don't know what is going to happen to them or to their neighbors, and consequently they are afraid. They don't know *how* to get involved, and so they *don't*. Instead they delegate responsibility for community problems to the public sector, which then hires professionals. But when people delegate responsibility for social problems to others, they begin to feel insignificant and powerless. The more insignificant and powerless they feel, the less inclined they are to become spontaneously involved in solving the problems of their community. It all becomes a self-sustaining cycle.

When people pass off their own responsibility, entire institutional systems are created to support the professionals to whom responsibility has been delegated. These systems become large, costly bureaucracies which all too often do little to solve the problems they were created to address. Even more alarming, these systems stand as barriers and road blocks between the community problems and the very people in the community who should be encouraged to take responsibility for solving them.

Delegation does not and cannot work—for a variety of reasons:

1. Currently, our service institutions act in a manner that implies that they, rather than the community at large, have the true responsibility for solving community problems. But history shows us that institutions do not solve specific problems: people must solve their own problems. I would contend that service institutions operate more effectively when they assist the people in voluntarily acting to solve their own problems.

2. Community problems do not belong to the professionals: community problems belong to the community. Where professionals do make a difference, they tend to make those differences as caring members or citizens of their community—not as professionals.

3. Professionals tend to operate on the principle of professional noninvolvement with their clients—the people. For example, they say "Schedule your problems, please. Our counseling hours are from 10:00 to 12:00 and 2:00 to 4:00." This posture is not conducive to trust or to promoting the feeling that people are significant.

4. Even if professionals could make a difference as professionals and could solve community problems, there is not enough money to get the whole job done. The problems we face are simply too big.

5. In the past, when we had new social problems, North Americans were always able to tap into new resources to meet those problems. Now, there are no more vast, untapped reserves of easily accessible resources. As we have new social problems or new emphases to address, we will have to take resources from one area and redistribute them to the area of increased concern.

6. Our current system uses limited resources inefficiently. When we pay a professional for an hour of problem solving, that is all we get—one hour. If we paid the same professional to spend an hour teaching carefully selected and managed volunteers, the hour invested could multiply itself many times.

7. Volunteers are often treated poorly: they are given tasks that professional staff do not have time to do or do not want to do or feel are nonessential. Volunteers are viewed and managed as an appendage to the "real tasks." Instead, volunteers should be seen as regular staff—the only difference between them and the paid staff should be the monetary element of compensation.

8. Professionals often think volunteers don't have enough sophistication or experience to understand, solve, or address community problems. Professionals think they can do it better. Empirical evidence suggests that they

often do it worse. Moreover, professionals often fear volunteers may take away their jobs. In fact, volunteer programs almost always create jobs.

9. Perhaps the largest single factor leading to the widespread lack of quality volunteer programming is that agency administrators misunderstand the complexity of volunteer management. The management of volunteers is much more complex than the management of traditional professional human services. A number of years ago, management gurus made a not so surprising discovery. They learned that the management of human service programs is more complex than the management of traditional businesses. The reason? In a traditional business, one manages the worker and the product. The administrator has only one human factor to manage. In most human service systems there are two human factors—the professional worker and the client. And in volunteer programming there is a third human factor—the volunteer.

Volunteer programs must have high priority if they are to be successful. Adding volunteers into any service system further increases its complexity. This creates a need to put the best management expertise in the driver's seat.

Transformation: The Church in Response to Human Need

The Wheaton '83 Statement

Introduction

For two weeks during June 1983 we have come together from local churches and Christian mission and aid agencies at Wheaton College in the USA from 30 nations to pray about and reflect upon the church's task in response to human need. Some of us belong to churches which are situated among marginalized peoples who live in situations of poverty, powerlessness, and oppression. Others come from churches situated in affluent areas of the world. We are deeply grateful to our heavenly Father for allowing us the privilege of sharing our lives with one another, studying the Scriptures in small groups, considering papers on aspects of human development and transformation, and looking closely at the implications of case studies and histories which describe different responses to human need. Because God hears the cries of the poor, we have sought each other's help to respond (Exod. 3:7-9; James 5:1-6). We rejoice at what we believe the Holy Spirit has been teaching us concerning God's specific purpose and plans for His distressed world and the part the church has to play in them.

As we have faced the enormous challenge before God's people everywhere to alleviate suffering and, in partnership together, to eliminate its causes, we are more than ever aware of the liberating and healing power of the Good News of Jesus. We gladly reaffirm, therefore, our conviction that Jesus Christ alone is the world's peace, for He alone can reconcile people to God and bring all hostilities to an end (Eph. 2:14-17).

We acknowledge, furthermore, that only by spreading the Gospel can the most basic need of human beings be met: to have fellowship with God. In what follows we do not emphasize evangelism as a separate theme, because we see it as an integral part of our total Christian response to human need (Matt. 28:18-21). In addition, it is not necessary simply to repeat what the Lausanne Covenant and the Report of the Consultation on the Relationship between Evangelism and Social Responsibility (CRESR, Grand Rapids, 1982) have already expressed.

254

What we have discovered we would like to share with our brothers and sisters throughout the world. We offer this statement, not as an attempt to produce a final word, but as a summary of our reflections.

Both Scripture and experience, informed by the Spirit, emphasize that God's people are dependent upon His wisdom in confronting human need. Local churches and mission agencies, then, should act wisely, if they are to be both pastoral and prophetic. Indeed the whole human family with its illusions and divisions needs Christ to be its Wisdom as well as its Savior and King.

Conscious of our struggle to find a biblical view of transformation that relates its working in the heart of believers to its multiplying effects in society, we pray that the Spirit will give us the discernment we need. We believe that the wisdom the Spirit inspires is practical rather than academic, and the possession of the faithful rather than the preserve of the elite. Because we write as part of a world full of conflict and a church easily torn by strife we desire that the convictions expressed in this document be further refined by God's pure and peaceable wisdom.

Some may find our words hard. We pray, however, that many will find them a help to their own thinking and an encouragement to "continue steadfast, immovable, always abounding in the work of the Lord, knowing that in the Lord your labor is not in vain" (1 Cor. 15:58).

I. Christian Social Involvement

1. As Christians reflect on God's intention for the world they are often tempted to be either naively optimistic or darkly pessimistic. Some, inspired by a utopian vision seem to suggest that God's Kingdom, in all its fullness, can be built on earth. We do not subscribe to this view, since Scripture informs us of the reality and pervasiveness of both personal and societal sin (Isa. 1:10-26; Amos 2:6-8; Mic. 2:1-10; Rom. 1:28-32). Thus we recognize that utopianism is nothing but a false dream (see the CRESR Report, IV.A).

2. Other Christians become pessimistic because they are faced with the reality of increasing poverty and misery, of rampant oppression and exploitation by powers of the right and the left, of spiralling violence coupled with the threat of nuclear warfare. They are concerned, too, about the increasing possibility that planet earth will not be able to sustain its population for long because of the wanton squandering of its resources. As a result, they are tempted to turn their eyes away from this world and fix them so exclusively on the return of Christ that their involvement in the here and now is paralyzed. We do not wish to disregard or minimize the extensive contribution made by a succession of Christians who have held this view of eschatology, through more than one hundred years, to medical and educational work in many countries up to the present day. Nevertheless, some of us feel that these men and women have tended to see the task of the church as merely picking up survivors from a shipwreck in a hostile sea. We do not endorse this view either, since it denies the

biblical injunctions to defend the cause of the weak, maintain the rights of the poor and oppressed (Ps. 82:3), and practice justice and love (Mic. 6:8).

3. We affirm, moreover, that, even though we may believe that our calling is only to proclaim the Gospel and not get involved in political and other actions, our very non-involvement lends tacit support to the existing order. There is no escape: either we challenge the evil structures of society or we support them.

4. There have been many occasions in the history of the church—and some exist today—where Christians, faced with persecution and oppression, have *appeared* to be disengaged from society and thus to support the status quo. We suggest, however, that even under conditions of the most severe repression, such Christians may in fact be challenging society and even be transforming it, through their lifestyle, their selfless love, their quiet joy, their inner peace, and their patient suffering (1 Pet. 2:21-25).

5. Christ's followers, therefore, are called, in one way or another, not to conform to the values of society but to transform them (Rom. 12:1-2; Eph. 5:8-14). This calling flows from our confession that God loves the world and that the earth belongs to Him. It is true that Satan *is* active in this world, even claiming it to be his (Luke 4:5-7). He is, however, a usurper, having no property rights here. All authority in heaven and on earth has been given to Christ Jesus (Matt. 28:18; Col. 1:15-20). Although His Lordship is not yet acknowledged by all (Heb. 2:8) He is the ruler of the kings of the earth (Rev. 1:5), King of kings and Lord of lords (Rev. 19:16). In faith we confess that the old order is passing away; the new order has already begun (2 Cor. 5:17; Eph. 2:7-10; Matt. 12:18; Luke 7:21-23).

II. Not only Development but Transformation

6. The participants at this conference have entered into the current discussions concerning development. For many Western political and business leaders development describes the process by which nations and peoples become part of the existing international economic order. For many people of the Two Thirds World it is identified with an ideologically motivated process of change, called "developmentalism." This process is intrinsically related to a mechanistic pursuit of economic growth that tends to ignore the structural context of poverty and injustice and which increases dependency and inequality.

7. Some of us still believe, however, that "development," when reinterpreted in the light of the whole message of the Bible, is a concept that should be retained by Christians. Part of the reason for this choice is that the word is so widely used. A change of term, therefore, would cause unnecessary confusion.

8. Others in our Consultation, because of difficulty in relating it to biblical categories of thought and its negative overtones, would like to replace "development" with another word. An alternative we suggest is "transformation," as it can be applied in different ways to every situation. Western nations, for

example, who have generally assumed that development does not apply to them, are, nevertheless, in need of transformation in many areas. In particular, the unspoken assumption that societies operate best when individuals are most free to pursue their own self-interests needs to be challenged on the basis of the biblical teaching on stewardship (Luke 12:13-21; 16:13-15; Phil. 2:1-4). People living in groups based on community solidarity may help these kinds of societies see the poverty of their existence.

9. Moreover, the term "transformation," unlike "development," does not have a suspect past. It points to a number of changes that have to take place in many societies if poor people are to enjoy their rightful heritage in creation.

10. We are concerned, however, that both the goals and the process of transformation should be seen in the light of the Good News about Jesus, the Messiah. We commit ourselves and urge other Christian believers to reject the cultural and social forces of secularism which so often shape our idea of a good society. We believe that notions alien to God's plan for human living are often more powerful in forming our opinions about what is right for a nation than the message of Scripture itself.

11. According to the biblical view of human life, then, transformation is the change from a condition of human existence contrary to God's purposes to one in which people are able to enjoy fullness of life in harmony with God (John 10:10; Col. 3:8-15; Eph. 4:13). This transformation can only take place through the obedience of individuals and communities to the Gospel of Jesus Christ, whose power changes the lives of men and women by releasing them from the guilt, power, and consequences of sin, enabling them to respond with love toward God and toward others (Rom. 5:5), and making them "new creatures in Christ" (2 Cor. 5:17).

12. There are a number of themes in the Bible which help us focus on the way we understand transformation. The doctrine of creation speaks of the worth of every man, woman, and child, of the responsibility of human beings to look after the resources of nature (Gen. 1:26-30) and to share them equitably with their neighbors. The doctrine of the Fall highlights the innate tendency of human beings to serve their own interests, with the consequences of greed, insecurity, violence, and the lust for power. "God's judgment rightly falls upon those who do such things" (Rom. 2:2). The doctrine of redemption proclaims God's forgiveness of sins and the freedom Christ gives for a way of life dedicated to serving others by telling them about the Good News of Salvation, bringing reconciliation between enemies, and losing one's life to see justice established for all exploited people.

13. We have come to see that the goal of transformation is best described by the biblical vision of the Kingdom of God. This new way of being human in submission to the Lord of all has many facets. In particular, it means striving to bring peace among individuals, races, and nations by overcoming prejudices, fears, and preconceived ideas about others. It means sharing basic resources like food, water, the means of healing, and knowledge. It also means working for a greater participation of people in the decisions which affect their lives,

making possible an equal receiving from others and giving of themselves. Finally, it means growing up into Christ in all things as a body of people dependent upon the work of the Holy Spirit and upon each other.

III. The Stewardship of Creation

14. "The earth is the Lord's and all that is in it" (Ps. 24:1); "The land is mine" (Lev. 25:23). All human beings are God's creatures. As made in His image they are His representatives, given the responsibility of caring wisely for His creation. We have to confess, however, that God's people have been slow to recognize the full implications of their responsibility. As His stewards, we do not own the earth but we manage and enhance it in anticipation of Christ's return. Too often, however, we have assumed a right to use His natural resources indiscriminately. We have frequently been indifferent, or even hostile, to those committed to the conservation of non-renewable sources of energy and minerals, of animal life in danger of extinction, and of the precarious ecological balance of many natural habitats. The earth is God's gift to all generations. An African proverb says that parents have borrowed the present from their children. Both our present life and our children's future depends upon our wise and peaceful treatment of the whole earth.

15. We have also assumed that only a small portion of our income and wealth, the "tithe," belongs to the Lord, the rest being ours to dispose of as we like. This impoverishes other people and denies our identity and role as stewards. We believe that Christians everywhere, but especially those who are enjoying in abundance "the good things of life" (Luke 16:25), must faithfully obey the command to ensure that others have their basic needs met. In this way those who are poor now will also be able to enjoy the blessing of giving to others.

16. Through salvation, Jesus lifts us out of our isolation from God and other people and establishes us within the worldwide community of the Body of Christ. Belonging to one Body involves sharing all God's gifts to us, so that there might be equality among all members (2 Cor. 8:14-15). To the extent that this standard is obeyed, dire poverty will be eliminated (Acts 2:42-47).

17. When either individuals or states claim an absolute right of ownership, that is rebellion against God. The meaning of stewardship is that the poor have equal rights to God's resources (Deut. 15:8-9). The meaning of transformation is that, as stewards of God's bountiful gifts, we do justice, striving together through prayer, example, representation, and protest to have resources redistributed and the consequences of greed limited (Acts 4:32–5:11).

18. We are perturbed by the perverse misuse of huge amounts of resources in the present arms race. While millions starve to death, resources are wasted on the research and production of increasingly sophisticated nuclear weapon systems. Moreover, the constantly escalating global trade in conventional arms accompanies the proliferation of oppressive governments which disregard people's elementary needs. As Christians we condemn these new ex-

pressions of injustice and aggression, affirming our commitment to seek peace with justice. In the light of the issues of the stewardship of creation we have discussed here, we call on the worldwide evangelical community to make the nuclear and arms trade questions a matter of prayerful concern and to place it on their agenda for study and action.

IV. Culture and Transformation

19. Culture includes world-views, beliefs, values, art forms, customs, laws, socioeconomic structures, social relationships, and material things shared by a population over time in a specific area or context.

20. Culture is God's gift to human beings. God has made people everywhere in His image. As Creator, He has made us creative. This creativity produces cultures. Furthermore, God has commissioned us to be stewards of His creation (Ps. 8; Heb. 2:5-11). Since every good gift is from above and since all wisdom and knowledge comes from Jesus Christ, whatever is good and beautiful in cultures may be seen as a gift of God (James 1:16-18). Moreover, where the Gospel has been heard and obeyed, cultures have become further ennobled and enriched.

21. However, people have sinned by rebelling against God. Therefore the cultures we produce are infected with evil. Different aspects of our culture show plainly our separation from God. Social structures and relationships, art forms and laws often reflect our violence, our sense of lostness, and our loss of coherent moral values. Scripture challenges us not to be "conformed to this world" (Rom. 12:2) insofar as it is alienated from its Creator. We need to be transformed so that cultures may display again what is "good and acceptable and perfect" (Rom. 12:2).

22. Cultures, then, bear the marks of God's common grace, demonic influences, and mechanisms of human exploitation. In our cultural creativity, God and Satan clash. The Lord used Greek culture to give us the New Testament, while at the same time He subjected that culture to the judgment of the Gospel. We too should make thankful use of cultures and yet, at the same time, examine them in the light of the Gospel to expose the evil in them (1 Cor. 9:19-23).

23. Social structures that exploit and dehumanize constitute a pervasive sin which is not confronted adequately by the church. Many churches, mission societies, and Christian relief and development agencies support the sociopolitical status quo, and by silence give their tacit support.

24. Through application of the Scriptures, in the power of the Spirit, we seek to discern the true reality of all sociocultural situations. We need to learn critically from both functionalist and conflict approaches to human culture. The "functionalist socio-anthropology" approach emphasizes the harmonious aspects of different cultures and champions a tolerant attitude to the existing structures. This position is often adopted in the name of "scientific objectivity." By contrast, the "conflict" approach exposes the contradictory nature of social

structures and makes us aware of the underlying conflicts of interests. We must remember that both approaches come under the judgment of God.

25. Given the conflicting ethical tendencies in our nature, which find expression in our cultural systems, we must be neither naively optimistic nor wrongly judgmental. We are called to be a new community that seeks to work with God in the transformation of our societies, men and women of God in society, salt of the earth and light of the world (Matt. 5:13-16). We seek to bring people and their cultures under the Lordship of Christ. In spite of our failures, we move toward that freedom and wholeness in a more just community that persons will enjoy when our Lord returns to consummate His Kingdom (Rev. 21:1–22:6).

V. Social Justice and Mercy

26. Our time together enabled us to see that poverty is not a necessary evil but often the result of social, economic, political, and religious systems marked by injustice, exploitation, and oppression. Approximately eight hundred million people in the world are destitute, and their plight is often maintained by the rich and the powerful. Evil is not only in the human heart but also in social structures. Because God is just and merciful, hating evil and loving righteousness, there is an urgent need for Christians in the present circumstances to commit ourselves to acting in mercy and seeking justice. The mission of the church includes both the proclamation of the Gospel and its demonstration. We must therefore evangelize, respond to immediate human needs, and press for social transformation. The means we use, however, must be consistent with the end we desire.

27. As we thought of the task before us, we considered Jesus' attitude toward the power structures of His time. He was neither a Zealot nor a passive spectator of the oppression of His people. Rather, moved by compassion, He identified Himself with the poor, whom He saw as "harassed and helpless, like sheep without a shepherd" (Matt. 9:36). Through His acts of mercy, teaching, and lifestyle, He exposed the injustices in society and condemned the self-righteousness of its leaders (Matt. 23:25; Luke 6:37-42). His was a prophetic compassion and it resulted in the formation of a community which accepted the values of the Kingdom of God and stood in contrast to the Roman and Jewish establishment. We were challenged to follow Jesus' footsteps, remembering that His compassion led Him to death (John 13:12-17; Phil. 2:6-8; 1 John 3:11-18).

28. We are aware that a Christlike identification with the poor, whether at home or abroad, in the North, South, East, or West, is always costly and may lead us also to persecution and even death. Therefore, we humbly ask God to make us willing to risk our comfort, even our lives, for the sake of the Gospel, knowing that "everyone who wants to live a godly life in Christ Jesus will be persecuted" (2 Tim. 3:12).

29. Sometimes in our ministry among the poor we face a serious dilemma: to limit ourselves to acts of mercy to improve their lot, or to go beyond that and seek to rectify the injustice that makes such acts of mercy necessary. This step in turn may put at risk the freedom we need to continue our ministry. No rule of thumb can be given, but from a biblical perspective it is clear that justice and mercy belong together (Isa. 11:1-5; Ps. 113:5-9). We must therefore make every possible effort to combine both in our ministry and be willing to suffer the consequences. We must also remember that acts of mercy highlight the injustices of the social, economic, and political structures and relationships; whether we like it or not, they may therefore lead us into confrontation with those who hold power (Acts 4:5-22). For the same reason, we must stand together with those who suffer for the sake of justice (Heb. 13:3).

30. Our ministry of justice and healing is not limited to fellow Christians. Our love and commitment must extend to the stranger (Matt. 5:43-48). Our involvement with strangers is not only through charity, but also through economic and political action. Justice must characterize the government's laws and policies toward the poor. Our economic and political action is inseparable from evangelism.

31. Injustice in the modern world has reached global proportions. Many of us come from countries dominated by international business corporations, and some from those whose political systems are not accountable to the people. We witness to the damaging effects that these economic and political institutions are having on people, especially on the poorest of the poor. We call on our brothers and sisters in Jesus Christ to study seriously this situation and to seek ways to bring about change in favor of the oppressed. "The righteous care about justice for the poor, but the wicked have no such concern" (Prov. 29:7).

VI. The Local Church and Transformation

32. The local church is the basic unit of Christian society. The churches in the New Testament were made up of men and women who had experienced transformation through receiving Jesus Christ as Savior, acknowledging Him as Lord, and incarnating His servant ministry by demonstrating the values of the Kingdom both personally and in community (Mark 10:35-45; 1 Pet. 2:5; 4:10). Today similar examples of transformed lives abound in churches worldwide.

33. We recognize that across the generations local churches have been the vehicle for the transmission of the Gospel of Jesus Christ, and that their primary, though not their only, role is a threefold ministry: the worship and praise of God, the proclamation in word and deed of the Gospel of the grace of God, and the nurture, instruction, and discipleship of those who have received Jesus Christ into their lives. In this way transformation takes place in the lives of Christians as individuals, families, and communities; through their words and deeds they demonstrate both the need and reality of ethical, moral, and social transformation.

34. All churches are faced at times with the choice between speaking openly against social evils and not speaking out publicly. The purpose for the particular choice should be obedience to the Lord of the church to fulfill its ministry. Wisdom will be needed so that the church will neither speak rashly and make its witness ineffective nor remain silent when to do so would deny its prophetic calling (1 Pet. 3:13-17). If we are sensitive to the Holy Spirit and are socially aware, we will always be ready to reassess our attitude toward social issues (Lk. 18:24-30).

35. Integrity, leadership, and information are essential for the transformation of attitudes and lifestyles of members of local churches. Churches are made up of people whose lives are pressured by the way their neighbors spend their money. They are often more aware of this than of the suffering and human need in their own and other countries. Often, too, they are reluctant to expose themselves to the traumas of global need and to information which would challenge their comfort. If church leadership fails to adequately stress the social dimensions of the Gospel, church members may often overlook these issues (1 Tim. 3:1-7; Heb. 13:17).

36. We should be sensitive and responsive to need within the local church. Widows, prisoners, the poor, and strangers are people who are particularly the responsibility of the local church (Gal. 6:10). We should attempt to be well informed about local human need and to seek God's will for us in meeting those needs. We should seek to minister to the poor in our local area who are not members of the church (James 1:27; Rom. 12:17).

37. Our churches must also address issues of evil and of social injustice in the local community and the wider society. Our methodology should involve study, earnest prayer, and action within the normative, ethical guidelines for Christian conduct set out in Scripture. Within these guidelines there are times, no matter the political system, when protest can be effective. Christians should carefully consider the issues and the manner in which they protest so that the identity and message of the church is neither blurred nor drowned.

38. The local church has however to be understood as being a part of the universal church. There is therefore a genuine need for help and sharing *(diakonia)* built on fellowship *(koinonia)* between churches of different localities and contexts. In this connection we considered a model for relating churches in different areas of the world. In such "church twinnings" the relationship should be genuinely reciprocal with giving and receiving at both ends, free from paternalism of any kind (Rom. 15:1-7).

39. Such reciprocal relationships in a spirit of true mutuality are particularly needed in view of the fact that every local church always lives on the edge of compromise with its context (Rom. 12:3-18). Some churches are immersed in the problems of materialism and racism, others in those of oppression and the option of violence. We may help each other by seeking to see the world through the eyes of our brothers and sisters.

40. With regard to the wider world community, Christian churches should identify and exchange people who are equipped through their personal

characteristics, training, and Christian maturity to work across cultures in the name of Christ and of the sending church. These men and women would go as servants and stewards characterized by humility and meekness; and they would work together with members of the Body of Christ in the countries to which they go.

VII. Christian Aid Agencies and Transformation

41. In reflecting upon the Christian response to human need, we have recognized the central place of the local church as the vehicle for communicating the Gospel of Jesus Christ both in word and deed. Churches around the world have throughout history displayed active concern for the needs around them and continue to serve the needy. We call upon the aid agencies to see their role as one of facilitating the churches in the fulfillment of their mission.

42. We recognize the progress which in recent years has been made in our understanding of the Gospel and its social and political implications. We also recognize, however, the deficiencies in our witness and affirm our desire for a fuller understanding of the biblical basis for our ministry.

43. We acknowledge that the constituency of the aid agencies is generally concerned with human suffering, hunger, and need. However, we recognize that this concern is not consistently expressed with integrity. In efforts to raise funds, the plight of the poor is often exploited in order to meet donor needs and expectations. Fund-raising activities must be in accordance with the Gospel. A stewardship responsibility of agencies is to reduce significantly their overheads in order to maximize the resources for the ministry.

44. We are challenged to implement in our organizations a positive transformation demonstrating the values of Christ and His Kingdom which we wish to share with others. We must, for example, avoid competition with others involved in the same ministry and a success mentality that forgets God's special concern for the weak and "unsuccessful" (Gal. 2:10; Ps. 147:6). We should continually review our actions to ensure biblical integrity and genuine partnership with churches and other agencies. Decisions on ministry policy, including how resources are to be used, need to be made in consultation with the people to be served.

45. We need to ensure that our promotional efforts describe what we are actually doing. We accept the responsibility of educating our donors in the full implications of the way Christian transformation is experienced in the field. The Holy Spirit has led us to this ministry. In accepting the responsibility of education we recognize the process may cause some to question our approach. We will strive to educate with a sense of humility, patience, and courage.

46. In all of our programs and actions we should remember that God in His sovereignty and love is already active in the communities we seek to serve (Acts 14:17; 17:23; Rom. 2:9-15). Agencies, therefore, should give adequate priority to listening sensitively to the concerns of these communities, facilitating a two-way process in communication and local ownership of programs.

The guiding principle is equitable partnership in which local people and Western agencies cooperate together. Many models for development have originated in the Two Thirds World. Christian aid agencies should in every way encourage these local initiatives to succeed. In this way the redeemed community of the Kingdom will be able to experiment with a number of models of transformation.

47. The agencies' legitimate need for accountability to donors often results in the imposition of Western management systems on local communities. This assumes that Western planning and control systems are the only ones which can ensure accountability. Since the communities these agencies seek to serve are often part of a different culture, this imposition can restrict and inhibit the sensitive processes of social transformation. We call on development agencies to establish a dialogue with those they serve in order to permit the creation of systems of accountability with respect to both cultures. Our ministry must always reflect our mutual interdependence in the Kingdom (Rom. 14:17-18; 1 Cor. 12).

48. In focusing on the apparently conflicting requirements of our action as Christian agencies, we are conscious of our sin and compromise. In a call to repentance we include a renunciation of inconsistency and extravagance in our personal and institutional lifestyle. We ask the Spirit of truth to lead us and make us true agents of transformation (Acts 1:8).

VIII. The Coming of the Kingdom and the Church's Mission

49. We affirm that the Kingdom of God is both present and future, both societal and individual, both physical and spiritual. If others have overemphasized the present, the societal, and the physical, we ought to confess that we have tended to neglect those dimensions of the biblical message. We therefore joyfully proclaim that the Kingdom has broken into human history in the Resurrection of Christ. It grows like a mustard seed, both judging and transforming the present age.

50. Even if God's activity in history is focused on the church, it is not confined to the church. God's particular focus on the church—as on Israel in the Old Testament—has as its purpose the blessing of the nations (Gen. 12:1-3; 15; 17; Isa. 42:6). Thus the church is called to exist for the sake of its Lord and for the sake of humankind (Matt. 22:32-40).

51. The church is called to infuse the world with hope, for both this age and the next. Our hope does not flow from despair: it is not because the present is empty that we hope for a new future (Rom. 5:1-11). Rather, we hope for that future because of what God has already done and because of what He has promised yet to do. We have already been given the Holy Spirit as the guarantee of our full redemption and of the coming of the day when God will be all in all (1 Cor. 15:28). As we witness to the Gospel of present salvation and future hope, we identify with the awesome birthpangs of God's new creation (Rom. 8:22). As the community of the end time anticipating the End, we pre-

pare for the ultimate by getting involved in the penultimate (Matt. 24:36–25:46).

52. For this reason we are challenged to commit ourselves to a truly vigorous and full-orbed mission in the world, combining explosive creativity with painstaking faithfulness in small things. Our mission and vision are to be nurtured by the whole counsel of God (2 Tim. 3:16). A repentant, revived, and vigorous church will call people to true repentance and faith and at the same time equip them to challenge the forces of evil and injustice (2 Tim. 3:17). We thus move forward, without either relegating salvation merely to an eternal future or making it synonymous with a political or social dispensation to be achieved in the here and now. The Holy Spirit empowers us to serve and proclaim Him who has been raised from the dead, seated at the right hand of the Father, and given to the church as Head over all things in heaven and on earth (Eph. 1:10, 20-22).

53. Finally, we confess our utter dependence on God. We affirm that transformation is, in the final analysis, His work, but work in which He engages us. To this end He has given us His Spirit, the Transformer *par excellence,* to enlighten us and be our Counselor (John 16:7), to impart His many gifts to us (Rom. 12; 1 Cor. 12), to equip us to face and conquer the enemy (2 Cor. 10:3-5; Gal. 5:22-23). We are reminded that our unconfessed sins and lack of love for others grieve the Spirit (Eph. 4:30; Gal. 5:13-16). We therefore fervently pray for our sins to be pardoned, for our spirit to be renewed, and for the privilege of being enlisted in the joyous task of enabling God's Kingdom to come: the Kingdom "of . . . justice, peace, and joy in the Holy Spirit" (Rom. 14:17).

For Further Reading

The questions this volume focuses on—questions on the relation of the gospel and social development and relief—have been addressed in several other publications and statements over the last ten years. Some of the more important among them are

"The Gospel and Culture." The Willowbank Report. Lausanne Occasional Papers no. 2. Wheaton, Ill.: Lausanne Committee for World Evangelization, 1978.

"Christian Witness Among the Urban Poor." Lausanne Committee for World Evangelization, 1982.

"Evangelism and Social Responsibility: An Evangelical Commitment." The Grand Rapids Report. Exeter: Paternoster, 1982.

Samuel, Vinay, and Chris Sugden, eds. *Sharing Jesus in the Two Thirds World.* Grand Rapids: Eerdmans, 1984.

Nicholls, Bruce, ed. *In Word and Deed.* (Papers from the Consultation on the Relationship of Evangelism and Social Responsibility, Grand Rapids.) (Exeter: Paternoster, 1985; Grand Rapids: Eerdmans, 1986).

Padilla, C. René, and Chris Sugden, eds. *Texts on Evangelical Social Ethics, 1974–83.* 2 vols. Bramcote, Nottingham: Grove Booklets, 1985.

In addition, René Padilla gives a commentary on many of the evangelical texts relating to transformation and development in "How Evangelicals Endorsed Social Responsibility," *Transformation* 2 (July-September 1985), also published under the title *Texts on Evangelical Social Ethics, 1974–1983,* vol. 2 (Bramcote, Nottingham: Grove Booklets, 1985). In general, the journal *Transformation—An International Dialogue on Evangelical Social Ethics,* edited by Tokunboh Adeyemo, Vinay Samuel, and Ronald Sider and published by the Unit on Ethics and Society of the Theological Commission of the World Evangelical Fellowship, seeks to provide further biblical and practical reflection on ministries of transformation from around the world. *Transformation* is available quarterly from The Paternoster Press, 3 Mount Radford Crescent, Exeter, EX2 4JW, U.K.

The "Transformation Newsletter" focuses particularly on issues of Christian involvement in development and serves to link those who wish to identify with the Transformation statement. It is published four times a year and is also available from The Paternoster Press, 3 Mount Radford Crescent, Exeter, EX2 4JW, U.K.

Wheaton '83 gave further scope to those who are concerned to continue the heart of the vision of the Lausanne movement—to continue to explore Christian mission as a partnership of proclamation and social responsibility. At Wheaton, mission theologians reflecting on the nature of mission and their partners working in missions through relief and development agencies were able to work together and learn from each other. The mixture was as explosive and creative as the Lausanne Congress had been in 1974, as is reflected by the papers in this volume first presented at the Wheaton conference and by the statement "Transformation" that resulted from it.

The "Transformation" statement has also been published with study questions in a twenty-page section, "Transformation—The Church in Response to Human Need," in *Texts on Evangelical Social Ethics, 1974–1983*, vol. 3 (Bramcote, Nottingham: Grove Booklets, 1986).

Contributors

Tom Sine is a consultant in futures planning and Third World development and was coordinator of the Wheaton '83 process.

Wayne Bragg is the former director of the Human Needs and Global Resources (HNGR) program at Wheaton College, Illinois.

Edward R. Dayton is vice president of World Vision International.

Tito Paredes is director of the Centro Evangelico Missiologico Andino Amazonico, which is concerned with enabling the Quechua Indians to maintain their own culture.

Miriam Adeney lectures at Seattle Pacific University and Regent College, Vancouver.

Robert W. Wall is professor of theology at Seattle Pacific University.

Vinay Samuel is executive secretary of Partnership in Mission Asia and a pastor in Bangalore, India; he was chairman of the Wheaton '83 Consultation.

Chris Sugden is registrar of the Oxford Centre for Mission Studies in England.

Maurice Sinclair is principal of Crowther Hall, Selly Oak Colleges, Birmingham, England.

Tite Tienou, from Upper Volta, lectures at Nyack College in New York State.

David J. Bosch is dean of the faculty of theology, the University of South Africa, Pretoria.

Vishal Mangalwadi is director of the Theological Research and Communication Institute, New Delhi.

Waldron Scott is former president of the American Leprosy Mission in New Jersey.

Chevannes Jeune is director of Integrated Rural Development, which works through the Evangelical Baptist Church in Haiti.

Samuel Baah is an evangelist and founder of Voices of Sacred Miracles in Ghana.

Robert Moffitt is the founder of HARVEST, a Christian organization enabling churches in the USA to partner other churches in Christian development.